Marx and the Failure of
Liberation Theology

MARX
and the
FAILURE of LIBERATION
THEOLOGY

ALISTAIR KEE

SCM PRESS

London

TRINITY PRESS INTERNATIONAL

Philadelphia

First published 1990

SCM Press Ltd
26–30 Tottenham Road
London N1 4BZ

Trinity Press International
3725 Chestnut Street
Philadelphia, Pa. 19104

British Library Cataloguing in Publication Data

Kee, Alistair
Marx and the failure of liberation theology.
1. Liberation theology
I. Title
261.8

ISBN 0–334–02437–4

Library of Congress Cataloging-in-Publication Data

Kee, Alistair, 1937–
Marx and the failure of liberation theology/Alistair Kee.
p.   cm.
Includes bibliographical references.
ISBN 0–334–02437–4
1. Liberation theology. 2. Marx, Karl, 1818–1883 — Religion.
I. Title
BT83.57.K445   1990
230′.046 — dc20   89–48336

Phototypeset by Input Typesetting Ltd, London
and printed in Great Britain by
Richard Clay Ltd, Bungay, Suffolk

Contents

Contents

Contents

Introduction

Marx and the Renewal of Religion

Latin American theology of liberation is widely assumed to be too Marxist: in reality it is not Marxist enough. It is frequently criticized for its unquestioned acceptance of Marx: on closer inspection there are crucial aspects of Marx's work which it simply ignores. In its rhetoric liberation theology submits all religion to the scrutiny of Marxist analysis: in fact it preserves its own theology as a no-go area which is beyond examination. It is in good standing with self-styled Marxists throughout the world in its denunciation of European capitalism: with friends like these it is small wonder that Marx once said prophetically, 'As for me, one thing I do know is that I am not a Marxist.' Liberation theology continually declares itself to be on the side of the oppressed: through its resistance to Marx it perpetuates an ideology of alienation.

This outburst may come as a surprise to those who think of me as a defender of the theology of liberation. It is almost twenty years since I first came across the work of Gustavo Gutierrez Merino and since that time I have continually argued for the importance of liberation theology. Its significance has now been long recognized throughout the world, and Christians in very different situations have attempted to face up to its challenge. In my own work I have been critical of European theology. In *The Way of Transcendence* I challenged its metaphysical presuppositions, and in *Constantine versus Christ* I exposed its ideological subversion. Liberation theology's criticism of European theology I have therefore found particularly helpful, especially coming as it does from outside our situation. I have nothing but admiration for the moral courage and spiritual insight of liberation theologians individually, and if I criticize their work it is certainly not to protect European theology in its self-congratulatory, triumphalist and alienated forms.

There is a balance to be struck. In the early years it was necessary to advocate and promote liberation theology, so that European theology might learn a word which it could not speak to itself. To criticize the movement would have given comfort to those interests which value the legitimation of a quiescent religion. This has been the effect, possibly unintended, of those who have criticized liberation theology for being Marxist. It has allowed many to ignore a message which they urgently needed to hear. Now that liberation theology is established, the balance has tipped in the other direction. I believe that Marx's criticisms of religion have to be accepted before there can be profound and long-overdue change in theology. I am also convinced that liberation theology has failed in this matter. It has not come to terms with Marx, and in this it has failed at an intellectual level. This failure, however, is of only relative significance. Much more importantly, it has failed the cause of the gospel of Jesus Christ in the modern world and consequently the very people it has attempted to serve.

In Europe there is a separation between academic theology and the life of the church. To many this is an unfortunate accident. On the contrary, it is but a symptom of the crisis of European Christianity. By contrast many Latin American liberation theologians divide their time between academic and pastoral work. This in turn is an expression of the new Christian reality in that continent. Inevitably the question arises whether their theology can help us with our problem. Or rather the question arises why it is that their theology cannot be applied to our situation. One way of answering would be to say that we have not been sufficiently open to Marx's criticism of religion. And in this book I shall argue that we should not only be acquainted with his criticism of religion, but should fully accept it. In order to do this I have found it necessary to deal with Marx's writings in detail in Part One. However, I do not accept the assumption behind the answer, namely that by contrast liberation theology has fully accepted Marx. In Part Two I examine the writings of nine of the leading Latin American liberation theologians. It would be quite impossible to provide an exposition of their several positions in such a restricted space. In any case the issue, their relationship to Marx's thought, can be dealt with separately at a methodological level.

Alfred Hitchcock reputedly heightened the suspense in his films by letting the audience know at the outset what was going to happen. In stating my conclusions at the beginning it may be that readers will be all the more intrigued to discover how they were reached. In Part Three I come to the conclusion that liberation theology has failed to take sufficient account of Marx, and that the way forward in our European crisis is not to seek to take onboard other people's theology, but to set about reconstructing our own as a matter of urgency. We too must 'drink from our own wells', and in this Marx is one of the most important springs of the European critical tradition.

It is not difficult to anticipate reactions to this study from three very different groups. In the first place those who have never valued Marx's work might consider that this in-house debate has nothing to do with them. In this I believe they are mistaken: Marx's non-ideological critical analysis has become an integral part of modern social theory. It is used even by those who are unconscious of his influence. It would be as well to clarify what they can take from Marx and what they specifically set aside. An uninformed rejection of Marx is itself ideological. In the second place there may be a reaction from some exponents of liberation theology. As previously indicated, I have learned a great deal from the movement and look forward any positive dialogue. What I should not welcome would be any repetition of the 'incommunication' of the international conference in Geneva in 1973. Then we Europeans were told that we should not be able to understand what liberation theology had to tell us. We were not told anything, except that we should not be able to understand it even if we were told it.

I have never disguised my admiration for those who vigorously hold self-consistent positions, even those with which I cannot agree. I should therefore welcome any positive responses from these two extremes. There is, however, a third group, whose reaction to this study might reflect only their own confusion and lack of commitment. They are theologians who used to speak well of Marx in previous decades when Marxism was more fashionable. But now in a period dominated by the resurgence of capitalism and its ideology, neo-liberalism, they have taken fright. Their bespoke theology has now been remodelled to reflect the values of the entrepreneurial culture. In this they stand in a historic tradition: when challenged with their previous associations with Marx's thought they are now quick to deny they ever knew him.

Why then is it both timely and necessary to write of Marx and liberation theology? William Temple once said that Christianity had not been tried and found wanting: it had never been tried. The same might be said of Marxism. As we shall see, Marx praised capitalism for its transformation and modernization of society. Ironically, the resurgence of capitalism in recent years has performed another positive function. Throughout the world what we are observing is the discrediting of regimes and systems which for too long have been taken to represent Marxism, but which fundamentally depart from Marx's own position. This opens up the real possibility of the vindication of historical materialism. Those who have made only a superficial analysis of the present situation, and who take fright at the collapse of what was taken to be Marxism succumb to their unenviable fate: being clasped to the bosom of capitalism. For those who take this route the privatization of religion will no longer by a danger but a virtue.

We are entering a new epoch characterized by the resurgence of capitalism in Europe and North America, its adoption by socialist economies and its extension into the third world. I believe that Christian theology needs to attend to Marx's philosophy to an extent which it has never done before. But we must be clear that in this liberation theology would be a completely inadequate and totally misleading guide.

PART ONE

Marx's Criticisms of Religion

1

Marx and Faith

(a) Positive experience of religion

A number of years ago I counted among my personal friends a man who was a committed Marxist. We co-operated amicably in practical matters, but although it was a period of Marxist-Christian dialogue, we were never able to discuss the things which motivated us. The reason was that although he came from a Jewish family, he himself was a thoroughly secular person. He genuinely did not understand what religion was about. Or rather he assumed it was a phase in cultural history beyond which as a Marxist he should have passed, and had indeed passed. What he could not understand was how anyone could be motivated by religion to share many of his personal values and social goals. Our friendship prevented him temporarily from making his normal generalizations about religion, but he probably regarded religion as my problem, not his. Yet fervent Marxist though he was, his relationship to religion was very different from that of Marx himself. Marx in his early years was both exposed to and influenced by religion, both Judaism and Christianity, and the culture within which he lived was deeply indebted to religion, morally and intellectually. Marx did not take my friend's view of religion, and ironically if it had been possible for him to do so, then Marxism itself could not have been developed.

Karl Marx was born in 1818 in the ancient Rhineland town of Trier. It had been founded by Caesar Augustus and had a distinguished history as an imperial centre. It has been Christian since the time of Constantine. Marx was descended from a long line of Jewish rabbis on both sides of the family. Among the most famous on his father's side were Joseph ben Gerson Hacohen, a distinguished sixteenth-century rabbinic scholar of Krakow, and Meyer ben Yitzchak Katzen-

3

ellenbogen, an older contemporary and chief rabbi of Padua. His mother, Henriette Presburg, was born in Nijmegen, Holland; also of a rabbinic family. According to Marx's daughter Eleanor her grandmother's family were Hungarian Jews who had fled to Holland in the sixteenth century.[1] Even though Marx rejected Judaism by the time he went to university, it is not surprising that its influence never left him. Although the views of his father, Heinrich Marx, were more the expression of the Enlightenment than orthodox Judaism, Heinrich was in no doubt as to the importance of religion, as indicated in the following advice to his son. 'But a great support for morality is pure faith in God. You know that I am anything but a fanatic. But this faith is a real requirement of man sooner or later, and there are moments in life when even the atheist is involuntarily drawn to worship the Almighty' (1.647). Heinrich Marx shared the liberal ethos of the Rhineland, which from Napoleonic times had been open to French democratic and egalitarian ideas. However, after the Congress of Vienna in 1815 the region came under the control of Prussia and became subject to laws which discriminated against Jews holding public office. In the following year the Minister of Justice ruled that Jews could not practise law. Heinrich Marx waited till his mother died and then was baptized into the Lutheran Church. He was then socially accepted, playing a prominent part in the Casino Club of Trier, and as a lawyer becoming the equivalent of a Queen's Counsel. His wife delayed baptism till after the death of her parents. The children were not baptized at birth, but Karl was baptized to allow him to attend elementary school. There was therefore no religious conversion to Christianity, but that did not prevent Marx from coming under the influence of religion as he grew up.

Marx attended the Friedrich Wilhelm Gymnasium in Trier, a state school which had formerly been a Jesuit college. The teachers were nearly all radical and progressive thinkers, pro-French and anti-Prussian, and Marx was exposed to moral and political judgments about the social conditions and government structures of the day. It is a sobering thought that not only do we possess his school-leaving certificate, but it has become the subject of public scrutiny. How many of us would welcome such attention! In view of his future development some details seem ironic. He is described as being 'of evangelical faith'. 'His knowledge of the Christian faith and morals is fairly clear and well grounded . . .' His 'moral behaviour towards superiors . . . was good.' His understanding of religion was good, his grasp of history poor (1.643–4). How prophetic!

In addition, we have the three essays which he wrote for his school-leaving examination. The first is entitled 'Does the Reign of Augustus

Deserve to be Counted Among the Happier Periods of the Roman Empire?' Although there is little of interest in it, those of us who are obliged to read student essays must sympathize with the notes written in the margin by one of Marx's teachers: '. . . the composition reveals a profound knowledge of history and of Latin. But what atrocious handwriting!' (1.758 note 199).

The second essay is on an exegetical theme: 'The Union of Believers with Christ According to John 15:1–14, Showing its Basis and Essence, Its Absolute Necessity, and its Effects' (1.636–9). The 'necessity' of which Marx wrote refers to his premise that 'man cannot by himself achieve the purpose for which God brought him into being out of nothing'. This he takes to be the lesson of history, 'the great teacher of mankind'. History, he tells us, teaches that not only peoples need union with Christ, but individuals also require it. Man alone in nature has a potential, intended by God, which is not fulfilled. But in the gospel, union with Christ means union with the other branches of the vine. 'Thus, union with Christ consists in the most intimate, most vital communion with Him, in having Him before our eyes and in our hearts, and being so imbued with the highest love for Him, at the same time we turn our hearts to our brothers whom He has closely bound to us, and for whom also He sacrificed Himself.' Our true life is fulfilled in 'sacrificing ourselves for one another' out of love of Christ. It is easy to be cynical about these sentiments, bearing in mind how critical of religion Marx will later become. But this is an arbitrary judgment. A more objective view is that Marx was deeply influenced by religion at a formative stage. We shall later review evidence that he never lost this understanding of religion, and indeed on occasion defended religion against those who would misuse it. Despite the Enlightenment assumptions which pervaded the school, the young Marx makes the point that the position he is describing does not follow from human reason, nor is it a natural expression of human behaviour. He concludes his essay with a statement which is profoundly different from Stoicism. 'Once man has attained this virtue, this union with Christ, he will await the blows of fate with calm composure, courageously oppose the storms of passion, and endure undaunted the wrath of the iniquitous, for who can oppress him, who could rob him of his Redeemer?'

It would, of course, be as unfair as it would be anachronistic to attempt to discover in these essays the first signs of historical materialism. He had not yet read Hegel, let alone begun his criticism on the master. He had not yet joined the Doctors' Club, let alone the Paris Commune. Yet it is interesting to note ideas which were already present to Marx at this stage in his development. Only ideological dogmatism could lead us to ignore them. For the present we might draw attention to four, to which we can refer later. The first is the historical and not simply metaphysical significance of Christ's sacrifice for others. The second is that man's life cannot be fulfilled as an isolated individual. The third is the premise that man cannot achieve his historic goal unaided. The fourth is that to the believer, the setbacks of this life do not have the last word.

The third essay by the young *Abiturient* is on the theme of 'Reflections of a Young Man on the Choice of a Profession' (1.3–10). The fact that in the Moscow Edition of the Collected Works it is placed at the very beginning, deliberately separated as far as possible from the exegetical essay, which is relegated to an appendix, has its own ideological significance. The assumption is that it is an example of early humanistic idealism, and yet it begins with precisely the same sentiments as the exegetical essay.

> To man, too, the Deity gave a general aim, that of ennobling mankind and himself, but he left it to man to seek the means by which this aim can be achieved; he left it to him to chose the position in society most suited to him, from which he can best uplift himself and society. This choice is a great privilege of man over the rest of creation, but at the same time it is an act which can destroy his whole life, frustrate his plans, and make him unhappy.

If we pay attention to what Marx actually says, then we see that the essay is not humanistic idealism, nor is it Enlightenment Deism. The four points to which I made reference in the exegetical essay recur here. 1. '. . . religion itself teaches us that the ideal being whom all strive to copy sacrificed himself for the sake of mankind, and who would dare to set at nought such judgements?' 2. 'If he works only for himself, he may perhaps become a famous man of learning, a great sage, an excellent poet, but he can never be a perfect, truly great man.' 3. '. . . the Deity never leaves mortal man wholly without a guide.' And finally, 4. 'If we have chosen the position in life in which we can most of all work for mankind, no burdens can bow us down, because they are sacrifices for the benefit of all; then we shall experience no petty, limited, selfish joy, but our happiness will belong to millions, our deeds live on quietly but perpetually at work, and over our ashes will be shed the hot tears of noble people.' In what sense Marx criticized religion we shall shortly examine, but these sentiments were to inspire his entire life, and justifiably earn him the grave-side eulogy of his life-long friend and colleague Friedrich Engels. Indeed both in its language and in its content the eulogy at the end of his life echoes the main themes of that essay written so many years earlier by a young man deciding not so much on a career as the values by which he shall live.

> And consequently, Marx was the best hated and most calumniated man of his time. Governments, both absolutist and republican, deported him from their territories. Bourgeois, whether conservative or ultra-democratic, vied with one another in heaping slanders upon him. All this he brushed aside as though it were cobweb, ignoring it, answering only when extreme necessity compelled him. And he died beloved, revered and mourned by millions of revolutionary fellow workers – from the mines of Siberia to California, in all parts of Europe and America – and I make bold to say that though he may have had many opponents he had hardly one personal enemy. His name will endure through the ages, and so also will his work.[2]

When Engels spoke these words in Highgate Cemetery, London, on 17 March 1883, he probably knew nothing of the sentiments of the schoolboy essays, but with hindsight we can see the connection, and only if ideology is allowed to overcome history can it be denied that early religious influences had a profound and continuing place in Marx's thought – and life. There was first of all the heritage of his family over more than four centuries. There was the example of his parents who in reverence for that tradition postponed baptism till after the deaths of their respective parents. There was the advice of Heinrich Marx to his son, between whom there was a close bond. And there was the environment and ethos of his school, deeply rooted in Christian faith in both its Protestant and Catholic forms. Choosing a career not for personal gain, but social good: do we take such values for granted, as if all forms of education subscribe to them equally? As I write this book, British government policies are being designed for both secondary and tertiary education which exactly reverse this order. Let us not think for a moment that as Marx entered university his values were anything other than those of Judaism, and more particularly of Christianity.

(b) Conversion

We may picture the young Marx leaving school under the heavy burden of choosing a career. Before Kierkegaard explored the depths of anxiety, Marx had already been there. It may seem ironic, therefore, that his father stepped in and told him that he should enroll at the University of Bonn to train in law, with a view to following his father's profession. So much for the crushing responsibility of choice! However, in the German essay Marx had actually acknowledged the place of parental advice in the choice of a career.

7

Marx's school-leaving certificate was issued in September 1835, and within a month he was a student at the University of Bonn. He was clearly ready for the freedom and the opportunities offered, and threw himself into his studies with great enthusiasm and energy. It may be surprising to those unfamiliar with his biography that Marx's main interest was poetry. His passion in this respect was fuelled by the Romantic movement, which was still much in evidence in Bonn, and (in lower case) by Marx's own romantic movement: he became engaged to Jenny von Westphalen in the summer of 1836. How history might have taken a different course if Marx had been a better poet! His father was no philistine, but recognized that the poetry was not first-class and required his son to move to the more 'serious' University of Berlin. Marx, always his own sternest critic, destroyed all the poetry of that period.

In Berlin Marx at least initially continued to compose, but in the midst of typical Romantic themes there are some indications of the continuing crisis in his life. The most curious are the eight Epigrams, particularly Epigram II, 'On Hegel' (1. 576–7). Of its four sections, the first three seem to be spoken by Hegel himself, though apparently expressing Marx's mixed views of the achievement of the master. In the first the density of Hegel's writings is attributed to his intention to cultivate obscurity. 'There I found me the Word: now I hold on to it fast.' The second begins with the same theme: 'Words I teach all mixed up into a devilish muddle.' But it is the third which is most curious.

> Kant and Fichte soar to heavens blue
> Seeking for some distant land,
> I but seek to grasp profound and true
> That which – in the street I find.

Few people have felt compelled to criticize the systems of Kant and Fichte in verse, but the more curious feature is that by contrast Hegel is represented as one whose starting point is the mundane. Marx was reading voraciously but had not been able to establish a position for himself. On the basis of study of the poetic corpus David McLellan makes this judgment:

In general, Marx's first contact with the university brought about a great change in the views he had expressed in his school-leaving essay. No longer was he inspired by the thought of service of humanity and concerned to fit himself into a place where he might be best able to sacrifice himself for this noble ideal: his poems of 1837, on the contrary, reveal a cult of the isolated genius and an introverted concern for the building of his own personality apart from the rest of humanity.[3]

The crisis when it came was therefore not the rejection of the religious position of his schoolboy days, but rather of the unreality of his life as a Romantic. The crisis was both academic and existential, as often happens among university students. The resolution is described in a letter which Marx wrote to his father in November 1837 (1.10–21).

The letter is quite unlike any end-of-term communication: it asks for no money. True, the young man does beg to be allowed to visit Trier, because of his mother's illness, because of his father's illness, and certainly not because he is desperate to see his fiancée. But the letter is unique in that it is almost entirely taken up with describing the development in Marx's philosophical position. (When did you last discuss Fichte with your father? 'A letter from Karl, dear. He's seems to be very critical of that nice Dr Schelling at the moment.') As indicated, the crisis was as much existential as academic, and it is of some interest that Marx describes what has happened to him as a 'metamorphosis'. His frustration and despair arose from the same feature which he encountered in poetry and in idealist philosophy, namely 'the same opposition between what is and what ought to be.' In philosophy he moved through Kant, Fichte and Schelling, but in each he met the same unreality. Not surprisingly he became ill and on medical advice moved out to the country, to the small village of Stralow, some twenty kilometres from Berlin. He had previously been put off Hegel's philosophy, finding it 'grotesque', but now as he recuperated he read the entire works. Some might think this a case of mistaking the disease for the cure, but this period was of fundamental importance to his development.

> A curtain had fallen, my holy of holies was rent asunder, and new gods had to be installed. From the idealism which, by the way, I had compared and nourished with the idealism of Kant and Fichte, I arrived at the point of seeking the idea in reality itself. If previously the gods had dwelt above the earth, now they became its centre.

Till the very last moment Marx struggled to find his own way without being drawn into the Hegelian orbit. But his final attempt was to no avail.

> I set about the task itself, a philosophical-dialectical account of divinity, as it manifests itself as the idea-in-itself, as religion, as nature, and as history. My last proposition was the beginning of the Hegelian system.

9

His best efforts to avoid the dreaded embrace simply delivered him into its clutches: 'this work, my dearest child, reared by moonlight, like a false siren delivers me into the arms of the enemy'.

Anyone familiar with the phenomenology of religious conversion will recognize Marx's metamorphosis. Common features include the following:

1. The experience is described as a rebirth, a dying and rising. Marx uses a traditional image: the veil of the old temple had been torn aside, 'my holy of holies was rent asunder, and new gods had to be installed'.

2. Although the subject experiences conversion as a sudden event, it is often the culmination of a long period of months, even years.

3. A peculiar characteristic of conversion is that it actually takes place in advance of complete knowledge, through a 'leap of faith'. That is to say, the new position is not adopted rationally after an objective demonstration that it can answer all questions and solve all problems.

4. Although the outcome of a conversion experience is relief and happiness, the experience itself can often be most unpleasant and distressing. It is often preceded by a period of strong, even desperate and angry, resistance. Far from being the result of wishful thinking, the final state is often the very last thing the subject wishes. It will often appear distasteful and entirely unacceptable right up to the last moment.

5. In such cases the emotional and psychological stress drains the subject's capacity to remain in control, and leads to a transmarginal state in which an ultra-paradoxical reversal takes place: at which point views or values previously rejected are now accepted.

6. The susceptibility is also increased if the subject is in any case physically debilitated in some way, for example through fatigue and or illness.

7. Just when we should expect the crisis to be over and peace to break out, some conversion experiences are accompanied by temporary impairment of the sensory and/or motor functions.

8. And finally there are feelings of blessedness, peace, joy and being well-disposed towards others.

9. Although the experience belongs to an individual, it is normally conversion to a position occupied by an existing group. One of the benefits is therefore membership of this community of like minded people.[4]

Historically the most famous conversion experience of this type is that undergone by Saul of Tarsus; but without any Procrustean enforcement it will be seen from a detailed study of Marx's letter that all of the above features of conversion were present in his 'metamor-phosis'. When soon after Marx became a member of the Doctors' Club, the association of Young Hegelians, he no doubt considered himself to be a scientific philosopher. But he was then what he remained throughout his life: a fervent man of faith. From evangelical Christianity he was converted to neo-Hegelian philosophy. Later he would undergo a further conversion to what is called historical materialism. The content would change in each case, but Marx was never content with a merely intellectual position. He required a faith which at the most general level disclosed the meaning of history and at the most particular gave him the courage to pursue his vocation in life.

2

Religion as Reconciliation

(a) Negative experience of religion

Even although in the letter to his father Marx discussed the way in which his career in law might develop, he also mentioned the possibility of eventually returning to university to teach. He seems to have been less interested in positive law than in jurisprudence and the philosophical issues underpinning it. Increasingly he devoted himself to philosophy, and when his father died in 1838 he began to concentrate his attention on the preparation of a doctoral dissertation, with the intention of becoming a university professor. Relations with his family became formal and for the next few years his closest friends and most influential associates were the members of the Doctors' Club. It was in this context that he decided upon his dissertation topic, 'The Difference Between the Democratean and Epicurean Philosophy of Nature'. The choice might seem eccentric or obscure, but throughout his life Marx was able to enter a discussion at an apparently remote point and quickly disclose its ongoing importance and contemporary relevance. The dissertation represented a significant stage in the development of Marx's critical philosophy, but for the present I wish to refer only to the Foreword, in which for the first time and quite unexpectedly some harsh criticisms are made of religion.

At the outset of this study we noted the four religious aspects of Marx's schoolboy essays. The new realism of the period of his dissertation is in contrast to the unreality of his writings while under the influence of the Romantic movement, especially during his time in Bonn. The metamorphosis, detailed in the letter to his father, describes a turning away not from the early religious idealism, but from Romanticism and transcendental idealism. But suddenly a new Marx appears in the Foreword to the dissertation (1.29–31), whose approach is entirely different in style and content. The early essays had been marked by what Marx's headmaster called a continual search for 'elaborate picturesque expressions' (1.733, note 1). The poems were characterized by the use of conventional romantic imagery and a languid, self-indulgent tone. Now in the dissertation the style is direct, abrasive and confrontational. Here speaks the youngest of the Young Hegelians, with all the brashness and irreverence which a previous Master of Trinity College, Cambridge, once alluded to in the aphorism: 'None of us is infallible, not even the youngest.' Marx is confident that he has solved a fundamental problem of Greek philosophy, in which no real progress had been made either by ancient or modern writers. The 'babbling' on the subject has gone on from Cicero and Plutarch, through the Middle Ages, here characterized as a 'period of realized unreason', to Gassendi, whose main interest is said to be the desire to 'accommodate his Catholic conscience to his pagan knowledge'. This is to be the contestational style of Marx throughout the remainder of his life, but in addition to the change in style, there is a marked change in the content.

A reference to Plutarch's critique of Epicurus's theology raises a point on which Marx apparently feels very strongly. It concerns the autonomy of philosophy, which must be allowed to carry on its work of exploration and criticism without reference to theology. The Foreword is only two pages long, but almost half of it pursues this point.

> In this respect it will be enough to cite, in place of all argument, a passage from David Hume: 'Tis certainly a kind of indignity to philosophy, whose *sovereign authority* ought everywhere to be acknowledged, to oblige her on every occasion to make apologies for her conclusions and justify herself to every particular art and science which may be offended by her. *This puts one in mind of a king arraign'd for high treason against his subjects.*' Philosophy, as long as a drop of blood shall pulse in its world-subduing and absolutely free heart, will never grow tired of answering its adversaries with the cry of Epicurus: 'Not the man who denies the gods worshipped by the multitude, but he who affirms of the gods what the multitude believes about them, is truly impious.' Philosophy makes no secret of it. The confession of Promotheus: 'In simple words, I hate all gods', is its own confession, its own aphorism against all heavenly and earthly gods who do not acknowledge human self-consciousness as the highest divinity. It will have none other beside.

Prometheus was chained to a rock by Zeus, condemned to suffer anew each day because out of compassion for human suffering he stole fire from the gods to bring help to mankind. In a Romantic poem Marx had sympathized with Hermes, the servant of the whims of the gods; now he makes a critical contrast.

But to those poor March hares who rejoice over the apparently worsened civil position of philosophy, it responds again, as Prometheus replied to the servant of the gods, Hermes:

> 'Be sure of this, I would not change my state
> Of evil fortune for your servitude.
> Better to be the servant of this rock
> Than to be faithful boy to Father Zeus.'

Prometheus is the most eminent saint and martyr in the philosophical calendar.

Whence comes this complete rejection of and violent attack upon religion? What caused Marx to turn away from the position of his youth? But on closer inspection this does not describe what is going on. With hindsight we can see that Marx was destined to become a Promethean figure, as already noted in the quotation from Engels' grave-side address. Out of compassion for the distress of the victims of the new urbanization and industrialization then beginning in Germany, his revolution in philosophy became a philosophy of revolution, leading to his persecution and exile. His life – and as a direct consequence, the lives of his wife and children – was to be marked for long periods by deprivation and suffering. And all this for a man who could have been successful in almost any career he had cared to choose. He could have followed his father into the legal profession and become an outstanding civil servant, rich and recognized. It is quite clear, therefore, that in the Foreword Marx is not rejecting the reflections of his early religious essays but rather committing himself to them.

His passionate outburst is rather against religious control exercised on creative and critical thought. In his new situation he began to experience religion in a much more negative way. Here as elsewhere he began with a subject remote in time and place, the control of philosophy by religion in ancient Greece, but applied it to developments in the contemporary Prussian state. Marx experienced the contradiction between his early religious ideals and the obstacle to their realization imposed by religion as a social institution. The surprise is not that he should now in his dissertation launch into this attack on religion as an institution of social control, but that it should have taken him so long to do so. After all, it had been a feature of his own early experience.

The alliance of conservative political and religious interests was to be one of the points on which Marx considered Germany to be less developed politically than France. McLellan has given some examples of the situation in Germany at that time.[1] It was as late as 1807 when the status of serf was finally abolished in Prussia. Up till then there had been feudal institutions in which the church participated. The feudal régime of the prince-archbishop of Trier was swept away by the French invasion of 1794. Although the more liberal people of the Rhineland welcomed the French initially and French ideas, the archbishop condemned the new socialist ideas from the pulpit. In the first half of the nineteenth century there were no political parties in Germany, but there was widespread support, both Catholic and Protestant, for a Christian state. We have already noted how this situation affected Heinrich Marx. The association of conservative religion and politics enforced conformity in society and led to censorship in education. The Trier Gymnasium was under suspicion as centre of radicalism. The same suspicion was directed towards the Casino Club, where pro-French, republican sentiments were expressed. Such was the association of religion and the Prussian state that to attack one was to undermine the other. The general situation is described by Marx's older contemporary, Heinrich Heine, also a 'convert' from Judaism. In *Memorials of Krähwinkel's Days of Terror*, he claims that the Prussian police prefer people to believe in God, since 'whoever tears himself away from his God will sooner or later break with his earthly superiors too'.[2]

We should not expect Marx to be specially conscious of these things in the days prior to going to university, but in joining the Doctors' Club he began to associate with men who were radical in political and religious matters. Their experience would bring home to him the realities of the situation. But it is at this point that we must make a careful distinction. The experience of religious control of society had been a constant part of Marx's life as he grew up, and yet it was in that very context that, as we have seen, he was deeply influenced by religious ideals and values. As his critical faculties developed he was able to discern that religion was not always as he had first perceived it. Religion, which he had experienced positively on the issue of a young man choosing a career, he now began to experience negatively as a form of social control. Religion, which had given him ideals and values which were to be important for him throughout his life, could also be experienced as narrow and bigoted.

Marx ends the Foreword to his dissertation by commenting on 'the apparently worsened civil position of philosophy'. After 1815 the situation was progressively worse, but just as Marx could begin from an analysis of a subject remote in time and place – in this case religious control in Greek society – and apply it to the contemporary Prussian

15

state, so he was given to generalizing from his own experience. The situation – his own situation – worsened as he became progressively involved in radical and political ideas.

(b) Hegel and the rational

It would be as well at this point to say something about Hegel. G.W.F. Hegel [1770–1831] considered himself to be a good Lutheran, and even if some should question his orthodoxy, there can be no doubt that he was deeply religious and that his philosophy was profoundly influenced by religion. As J. N. Findlay confirms, 'Hegel developed his ideas, not so much in reaction to the opinion of philosophers, as in deep ponderings on the meaning of the Christian religion . . .'[3] He considered it one of the great achievements of his system that he had finally reconciled philosophy and religion. This is a recurring theme in Hegel's major works, and can be easily appreciated when we understand his ontology. In the *Logic* he describes the dialectical movement by which the Spirit externalizes itself, becoming alienated in the material world, before proceeding through a series of 'moments' to return, now in full self-consciousness.

> The Idea is essentially a process, because its identity is the absolute and free identity of the notion, only in so far as it is absolute negativity and for that reason dialectical. It is the round of movement, in which the notion, in the capacity of universality which is individuality, gives itself the character of objectivity and of the antithesis thereto; and this externality which has the notion for its substance finds its way back to subjectivity through its immanent dialectic.[4]

The Christian doctrine of the Incarnation was so central to Hegel's thought that while he presents religion as an illustration of the dialectic of the Spirit, it could equally well be argued that it is in fact his philosophy which is an extrapolation of this religious model. In the following passage from *The Phenomenology of Mind* we see the interconnection as he discusses the *kenosis*, the idea that 'The Divine Being empties Itself of Itself and is made flesh'.

> This figurative idea, which in this manner is still immediate and hence not spiritual, i.e. it knows the human form assumed by the Divine as merely a particular form, not yet as a universal form – becomes spiritual for this consciousness in the process whereby God, who has assumed shape and form, surrenders again His immediate existence, and returns to His essential Being. The essential Being is then Spirit, only when it is reflected in itself.[5]

Hegel therefore reconciled philosophy and religion, and in this he was critical of the Enlightenment view that philosophy had rendered religion obsolete and redundant. Especially in the cult, religion has a continuing contribution to make. As Taylor points out, 'The union with God which is philosophy thus requires the union with God in heart and feeling which religion provides; and this not just as a temporarily prior stage which is destined to be left behind, but in a continuing way, since the union in thought can only continue if the union in life persists.'[6]

Because of the organic nature of Hegel's ontology, everything can be reconciled to everything else, since dualism is overcome in the dialectic. Everything is a moment or mode in the progressive self-realization of Spirit. We have seen this in the case of religion; it is also true of the state. In Hegel's philosophy everything is deduced, nothing merely described. In the *Phenomenology* he can deduce the material world; in the *Encyclopedia* he can deduce gravity. So the state is not described as a merely contingent, historical entity. It too is an expression of the Idea, under certain conditions. 'The Idea is the inner spring of action; the State is the actually existing realized moral life.[7] Hegel rejects Rousseau and Hobbes alike as they define the relationship of the individual to the state. Instead, 'all worth which the human being possesses – all spiritual reality, he possesses only through the State'.[8]

If philosophy and religion have been reconciled, and if philosophy and the state have been reconciled, it is not surprising that religion and the state have also been reconciled. Religion is the expression of the divine truth, and for Hegel the state – and thus its laws, duties and responsibilities – is ultimately founded also on the divine will. Of course there have been enighted forms of religion, and examples of religion of an extreme libertarian form. In the *Philosophy of Right* Hegel discusses the relationship between true religion and the state. It does not view the state in a negative way. 'It rather recognizes the state and upholds it, and furthermore it has a position and an external organization of its own.'[9] In other words, the state also has an obligation to recognize and protect religion and its integrity.

The task of philosophy is therefore ontology, to learn from history and to discern in its advance the Idea which is coming to more and more comprehensive expression. Hegel was therefore perfectly aware of the deficiencies of previous forms of religion and previous forms of the state. But they were stages in the long process. And although they were inadequate expressions of the Idea, they were not 'mistakes'. Viewed from the outside, historical events might have been otherwise, but as the embodiment of the Idea they have their own necessity. Thus we cannot say that it would have been better if stage G had been achieved without stage F. Each stage is organically related to its predecessor. It is for this reason that Hegel constantly describes this movement by the term *Aufhebung*, usually translated as 'supersession'. In the *Phenomenology* he tells us that 'to supersede (*aufheben*) is at once to negate and to preserve'.[10] while in the *Logic* he contrasts it with 'the mere 'either – or' of understanding'.[11] It is of crucial importance to Hegel's position that no stage could be reached ahead of its time. It is not possible to leap-frog one's time and place, which is the meaning Hegel gives to the ancient proverb *Hic Rhodus, hic saltus*. For this reason the *Philosophy of Right* 'must be poles apart from an attempt to construct a state as it ought to be. The instruction which it may contain cannot consist in teaching the state what it ought to be; it can only show how the state, the ethical universe, is to be understood.'[12]

It is in this context that we should understand the contentious aphorism: 'What is rational is actual and what is actual is rational.'[13] It was restated in the *Logic* as 'What is reasonable is actual/What is actual is reasonable.'[14] It is commonly translated as, 'What is real is rational, and what is rational is real', but this invites misunderstanding. Given the Hegelian ontology, we are directed to those phenomena which manifest the Idea, or Reason. In the *Logic* Hegel attempts to distinguish between the actual and the merely fortuitous or transient, but since everything happens of an inner necessity we may doubt whether this distinction is proper and if proper whether it is practical. Instead we should say that at our stage in the historical process we can distinguish between those aspects of a phenomenon which seem to us to embody reason, and those which still reflect a previous and inadequate phase. It may be that at some future stage elements which we took to be fortuitous or transient will be seen to be essential. Hegel was therefore defensive about this aphorism, because out of context it could be taken as a motto for political conservatism: what is is what should or must be. As we have seen, Hegel was quite capable of distinguishing between the rational, the manifestation of the Idea at a particular stage, and what contradicted it. However, even although his position was not conservative in this way it still had an overall conservative ethos. As we have just noted, he did not think it possible to produce a blueprint of the next stage in development. Philosophy, the rational discernment of universal reason, is a retrospective activity. Only when a historical epoch is coming to the end of its natural term can philosophy with the advantage of hindsight understand what has been achieved. 'The owl of Minerva spreads its wings only with the falling of the dusk.'[15]

Philosophy interprets history as an inherently rational process. It is concerned with the past and the present, but not with the future. This gives Hegelian philosophy a conservative aspect. Yet Hegel was committed to a positive evaluation of radical movements. An alternative way of describing the movement of world history is to see it as 'the progress of the consciousness of Freedom . . .'[16] The Reformation therefore has a particularly important place in the establishment of the freedom of faith against ecclesiastical authority. And the Enlightenment carries forward this development in the assertion of human freedom from all forms of externally imposed control. Valuable though the assertion of absolute autonomy is, Hegel saw its limitations. It was the basis of his rejection of Kant's assertion of ought over is. Because it was not rooted in Hegel's ontology it remained abstract and formal, lacking in content. Similarly, the outcome of the Enlightenment was the French Revolution, with its inevitable consequence, the Terror.

> In this case it is not private interest nor passion that desires gratification, but Reason, Justice, Liberty; and equipped with this title, the demand in question assumes a lofty bearing, and readily adopts a position not merely of discontent but of open revolt against the actual condition of the world.[17]

There are conflicting ontologies here. For the men of the Enlightenment it is possible to conceive of, for example, an ideal state and to take appropriate steps to create it. The state will then embody human reason. For Hegel, human reason at its best reflects universal absolute reason. But reason is already present in the world, in the actual. It is neither necessary nor possible for men to oppose their will or reason to the progressive embodiment of reason itself. The attempt is futile but also disastrous. But from human futility the cunning of reason is able to bring forth its own ends.

> It is not the general idea that is implicated in opposition and combat, and that is exposed to danger. It remains in the background, untouched and uninjured. This may be called the *cunning of reason* – that it sets the passion to work for itself, while that which develops its existence through such impulsion pays the penalty, and suffers loss.[18]

Since infinite Spirit recognizes itself through finite spirits, it is the work of philosophers to understand the past and the present. That is their contribution to the future. They cannot know reason better than reason knows itself, hence they cannot anticipate the future with plans of their own. The function of philosophy is to reconcile people to the rational, to the actual.

Reconciliation is therefore the underlying feature of Hegel's philosophy. Because of his ontology everything is organically related to everything else, and because each phenomenon to a degree embodies immanent reason, all have a common foundation. Nothing is finally rejected: through supersession even the negative is negated in the dialectic and eventually reconciled to its opposite.

(c) Atheism and treason

Not surprisingly Hegel left no successor, but his many disciples understood their responsibilities to lie in the further elaboration and application of the system of the master. Since they perceived the keystone of that arch to be the reconciliation of Christianity and the Prussian state, Hegelian philosophy promised religious and political tranquility. The situation did not last long. Within four years the attacks began, and were soon to become more extreme on both counts. The first was mounted by David Strauss, whom for the purpose of this study I should include among the Young Hegelians. After studying with F. C. Baur in the seminary at Blaubeuren, Strauss went on to study at the University of Tübingen. Both in a prize essay which he wrote in the Catholic Faculty and in his doctoral dissertation presented to the Protestant Faculty the influence of Hegel is increasingly evident. In 1831 he arrived in Berlin finally to study with Hegel himself. He attended two lectures on the first day, 15 November. Hegel died of cholera that evening. In 1835 at the age of twenty-seven Strauss published his epoch-making work *The Life of Jesus Critically Examined*. Seventy years later Albert Schweitzer was fulsome in its praise.

> Considered as a literary work, Strauss's first *Life of Jesus* is one of the most perfect things in the whole range of learned literature. In over fourteen hundred pages he has not a superfluous phrase; his analysis descends to the minutest details, but he does not lose his way among them; the style is simple and picturesque, sometimes ironical, but always dignified and distinguished.[19]

Horton Harris tells us that for the theological world the century was split into two, before and after Strauss.

> It is not surprising that the orthodox were enraged, for the Bible, which had previously been accepted as a strong and impregnable fortress had now, so it appeared, been almost reduced to a heap of rubble.[20]

There had of course been literary criticism of the Bible for some sixty years before that, culminating in the work of the Heidelberg scholar H. E. G. Paulus. In its time Paulus's work had been regarded as critical, but it was as nothing compared to the damage done by

Strauss. His work was hailed by orthodoxy as a new betrayal of Christ. Eschenmayer entitled his reply to Strauss 'The Ischariotism of our Days', and later pictured Satan rewarding the one who had done most for his cause on earth. The elderly Paulus comes forward confidently: 'What has this young puppy to point to in comparison with my service?' But Strauss elbows him aside, claiming, 'For what the old man allowed to remain, I have completely wiped out . . .' The final placings are announced, not in reverse order. 'And now the youth receives the prize and the old man the "highly-commended".'[21]

In the main body of the work Strauss subjected section after section of the Gospels, verse after verse, to the most erudite scientific criticism, concluding that the material of the Gospels is not historical but mythical, arising not from facts or events but from the religious hopes of the first Christians, expressed in narratives and images from Old Testament sources. He rejected the traditional, orthodox supernaturalist reading of the texts as untenable in the modern world. But he also rejected the naturalism of Paulus, the rationalist attempt to remove the offence of the miraculous. Instead he proposed a third hermeneutical principle, the mythical. As a principle it was valuable, as long as it was justified by the evidence. But it is not the vocation of youth to exhibit moderation and balance in such matters. As Schweitzer commented, 'Who ever discovered a principle without pressing its application too far?'[22] A lesson which was not lost on Marx.

But if Strauss can justifiably called the first major critic of Hegel, it was not because of his tireless historical examination of the Gospel texts. The criticism comes in the final section of the book in which he undertakes 'to re-establish dogmatically that which has been destroyed critically.'[23] It is here, with some help from Schelling, that he divorces the truth of Christianity from any historical basis. It is not an expression of the immanent Idea. To this point, the substance of his break with Hegel, we shall return when considering the development of Marx's theory of religion, but our interest at this point is to understand Marx's criticism of religiion as an institution of social and political control.

Earlier I quoted the final challenging aphorism with which Marx concludes the Foreword to his dissertation: 'Prometheus is the most eminent saint and martyr in the philosophical calendar.' He refers here not to philosophy in general nor even to the philosophy of Hegel in particular but to the new critical philosophy of the Young Hegelians, the group which Strauss was to refer to as the left-wing Hegelians. And if when Marx wrote these words they had no Promethean martyrs, by 1841 they already had some confessors, philosophers who had suffered for their beliefs. When Strauss wrote his *Life of Jesus Critically Examined*, he could not have been surprised that he was immediately dismissed from his post in the seminary at Tübingen. As an observer at that time noted: 'Strauss wrote the book well-knowing that in so doing he was casting away any chance of an appointment to Berlin – a great honour which would certainly have come to him at the next opportunity.'[24] Strauss was a deeply committed Christian, and was particularly hurt that he should have been represented as undermining the faith when, as he saw it, the alternatives of supernaturalism and naturalism made it unworthy of belief in the modern age.

Given the reconciliation in Hegel's system, it is not at all surprising that the first step in the revolution in theory, the first step towards what would become a theory of revolution, should be in the criticism of religion. At the outset the Young Hegelians were loyal to Hegel's doctrine of the state, and merely critical of the control exercised by religion. If for our purpose here religion and politics formed a spectrum, then we might say, if we adopted the aphoristic style of the movement itself, that the persecution of the Young Hegelians began with those who undermined the absolute form of the state religion, and ended with those who undermined the religious form of the absolute state.

If we enquire into how it was that Marx so quickly moved from his early religious sentiments to an overtly irreligious stance, then we must remember that it was not after all to original Hegelianism that he was converted. He came too late for that. When he entered the Doctors' Club, the Young Hegelians had already experienced the first of what was to become a series of persecutions. Criticism had shattered in a moment the reconciliation which it had taken a lifetime to formulate. The next target was Bruno Bauer.

Bauer had been a student of Hegel, and in 1834 began to lecture in theology in Berlin. He was highly regarded by orthodox Hegelians as a loyal interpreter of the master. When Strauss's book was published he was still loyal enough to Hegel to attempt to justify the historical value of the Gospels. However, by 1839 his position had completely changed. In a rash step he criticized the Berlin establishment, and as a result was moved to the University of Bonn. But in 1841 the publication of his *Kritik der Evangelischen Geschichte der Synoptiker* led to him his dismissal by the Minister of Culture. Strauss wished to defend the truth of Christianity, but on a new philosophical basis; in his new work on the Synoptic Gospels Bauer wished to undermine Christianity, which he now regarded as merely reflecting the level of consciousness of the period in which the Gospels were written. There could be no reconciliation between critical philosophy and religion. Although Christianity had contributed to the development of consciousness at a certain stage, to remain with institutional forms of religion would be to remain with the level of consciousness of that stage. Bauer considered that with his work the criticism of religion was complete.

The Young Hegelians were under attack for their new critical philosophy which undermined both religion and state, but Bauer in the same year published a provocative piece in which he claimed to reveal the real Hegel. *Die Posaune des Jüngsten Gerichts Über Hegel den Atheisten und Antichristen: Ein Ultimatum* is written in apocalyptic language, presenting Hegel as a demonic figure, both atheist and antichrist. Why should the Young Hegelians still develop their criticism within the premises of orthodox religion and conservative politics?

> As though Hegel had not attacked religion with a hellish rage, as if he had not set forth upon the destruction of the established world. But his *theory* is *praxis* and for that very reason most dangerous, far-reaching and destructive. It is the revolution itself.[25]

Given Hegel's affirmation of religion, constitutional hereditary monarchy and his criticism of the Terror, the position described was certainly not his, but Bauer's intention was not to repeat Hegel but to supersede him.

The important element in Bauer's work which separated him from Hegel and which was later to influence Marx was the reintroduction of Englightenment dualism. Marx, it will be recalled, had been attracted to Hegelian philosophy because it reconciled the is/ought dualism of Fichte and Kant. But now in Bauer what is does not necessarily embody reason. Reason stands over against the actual to judge it. At this stage Bauer was politically radical and his position encouraged Marx to introduce the righteous anger of prophetic judgment on existing institutions, both religious and political.

However, at this point we are not considering the influence of Bauer on Marx's own position, which was considerable especially in the dissertation, but rather how Bauer's experience confirmed Marx in his new negative view of religion. Marx had attended lectures by Bauer in Berlin, and through the Doctors' Club, where Bauer was one of the leading figures, the two were close friends. As already indicated, Marx turned from a possible legal career to write his dissertation with a view to rapidly entering university teaching. Things looked to be going very well. Bauer was keen to have him as a colleague in Bonn, and even began to discuss what Marx might teach. However, all such hopes were dashed with Bauer's dismissal twelve months after Marx submitted his dissertation. Marx's position was so closely identified with Bauer's that he had to give up all thought of a university career, not just at Bonn. It may well be that in the long term Marx's real profession, his religious vocation of a life dedicated to the service of others, was better served by the closing of the door to university teaching (if not providence, then at least the cunning of reason!), but in the short term the experience of Bauer, and consequently of Marx himself, must have confirmed the Young Hegelian criticism of the alliance of church and state, the control of society through institutional religion.

Nor would the case of Edgar Bauer do anything to ameliorate this view. Edgar Bauer was eleven years younger than his brother Bruno. He wrote in support of his brother after he had been dismissed from his university post. *Bruno Bauer und Seine Gegner* polarizes and politicizes the dismissal and advocates an extreme, anarchistic resolution. In 1844 he published *Der Streit der Kritik mit Kirche und Staat*, in which he deplored the fact that the French Revolution had not been revolutionary enough. His position is guided by a perspective of anarchy, in the strict political sense. That is so to say, he attributes the ills of society to the distortions of relationships imposed by institutions. Thus it is monarchy which is the enemy, not the king. Marriage causes prostitution. Somewhat in advance of his time he is sensitive to the domination of women, which is prevalent in a society which expects one group to lord it over others.

Many of Bauer's ideas were later to be echoed by Marx, though not in their anarchist setting. Thus philosophy cannot provide a blueprint for the new society. No one can determine it in advance of revolutionary action. The new consciousness of the revolution will create a society which previously could not exist, but it will be without private property, which Bauer regarded as the basis of many of the ills and crimes of society. 'From now on history is a *self-conscious* history, because mankind knows the principles by which it moves forward, because mankind has history's goal – freedom – in sight.'[26] He could not have been surprised that the book produced no revolution, nor that because of it he was sentenced to four years in the special political prison of Magdeburg.

A fourth example of a Young Hegelian who suffered the consequences of his criticism of religion was of course the most influential philosopher of the group, Ludwig Feuerbach. Like Hegel and so many of his followers, Fuerbach had originally been a student of theology. He transferred from Heidelberg in 1824 to study under Hegel. After two years he moved to Erlangen where he eventually presented his dissertation. From 1928 he lectured in philosophy at Erlangen, and seemed set for a career in university teaching. The next year, however, he published (anonymously) a pamphlet on *Gedanken Über Tod und Unsterblichkeit*. In circumstances which were to be soon repeated in the case of Strauss, the work brought him instant notoriety and dismissal. Although Feuerbach continued to publish in philosophy works which were well reviewed and well received, he was never appointed to a university position again. The essay, apparently on the religious themes of death and immortality, was not yet a critique of Hegel, but it made an important start in the process which Feuerbach was later to complete, namely standing Hegel on his head. Feuerbach summarized the intention of the essay in this way: 'To cancel above all the old cleavage between this side and the beyond in order that humanity might concentrate on itself, its world and its present with all its heart and soul.'[27]

Feuerbach's most famous work, *The Essence of Christianity*, was published in 1841, a very busy year for the Young Hegelians. It gained him the leading place in the movement. David Strauss acknowledged this: 'Today, and perhaps for some time to come, the field belongs to him. His theory is the truth for this age.'[28] And Ernst Renan, often misleadingly identified as the French David Strauss, claimed in the kind of understatement which he made his own, 'If the end of the world were to come in the nineteenth century, then, of course, he would have to be called the Anti-Christ.'[29] *The Essence of Christianity* created another storm of protest, but the author could not be dismissed. Through royalties and marriage, he had become man of independent means. As Marx might have said if he had thought of it: Feuerbach had become fire-proof. We shall discuss Feuerbach's influence on Marx in more detail later.

Another figure influential on the development of the young Marx was Arnold Ruge, who taught at the University of Halle, and edited the *Hallische Jahrbücher* which was first published in 1838, a forum for the views of the Young Hegelians. The journal was banned in Prussia in June 1841, though it continued for another two years as the *Deutsche Jahrbücher*, published in Dresden. Ruge was the most politically active of the group. He had been a member of a radical student organization and spent six years in prison, time which he spent studying Hegel. Like Bruno Bauer, he lost faith in the Hegelian claim that reason was becoming progressively embodied in the world. In his writings reason was turned upon the Prussian state which, even under Frederick William IV, continued traditional forms of religious discrimination and censorship. At the outset Ruge wished only for a reform of the state, but increasingly his position was critical of the whole institution of the Christian state. In discussing the Foreword to Marx's dissertation I noted the sudden change in style as well as in content. If Marx was converted to the movement, then why not also to its premises and its literary style? Rosenkranz deplored the direction in which Ruge's publication was developing. 'The *Jahbücher* has come to the point where no contribution is accepted unless it is written in a brusque, dictatorial, atheistic and republican tone.'[30] But the 'atheism' of the movement, as we have seen, was for the most part the rejection of the reconciliation of philosophy and institutional religion, the exercise of religious control on thought as well as behaviour. Censorship provides us with the final incident I might mention which must have confirmed Marx that his new friends were right to oppose religion in such strident terms.

(d) Prometheus bound

In June 1840 Frederick-William IV succeeded to the throne, and it seemed for a time that the hopes of the middle classes for a more liberal state would be realized. A new instruction on censorship was passed the following year, overtaking the very restrictive law imposed in 1819 after the defeat of Napoleon. At first things seemed to be moving in the right direction. Marx knew better, though since being proved right was at considerable personal cost it could have given him little satisfaction.

'Comments on the Latest Prussian Censorship Instruction' (1.109–131) was Marx's first article in political journalism, and in it he subjected the text to detailed criticism, claiming that the new censorship law was in important respects more not less repressive than the old. It was intended for publication in Ruge's *Jahrbücher*, but in ironic confirmation of Marx's argument, the censor would not allow its publication. Our sole concern here is with the discussion of institutional religion and social control, but in any case this subject is central to Marx's criticism of the new law.

The instruction, it was claimed, was not intended to inhibit 'serious and modest investigation of truth', but was rather against 'anything aimed in a frivolous or hostile way against the Christian religion in general, or against a particular article of faith . . .' The older law had tried to protect religion in general, but Marx saw in this new instruction an identification (reconciliation) of interests between politics and religion. He addressed those 'who base the state even in details on faith and Christianity, who want to have a Christian state . . .' It was the inconsistency of the instruction which concerned Marx: politics and religion were not indeed separated; they were intentionally brought together, but only in a certain way, to serve certain interests.

> Hence either forbid religion to be introduced at all into politics – but you don't want that, for you want to base the state not on free reason, but on faith, religion being for you the *general sanction for what exists* – or allow also the *fanatical* introduction of religion into politics. Let religion concern itself with politics in *its own way*, but you don't want that either. Religion has to support the secular

26

authority, without the latter subordinating itself to religion. Once you introduce religion into politics, it is intolerable, indeed *irreligious*, arrogance to want to determine *secularly how* religion has to act in political matters. He who wants to ally himself with religion owing to religious feelings must concede it the decisive voice in all questions, or do you perhaps understand by religion the *cult of your own unlimited authority and governmental wisdom*? (1.118).

I have quoted this passage in full because it is not only of central importance to the particular article under consideration, but confirms my general thesis about the precise subject of Marx's criticism of religion. I have commented on the speed at which Marx adopted the irreligious criticism charactersitic of some – though not all – of the Young Hegelians, in the style exemplified and favoured by Ruge for his contributors. Religion in this context is consistently attacked as a negative influence in society. But this is not at all the case in the passage before us. In it Marx does two things at once. In the first place he clarifies the subject of attack, namely the use of religion by the political powers. But in the second place, by showing this use to be in fact an abuse, he defends religion against the state. Six years after his schoolboy essays he still knows about religion in its own profound terms. That he does not attack, but now defends, though not of course as a believer.

It is not difficult to understand the points Marx makes: they seem very familiar in the contemporary world. Is it the intention of the political powers to keep religion out of politics? By no means. They wish to deliberately mix the two. But at the same time they wish to control the way in which the two are engaged. Religion has to become involved in politics not on its own terms but on terms dictated by the state. 'Religion' in this arrangement is 'the general sanction for what exists'. Here is the reconciliation of what is and what ought to be, but now legitimized in the name of a higher power, in direct contrast to Hegel's meaning. Religion has to perform this function for the state, but the state has no intention in return of submitting to religion. There is no question of religion being allowed to question or propose changes to what is, to bring about a true and religious reconciliation with what in the purposes of God ought to be. Religion, in other words, must perform no critical or prophetic task on its own account. And it is here that we see a move which will become characteristic of Marx's debating style. The liberal censorship instruction is not better than the old authoritarian law, but worse; in purporting to defend Christianity it undermines it. Marx is able to drive a wedge between the present false accommodation of politics and religion precisely because he can envisage a true relationship. The present accommodation is a secular use of religion, for political ends. Religion, as everything else in the social and political sphere, is expected to serve the good of the state. But for the religious person this cannot be right. Marx identifies such a person as one who is motivated by 'religious feelings', that is, by religious faith, convictions or commitments. For such a person it is always necessary to obey God, and on occasion that may mean to obey God rather than men. But the instruction on censorship is not intended to defend, let alone promote, such prophetic Judaeo-Christian religion. Rather, it is to be enforced to promote civil religion, 'the cult of your own unlimited authority and governmental wisdom'.

What a defence of religion! One of the characteristics of Marx's writings to which we have already referred is his ability to take a historical subject and demonstrate its contemporary relevance. Correspondingly, one reason why his works are still read is because even although they themselves have become historical, they often anticipate, in a prophetic way, issues of our own time and place. Throughout the modern world political authorities wish to use religion, not on its own terms but theirs. But worse than that, many religious people acquiesce in this because their own interests are served by such legitimations. It is ironic that it is Marx, the irreligious critics, who steps forward without hesitation to expose this abuse, to defend the integrity and autonomy of religion, and thereby challenge those who claim to be motivated by religious feelings, to obey God rather than men.

Although Marx was highly critical of the new censorship arrangements, initially they did lead to a liberalization. As he was writing his critical article, a consortium led by Moses Hess was setting up a new publication, the *Rheinische Zeitung*, which was to become the main instrument of the Young Hegelians. Marx came to be closely associated with it, and in October 1842 was appointed editor. Circulation increased rapidly, but for reasons which only brought it under further scrutiny by the authorities. In January 1843 it was decided to suppress both the *Deutsche Jahrbücher* and the *Rheinische Zeitung*. The Young Hegelians in Berlin associated with Bruno Bauer continued to be critical, but at a purely theoretical level. The others, associated with Ruge and including Marx, were further radicalized by the experience and moved towards the integration of Germany theory and French revolutionary praxis.

Appropriately, therefore, it was not in theory but in practice that Marx became a bitter critic of religion. He had seen religious interests destroy the careers and the lives of his associates and he had suffered more than most. But the object of his attack was not religion itself so much as the unholy alliance of political and religious interests. When he learned that the *Rheinische Zeitung* was to be banned he observed in a letter to Ruge that it was to be allowed to continue briefly, but under strict control, 'and if the police nose smells anything un-Christian or un-Prussian, the newspaper is not allowed to appear' (1.398). In March, as the paper closed, Marx revealed to Ruge some of the personal cost of his struggle. He refers in particular to his fiancée, Jenny, her family and their aristocratic and ecclesiastical connections.

In passing I might expand on their relationship. Jenny was an intelligent, witty and beautiful young woman, a few years older than Marx. After the death of his own father, Marx became very attached to her father, the Baron Ludwig von Westphalen, to whom he dedicated his doctoral dissertation. The Baron was an important government official, of distinguished family. His father Philipp had been chief of staff to the Duke of Brunswick and had married Jeanie Wishart, daughter of an Edinburgh minister. The Wisharts were an old Scottish family: on her mother's side she was a Campbell, and on her father's side she was descended from Archibald, Duke of Argyll, executed for his part in the rebellion against James II. Thus it was that the Baroness Jenny von Westphalen, wife of Karl Marx, inherited some of the Argyll family silver (and subsequently Marx came under question when he tried to pawn some of it when living in London).[31] I have thought it worth mentioning these details not from any voyeuristic motive but because it will be relevant later when we consider the circumstances in which Marx's philosophy was developed.

Here as elsewhere in Marx's writings the occasional note of bitterness comes not from the way in which he was treated – he knew well how to defend himself – but from the way in which the defenceless and the innocent were abused.

> I can assure you, without the slightest romanticism, that I am head over heels in love, and indeed in the most serious way. I have been engaged for more than seven years, and for my sake my fiancée has fought the most violent battles, which almost undermined her health, partly against her pietistic, aristocratic relatives, for whom 'the Lord in heaven' and the 'lord in Berlin' are equally objects of religious cult, and partly against my own family, in which some priests and other enemies of mine have esconced themselves. For years, therefore, my fiancée and I have been engaged in more unnecessary and exhausting conflicts than many who are three times our age . . . (1.399).

Yet it was also characteristic of Marx, as noted by Engels in the grave-side oration, that although he did not hold back in intellectual debate, yet one to one he bore no grudges. The same letter ends with a glimpse of Marx's relations with religious people in practice and in abstraction.

> I have just been visited by the chief of the Jewish community here, who has asked me for a petition for the Jews to the Provincial Assembly, and I am willing to do it. However much I dislike the Jewish faith. Bauer's view seem to me too abstract (1.400).

Did this orthodox Jew know something that Marx's critics did not know, which encouraged him to ask Marx for his help? And did Marx know something which many of his followers ignore: do not strengthen your enemy by delivering your friends into his camp? The enemy was not religion but the use of it, especially its abuse by the state and its supporters. In a drawing representing the banning of the *Rheinische Zeitung*, the figure of Prometheus stands bound to his printing press unable to help the suffering of the people who surround him (1.374).

(e)   Opiate of the poor

Heinrich Marx wished his son to become a lawyer. Karl Marx in the choice of a career wished to fulfil his destiny by dedicating his life to the service of others. He hoped to do this through teaching, but that door was soon barred to him. Alternatively he sought to pursue it through journalism, but with the suppression of the two journals in which he could express his views that way forward was also barred, at least in Germany.

Although the problem might seem to be a personal and practical one for Marx, where to work and how to support himself and his wife, it was symptomatic of the crisis faced by the Young Hegelians in general. At the outset they had shared Hegel's doctrine of the state, seeking to free it from the control of religious interests. But as we have just seen in the discussion of the censorship instruction, the real nature of the situation had now been uncovered. It was not that the state was moving in a progressive direction, deflected only by religion. Rather it was that the state, even under – or precisely under – Fredrick-William IV, was consciously using religion to prevent any progress. The Prussian state showed no signs of approximating to Hegel's rational state. Marx's attention therefore turned from religion to politics, and during the summer following the suppression of the journal he worked on a criticism of Hegel's *Philosophy of Right*, with particular attention to the third part, in which Hegel deals with civil society and the state.

A corollary to this recognition of the disparity of what is and what ought to be was that the rational state was not being realized by an advance in self-consciousness. What ought to be would not replace what is by the advance of reason, but only by action for change. To German critical theory there must be added French revolutionary praxis. In so far as they could be part of the progressive force for change, Ruge and Marx were agreed that what was needed was a *Deutsch-Französische Jahrbücher*. This could not be published within Germany: Zürich at first seemed a possibility, and then Strasburg. Brussels was also considered, but inevitably it was to Paris that the group went, the centre of radical political thought and revolutionary experience, described by Marx in a letter to Ruge as 'the new capital of the new world' (3.142).

This inability to make a practical decision about the location in which to be practical might seem somewhat ironic, but it was not the only or the greatest internal contradiction exhibited during the venture. In the first place, like magi from the East they came bearing gifts: the criticism of religion, the criticism of philosophy, the criticism of the state. Through Hess's contacts they could expect their offerings to be snapped up by the active but unschooled communards. Sadly this was not the case. The gifts were marked 'German – not for export'. Their criticism was modern, the subject dated. They were describing a situation which had been swept away by the revolution of 1789. And this is relevant to our study. The Young Hegelians had considered religion as an institution of social control, or as providing a legitimation for the state. But it no longer performed that function in France. More to the point, religion had a place within the lives of French people. The Young Hegelians, with the notable exception of Feuerbach, had paid no attention to this form of religion. Significantly, Feuerbach did not join them in Paris nor did he contribute to the new journal, even though Marx in a rather grovelling letter had strongly urged him to send a contribution, perhaps on 'the unholy Schelling' (3.350).

The second internal contradication was that there were no French contributors to the Franco-German Yearbook. (We may leave aside the further matter that strictly speaking a publication which achieves a run of one-in-a-row hardly constitutes a 'yearbook'.) This would not have been decisive if at least the German contributors had been influenced by the situation in France. Nor was this the case. The contributions were for the most part already written, and certainly already conceived of before they reached Paris. (In the letter to Feuerbach Marx invited him to send something that had already been written.) Ironically the only French element in the yearbook was that the contributors were Bourbon-revolutionaries: they had learnt nothing and forgotten nothing. The essays were entirely about Germany, written by exiles who cared only for Germany. A final contradiction might be seen in the fact that the *Deutsch-Französsische Jahrbücher* was to be the rallying-point of a new movement: in reality it was the deathnell of an old movement. The journal was published in February 1844, and within a few weeks Ruge and Marx had parted company. This was simply confirmation that the Prussian authorities had defeated the Young Hegelians. But if the new comes not from the old, nor from the best of the old, but from the death of the old, then it was a good thing that the group ceased to exist. What could have been more tragic and more ineffectual than a group of aging émigrés (at least that would have been French) sitting in Parisien cafés plotting the downfall of the Prussian monarchy? But in one important respect the death of one association marked the beginning of another. Although Marx had first met Engels in November 1842, the two had not worked together. But from this point on their co-operation would enable them jointly to contribute to the development of socialism, not in one country but throughout the world, not in their own time alone, but for generations to come.

As we pursue our investigation of how Marx came to adopt an abrasive, dismissive approach to religion we turn to our last document, one of two which Marx wrote for the ill-fated yearbook: 'Contribution to the Critique of Hegel's Philosophy of Law: Introduction'. Although the essay is highly critical of the political situation in Germany, Marx still writes of Germany, its problems and its future. One of its most striking features is its opening tirade against religion: the criticism of religion is given a place which it will never again have in his writings.

Later we shall return to this essay in discussing another criticism which Marx makes of religion, but for the moment we must pursue the theme of reconciliation, the social control exercised by religion and religion's capacity to reconcile what is and what ought to be, at least in appearance. Before leaving Kreuznach for Paris, Marx in a letter to Ruge, had assessed the situation in Germany. 'There are two kinds of facts which are undeniable. In the first place religion, and next to it, politics, are the subjects which form the main interests in Germany today . . .' (3.143). In the essay he is about to write of political change, and not surprisingly both issues must be dealt with at the same time. 'The struggle against religion is therefore indirectly a fight against the world of which religion is the spiritual aroma.' (3.175). Religion on this view performs the function of legitimation, convincing people that this world is as it ought to be. This leads directly to one of the best known passages in Marx's writings:

Religious suffering is at the same time an expression of real suffering and a protest against real suffering. Religion is the sigh of the oppressed creature, the heart of a heartless world, and the soul of soulless conditions. It is the opium of the people.[32]

Understandably attention is focussed directly on the final assertion, one of the most famous aphorisms in European literature. It pursues the theme of the function of reconciliation effected by religion. Looked at more closely, however, the passage is not as dismissive as it first appears. We saw in the essay on the censorship instruction that Marx could still recall that religion can perform a very different function, that it can be autonomous and prophetic. Now he tells us something about religion and the real, not the unreal.

We have just had an example of Marx in full flight, lashing out at religion: the spiritual aroma which covers over the rottenness of the world. Suddenly we are addressed in a very different tone. The subject is not so much religion as the suffering of the poor. It is Marx's vocation to speak in their defence, to come to their assistance if he can. We should expect him to continue his attack on religion by blaming it for causing suffering, but that is not what he says. Religion actually gives expression to real suffering. But more than that, religion is a protest against this suffering. In this he comes close to a recognition of the prophetic form of religion which denounces the rich and their exploitation of the poor, which gives voice to the cry of the oppressed. Marx seldom admits that religion historically has also performed this function, perhaps because in his own time that prophetic voice was largely silent. Who in Germany cared for the plight of the poor in the worst days of the industrial revolution? Not the king and not the aristocracy. Not the bourgeois classes who were promoting and bene-fitting from these conditions. And certainly not the philosophy of reconciliation: it was not after all Hegel who called to him all those who were heavy laden and over-worked. In the midst of real suffering there was religion, not the religion of the imperial cult but of one who suffered in all things as we do. For some quite unexpected reason Marx chooses this moment to acknowledge that religion has played more than one part in society. It has been the caring heart in social indifference. It has preserved the spiritual in dehumanizing conditions.

In addition it has been the opium of the people. This aphorism is taken to be the final dismissive judgment on religion, but read in this context it is more ambiguous. Opium was widely used in the nineteenth century, Victorian values notwithstanding.[33] At a time when medical science could diagnose without being able to cure, it provided the only means by which many people could continue to live out their lives in face of constant pain. Opium was there, and many were grateful for it. And religion was there, Marx tells us. Who is he to dismiss it? Yet this compliment is at the same time a final criticism. Religion makes the intolerable tolerable. In the short term this is a considerable contribution, but in the long term it is a grave disservice. It heals the wound too lightly; it weakens the necessity for finding a cure. On this view religion steals from the mind the imagination that there must be another and better order of things: it drains from the heart the courage to fight for such a goal.[34]

Having momentarily praised religion because it descended into the real world of human suffering, Marx adopts his stern approach again.

> To abolish religion as the illusory happiness of the people is to demand their real happiness. The demand to give up illusions about the existing state of affairs is the demand to give up a state of affairs which needs illusions. The criticism of religion is therefore in embyro the criticism of the vale of tears, the halo of which is religion (3.176).

The aroma has become the halo: religion legitimates an unjust world order. But if philosophy sought to reconcile what is and what ought to be, religion on Marx's view performs this function on its own account and with even more powerful resources. Religion can reconcile people to the sufferings of this world by asserting that God's will is always done, and by assuring them by Christ and by Kant that the injustices of this world would be recompensed in the life to come.

Borrowing some further images from Bruno Bauer, Marx draws his final conclusion. 'Criticism has torn the imaginery flowers from the chain not so that men shall wear the unadorned, bleak chain but so that he will shake off the chain and pluck the living flower' (3.176). Religion is the aroma, the halo, the flowers, but not the chains. Man need no longer be reconciled to his lot. Three years later the proclamation will ring out: 'The proletarians have nothing to lose but their chains. They have a world to win. Workers of the world unite!' (6.519).

Marx is known to make a criticism of religion. In fact he offers three very different critiques. We have just examined the first, that religion reconciles man to an evil world, as if it were the world that God willed. Stated thus, it is clear that Marx is not rejecting religion so much as the abuse of religion. From his youth, up to and including the article on censorship, he knew of a prophetic form of religion which exposed and denounced the evils of society. He knew that religion true to itself must obey God rather than men. Hegelian philosophy was a system of reconciliation, but one which declined to call evil by its name. Christianity is fundamentally a religion of reconciliation, but one which recognizes evil and condemns it. 'God was in Christ, reconciling the world to himself.'[35] But this reconciliation was achieved through the suffering of Christ. It would be blasphemous if the Christian religion

34

should allow itself to be used or misused to support the claim that God is reconciled to an evil and oppressive order. He has reconciled the world to himself: he is not reconciled to injustice. Those who are concerned for the truth and integrity of religion, of Christianity in particular, should take Marx's first criticism to heart.

(f) Liberation by redemption

It would seem that an element in Marx's conversion to the position of the Young Hegelians involved his acceptance of their view of religion. As we have seen in the Foreword to his dissertation, he had already adopted the required 'brusque, dictatorial, atheistic and republican tone.' Religion was used by the state in order to legitimize the present order. It participated with Hegelian philosophy and Prussian politics in the apparent reconciliation of what is and what ought to be. But regardless of the dictatorial tone it is quite clear that the subject was narrowly conceived. It was not after all religion, as practised by individuals or within religious communities. It was not religion as found in the Middle East, India or Japan. It was not necessarily Christianity as experienced within other European countries. It may be that this was brought home to Marx only when he moved to Paris, thus gaining a new perspective on the parochialism of a critical philosophy which thought that all it had to undertake was a revision of the absolute system of Hegel himself. In the 'Critique of Hegel's Philosophy of Law: Introduction' we see that it is with dismay that he discovered that the analysis of politics and religion he proposed to carry out was, by French standards, an 'anachronism'. 'If I negate the German state of affairs in 1843, then, according to the French computation of time, I am hardly in the year 1789, and still less in the focus of the present' (3.176).

Marx certainly knew better when he was at school. At that time he exhibited a sensitivity to some of the most profound aspects of religion, not in an alienated form, but as they affected the life of the individuals and their relationships within society at large. But this proper understanding of religion was submerged in the dogmatism of the Doctors' Club. Yet, as we have seen, it was not totally lost. In discussing the instruction on censorship he clearly understood the autonomous and prophetic function of religion, a function which did not at all correspond to the theory of the Club. This prior understanding reappears in the beginning of the 'Introduction', when Marx deals with religion and real suffering. At the end of the discussion of his early and formative days we noted four religious ideas which were to remain with him throughout his life. It is of some significance that in the essay in which his adopted view of the nature of religion is shown to be inadequate, one of these issues reappears. At the outset we formulated the point as 'the historical and not simply metaphysical significance of Christ's sacrifice for others.'

The issue appears at the end of the essay, but it requires a context, which can be briefly described. One of the most important influences on Marx's development was the work of Feuerbach. Marx was not primarily interested in Feuerbach's reinterpretation of religion but rather in his humanism. Marx wrote a letter to Feuerbach from Paris in the most ingratiating terms, claiming that Feuerbach's two works, the *Philosophie der Zukunft* and the *Wesen des Glaubens* were of 'greater weight than the whole of contemporary German literature put together. In these writings you have provided – I don't know whether intentionally – a philosophical basis for socialism and the Communists have immediately understood them in this way' (3.354). Whether Feuerbach was encouraged or appalled at this report we need not decide, but in *The Essence of Christianity* Feuerbach had certainly presented man as a social being, a species being. He begins with the assertion that: 'Consciousness in the strictest sense is present only in a being to whom his species, his essential nature, is an object of thought.'[36] A definition of the uniqueness of the human over against nature which focussed on consciousness was of course what Young Hegelians would wish to hear, but that is not the most important aspect of Feuerbach's work. He goes on to say that 'man has both an inner and an outer life.'[37] 'Man is himself at once I and thou . . .'[38] Man has the capacity to compare himself by another standard outside himself. Feuerbach refers to this outside standard of reference as the species; perhaps a more manageable entity would be society. But there is more to it than that. It transpires that Feuerbach has in mind not an empirical entity with its communal faults and failings. The 'species' becomes, rather, a pseudo-empirical way of speaking about human ideals, but without appearing to regress into speculative idealism: an important consideration for the holder of the accolade 'father of German materialism'. It is in this context that we must understand his projection theory of religion: the attributes of God are in fact but the projected attributes of man, and if not actual men, then at least the ideal attributes of the species. 'All divine attributes, all attributes which make God God, are the attributes of the species . . . The history of mankind consists in nothing else than a continuous and progressive conquest of limits, which at a given time pass for the limits of humanity, and therefore absolute insurmountable limits.'[39] The predicates of God are therefore on this view the attributes of mankind. Feuerbach stands in the idealist tradition, with little interest in history.

It may well be that Feuerbach took this model from David Strauss, the first of the young critics of Hegel. While Strauss accepted the idea of the God-man found in early christology he could not, on his terms accept it as a historical incarnation. He proposes a different approach.

And is this no true realization of the idea? Is not the idea of the unity of the divine and human natures a real one in a far higher sense, when I regard the whole race of mankind as its realization, than when I single out one man as such a realization? Is not an incarnation of God from eternity, a truer one than an incarnation limited to a particular point in time. This is the key to the whole of christology, that, as subject of the predicate which the church assigns to Christ, we place, instead of an individual, an idea; but an idea which has an existence in reality, not in the mind only, like that of Kant.[40]

With this parenthetic swipe at the vacuousness of the Kantian moral law, Strauss still displays his Hegelian pedigree, but his position differs from that of Feurerbach in two important respects. The first is that the hope of mankind and the goal of mankind are represented not by the broad category of the predicates of God, but more specifically by the attributes of Christ. What are these attributes? They would include the willingness to suffer for others, the power to defeat evil by the refusal to adopt the ways of evil. The second distinguishing point is that for Strauss these predicates refer to a historical reality, not merely to imagination or longing.

We return now to the end of Marx's essay 'Critique of Hegel's Philosophy of Law: Introduction', to a passage which requires some explanation. His main concern is still with the future of Germany, but he can learn something from French history. If he must now turn away from the hope, or assumption, that the rational state will appear necessarily, he must now enquire about the historical process by which it can be realized. One kind of revolution would involve the most oppressed class in society replacing the class which has oppressed it. But this is not what Marx seeks. In Germany no class embodies the evils of society to such an extent that all oppression would be overcome by its defeat. Nor is there any existing class which could in any case undertake such a revolution. And beyond that, it is clear that Marx does not think the replacing of an oppressing class by one which takes its place is the goal: it does not constitute liberation for society as a whole. The history of France suggests a sequence by which successive revolutions have been led by classes further and further down the social, political and economic scale. The important point is that the kind of liberation effected changes in this process.

Liberation from particular ills connected with political society is necessary, but essentially negative. Marx ends the essay with a more fundamental question: 'Where, then, is the *positive* possibility of a German emanicipation?' (3.186). The answer divides into two parts:

> A class must be formed which has *radical chains*, a class in civil society which is not a class of civil society, a class which is the dissolution of all classes, a sphere of society which has a universal character because its sufferings are universal, and which does not claim a *particular redress* because the wrong which is done to it is not a *particular wrong* but *wrong in general*. There must be formed a sphere of society which claims no *traditional* status, but only a human status, a sphere which is not opposed to particular consequences but is totally opposed to the assumptions of the German political system;

This is idealism, retaining a reference to the Hegelian universal: it is also humanism. Marx is speaking not of an existing social class, with specific ills and specific objectives with respect to these injustices. He is beginning to envisage not simply a new social order, but a new humanity. If this is the work, the quotation continues as he goes on to describe the person.

> . . . a sphere, finally, which cannot emancipate itself without emancipating itself from all the other spheres of society, which is, in short, a *total loss* of humanity and which can only redeem itself by a *total redemption of humanity*. this dissolution of society, as a particular class, is the *proletariat*.[41]

Feuerbach projected the eternal attributes of God on to an ideal and non-existent species. Strauss broke with idealism to the extent that he projected the historical attributes of Christ on to an ideal and non-existent species. Marx has taken the further step of projecting the historical attributes of the work of Christ on to a non-existent historical social class. He sees what has to be done, and understands the attributes that will be required for such a work of liberation. But in all honesty he sees that there is no existing social class capable of performing it. He is not after all dealing with an actual historical class. The work and the character of the person required do not come to Marx from observation of any class, not even the industrial working class. His understanding of the work and the person comes to him from religion: christology provides him with the model. This is not now the alienated form of religion which performs a legitimizing function to perpetuate oppression. Nor is it simply a different task which has to be performed by a new social group. The matter is more profound than that. He understands that the person and the work go together.

Oppression cannot be ended by the oppressors, just as the power of evil cannot be defeated by the wrong-doer. The liberation of mankind can be brought about only by the appearance of one (in his case a class) who is oppressed but who will not become an oppressor, one who is wronged but will not use the power of evil to attempt to overcome that wrong. And it is significant that at this point Marx refers to this action on behalf of humanity as 'redemption'.[42]

Both the problem and the answer, the person and the work come not from political analysis or observation, but from a profoundly religious model. Marx had never observed a social class which could perform this work of redemption. He may well have underestimated the super-human demands which would be placed upon those who were to create the new humanity through their own redemptive suffering. Unfortunately the history of all political revolutions since that time simply confirms that no actual social class has possessed the required attributes. But before Marx's detractors take too much smug comfort from this observation, we might reflect on why it is that Marx had to pin his hopes for the reconciliation of mankind to a non-existent class rather than ever-present Christian church.

(g) Reconciliation in Christ

Marx's first criticism of religion is that it performs a reconciliation of what is and what ought to be, or rather that it uses its authority to persuade people that what is is what ought to be. In an evil world this inevitably means that religion functions as a legitimation of oppression and injustice, and aligns itself with the values and interests of the oppressors against the oppressed. This is not so much an attack on religion as an exposing of the abuse of religion and an indictment of religious people when they consciously or unconsciously participate in such situations. It is a positive criticism in two important respects.

The first is that it challenges religious people to be more truly religious; specifically it challenges Christians to be more truly Christian. Religion should always be personal but never private. The ending of religious legitimation cannot be brought about simply by the good intentions of individuals. Marx points out the social reality of religion, and it is clear that if the abuses of religion to which he points are to be eliminated, then certain structural changes and re-alignments will have to be effected. This is the first challenge, and we should not underestimate the difficulties involved nor the resistance it will arouse.

The second challenge is even more demanding. The criticism which we have been examining is important, but at the same time limited. We have seen that Marx was aware of this abuse of religion because of the pressure on his family, his personal experience and that of his friends and colleagues. It was historically important in Germany at that time, and Marx was right to say that no emancipation could take place until the issue of religion had been settled. The criticism was important but limited, and we have noted points at which Marx knew better. Religion has performed more than one function in society. It has exhibited priestly reconciliation but also prophetic denunciation. Marx felt no obligation to be fair to religion in this respect: there was no evidence to suggest that the prophetic tradition would solve the problem by itself, as if it was an internal matter to religion.

And yet when Marx looked to the long-term solution, to the goal of a new humanity, it was to a religious model that he turned. In an evil world evil is not exclusively the property of the property-owning classes. He saw the work, but could not find the person to carry it out. And this provides the second challenge to Christians. In his religious essays on leaving school Marx wrote of the union of believers with Christ the Redeemer, the second of the four continuing religious issues to which we have pointed. If this redemption is to be a historical and not merely a metaphysical reality, if it is to be political and not merely pious, then Christians must exhibit as a social sphere the first signs of the liberation for which Marx looked.

3

Religion as Reversal

(a) Religion as projection

In Chapter 1 we considered Marx's involvement in religion and his conversion to a life philosophy. In Chapter 2 we dealt with his criticism of the abuse of religion in the legitimation of the state. We now turn to a third element, which by comparison is more theoretical, in two senses. First of all it is a theory about the origins and nature of religion. But secondly, this theory about religion proved decisive in the development of Marx's philosophy in general. We begin with the theory of religion, that religion reverses reality.

This theory of religion was not devised by Marx: he took it over from Ludwig Feuerbach, whose work I have already mentioned. Feuerbach is today remembered as the author of *The Essence of Christianity*, in which he proposed a projection theory of religion. Others, notably Freud, have used the basic idea, but it is difficult now to appreciate how important was the work of Feuerbach in his own time. He was regarded as the father of German materialism, the former disciple of Hegel who turned the system on its head. But he has also been important in the development of the social sciences because of his analyses of alienation and reification. And I have already quoted a letter in which Marx saw Feuerbach's work on man as a species being as fundamental to the development of socialism and communism. Ironically his criticism of religion, for which he is now almost exclusively remembered, was the least important aspect of his work so far as Marx was concerned. Nevertheless, in this the second of Marx's criticisms of religion, Feuerbach was of fundamental importance.

It was appropriate that the radical Hegelians had a dialectical relationship to the master. Hegel's treatment of history is more convincing in the macro- rather than the micro-scale. Its credibility is in

41

inverse proportion to the particularity of its subject. As we have seen, the great sweep of history is interpreted as the incarnation of Spirit or Mind (*Geist*). Spirit externalizes itself into the material, thus becoming alienated. By a long and convoluted series of moments, epochs or stages, it finally achieves reintegration. In its self-realization it overcomes the alienation of subject and object. In religion God is the highest of the immediate forms in which Spirit is represented.

Feuerbach's philosophy is based on the recognition of a dialectial movement, not within history, but within human consciousness. He applied it first to religion, but its lasting importance has been in its application to other social phenomena. In fact the dialectical movement appears in two forms in Feuerbach's analysis of religion: one materialist and reductionist, the other more idealist and Hegelian. The reductionist form comes first. 'Man – this is the mystery of religion – projects his being into objectivity, and then again makes himself an object of this projected image of himself, thus converted into a subject.'[1] The movement is not peculiar to religion, but for Feuerbach it is well-illustrated by religion. Man projects aspects of his being, for example ideals or desires, away from himself. These become objectified as the attributes of God. Since this is an unconscious activity, man is not aware that these attributes are actually human. The attributes now belong to God and not man, and in their alienated and reified form act back on man to control and govern his life. In this reductionist interpretation of religion there is a reversal of reality: man the subject has become the object, while the human predicates have become the divine subject. Alternatively it is a reversal of the order of man and God: man the subject and creator has now become the subject of God, his creation.

It will be clear to what extent Feuerbach was indebted to Hegel, and yet his position involves a fundamental change of perspective. The subject is no longer the absolute Mind in its movement of externalization, alienation and return. Instead Feuerbach deals with the human mind and its parallel movement. For Hegel Mind produces the world and world history is the process of achieveing self-consciousness. For Feuerbach the human mind produces religion in a parallel process. For Hegel the Infinite Spirit comes to self-consciousness through finite spirits. For Feuerbach man achieves self-consciousness through God. Religion is a mystery, not a mistake, and through it man comes to understand himself.

Feuerbach's reversal of subject and predicate in the case of religion can be applied to Hegel's idealism more generally. Whereas the human world is merely posited by the divine Mind, now for Feuerbach the divine is generated by the human. In the Preface to the second edition

Feuerbach made clear the parallel: 'I found my ideas on materials which can be appropriated only through the activity of the senses. I do not generate the object from thought, but the thought from the subject.' Before writing the book he had embarked on further study at Erlangen in anatomy and physiology, consciously attempting to compensate for the one-sidedness of the Hegelian idealism. In the Preface he could assert, 'I am nothing but a natural philosopher in the domain of the mind.'

Since few people today are Hegelians, it is difficult for us to understand the dramatic impact which Feuerbach's work had on his contemporaries. At that stage the Young Hegelians who criticized religion were still loyal to Hegel's philosophy in general. As we have seen, the criticism of religion as reconciliation was not a theory of religion, and rejecting religion in this distorted form did not in itself undermine philosophy. However, if this materialist perspective could be successfully applied to religion, presumably it could be applied to other social forms, thus dismantling the foundations of philosophy. Materialism or natural philosophy was in the air at that time: it was the subject of Marx's dissertation. What is not clear is how Feuerbach came to apply it to religion. The question is important in view of Marx's later break with Feuerbach. Did Feuerbach begin with religion and form this explanatory theory, which he then applied to Hegelian philosophy? Or did he begin with his criticism of idealist philosophy and, for political reasons, expound it first as an indirect critique by applying it to religion?

It is not difficult to see where his criticism might have come from if he began with religion. Schleiermacher, the most influential theologian in the modern world, taught in Berlin at the same time as Hegel. Their systems were completely different and Hegel was very critical of what he perceived to be Schleiermacher's lack of commitment to a rational ontology. In 1799 he had published his first major work, *On Religion: Speeches to its Cultured Despisers*. As a leading figure in the Romantic movement, he expressed sympathy with those who were alienated from religion, but at the same time made a very important distinction. 'At all times but few have discerned religion itself, while millions, in various ways, have been satisfied to juggle with the trappings.'[2] They are alienated from certain objectifications, certain institutional forms, but they must not think that these are religion itself. 'If you have only given attention to these dogmas and opinions, therefore, you do not yet know religion itself, and what you despise is not it.'[3] These manifestations are human attempts to give sensuous, material or conceptual form to the essence of religion, an essence incidently which is the same in all religions. The human capacity for religion arises not from adherence to these externals, but rather from the core of religion itself: 'true religion is sense and taste for the Infinite.'[4] For the purposes of his approach to the Romantics Schleiermacher does not wish further to define the Infinite. 'The analogy with the human conception of the Highest Being and the analogy with the earthly remains the shell of the hidden kernel.'[5]

Certain elements in Schleiermacher's position were important for Feuerbach. The first is the reversal of direction. The enquiry into the nature of religion begins with man rather than God, life in this world in all its variety and sensuousness. Religion is presented as a distinct mode of human behaviour, *sui generis* and not an alternative form of philosophy or morality. It belongs to being human, indeed is constitutive of it, and is therefore important in human development. Second, its core is human feeling, human experience. Feuerbach was prepared to take this over in a reductionist way, as if religion were nothing but the expression of human feelings, needs and desires. And finally, as in the last quotation, the analogy between God and man was one way in which these feelings could be manifest. Thus in *The Essence of Christianity* Feuerbach would seem to be borrowing from Schleiermacher when he claims that 'God is pure, unlimited, free Feeling'.[6] And he is justifying his approach by reference to Schleiermacher in saying, 'If, for example, feeling is the essential organ of religion, the nature of God is nothing else than an expression of the nature of feeling.'[7] This was not at all what Schleiermacher meant, but it was how Feuerbach appropriated it.

Schleiermacher began with actual religion, with experience, and if Feuerbach began with Schleiermacher then at one remove this too was his starting point. It was possible, however, that he began with his critique of idealism, and subsequently applied the criticism to religion. To this point we shall return. In any case he seems to be following Schleiermacher in the distinction he makes between the two parts of his work. The first is 'The True or Anthropological Essence of Religion' while the second part is on 'The False or Theological Essence of Religion'. He wished to investigate the anthropological, the human aspects of religion. His rejection was of the theological, the aspects of religion which did not refer to man. 'Certainly, my work is negative, destructive; but, be it observed, only in relation to the unhuman, not to the human elements of religion.'[8]

This is the first dialectical movement identified by Feuerbach, the reduction, and Marx simply took it over as a second critique of religion.

(b)   Inverted world

Marx began the 'Contribution to the Critique of Hegel's Philosophy of Law: Introduction' with some very abrasive assertions about religion. We have already examined those which constitute part of his reconciliation view of religion. These are interspersed with a very different criticism, one largely taken from Feuerbach. 'The basis of irreligious criticism is this: *Man makes religion*, religion does not make man' [13.175]. This presupposes Feuerbach's projection theory of religion, without spelling it out. The tone however is quite different. For Feuerbach the projection was the source of a mystery; for Marx it is the source of an error.

> Man, who looked for a superhuman being in the fantastic reality of heaven and found nothing there but the *reflection* of himself, will no longer be disposed to find but the *semblance* of himself, only an inhuman being, where he seeks and must seek his true reality.' (3.175).

As Feuerbach fundamentally departed from Scleiermacher's intention when he appropriated his work, so Marx now vulgarizes Feuerbach's position. Marx says of religion what Feuerbach said only of theology. Feuerbach was far from saying that religion is without value. It is a mode of expressing something mysterious about man and is not overtaken in the modern world. He declares that 'religion is man's earliest and also indirect form of self-knowledge. Hence religion everywhere precedes philosophy, as in the history of the race, so also in that of the individual.'⁹ Religion enables man to express and recognize that which otherwise would be hidden from him. Cumulatively the race or a culture has defined itself in relation to those values which it recognizes as the attributes of God. The last thing Feuerbach had in mind was that the projection theory discredited these attributes. 'Hence he alone is the true atheist to whom the predicates of the Divine Being – for example love, wisdom, justice – are nothing; not he to whom merely the subject of these predicates is nothing.'¹⁰ Before philosophy, religion defines and then defends the values which make man human, and humanize society. Nor does religion simply say in mythical terms what philosophy can then state objectively. Feuerbach illustrates this by reference to forgiveness and suffering love. Marx claims in this quotation that religion dehumanizes man: this is the opposite of Feuerbach's view.

But if Feuerbach was offended at being described as an atheist, Marx had by this time, under the influence of Bruno Bauer, adopted it as one of the necessary conditions of being 'critical'. The fact that

Feuerbach was by 1844 the leading intellectual force among the Young Hegelians counted for nothing in this respect. Feuerbach was deeply concerned with religion and continued to be so throughout his life. From the time he joined the Doctor's Club Marx had lost interest in religion and came to see it only as an obstacle to be overcome and an enemy to be defeated.

However, as already noted, Feuerbach had applied the reversal theory not only to religion but too idealist philosophy. This was more significant for Marx, since he had been converted to a form of Hegelianism. In this sense Feuerbach's critique of Hegel made an impact on Marx similar to the impact which his critique of religion might have made on a believer. But the reversal theory was even more important for Marx than that. If it could begin with religion and be applied to the philosophy of Mind, could it be further extended to apply to other social institutions? This was to be the starting point of Marx's own critical philosophy. And it is for this reason that the essay, apparently on the philosophy of the state, begins with the criticism of religion.

The essay begins with this brisk and confident assertion. 'For Germany the *criticism of religion* is in the main complete, and criticism of religion is the premise of all criticism' [3.175]. The phrase 'for Germany' simply refers to the group to which Marx belonged. Strauss, Bauer, Feuerbach, but also Ruge, Stirner, Hess and Marx himself had all directed their criticism against religion. It was complete in the sense that so much ink had been spilt on it. But in a practical sense, now that all avenues had been closed to them in Germany the criticism had no further scope. And now in Paris Marx had suddenly realized that nothing more need be said. But most importantly of all, he came to see that the criticism of religion was a model for other forms of criticism. In that sense it had served its purpose. For Feuerbach it might be a crutch: for Marx it was but a ladder now to be kicked away: 'the criticism of religion is the premise of all criticism.' Feuerbach's analysis had illustrated how the dialectic of human consciousness produced religion. Religion was not the root of the process but an example of it. It is the same man who creates religion who creates other social institutions.

> But *man* is no abstract being encamped outside the world. Man is the *world of man*, the state, society. This state, this society, produce religion, an *inverted world-consciousness*, because they are an *inverted world* (3.175).

Religion is not the source of the reversal of reality, but an example of a human capacity and tendency. Yet given the place which religion has within society (and Marx was still thinking of German in the 1840s), the religious inversion of reality makes other inversions possible and credible. 'Religion is the general theory of that world, its encyclopaedic compendium, its logic in popular form . . .'(3.175). Anyone who is involved in religion, who accepts its reversal of reality, is more likely to accept other forms of reversal.

In his dissertation Marx discussed the philosophy of Epicure, coming as it did after the all-embracing system of Aristotle. He and his colleagues faced something of the samer crisis after the death of Hegel. Hegel's philosophy, as we have seen, dealt with history and the present. This was not simply a practical limitation of a huge subject. 'The owl of Minerva spreads its wings only with the falling of the dusk.' Philosophy, according to Hegel, has nothing to say about the future. The actual is rational and it is philosophy's task to discern that rationality at its own particular stage of history. But we have also seen that the Young Hegelians, notably Bauer and Ruge, now pitted reason against what exists, thus reintroducing the Enlightenment perspective to which Hegel objected so strongly. Criticism was no longer the discernment of the rationality of the actual, but the exposing of the disparity between the essence and existence of social institutions such as religion or the state. What was left for the Young Hegelians to do? How could they break free of Hegel? His work, the recent history of philosophy, was in a real sense the philosophy of history. But, if we may adopt the aphoristic style of the movement, the future of philosophy must be a philosophy of the future. Not now a philosophy which assumes that the actual is rational, thus both justifying the present and providing an argument for its continuation, but a philosophy, which in exposing the irrationality of the present, disputes the present and calls for a new future. (Were the Young Hegelians here superseding the master? No. They were reverting to the Enlightenment tradition which, he had already warned, led first to criticism of what is in terms of abstract ideals, then to Revolution and finally to the Terror. And if Marx perpetrated no terror himself, he at least opened a door which Hegel had already warned his apprentices must remain closed.)

One of the most ambiguous but influential contributions to the debate came from the Polish-born August von Cieszkowski. A few years older than Marx, he had studied in Berlin just after the death of Hegel. In 1838 he published a work entitled *Prolegomena zur Historiosophie* in which he took up the challenge. Although Hegel had dealt with teleology in history (to which we shall later refer in Chapter 5), he had not enquired into the implications of this dynamic for the future. In this Cieszkowski brought together two elements not found in Hegel. The first was from the recently published work by Philippe Joseph Buchez *Introduction à la Science de l'Histoire*, namely the concept of organic laws of history.[11] Since the future is but the next link in the past and present, it will be produced by the same dynamic. The second was from the influence of French utopian socialism. Thus those who know the laws of history can shape the future to their social ends. Since the laws of historical motion have been discovered by philosophy, its task with regard to the future is essentially practical: it must become applied philosophy. Fundamental to Cieszkowski's position is the deed. Praxis no longer refers to the activity of critical theory, but to the intervention which guides and changes history. The task of philosophy is 'to become a practical philosophy or rather a philosophy of practical activity, of "praxis", exercising a direct influence on social life and developing the future in the realm of concrete activity'.[12] Heady stuff, but how was this to be done? Where was the point of entry? But now Marx had solved that problem. As we have seen the criticism of religion was an important practical matter for a philosophy of the future. But now a very different criticism of religion proved to be the premise of all other forms of criticism.

It is in this context that we should understand one of the most important and programmatic statements in Marx's early works. The criticism of religion, that it is error, illusion, fantasy, is necessary, but its achievement is very limited. Since religion is not the source of the tendency to reversal, even the elimination of religion would not end other forms of reversal. But at least the elimination of religion would expose the other, secular forms of reversal for what they are. They would have no religious context in which to seem more credible. Marx sees that with this his work has not ended, it has scarcely begun, at least he is now standing in the right place.

> It is the *task of history*, therefore, once the *other-world of truth* has vanished, to establish the *truth of this world*. The immediate *task of philosophy*, which is in the service of history, is to unmask human self-alienation in its *secular form* now that it has been unmasked in its *sacred form*. Thus the criticism of heaven is transformed into the criticism of earth, the *criticism of religion* into the *criticism of law* and the *criticism of theology* into the *criticism of politics*.[13]

The criticism of religion is complete, and necessary, but it merely clears the decks for all other forms of criticism to be undertaken. It was an important and exciting moment for Marx: he could see how his critical philosophy of the future would develop, and how it would be capable of practical application. Philosophy in itself would not change the present, but now at least this was to be its objective. 'The weapon of criticism cannot, of course, replace criticism by weapons, material force must be overthrown by material force; but theory also becomes a material force as soon as it has gripped the masses' (3.182).

It will be clear why this theoretical criticism of religion, religion as the reversal of reality, was in the long run more important to Marx than the practical criticism, religion as reconciliation. It is in its paradigmatic form that the criticism of religion was important. What started as a narrow atheistic dismissal of religion as error has been transformed from a negative task, to a positive enterprise, what Marx refers to as 'the resolute positive abolition of religion' (3.182).

With this Marx's own criticism of religion is complete. He refers to religion from time to time in his later writings, but as instances of reconciliation or reversal.

(c) Secular reversals

As we have noted, Feuerbach identified in religion a particular instance of a general human capacity. I have referred to this analysis as the reductionist dialectic. Man unconsciously projects aspects of his being into objectivity. These human predicates then take on objective and independent existence. Finally they become the subject, acting back upon man. This is what Feuerbach identified as the reversal of subject and predicate. It takes place in religion, but he was able to apply the same analysis to Hegel's philosophy. In this the idea, originally a human predicate, takes on objective existence. It becomes more real than human being as individuals or groups and acts back to control human existence.

Since Marx was not fascinated by religion he simply took over Feuerbach's critique without further comment. However, it was Feuerbach's application of the analysis to Hegel which proved of fundamental importance to the development of Marx's own philosophy. From 1843, in a series of essays he explored a variety of subjects, and in each case the reversal of subject and predicate was the turning point. According to Feuerbach the projection and reversal produce alienation. Man is estranged from his true life, his species life. As he moved from subject to subject Marx developed this into a general theory of alienation. In this sense Feuerbach laid the foundations of Marx's socialism.

In 1820 Hegel prepared a text-book for his lecture course on the Philosophy of Right. It dealt with right/law itself and with morality. In the third part it discussed the progression from the family, through civil society to the state. It was of course the fundamental source of his political philosophy and as such very influential on his followers. In the summer of 1843, after the closure of the *Rheinische Zeitung* and before his move to Paris, Marx made a very close, section by section, study of the *Rechtsphilosophie*, or at least the part dealing with the state. It is all too easy in such a commentary to become lost in the welter of detail, but its constant feature is the exposure in Hegel's philosophy of the state of the same reversal to which Feuerbach had drawn attention to in religion.

According to Hegel the state cannot be properly understood simply by examining its constituent features regarded as the outcome of historical accident or contingent events. The state, being actual, is rational: it is the incarnation of the Idea. In this Marx detected an 'inversion of subject and predicate'.

> The genuine thought is this: the development of the state or the political constitution into distinct aspects and their actualty is an *organic* development. The *actual distinct aspects* or *various facets of the political* constitution are the premise, the subject. The predicate is their characterization as *organic*. Instead of this, the idea is made the subject, and the distinct aspects and their actuality are conceived as the idea's development and product; whereas, on the contrary, the idea has to be developed from the actual distinct aspects (3.12).

According to Marx, in Hegel's approach to the issue 'The correct method is stood on its head' (3.40). Historical events are no longer understood by reference to human motives and decisions, but rather in the light of the progressive outworking of the immanent Idea, what in a notebook written in Kreuznach Marx described as 'political teleology' (3.130). Human essence is thus defined apart from human existence as the embodiment of the Idea. The human significance and meaning of events is replaced by something which either is, or at least creates the impression of being, profound. 'It makes a deep mystical impression to see a *particular* empirical existent posited by the idea, and thus to meet at every stage an incarnation of God' (3.39).

It is possible to illustrate the movement either as embodiment or as incarnation because of the extent to which Hegel's philosophy was based on essentially religious structures of thought. Marx looks in passing to the Old Testament and chooses to illustrate his criticism by reference to the law. 'Man does not exist for the law but the law for man . . .' (3.30), a form which would recall for many the words of Jesus about the sabbath.[14] In all this Marx takes up the reversal theory of religion and applies it to Hegel's political philosophy.

> Hegel starts from the state and makes man the subjectified state; democracy starts from man and makes the state the objectified man. Just as it is not religion which creates man but man who creates

religion, so it is not the constitution which creates the people but the people which creates the constitution (3.29).

The parallel is clear. In this case we are dealing with ideas about social order and social relations which have been projected away from man. These predicates have become objectified, gaining independent existence over against man. And then they act back. Man 'forgets' that he created the state. But now the creator must submit to his creature: the state defines who is a citizen, and bestows or withholds civil rights. So now man as a citizen is alienated from his true or social being. He exists not in virtue of his membership of society, but as an individual in the eyes of the state (3.77).

Although Hegel gave the impression that his political philosophy was the exposition of purely rational principles when it comes to contentious issues of the day, he seemed to be simply legitimizing the political *status quo*. Thus he argued, or perhaps simply asserted, that hereditary monarchy was a truer expression of the Idea than elected government. Marx did not lose the opportunity of pointing up the contradiction in this position. Election is associated with human freedom and conscious choice, heredity with the accident of physical birth. 'Hegel descends everywhere from his political spiritualism into the crassest *materialism*' (3.105). It will be recalled that Feuerbach broke with Hegel because the latter was so one-sided in his philosophy. Marx sees a certain natural justice here. 'Nature avenges itself on Hegel for the contempt he has shown it' (3.105).

Under the influence of Feuerbach's reversal theory of religion Marx came to see the reversal of subject and predicate as endemic in Hegel's thought. The study of the *Rechtsphilosophie*, which Marx entitled 'Contribution to the Critique of Hegel's Philosophy of Law', was not published; indeed it was not published anywhere till 1927, but it laid the foundations for the further development of his new position. He went on to write an article 'On the Jewish Question', which was published in the *Deutsch-Französische Jahrbücher* the following year. It is in two parts, responding to the issues raised in two articles on the subject written by Bruno Bauer. The first part of the essay continues his previous discussion of political and civil societies. The second part of the essay sees another application of the reversal theory of religion.

Marx was greatly influenced by the Young Hegelians, but he was also an original thinker and, as we have seen, he could transform traditional or even contemporary studies by his distinctive approach. We have already noted the discrimination against Jews in Prussian law. Bauer tackled the issue in an essay entitled 'The Capacity of Present-day Jews and Christians to Become Free.' His position was so changed by this time that his solution was for Jews and Christians to give up their religions. Although Bauer was now an atheist he could not conceive of the issue in other than theological terms. But for Marx that was the necessary starting point: how could the issue be reconceived in other terms?

> For us, the question of the Jew's capacity for emancipation becomes the question: What particular *social* element has to be overcome in order to abolish Judaism? (3.168).

This is certainly a new approach to the issue: new to Bauer, but new also to Marx. It suddenly appears without warning and without explanation. Why should we deal with Judaism, or any other religion, by seeking a 'social element'? And there is a prior question: what does it mean? On this point Marx is as brief as he is brusque and it is not at all clear what he has in mind. But since at the end of the argument he presents us with an example of reversal, we might enquire whether this lies behind his enigmatic assertion.

If religion ends up with an inversion of reality, it is because it has started out with the projection of certain predicates. Although Feuerbach seemed to suggest that man projects his whole being into objectivity, it transpires that he thought man projected only certain aspects. These would normally be what man – or in particular a race, culture or society – either admired or feared. One of the fundamental factors leading to the great divergencies among religions would be what the particular society admired or feared. That could vary from culture to culture, age to age, environment to environment. On a reversal theory of religion therefore the first step towards the emancipation of a people would be to identify from their religion what it was that most concerned them.

Two further qualifications would have to be added. First, since the projection identifies an aspect of the species being of the society in question, the answer Marx seeks will be a social element. Second, and reminiscent of Feuerbach's distinction between religion and theology, Marx directs attention not to orthodoxy but to popular religion. Along these lines I believe it is possible to understand Marx's intention. However, it hardly prepares us for the crass and apparently anti-semitic answer he gives to his own question.

> Let us consider the actual, wordly Jew, not the *Sabbath Jew*, as Bauer does, but the *everyday Jew*. Let us not look for the secret of the Jew in his religion, but let us look for the secret of his religion in the real Jew. What is the secular basis of Judaism? *Practical* need, *self-interest*. What is the worldly religion of the Jew? *Huckstering*.

What is his worldly god? *Money*. Very well then! Emancipation from *huckstering* and money, consequently from practical, real Judaism, would be the self-emancipation of our time (3.170).

This represents an extraordinary outburst, especially when we consider the distinguished traditions of Marx's family and the gracious example of his parents. Since our interest here is solely in the development of theory, we might restrict ourselves to pointing out that at this point Marx has not departed from his master. He accused Hegel of a reversal: he had dealt not with real men but with abstract men who were the exemplification of pre-established ideas. Marx's definition of the social basis of Judaism does exactly the same for actual Jews, misrepresenting both them and Judaism itself. Having said that, we can see that Marx is attempting to understand a religion by reversing its original projection. In this case what he considers to be the original projection might be questioned.

From what we have seen of Marx it is unlikely that he would rest content with the analysis of a particular religion, or even with the generalization of the analysis. In his critique of Hegel's philosophy of the state he used the religious example to clarify the secular inversion. Marx now procedes to a similar application.

Money is the jealous god of Israel, in face of which no other god may exist. Money degrades all the gods of man – and turns them into commodities. Money is the universal self-established *value* of all things. It has therefore robbed the whole world – both the world of men and nature – of its specific value. Money is the estranged essence of man's work and man's experience, and this alien essence dominates him, and he worships it (3.172).

Marx only started with Judaism because he was responding to an article by Bauer, but he has ended with a position which is quite independent of his comments on Judaism. By a rather convoluted route he has arrived at a conclusion which makes a further contribution to his new critical philosophy. He was discovered a new inversion of reality in that series which began with Christianity, proceeded through Hegel's philosophy, and continued by way of the criticism of Hegel's doctrine of the state and the monarchy. Now in money we are presented with yet another example. Money is not part of the natural world, although successive generations of teenagers believe it grows on trees. Nothing brings its conventional nature to our attention more effectively than the sight of some foreign banknotes which we brought home with us from a holiday abroad. Notes which would a week before have earned us smiles of welcome in a bar or bazaar now seem like samples of wallpaper. Money is a human creation. But now, on the reversal model, it has become more real than those who devised it. The creature now controls its creator. But in this case Marx points out the further alienation. Money has now become independent of its creators. It acts back to bestow not their, but its value on everything – and everyone. Man, the human world, and even the natural world now exist on its terms. It takes from man his human value: merely human values are now degraded, even derided. 'What is this field worth?' 'This house?' 'What was he worth when he died?' Money on the reversal theory, alienates man from his species being, his true life, his human life.

(d) Economic reversals

Earlier I quoted a programme which Marx set out for dealing with human alienation in its profane forms now that he had unmasked it in its sacred forms. This appeared in the essay a 'Contribution to the Critique of Hegel's Philosophy of Law: Introduction'. By the beginning of 1844 Marx had made preliminary attempts to deal with the reversals and hence the alienations present in philosophy, history, and politics. But if his critical philosophy was to become applied philosophy then he has to tackle the very different subject of work.

It was in Paris that the third main ingredient was added to his new philosophy. German critical theory, French revolutionary praxis, and now Scottish political economy. In the summer following his arrival in Paris Marx produced three studies, largely to clarify his thinking in this new area: they are usually referred to as the 'Economic and Philosophical Manuscripts of 1844'. I have already observed that although Marx was an original thinker, he often took as his starting point some existing study. It was then for him to question its underlying assumptions. This was true of Hegel's treatment of the state, of Bauer's approach to the emancipation of the Jews, of 'a Prussian's' view of the Silesian weavers' revolt. So now in the Paris Manuscripts, as Marx enters what for him is a relatively new field, he begins with the main authorities in political economy at that time. Indeed his treatment of wages, capital, profit and rent consists largely of a series of lengthy quotations, mainly from Adam Smith's foundation work *The Wealth of Nations*. (The original was published in 1776 and Marx used a French translation published in 1802.) Marx could hardly have looked for a better statement of bourgeois political economy. Adam Smith, Professor of Moral Philosophy at the University of Glasgow, was the founder of modern political economy. As Alexander Gray puts it: 'Before Adam Smith there had been much economic discussion; with him we reach the stage of discussing economics.'[15]

Marx makes almost no critical comments during what turns out to be but an exposition of current economic theories. But he then makes it clear that he disagrees with certain basic premises from which they begin.

Political economy starts with the fact of private property; it does not explain it to us. It expresses in general, abstract formulas the *material* process through which private property actually passes, and these formulas it then takes for *laws* (3.270).

Humanism is probably the best term to describe Marx's position, from the days of his schoolboy essays he was motivated by the desire to assist people to live truly human lives. The various obstacles to that goal were his enemies. Political economy, as Marx presents it, describes certain relationships and processes which result in the dehumanizing of industrial workers. That is not the concern of the economics, but it is Marx's concern. They describe the laws which govern economic activity: he is concerned with the intrinsic connection among economic relationships which bring about human alienation. They take for granted what he wishes to challenge.

The economist assumes in the form of a fact, of an event, what he is supposed to deduce – namely, the necessary relationship between two things – between, for example, division of labour and exchange. Thus the theologian explains the origin of evil by the fall of man: that is, he assumes as a fact, in historical form, what has to be explained (3.271).

Marx directs his attention to something which is of no consequence to the economist, namely, the relationship between the worker and the product of his labour. At once we see an example of reversal. Under the circumstances of modern capitalist production the worker produces a commodity which not only objectively embodies his labour, but in becoming a commodity becomes alienated from him. It increases in value, but he decreases.

For on this premise it is clear that the more the worker spends himself, the more powerful becomes the alien world of objects which he creates over against himself, the poorer he himself – his inner world – becomes, the less belongs to him as his own. It is the same in religion. The more man puts into God, the less he retains in himself (3.272).

In addition to this form of reversal which arises from the relationship of the worker to the product of his labour, there is a second inversion of reality which arises from the act of production itself. Once again this is an issue only for the humanist, and not for the economist. The alienated product arises fron activity which is itself alienated. It is what Marx calls 'forced labour'. Alienated labour does not express a creative potential: its motive has nothing to do with human needs. The reversal is that while labour should be carried on to satisfy a human need, under the conditions of alienated labour it becomes merely a means to satisfy animal needs, such as eating and drinking. The end becomes merely a means to another end.

Although Marx makes this thought his own, it owes a good deal to Hegel, for example in the *Philosophy of Right*, where in his profession a man 'actualizes himself',[16] and more extensively in the famous master/slave passage in *The Phenomenology of Mind*. In passing we might note that the reversal of the advantage of the master and the slave provides a parallel with our earlier discussion of the transformation which Marx envisaged in the proletarian revolution. Hegel's point of interest is of course in the development of consciousness, yet it is an instance of the general movement of spirit into the material world. 'Through work and labour, however, this consciousness of the bondsman comes to itself.' Richard Norman underlines the importance of 'the recognition that self-consciousness requires not just that a man gets to know himself, but that he actively produces himself. Self-consciousness becomes self-realization'[17] At the end of the Paris manuscripts there is a section modestly entitled 'Critique of the Hegelian Dialectic and Philosophy as a Whole'. There Marx draws attention to this point, which he regards as 'the outstanding achievement of Hegel's *Phänomenologie*', namely that Hegel 'grasps the essence of *labour* and comprehends objective man – true, because real man – as the outcome of man's *own labour*' (3.333). In alienated labour this self-production of true life does not take place: man is not motivated by inner human needs, but by external forces.

> Just as in religion the spontaneous activity of the human imagination, of the human brain and the human heart, operates on the individual independently of him – that is, operates as an alien, divine or diabolical activity – so is the worker's activity not his spontaneous activity. It belongs to another; it is loss of his self (3.274).

But there is a third respect in which man in alienated in the modern conditions of production. It is in his conscious, creative activity that man is distinguished from the beasts. Unlike the beasts, man makes things even when he had no merely biological needs, and creates works of beauty. Like the animals man works on the natural world, but as he does this he expresses not his animal, but his truly human life.

The object of labour is, therefore, the *objectification of man's species-life*; for he duplicates himself not only, as in consciousness, intellectually, but also actively, in reality, and therefore sees himself in a world that he has created (3.277).

This is the worst form of the reversal, that man's species life becomes simply the life of the individual, both alienated from his own true life and alienating him from his fellow men.

Thus Marx applies the inversion of reality model, which he first learned from Feuerbach's criticism of religion, to labour and the life of the proletariat. At the outset he realizes that he is going to be raising issues for which economists take no responsibility whatsoever. Political economy deals with man at work, as it might deal with a horse. 'It does not consider him when he is not working, as a human being; but leaves such considerations to criminal law, to doctors, to religion, to the statistical tables, to politics and to the poor-house overseer' (3.241). There is one final example of the application of the reversal theory, and that concerns private property.

When I was an undergraduate in the Department of Political Economy, Marx was hardly mentioned. In one sense this was understandable, in another ironic. It was understandable since Marx did not share the fundamental premises of much of the political economy of his day. He was not an economist and arguably did not aspire to be one on the narrow definition of the subject offered then, as now. He was a moral philosopher, always seeking the human basis of actions and institutions. The social sciences aspire, rightly or wrongly, to being value-free. Marx was highly critical of economics not for being a moral science, but for not acknowledging the fact, or rather for covertly advocating moral values which he regarded as dehumanizing (3.309). But in another sense it was ironic that in the University of Glasgow Marx should not be mentioned, because Marx was deeply influenced by our own Adam Smith. Smith, too, was a moral philosopher, and this was carried into his economics.

We have seen that Marx focussed on the human essence of the relationship between labour and commodity, the product of labour. The product considered in a purely objective sense without reference to its human origins was simply another example of the reversal of subject and predicate, the setting up of an alien power over against man, distorting man's truly human life. This is of no concern to the economist as he deals with the relationship of labour to the production of commodities. Such commodities become private property, and once again economists are concerned with private property only in an objective sense. Thus for Marx private property can be seen as part of that

57

whole inverted world which he can describe in various ways, including religious.

Marx claims that it is in the work of Adam Smith that he discovered the real essence of private property, the human, subjective essence in contrast to the alienated objective approach of less enlightened economists.

> To this enlightened political economy, which has discovered – within private property – the *subjective essence* of wealth, the adherents of the monetary and mercantile system, who look upon private property *only as an objective* substance confronting men, seem therefore to be *fetishists, Catholics*. Engels was therefore right to call *Adam Smith the Luther of Political Economy*. Just as Luther recognized *religion – faith –* as the substance of the external *world* and in consequence stood opposed to Catholic paganism – just as he superseded *external* religiosity by making religiosity the *inner* substance of man – just as he negated the priests outside the layman because he transplanted the priest into laymen's hearts, just so with wealth . . . (3.290).

Viewed objectively, private property, or wealth, simply happens to exist, and economics is the 'cynical' science which explains how it comes about. But to the humanist, to the moral philosopher, who understands its subjective essence, its relation to man, it becomes 'a world-historical power' (3.293). In a secular and non-mythological sense Marx is referring to an inverted world in which man is enslaved and subjected to alien powers, the rulers of this world.

It would be tempting, but facile, to say that Marx's solution to the problem of private property was communism. In the Paris Manuscripts Marx knew communists who regarded the abolition of private property as their primary goal. Not surprisingly they had not arrived at this position along the lines of Marx's analysis. They did not understand about the subjective essence of labour, or the subjective essence of private property. Consequently they shared the common assumption of the objective nature of private property. For them the question was whether private property could be commonly owned or not. And if not, it was to be destroyed. Nothing could have been further from Marx's view. He criticized this 'crude and unreflective communism' in three respects.

First, because it has not understood the relationship between work and alienated labour, this form of communism is not guided by the desire to achieve the species life. Its vision is not the release, exercise and expression of creative talents, not the delight in beauty or the enjoyment of skills. Thus alienated labour is not only maintained, but generalized.

Secondly, because it has not looked into the subjective essence of private property, namely labour, the abolition or retention of specific commodities as property does not address the fundamental problem. 'General envy constituting itself as a power is the disguise in which *greed* re-establishes itself and satisfies itself, only in *another* way' (3.295). By treating private property in this objective and crude manner, Marx considers that this kind of communism negates the world of culture and civilization; far from raising the level of the poor, it proceeds by a levelling-down process to degrade them to an even lower level of human existence than before.

Thirdly, because the roots of alienated labour and the relationship between commodity production and private property have not been explored, when it comes to wages the communist system merely transforms the person of the employer, creating 'the community as the universal capitalist'.

In passing we might note the irony that several countries which claim Marx for the inspiration of their communist revolutions exhibit precisely that form of state capitalism which Marx condemned as being more dehumanizing than capitalism itself. After Marx criticizes various forms of communism he proposes another. It does not yet exist, and is based on his own position, which takes into account his whole critical philosophy and his analysis of economic relations. It is not a negative, destructive movement, but a positive overcoming of all forms of human alienation.

> *Communism* is the *positive* transcendence of *private property* as *human self-estrangement*, and therefore as the real *appropriation* of the *human essence* by and for man; communism therefore as the complete return of man to himself as a *social* (i.e., human) being – a return accomplished consciously and embracing the entire wealth of previous development. This communism, as a fully developed naturalism, equals humanism, and as fully developed humanism equals naturalism (3.296).

There is one final feature of existing forms of communism which Marx criticises, atheism. As we come to the end of this section on Marx's criticism of religion as a reversal of reality, we recall that the model of reversal arose from the critique of religion. It was then applied to various other human spheres, from philosophy to economics. The criticism of religion is the 'premise of all criticism', but only in a historical, contingent sense. It is not the premise in the sense

59

of the first step in an argument which must be constantly reaffirmed each time the argument is used.

> *Atheism*, as the denial of this unreality, has no longer any meaning, for atheism is a *negation of God*, and postulates the *existence of man*, through this negation; but socialism as socialism no longer stands in any need of such a mediation (3.306).

It is very significant that Marx at this point places religion in the same category as private property. Atheism and communism deal with alienations created by inverted worlds. The denial of religion and the rejection of private property are merely stages in a process.

> Socialism is man's *positive self-consciousness* no longer mediated through the abolition of religion, just as *real life* is man's positive reality, no longer mediated through the abolition of private property, through communism. Communism is the position as the negation of the negation, and hence is the *actual* phase necessary for the next stage of historical development in the process of human emancipation and rehabilitation. *Communism* is the necessary form and the dynamic principle of the immediate future, but communism as such is not the goal of human development, the form of human society (3.306).

How many of those who have called themselves followers of Marx have practised the state capitalism which he condemned? And how many, in spite of his objections, have made atheism the dogmatic foundation of their communism? But how few have understood that communism is not even the goal? The criticism of private property, like the criticism of religion, is a distraction when viewed objectively. It must be related to the development of the species life of mankind.

(e) Human essence of religion

It is time now to make an assessment of Marx's criticism of religion. At first sight this might seem as useful as enquiring about a gardener's view of weeds. Those who know nothing about Marx, and some who know a great deal about him, assume that Marx utterly rejected religion and that nothing more need be said. One of the most popular books containing extracts from his writings is entitled *K. Marx and F. Engels: On Religion*. It was prepared in the Institute of Marxism-Leninism in Moscow and no doubt is intended to make available in convenient form Marx's most critical and dismissive words on the subject of religion. However, it will be clear from our coverage of the matter that determining Marx's understanding of religion is a much more complicated affair than collecting some passages in which religion is mentioned.

So far as Marx's reversal theory is concerned, the criticism of religion is integral to the development of his whole philosophy: it cannot simply be extracted and dealt with as a discrete social institution. As the premise of all criticism it is essential for understanding all subsequent disclosures of reversal. For this reason Marx, in his early writings, refers to religion more than any other single subject, with the exception of Hegel's philosophy. I have therefore taken the trouble to follow the development of his philosophy from the criticism of religion through the criticism of philosophy, the state, money, alienated labour and private property. It is in this context that an assesment of his position must be made.

If we wish to avoid the flash-card automatic response, the knee-jerk reaction to the association 'Marx – religion', then we must perform a task which to my knowledge has never been undertaken. We must present Marx's criticism of religion as one example in the series of reversals which we have already examined. If, as Marx claimed, it is the premise of all other forms of criticism, it should be possible to understand it as a typical example in the sequence. If this has never been previously undertaken, it is because Marx did not himself undertake it, for three reasons.

1. The first is a practical reason. Since religion came as the first in the series, it appears before a pattern has been established. No one has taken the trouble to go back again to see how well the original analysis fits the emerging pattern.

2. From the time of his entry into the Doctors' Club, and possibly under the influence of Bruno Bauer, Marx was an atheist, and had no personal interest in religion. While he was intensely interested in what lessons could be drawn from uncovering reversals in their secular forms, he had no such interest with regard to religion.

3. The third reason is more concerned with the theory itself, and its implications are much more important. It arises from a fundamental flaw in Marx's assessment of Feuerbach's account of religion. We must explore this third reason in more detail.

Now, dear reader, I must admit that in one important respect I have misled you. I have said that Feuerbach stood Hegel's system on its head. This is what Feuerbach thought he had achieved. It is what Marx thought Feuerbach had achieved. And this view has been passed on by scholars from decade to decade, carefully preserving the tradition. Alas, it is not so. Feuerbach was a brilliant pupil of Hegel. His account of religion is not an attack upon the Hegelian system, but rather an example of it. Far from standing Hegel on his head, it is an offering laid at his feet. But how can this be? In many spheres of life we see bitter conflict: two individuals or groups attack each other's positions. They are diametrically and irreconcilably opposed. Or at least that is how it appears to them. To the outsider the two positions are simply variations on a theme. They are characterized from the outside, not by what divides them but by what they have in common. Neither group notices that they share assumptions which not only unite them, but distinguish them from many other groups in society. Feuerbach's position was shocking to orthodox Hegelians. And that is the point. The Young Hegelians were young *Hegelians*. They could shock those who shared with them basic Hegelian premises. This was an in-house controversy, the kind which is notoriously bitter. In what sense, then, was Feuerbach still a Hegelian?

In Hegel's *Phenomenology of Mind*, objects in the social world are regarded as phenomena, as the products of consciousness, with religion, as Richard Norman puts it, 'being the means by which a society attains to self-consciousness and expresses to itself its own nature'.[18] And did Feuerbach think he could actually supersede Hegel? In the *Phenomenology* Hegel had already dealt with that one-sided form of enlightenment which considered that whatever reality belief held to be absolute was 'a being that comes from belief's own consciousness, is its own thought, something produced from and by consciousness'.[19] In *The Essence of Christianity* Feuerbach presents religion as the product of mind, the accumulated sedimented consciousness of a whole society or culture. To the orthodox it might have been shocking that in this case the phenemenon of religion is produced by human consciousness, rather than the divine Mind. But to the outsider what matters the case of the letter, be it Mind or mind, compared with the unfounded and unjustified assumption that objects in the social world are created in the course of a dialectial movement in consciousness?

There is, of course, a reversal in Feuerbach's projection: whereas previously the divine Mind created man, now the human mind creates God. But it is not a reversal in reality, merely a reversal within the Hegelian order. Looked at more closely this is not the reversal which Marx identifies when he turns to the social institutions of the state, money, labour and property. Take, for example, his criticism of the state. If Marx had actually applied Feuerbach's account of religion then he would have replaced the Hegelian view that the state is produced by the divine consciousness, by a Feuerbachian counter that the state is produced by human consciousness. This he does not do. Man creates the state, but out of a long and ambiguous historical process which shows to date no sign of being rational. There is a reversal, but it is not Feuerbach's reversal, not an exchange of places within the Hegelian system.

When, therefore, we seek to evaluate Marx's criticism of religion as reversal, we encounter a double ambiguity. In the case of the state Marx contrasts the Hegelian idealist doctrine with the actual historical state. By contrast, when he deals with religion he begins with the Hegelian view of religion and ends with the Young Hegelian view of religion. Neither at the beginning nor at the end does he deal with actual historical religion. The second ambiguity inevitably follows from this. The reversal in the case of religion is not the reversal which Marx discovers in the secular examples. It is not a reversal in reality, but merely within the Hegelian extended family. Although Marx's inversion of reality model therefore arose from religion and was applied in all other spheres, it was never properly applied to religion itself.

If we therefore seek to apply the reversal theory to religion we must form a systematic view of how that theory was developed with regard to the secular examples. Following that, we can apply the general form of the theory to religion, something which Marx did not attempt. We begin, therefore, with the general theory of reversal, as characterized by the analysis of the state.

1. Following his normal practice Marx does not begin with the state, the actual state, a contemporary instance of the phenomenon. Rather he begins with Hegel's political philosophy.

2. The reversal which emerges does not lie inevitably within the state, but rather in Hegel's presentation of it.

3. Little interest is shown in the origins of the state, the historical, geographical or cultural factors involved.

4. Consequently Marx is not concerned with the distinctive character of particular states, but with the essence of the state.

5. The essence of the state is man. This is not a self-evident proposition and conflicts with the traditional view of the state held by its supporters and by its critics.

6. The reversal theory is therefore that the human essence of the state has been replaced by a non-human, alienated and alienating essence. At this point and without telling us, Marx has moved from a description of the Hegelian view of the state to a description of the effect that holding this view has on those who participate in it.

7. The solution is for the reversal to be reversed, a negation of the negation.

8. The state is not abolished, but is now understood in its human essence.

9. The transformation from the state in its alienated form to its essential form cannot be effected at the level of consciousness only.

10. The reversal in theory must be allied to a revolution in praxis.

If this is an example of the general theory of reversal, my proposal is that it should now be applied to religion. We can do this simply by substituting the word 'religion' for 'state' throughout each proposition.

1. Following his normal practice Marx does not begin with religion, actual religion, a contemporary instance of the phenomenon. Rather he begins with Hegel's religious philosophy.

2. The reversal which emerges does not lie inevitably within religion, but rather in Hegel's presentation of it.

3. Little interest is shown in the origins of religion, the historical, geographical or cultural factors involved.

4. Consequently Marx is not concerned with the distinctive character of particular religions, but with the essence of religion.

5. The essence of religion is man. This is not a self-evident proposition and conflicts with the traditional view of religion held by its supporters and by its critics.

6. The reversal theory is therefore that the human essence of religion has been replaced by a non-human, alienated and alienating essence. At this point and without telling us, Marx has moved from a description of the Hegelian view of religion to a description of the effect that holding this view has on those who participate in it.

7. The solution is for the reversal to be reversed, a negation of the negation.

8. Religion is not abolished, but is now understood in its human essence.

9. The transformation from religion in its alienated form to its essential form cannot be effected at the level of consciousness only.

10. The reversal in theory must be allied to a revolution in praxis.

The implications of the reversal theory when applied to religion are not immediately clear, but then neither are the implications for the state immediately clear. One of the problems with Marx's method is that he begins not with the phenomenon itself, but with a theory about it. Half-way through there is a significant change. But even here it is not that he begins to address the phenomenon as it is, rather that he forms a new theory about how it ought to be. While in the case of the state he was interested enough to go on to say something about how it ought to be, he had lost interest in religion and did not pursue this side of the reversal of the reversal. To clarify the implications we must further analyse the position of Feuerbach, whose theory he was using.

In the tradition of Hegel, and in common with the other Young Hegelians, Feuerbach began his critical work with reflections on human consciousness. But consciousness is always consciousness of something; it locates man in a field of experience. This is the weakness of Feuerbach's approach to religion: he does not begin with experience, with religious experience or that experience which gives rise to religion. Rather he begins with consciousness – of the species. But on closer inspection this is a fiction. No one is conscious of the species. At most we are conscious of our family, colleagues, society around us. Through the media and education we are aware of other people and cultures around the world and throughout history. But of the species we are not aware, nor if we could be would it be any different from aspects of the sub-groups mentioned.

In Feuerbach's philosophy the species is simply a fiction to represent human ideals and values. Man is not as he should be: we are all a mixture of good and evil. It may well be that men in association are more evil than they are individually: 'moral man and immoral society' (Niebuhr). Be that as it may, the species, if we could form a meaningful view of it, would share the evil as well as the good of individuals. For Feuerbach the species represents and indeed embodies only the good. The species-life is man as he ought to be. Feuerbach never deals with man as he is, with human experience. His subject is always man as he ought to be. The 'father of German materialism' was never anything but an idealist. His critique of Hegel was that idealism should begin with man. It is man who generates his ideals and values and who is responsible for pursuing them. But his criticism of Hegelian idealism should not disguise from us the fact that he was no materialist, nor even empiricist. He did not begin with human experience as it is, with states of consciousness, but consciousness of ideals.

When Marx took over Feuerbach's projection theory of religion he got less than he bargained for. It is not much of a theory of religion, and it is based on an inadequate view of man. However, since Marx did not want to reform, refine or perpetuate religion, as Feuerbach did, this inherent weakness did not occur to him, at the time.

In a restricted context Feuerbach's projection theory of religion contains a very important observation. Religion and culture advance together. It is no coincidence that the attributes of the gods correspond to the character of their peoples.

Physical strength is an attribute of the Homeric gods: Zeus is the strongest of the gods. Why? Because physical strength, in and by itself, was regarded as something glorious, divine. To the ancient Germans the highest virtues were those of the warrior; therefore

65

their supreme god was the god of war, Odin . . . Not the attributes of the divinity, but the divineness or deity of the attributes is the first true Divine Being.[20]

The doctrine of God current in a society tells us a great deal about the level of moral or cultural development of the age. In the rather heroic style of George Eliot's translation: 'As thou thinkest God, such is thy thought; – the measure of thy God is the measure of thy understanding.'[21] Regardless of what ought to be, it is a matter of observation that very often to speak of God is simply to speak of man in exalted tones. However, Feuerbach said more than this. That which is projected away from man becomes objectified as the attributes of God, as the will of God. It then acts back on man, to control his life. This is the source of the reversal, and of alienation. Man now lives in a world within a world. The human world has lost its own meaning, value and significance. It is now to be understood only *sub specie aeternitatis*. And yet if the projection theory is substantially correct, much if not all of this divine context is a human construction. It does not exist outside of human inventive consciousness. The world is no longer an object, but a phenomenon, an expression of the divine mind. History is no longer human history, but the outworking of the divine purpose. In other words the human essence of the world has been lost in religion just as much as in the Hegelian state.

The question is, therefore, what is the human essence of religion? Marx was not interested in reforming religion and so he gives us no help. Feuerbach should be of use, but as we have seen his approach is flawed. The essence of Christianity for him is a movement in human consciousness: of the human essence of religion he tells us nothing. He confidently tells us that he does not deny the divine predicates but the divine subject of the predicates. Looked at more closely, the projection theory, far from denying the existence of God, actually presupposes it. An elementary understanding of projection tells us that without a screen there is no image. Feuerbach's projection theory tells us something important about the doctrine of God, but not about the origins of belief in God. In particular it tells us nothing about the human essence of religion, about those experiences which give rise to religion.

I earlier referred to the projection theory as reductionist. The characteristic of reductionism is a phrase such as 'nothing but'. For example, religion is nothing but the longing for the father (Freud). Or again, religious assertions are nothing but the announcement of allegiance to set of moral principles (Braithwaite). Religion may also be these things, or may be for some people or at some periods of their lives.

But such reductionism discounts the mass of evidence which shows that religion arises from very different human experiences.

Marx thought that he was taking over a materialist account of religion; what he got was but another idealist interpretation. For personal reasons he wished for an explanation of religion which would enable him to dispense with it. But Feuerbach was, if anything, more committed to the maintenance of religion than Hegel himself. When an author publishes a book it enters the public domain and he has no proprietary rights over its interpretation. Marx propounded a theory of reversal and the fact that he did not apply it correctly to religion cannot prevent us from attempting to do so. In no other instance did he draw the conclusion that an inversion of reality meant that the phenomenon should be completely dismissed. In each case he assumed that it must be rescued, for the sake of man's true life. Thus on Marx's own terms religion exists and has a perfect right to do so, if and only if its human essence can be restored. But this is what Schleiermacher attempted to do. What is taken to be religion are the objectifications of the human essence of religion. Now it is notoriously difficult to identify that human essence, the distinctive core of religious experience, but that need not detain us for the moment. Schleiermacher would seem to have anticipated Marx, which is hardly surprising since he was so influential on Feuerbach. Schleiermacher does not reject religion any more than Marx rejects the state. But he rejects religion in its objective forms when they have become alienated from their human essence. That is to say, when they have attained an existence independent of human experience.

We cannot accept Feuerbach's position, not because it is critical of religion, but because it does not even begin to deal with its human essence. But it will be clear from all this that we are not rejecting Marx's criticism of religion as reversal, as an inversion of reality. If at the outset we are not in a position to accept it, it is because Marx does not provide us with the criticism in its fully developed form. He takes the criticism of religion and uses it as a model for application to other social institutions. But he did not care to return to apply it comprehensively to religion. That is the task which we have decided to undertake.

In seeking to apply Marx's general theory of reversal to religion we are actually attempting to go beyond Marx himself in two respects. In the first place we are applying it more extensively to religion than he cared to. But in the second place we are questioning his distinction between the reversal which takes place in the sacred sphere and the reversals which take place in the profane. That distinction is itself theological and presupposes the very alienated world view which he wishes to dismantle. In other words, fully to accept Marx's theory of reversal as applied to religion it is necessary to do two things. First, to apply it to religion more comprehensively than Marx himself did. Second, to regard religion as a secular sphere; or rather to dispense with that world-view in which religion is by nature and necessity a source and expression of human alienation.

There is a choice of priorities here. Is the priority to defend religion in its traditional form, acknowledging that it necessitates an inversion of secular reality? Or is the priority to overcome the reversal of reality in order to uncover the reality of the secular? It should be emphasized that in the latter case the focus of attention is then those human experiences which in the past have been objectified into alienated religious forms. It cannot be stressed sufficiently – though inevitably the point will be ignored – that these experiences, the human essence of religion, include the awareness of that which transcends human existence. The priority is to seek the essence of religion in its secular mode, and to avoid new reifications which would in turn produce new or reconstituted institutions of alienation.

The first of Marx's criticisms of religion, that it reconciles people to an evil world, is a moral criticism, and it should be accepted for the sake of what is right. The second criticism of religion which I have now presented, that it produces an inversion of reality, is an ontological criticism and it should be accepted for the sake of what is true. Of all the reversals we have considered, there is one which would be ironic indeed. Marx's criticisms of religion are abrasive and in important respects ill-thought-out. Yet it would be ironic if they should have the very opposite effect from the one intended. If they were accepted, in good heart, then instead of leading to the disappearances of religion, they might contribute to the renewal of religious integrity and credibility in the modern world. To this subject we shall return in Chapter 12.

4

Religion as Ideology

(a) The Holy Family

The move to Paris distanced Marx physically from Germany, though
for some time it continued to be the focus of his attention. It also
marked the beginning of the process by which he distanced himself
from those Young Hegelians who had formerly been his closest associates. He had been greatly influenced by them in their criticism of
religion and then of Hegelian philosophy, but as his own position
developed into a further decisive phase, he became increasingly aware
of the limited extent to which they had actually broken with the
old philosophico-theological approach. In the Preface to the Paris
Manuscripts Marx expresses his reservations:

> On close inspection *theological criticism* – genuinely progressive
> though it was at the inception of the movement – is seen in the final
> analysis to be nothing but the culmination and consequence of the
> old *philosophical* and especially the *Hegelian transçendentalism*,
> twisted into a *theological caricature* (3. 233).

In the autumn of 1844 Marx and Engels collaborated in a work
intended to settle their account with those whom they regarded as
'theological' critics. After the break-up of the Young Hegelians Bruno
Bauer had become more conservative philosophically and more quietist
politically. He had withdrawn into a position which was referred to by
the rather grand title of 'critical criticism'. It was this new position
which Marx and Engels exposed in a work entitled *The Holy Family
or Critique of Critical Criticism: against Bruno Bauer and Company*.
Bruno Bauer had at one time been a close friend and mentor of the
young Marx, but that did not save him from an attack which though
intellectually penetrating is constantly mocking and often scurrillous.

Far from departing from Hegel and the reconciliation of philosophy and religion, Bauer saw himself completing or going beyond Hegel. Marx was thus able to represent Bauer's position as if it were a cult, one in which the idea of critical criticism was incarnate in the person of Bruno Bauer himself, capably supported by his brother Edgar.

> Critical criticism is in its own eyes the *Absolute Subject*. The Absolute Subject requires a cult. A *real* cult requires other believing individuals. The *Holy Family of Charlottenburg* therefore receives from its correspondents the cult due to it [4. 144]

In the following pages the metaphor is extended by the application of the terminology of redemption, grace, faith, catechumen and Last Judgment. Those who oppose the cult can be excommunicated. In a later work Marx carries this aspect further, as he comments on the wrath of 'Saint Bruno' directed against the authors of *The Holy Family* and others such as Moses Hess who have not submitted to his Inquisition. 'But as these accused have been busying themselves with "worldly affairs" and, therefore, have failed to appear before the Santa Casa, they are sentenced in their absence to eternal banishment from the realm of the spirit for the term of their natural life' (5. 96).

This distinction characterizes the new interests of Marx. He rejects idealism in favour of materialism, the life of the spirit in favour of the life in this world; he rejects the primacy of ideas over the concerns of ordinary men and women in their daily lives. And they, the masses, are also seen by critical criticism as its opponents. Marx is happy to be on their side against the cult.

> Bruno Bauer . . . proclaims *criticism* to be Absolute Spirit and *himself* to be *criticism*. Just as the element of criticism is banished from the Mass, so the element of the Mass is banished from criticism. Therefore *criticism* sees itself incarnate not in a mass but exclusively in *a handful* of chosen men, in Herr Bauer and his disciples . . . On the one side is the Mass as the passive, spiritless, unhistorical, *material* element in history. On the other side is the Spirit, *criticism*, Herr Bruno and Co. as the active element from which all *historical* action proceeds (4. 86).

If Marx was by this time critical of Hegel, this was worse than Hegel. Critical criticism was a 'ruminant animal' which chewed 'the old Hegelian cud' [4. 103]. Once again history was formed by the incarnation of ideas, and not by people in their active, working lives. Except that in the system of absolute criticism the Spirit directs history against the interests of the masses.

The critique of critical criticism was therefore essential for Marx as he clarified the nature of religious thinking and philosophy which was founded upon it. Bauer, with his stress on the primacy of consciousness, now self-consciousness, was still what he had always been, a theologian.

In *The German Ideology*, as already indicated, Marx again returned to deal briefly with 'Saint Bruno'. At the same time he dealt more extensively with another position within the Berlin Young Hegelians, represented by Max Stirner and *Die Freien*. Max Stirner (Kaspar Schmidt) was, like Feuerbach, educated at Berlin and Erlangen. He was one of *Die Freien*, the more outrageous members of the Berlin group of Young Hegelians, noted for his advocacy of atheism and the rejection of the conventions of bourgeois life. In 1844 he published *Der Einzige und Sein Eigentum*, a title so illustrative of the obscurity of the book that is has been translated as *The Ego and His Own*, and in the Moscow edition as *The Unique and His Property*. It is a book which has been in turn influential on anarchists, existentialists and fascists, with its advocacy of an extreme form of individualism. 'My concern is neither the divine nor the human, not the true, good, just free, etc., but solely what is *mine*, and it is not a general one, but is – unique, as I am unique. Nothing is more to me than myself.'[1] His position is neatly summarized by Kolakowski as follows.

> The Ego's desires or whims are its own law; it is not bound by any state ordinances or 'rights of man'. It seeks no justification from society and acknowledges no obligation towards it; it has a right to everything it can lay hands on.[2]

Once again Marx brings out the inherently religious structure of Stirner's thought by the constant use of religious metaphors. His book is the holy book, which has fallen from heaven. The continuing idealist movement of his thought it illustrated in the following passage:

> The thoughts became themselves *corporeal*, they were spectres like God, the Emperor, the Pope, the Fatherland, etc.; by destroying their corporeality, I take them back into my own corporeality and *announce:* I alone am corporeal. And now I take the world as it is for me, as *my* world, as my property: I relate everything to myself (quoted 5. 125).

Marx's detailed critique of Stirner seems excessive, over 350 pages long, but in the course of its his own position emerges by contrast and we see some of the features which will increasingly characterize his later work. For example, although like the other Young Hegelians Stirner speaks constantly of consciousness, what now strikes Marx is that it is always the consciousness of the individual in abstraction. 'The physical and social changes which take place in the individuals and produce an altered consciousness are, of course, of no concern to Stirner' (5. 128). Stirner's view of consciousness pays no attention to 'historical epochs' or nationalities. And if it does relate to class, it is of course the class of the writer.

In familiar idealist fashion Stirner 'stands facts on their heads, causes material history to be produced by ideal history . . .' (5. 137). This Marx now sees to be typical of both idealist and religious approaches. In contrast, we see Marx advocating a much more materialist view of religion, for example. People have previously regarded religion as *causa sui* 'instead of explaining it from the empirical conditions and showing how definite relations of industry and intercourse are necessarily connected with a definite form of society, hence, with a definite form of state and hence with a definite form of religious consciousness' [5. 154]. Many people have failed in this respect, and to the list of names that of Stirner should be added, together with Marx himself. Following Feuerbach, Marx had failed to deal with actual religion in its socio-historical context. Here he is looking to factors which might explain religious consciousness. But even if he is not attempting to understand the empirical roots of religion, at least he is acknowledging the human essence of religion. Marx did not develop this line of enquiry.

It would seem, therefore, that the criticism of Stirner was probably more important in clarifying Marx's own position on these important matters than in anything which he gained directly from Stirner's position. However, Stirner did influence Marx on one issue which proved decisive for his development. It was because of Stirner that Marx finally understood the true nature of Feuerbach's work. Stirner was highly critical of communism[3] and, as we have seen, Marx regarded Feuerbach as having provided its philosophical basis. But in addition to this, Stirner pointed out that Feuerbach's position, far from signifying the end of religion, was in fact its continuation by other means. 'Man, spirit, true individual, personality, etc. are statements or predicates which abound in a fullness of content, phrases of the highest matter. The unique one is, in contrast to those holy and sublime phrases, the empty, unpretentious, and thoroughly common phrase . . .'[4]

So far I have presented the first part of Feuerbach's work, the reductionist use of the dialectic. I must now illustrate the second movement: not that theology is anthropology, but that after all anthropology is theology, again. The divine predicates were human predicates, but for Feuerbach these human predicates were not actual predicates but ideal predicates of the species. So hostile was Marx to Stirner that in the exceedingly long and detailed analysis of Stirner's position Marx makes no substantial reference to Feuerbach, but by the time the analysis was complete Marx had implicitly accepted Stirner's judgment against Feuerbach. That freed him from the last 'theological' influence on his developing position.

(b)   Farewell to Feuerbach

It is an indication of Marx's single-mindedness and intellectual integrity that although he owed so much to Feuerbach, he should finally dissociate himself from the position which he had so openly and at times extravagantly praised. With hindsight what is surprising is not that he should have eventually made the break, but that it should have taken him so long. With the Paris Manuscripts there is a definite transition: from Germany to France, from continual philosophical analysis to the sphere of economics, from consciousness to labour. Yet in the midst of this move Feuerbach is still being hailed as the inspiration of the new materialism and even communism.

In the Preface to the Paris Manuscripts, in terms which clearly describe his own position, Marx acknowledged Feuerbach's unique position among critical philosophers,

> It is only with *Feuerbach* that *positive*, humanistic and naturalistic criticism begins. The less noise they make, the more certain, profound, extensive, and enduring is the effect of *Feuerbach's writings, the only writings since Hegel's Phänomenologie and Logik* to contain a real theoretical revolution (3. 232).

At the end of the Third Manuscript there is a section headed 'Critique of the Hegelian Dialectic and Philosophy as a Whole', to which we have already alluded. The point of reference in the current ferment is Feuerbach, who 'both in his "Thesen" in the *Anekdota* and, in detail, in the *Philosophie der Zukunft* has in principle overthrown the old dialectic and philosophy . . .' (3. 327). In view of what was soon to come it is almost embarrassing to read Marx's assessment of the contribution of Feuerbach.

> *Feuerbach* is the only one who has a *serious, critical attitude* to the Hegelian dialectic and who had made genuine discoveries in the field. He is in fact the true conqueror of the old philosophy. The extent of his achievement, and the unpretentious simplicity with which he, Feuerbach, gives it to the world, stand in striking contrast to the opposite attitude (of others) (3. 328).

We now know what Marx thought of 'the others', but Feuerbach's achievements are listed as 'the proof that philosophy is nothing else

but religion rendered into thought', 'the establishment of *true materialism* and of *real science* by making the social relationship of "man to
man" the basic principle of the theory', and his positive 'opposing of
the negation of the negation' (3. 328). I have already commented on
the letters of Marx to Feuerbach, in which Feuerbach is credited with
having provided 'a philosophical basis for socialism'. In the *Grundsätze
der Philosophie* Feuerbach tells us that 'without egoism you have no
head, and without communism no heart'.[5]

Even in *The Holy Family*, in which Marx began to distance himself
from the others, from the theological critics, Feuerbach is not included
among them. He is not criticized at all. Indeed Marx still identifies his
position so closely with that of Feuerbach that he frequently refers to
Feuerbach both to defend him against the others and to call on his
support in Marx's defence of his own position. The decisive step had
been taken but apparently not by Marx: 'The old antithesis between
spiritualism and materialism has been fought out on all sides and
overcome once and for all by Feuerbach' (4. 94).

And yet although no direct criticism appears, it is possible that Marx
had begun to sense a certain limitation in Feuerbach's position. 'But
just as *Feuerbach* is the representative of *materialism* coinciding with
humanism in the *theoretical* domain, French and English *socialism* and
communism represent *materialism* coinciding with *humanism* in the
practical domain' (4. 125).

Indeed the early suspicion is to be found in the first quotation given
above, from the Paris Manuscripts. The work of Feuerbach was 'a real
theoretical revolution'. At the outset this was a considerable achievement, but was it also an obstacle to further progress? If we were to
adopt the style of the movement itself, we might say that the theoretical
revolution never became a revolutionary theory. Feuerbach after all
did not contribute to the agenda indicated by Cieszkowski: his philosophy of the future did not become applied philosophy. Always a
philosophy of consciousness, it never descended to the realms of praxis.
Even if he suggested the philosophical basis of socialism, he declined
to take responsibility for building on that foundation. It was not that
Feuerbach discounted sensuous human experience, but rather that he
was never able to make it decisive in his philosophy. Marx was later
to highlight the dichotomy. 'As far as Feuerbach is a materialist he
does not deal with history, and as far as he considers history he is not
a materialist' (5. 41).

This is true of Feuerbach's position as I have already outlined it,
but the continuing religious dimension of his work makes it even more
obvious. At the beginning of the last chapter I said that Feuerbach
applied the dialectic in two different directions. Largely through

Stirner, Marx eventually came to see that the reductionist application was not fully materialist. I can now briefly indicate the form of the other application, not reductionism but exaltation. It is difficult to see how Marx could have defended Feuerbach so long in view of this part of his work.

In Feuerbach's theory of projection, the attributes of God are seen to be aspects of human consciousness objectified. The reduction is therefore reclaiming the divine attributes for man. But which man? The divine attributes had never been real attributes, merely the imaginings of the human mind, the longings of the human heart. 'The fundamental dogmas of Christianity are realized wishes of the heart: the essence of Christianity is the essence of human feelings.'[6] It is for this reason that the process of projection is not an error, but a mystery. At a stage prior to the level of abstract thought typical of philosphy, religion was able to describe not how man is so much as how man ought to be. And by projecting these ideals, by objectifying them, man was unconsciously attempting to recognize them and declare them to be of ultimate value. In other words he worshipped them. Nor was he wrong so to do.

The age of reason might have taken as its motto the aphorism of Protagoras: 'Man is the measure of all things, of the reality of those that are, and the unreality of those that are not'[7] This saying, which originally expressed a certain sophistic pessimism and resignation characteristic of the fifth century BC, could have expressed in the eighteenth century the self-confidence of modern man. One example was atheism: the declaration of the unreality of God. To many it seemed obvious that Feuerbach was an example of this movement, but this he deeply resented.

> Whoever knows to say no more about me than that I am an atheist, says and knows as good as nothing about me. The question concerning whether God exists or not, the opposition of theism and atheism, belongs to the eighteenth and seventeenth centuries, but no longer to the nineteenth. I negate God, but for me that means I negate the negation of Man . . . The question about the being or non-being of God is for me simply the question about the being or non-being of Man.[8]

The true atheist is the man who denies not the subject of the predicates, but the predicates themselves. Not the man who has no faith in a supernatural Being, but one who has no faith in those ideals for which men should live and if necessary die.

Nor has philosophy now overtaken religion. Man may be the measure – or the scientific measurer – of all things, but through religion we can still learn of that which goes beyond philosophy. God forgives. In this we are to understand that forgiveness is a higher form of morality than the justice of the moral law within. In the cross of Christ we are to understand that which constitutes the highest form of human love.

> God suffers – suffering is the predicate – but for men, for others, not for himself. What does that mean in plain speech? Nothing else than this: to suffer for others is divine: he who suffers for others, who lays down his life for them, acts divinely, is a God to man.[9]

Since he has been hailed as the father of German materialism for his reduction of theology to anthropology, it is therefore unexpected that Feuerbach ends with a reversal (sic!), so that anthropology becomes theology. Not now in its alienated form, as referring to a being over against man whose existence causes and perpetuates human alienation, but as a recognition of that which is human only in the sense that it lies before man, ahead of man if he wishes to discover his true (species) life.

> He who has an aim, an aim which is in itself true and essential, has, *eo ipso*, a religion, if not in the narrow sense of common pietism, yet – and this is the only point to be considered – in the sense of reason, in the sense of the universal, the only true love.[10]

It transpires that Feuerbach was a deeply religious man, and never wished to be anything other. He had formally departed from Hegel's system, but we can see continuing elements not least is the fact that philosophy must be supplemented by religious devotion. The surprise is not that his position is confused and confusing, but that he was able to say so much given the ambiguities of his terminology and the constrictions of the dialectical method. His work was immensely important for many of his contemporaries. He preserved the possibility of religious devotion for those who experienced the alienation inherent in traditional religious forms.

Feuerbach had been the greatest single influence on the development of Marx's critical philosophy and it is fitting as well as typically ironic that the final major development of his system should begin with his critique of Feuerbach. Unfortunately for his friends Marx extended his system by sharpening his thought on their contributions. Religion was the first victim of Marx's developing philosophy, soon to be followed by Hegel himself. And before long there was a procession of those who had been his early influences, the founders of the revolutionary theory. Bruno and Edgar Bauer, Stirner and now Feuerbach himself. In his intellectual life, as opposed to his personal life, Marx raised biting the hand that feeds you to an art form. He would have been well in line for the gold if it had been accepted as a demonstration sport.

(c) A second conversion

We should not lose sight of the continuity between the development of Marx's philosophy and his life experiences. We have already noted the effect of his virtual exclusion from the prospect of university teaching and the silencing of the *Rheinische Zeitung*. Consciousness was the constant theme of the Young Hegelians, but Marx's consciousness was being daily affected by these practical circumstances. In addition we have seen the extent to which living in Paris and contact with the communards moved him in an increasingly materialist direction. In February 1845 he moved to Brussels, following his expulsion from France by the Guizot government. In August 1845 Marx and Engels began a major two-volume work which was to mark their final break with the Young Hegelians and the old Hegelian approach. *The German Ideology* was finished in August 1846. More than a decade later Marx described the circumstances in which it was written: 'We resolved to work out in common the opposition of our view to the ideological view of German philosophy, in fact, to settle accounts with our erstwhile philosophical conscience.'[11] The lengthy work was not published at that time (indeed not till 1932), but it served an important function. 'We abandoned the manuscript to the gnawing criticism of the mice all the more willingly as we had achieved our main purpose – self-clarification.'[12]

In 1888, some years after the death of Marx, Engels agreed to write an article entitled 'Ludwig Feuerbach and the End of Classical German Philosophy'. Since *The German Ideology* contains an extensive criticism of Feuerbach he looked out the old manuscripts as part of his preparation. He did not use it, but in the process discovered one of Marx's old notebooks, the kind in which he wrote in longhand both preparatory materials and finished articles. Engels reports that in the notebook he found eleven brief theses on Feuerbach. They were written in Brussels in the spring of 1845 and were of course overtaken in the longer book, but Engels saw in them something which has given them a unique place in Marx's writings. 'These notes hurriedly scribbled down for later elaboration, absolutely not intended for publication, but invaluable as the first document in which is desposited the brilliant germ of the new world outlook.'[13] These notes, which would seem to be in the form of classical German discussion theses, which were 'absolutely not intended for publication', Engels immediately published as an appendix to his essay on Feuerbach. They form the bridge to the new world outlook of historical materialism.

We have already noted that the surprising thing is not that Marx should have parted company with Feuerbach, but that it should have taken him so long; not that he should have criticized Feuerbach, but that he did not include Feuerbach in his critique of the Bauer brothers and Max Stirner; not that he was reluctant to single Feuerbach out for criticism but rather that to the end he actually defended Feuerbach as if their positions stood or fell together. To the end: and the theses mark this point. Earlier we discussed the characteristics of Marx's conversion to a Hegelian position. Now it was a de-conversion experience, which took place with the same abruptness, with the same total conviction. Suddenly Feuerbach was history, the last link severed with the old approach. In the course of a few months the simmering doubts had boiled over into new convictions. These theses (5. 3–5) may not have been intended for publication, but in any case they do not represent the struggle, the pain of recognition. All that had already taken place and Marx was back to his self-confident assertive style. 'The chief defect of all previous materialism (that of Feuerbach included) is that things (*Gegenstand*), *reality, sensuousness are conceived only in the form of the object of contemplation*, but not as *sensuous human activity, practice, not subjectively*' (Thesis 1).

It was a revolutionary step, as we have already noted, that Feuerbach should focus not on the absolute Mind, but on human consciousness. He began with this world and not the perspective of another. But even so, it was with thought that he began, not with life. Knowledge was not derived from the course of events, from the experience of people living their daily lives. But for Marx this is still a reversal, still the old religious, the old scholastic way. The truth of this world does not exist independently, available to pure reason. It is derived from living in the world, and it is tested against actual experience. And above all, the truth of the world is subject to change, because through their active lives men and women change the world. Hegel had said as much. As Marx outgrew his former teachers and those whose positions had influenced him, eventually there was only one left whose work he never fully or finally rejected, Hegel himself. As we shall see, this dependence on Hegel became more, not less, obvious as he developed his own distinctive position.

Feuerbach took as his subject the human as opposed to the divine, except that he converted the human into the divine, that is to say, he perpetuated the alienation of consciousness and hence alienation in general. 'His work consists in resolving the religious world into its secular basis. But that the secular basis lifts off from itself and establishes itself as an independent realm in the clouds can only be explained by the inner strife and intrinsic contradictoriness of this secular basis' (Thesis 4).

Feuerbach wrote of the human life, but not actual lives; about this world, but not in its worldliness. In each case he just failed to make the breakthrough. This is so in a third and even more important respect. Although he wrote of man as a species-being, for which Marx praised him extravagantly, yet Feuerbach did not present life as social life. Man even as a species being is still viewed contemplatively. 'Feuerbach resolves the essence of religion into the essence of man. But the essence of man is no abstraction inherent in each single individual. In its reality it is the ensemble of the social relations' [Thesis 6]. What Feuerbach in an idealist manner takes to be religious sentiments are, like everything else, socially produced.

With these three issues – the sensuous life, the secular life and the social life – Feuerbach's materialism is exposed as a continuation of the old religious idealism. The break is made dramatically in ten short theses. In the manuscript there is then added a further sentence. By itself it says little, nor is it in any sense a summary of the fundamental issues covered by the first ten points. But perhaps because few people now are concerned to understand the complexities of the break with the old German philosophy, and perhaps because it is in the form of an aphorism, it has become the second most quoted sentence in the whole of the Marx corpus. The Eleventh Thesis on Feuerbach: 'The philosphers have only *interpreted* the world in various ways; the point is to *change* it.'

(d) False consciousness

The German Ideology was written jointly by Marx and Engels, but since my purpose is to review and assess what Marx thought, I shall assume that he agreed with everything in it, whether it originated with him or with Engels. The first volume is the Critique and in it the phrase 'the German ideology' referred to the philosophy of Feuerbach, Bruno Bauer and Stirner. (At one stage it had also been intended to include a chapter on Arnold Ruge by Moses Hess). They had been credited with effecting a revolution in Germany, but Marx considered them to be sheep in wolves' clothing. They had simply exchanged one set of concepts for another. The Preface begins with a famous assertion which is more than a little ironic, since it describes the work of Feuerbach, making use of the very analysis which Marx had learned from Feuerbach in the criticism of religion and idealist philosophy.

Hitherto men have always formed wrong ideas about themselves, about what they are and what they ought to be. They have arranged their relations according to their ideas of God, of normal man, etc. The products of their brains have got out of their hands. They, the creators, have bowed down before their creations (5. 23).

The philosophers have interpreted the world in various ways, and the theologians, too. These interpretations are specific forms of the reversal theory which we have already examined. Ideas about the world, about social relations, have been objectified and given independent reality over against man. They have been personalized as the divine purpose or the expression of reason. In these forms they have acted back, to control human lives. This analysis we have met before, but now as Marx becomes more truly materialist he enquires not how this reversal takes place, but why. Why do inversions occur in their specific forms? They may arise within human consciousness, but this does not account for them. There is a mental element in the process, but surely it has a material basis. The Young Hegelians now criticized by Marx had focussed attention on the creative activity of consciousness, but they were essentially conservative politically. With Hegel they assumed the inherent rationality of what is. As a materialist Marx no longer shared that assumption. These mental constructions are illusions. They do indeed create new states of consciousness, but since they are fantasies what they produce is false consciousness.

This is the basis of Marx's theory of ideology. An ideology is a mental construction providing a picture of the world, a system of ideas about the world and social relations, and it may include moral and aesthetic values. As such it explains how things are, bestowing on them meaning and significance. The term ideology was originally used by a group of French senators, lead by Destutt de Tracy, who wished to develop a 'science of ideas', discovering how they were formed and perpetuated. Since they were critical of the continuing influence of the Catholic Church after the Revolution they were clearly suspicious of the ideas they wished to study. But Napoleon was suspicious of the movement itself, referring to them dismissively as 'idéologues'. In the *Philosophy of History* Hegel refers to 'idéologues and abstract-principle men'.[14] It is therefore in its perjorative sense that Marx used the term ideology. It is not a true picture. not a picture of the real world. Those who participate in projection and reversal are said to be unconscious of their actions; so now those who live within an ideological system are unaware that they have inherited false consciousness. Everything seems to be in order as it is, and it does not occur to them to question the ideological picture.

However, this theory of ideology still does not answer the question; Why do such mental constructs occur? Marx has still to relate them to their material base. The division of labour is fundamental to Marx's developing understanding of economics, and it is to this that he attributes the rise of ideologies, the division of mental and material labour. In any age there are 'active, conceptive, ideologists' (5. 60), whose task it is to produce the illusions of that society. In the previous forms of the theory (projections, reversal) the mental activity was performed unconsciously or unintentionally. Marx is now suggesting that ideologies are formed consciously. This is probably to attribute too high a level of self-consciousness to the process, but he may well take this view because of the final element which is now added. That element is 'suspicion'. Ideologies are constructed by a sub-class whose task it is to produce them, but this still does not relate a particular ideology to its specific time and place. What is lacking is the motive, and that is now added. The ideology of the specific time and place suits the material interests of those who are responsible for its production.

> The ideas of the ruling class are in every epoch the ruling ideas: i.e., the class which is the ruling *material* force of society is at the same time its ruling *intellectual* force. The class which has the means of material production at its disposal, consequently also controls the means of mental production. (5. 59).

An ideology therefore produces false consciousness. It constructs, circulates and maintains a mistaken picture of reality. It may be based on a mistake, but it is not a simple mistake. It is not by chance that the false picture furthers the material interests of those who produce and promote it. Not that the rulers of society are themselves capable of such a creative work, but they can employ others who are prepared to work for them or who have come to associate their own interests with those of that class. I believe it is an improbable scenario to imagine that the rulers of a society would call in a firm of ideologists, providing them with the general specifications of the required product. But we have already noted that Marx was a moral philosopher, motivated by service to others, especially the exploited. Since an ideology is a means by which exploitation is both disguised and legitimized, Marx clearly saw it as morally evil. He was therefore quite prepared to think the worst of those who gain from it, and perhaps inclined to attribute more intentional creativity to them than is justified. However that may be, the effect is the same.

An ideology disguises the true motivation behind the social construct: it deliberately breaks the connection between it and the material basis of its production. The effect of this is to distract attention from the inherent injustices of the social, political and economic system which it legitimates. This can be done in several ways. For example it can present a picture of a society unified in the pursuit of embodying certain ideals. In the national interest the majority may be prepared to suffer hardship. If they only knew, it is not the national interest which is served, but only the interest of a minority ruling class. However, it is one of the ironies of ideology that those who suffer most under it are often most loyal to it: note the hostility of many women towards feminism, or the rather touching loyalty of the working class in the East End of London towards the Royal Family. Alternatively, the ruling ideology may present their own motives in highly idealistic form. Marx recognized this pattern: 'that during the time aristocracy was dominant, the concepts honour, loyalty, etc., were dominant, during the dominance of the bourgeoisie the concepts of freedom, equality . . .' (5. 60). An ideology therefore gives the clear impression that history is guided by ideas: it certainly does not allow the true, material basis to appear. In that case the game would be up: the supposed moral legitimacy of the present order would be destroyed and revolution would ensue. It was Marx's vocation to perform exactly this function, so that his critical philosophy would become a material force.

(e) Religion and the ruling class

Just before I sat down to write this section I heard the end of a radio programme which caught my attention. The former cabinet minister Mr Tony Benn was the latest in a long series of unfortunates to be a castaway on a desert island. Those who are familiar with the long-running series, *Desert Island Discs*, will know that at the end of the programme, having selected eight records which will by chance be preserved from the ship-wreck, the survivor will find that he has a book of his choice, in addition to the Bible and Shakespeare. Mr Benn, unlike many of the good and the great who have shared this fate in the past, seemed to hint that he would actually welcome having both the Bible and Shakespeare. But as a fearless socialist he bravely called for a copy of *Das Kapital* as the book of his own choice, claiming that few people had read it, and that from it he would expect to understand much better the society from which he had been so recently and so tragically cut off.

I am sure that Tony Benn, who belongs within the broad tradition of Christian socialism rather than anti-religious communism, would find the multi-volume work fascinating, if not exactly a good read. Since by 1867 Marx had come to regard his work as 'scientific' it is not surprising that *Capital* is full of empirical materials, either from government published statistics or from independent economic or social surveys. Nevertheless the tone of the work is quite different from other works on economics. We saw that it was Marx's early humanism, his vocation to serve others, which led him back beyond philosophy into economics. As a moral philosopher investigating economic relations his work is written with righteous anger. He is concerned with accumulated capital, but only to understand how it produces conditions of exploitation; he is concerned with levels of poverty, but never losses sight of the poor whose real suffering is eliminated from the statistics. For example he deals with the 'gang-system' of labour in England at that time, whereby in rural areas gangs of perhaps fifty people were contracted out to work on the land. His interest is less in the efficiency of the system by which 'the driver' holds together like the Pied Piper the ragged group, but on the misery of the children used in this way, the immorality, the opium addiction and the high level of illegitimacy which automatically accompanied the system.[15]

Most of the examples which arouse Marx's indignation, however, are concerned with the effects of industrialization on those who were drawn into the cities. He includes a lengthy extract from a report which appeared in 1866 on conditions in some London boroughs. It includes harrowing accounts of families who despite all their best efforts were dragged down into poverty and despair. The following account, not by Marx, describes one typical situation. 'Nineteen weeks of enforced idleness had brought them to this pass, and while the mother told the history of that bitter past, she moaned as if all her faith in a future that should atone for it were dead . . .'[16]

Such reports seem to confirm Marx's views of the place and function of religion in nineteenth-century industrial Europe. It was an opiate which enabled people to bear their burden rather than encouraging them to cast it off; it was a reversal which convinced them that arbitrary conditions were their 'lot', as if such arrangements were the divine will. This was the subject of the two previous chapters which dealt with religion as reconciliation and religion as reversal. The present discussion extends these criticisms into a third form, religion as ideology. This application can be discussed at two levels.

At the first level, having reviewed Marx's theory of ideology, we can see how religion functions as a source and form of false consciousness. Religion is a particularly powerful factor in the creation of a world-view. It provides a cosmic setting for the contingent. Every aspect of the natural world and the social world can be understood in relation to an order which is non-human in origin. Political institutions, social and economic relations which have evolved from processes which are directly related to such considerations as geography, climate, famine, need, greed, ambition, are legitimized as natural phenomena, created by the divine will. Although religion is therefore but one agent in reconciliation and reversal, because of its cosmic dimension it has been perhaps the most powerful of all.

Religion has been central in the production of ideology, but it has also been crucial in its maintenance. When faced with intolerable and unjustifiable conditions people experience a reality slip: the arbitrariness of the world-view is exposed. Or it would be if religion did not intervene to re-enforce its legitimacy. In European history institutional religion has dealt most harshly, not with those who break the rules (they can be forgiven, under certain specified arrangements) but rather with those who have doubted and publicly questioned the basis of the rules, the authority by which the system is maintained. The enemies of institutional religion have not been those sinners who have fouled this or that detail of the great canvas of life, but those sceptics who have declared the whole picture a fraud.

We need not spend any more time on the application of the theory of ideology to religion at this, the first level. It explains a good deal of the social, non-theological, history of European religion including the persecution of scientists, witches and free-thinkers. Important though this application is, there is a second level, an application more incisive and if anything more damaging.

At a deeper level we are faced with Marx's question, 'Why?' Not, 'How has religion performed these functions or reconciliation and reversal?', as if the interest was merely in the mechanism. We have seen in Marx's analysis that the creation and maintenance of an ideology is not simply a theoretical matter. With the injection of the element of 'suspicion' it becomes a moral issue. Ideology as false consciousness uncovers a mistake, but, as we have already commented, not a simple mistake. The production and maintenance of an ideology are directly related to the interests of a particular social class. If religion is an ideology, then it has consciously or unconsciously thrown in its lot with the ruling class. In particular circumstances, such as Egypt in the Middle Kingdom, the ruling class might be the priests of the imperial cult. But more generally religion makes a fundamental and crucial contribution to the production and maintenance of the ideology of the secular ruling class. Religious leaders then form that sub-class to which I referred earlier which provides or enhances the ideology required by the rulers. These religious leaders assume an identity of interest which the ruling class and therefore by definition take sides against the interests of lower classes.

In my earlier study, *Constantine versus Christ*,[17] I indicated how the leaders of the church in the fourth century identified the values of the emperor with those of Christ. Or rather, how the values of the emperor replaced the values of the primitive church. From that time a process gathered momentum by which Christianity became the imperial cult of the Roman Empire, the bishops became civil servants, wearing the royal purple, living in palaces and taking the name 'prince' and 'lord'. It would be fascinating and instructive if further studies were to be made of the outworking of this process, down through the Middle Ages to the present day. Nor has it been exhausted: I mention only two contemporary examples. The first is simply the fact that bishops of the Church of England sit in the House of Lords. The second is more specific, and concerns a meeting several years ago in Glasgow at which the main speaker was the Moderator of the General Assembly of the Church of Scotland. One questioner was much exercised by the fact that so many working-class people identified the church with the ruling class. The Moderator in a sympathetic response said that he could not imagine why this should be. At the time he was wearing the traditional moderatorial dress, which includes a white ruffled shirt with elaborate lace cuffs, black tail coat, knee breeches and buckled shoes, a form of dress which I understand was worn in the eighteenth century by those being presented at court to the monarch.

Is that the whole story? And before we say, 'No,' let us pause to reflect on just how much of the story it has proved to be so far. But it is not the whole story, in the sense that there have been other examples. There have always been prophets and denouncers who have condemned this identification of interest with the ruling class against the interests of the poor. There have been individuals and groups who have attempted to change sides. And of course there has been the work and witness of the churches themselves, in defending the interests of the poor against their exploiters. Taken together, what has this amounted to, or rather why has it amounted to so little? The answer will already be clear to anyone who has helped those less fortunate, clear to anyone who has been in a position to defend the poor or pull a few strings to get things done, cut through red tape to ensure a decision is made and action taken. In order to promote the interests of the poor in such circumstances it is necessary to accept the reality of the existing social ideology. And let us not be naive enough to think that to 'use' the system in this way does anything else except reinforce its strength and credibility. In the final analysis an ideology is not constructed to establish the metaphysical truth of the universe. It is purely functional, and even ameliorative action demonstrates just how well it works.

In other words the problem lies at a deeper level. Many Christians would accept Marx's criticism of religion as reconciliation. They accept the moral criticism. But so long as Marx's second criticism is not accepted, as long as religion functions as a reversal of reality, then it will perform an ideological function within society. This is why so little has been achieved. The problem is not a moral problem and cannot be solved at the level of behaviour or allegiance. Of course Christians as individuals, groups or even at an institutional level can identify with and support proletarian interests on specific matters, and their support may be valuable. But as long as religion is a reversal of reality, their religious commitments constitute an obstacle to the advancement of the cause they think to espouse. In their mental and spiritual lives they daily affirm that alienation without which ideology could not exist. They are the secret ambassadors of the ideology of the ruling class, even if that role is kept secret also from them.

Students who first hear an exposition of Marx's critique of religion sometimes ask when they are to get 'the answer'. Marx, it would appear, needs to be answered. This assumes that religion is all right as it is, and Marx must be shown to be mistaken. But as we have seen, Marx set out to serve the interests of the poor and to uncover the sources of exploitation. The answer to Marx would be to end these conditions. The answer to Marx on religion would be to end participation of the religion in the process. That is indeed an 'answer' that would have delighted Marx. But there were those in his time who sought to oppose him and his kind, not for the sake of the exploited, but only to protect the future of Christianity, like the writer in the *Rheinischer Beobachter* who protested: 'If only those whose calling it is to develop the social principles of Christianity do so, the communists will soon be put to silence.' To this Marx was quick to respond.

> The social principles of Christianity have now had eighteen hundred years to be developed, and need no further development by Prussian Consistoral Counsellors. The social principles of Christianity justified the slavery of antiquity, glorified the serfdom of the Middle Ages and are capable, in case of need, of defending the oppression of the proletariat, even if with somewhat doleful grimaces. The social principles of Christianity preach the necessity of a ruling and an oppressed class, and for the latter all they have to offer is the pious wish that the former may be charitable (6. 231).

At a moral level the answer to Marx is to change the moral basis of Christianity, or, depending on your understanding of history, revert to the values of the early church. But while we should not underestimate the difficulties and even the improbabilities involved in giving that answer, we should not make the mistake of thinking that it is possible to fully answer Marx by such moral reformism, however sincerely undertaken and extensively carried through. Marx's fundamental criticism is ontological: as long as religion continues in its present form it will reinforce and legitimize all forms of the inversion of reality, and will consciously or unconsciously support the ideology of the ruling class. The ontological problem cannot be solved by moral means.

5

Historical Materialism as Religion

(a) Materialism

In Part One we have been dealing with Marx and religion. In chapters 2–4 we have discussed Marx's three criticisms of religion, as reconciliation with evil, as reversal of reality and as ideology. In Chapter 1 we reviewed Marx's early involvement and interest in religion, and at that stage I indicated that certain elements were to be influential throughout his career. We now turn from his criticism of religion, to the religious dimension of his own position.

This might seem unlikely, precisely at the stage at which Marx became a materialist. This term however is ambiguous. Feuerbach was called a materialist because he substituted human consciousness for the divine predicates. Yet he was never anything other than an idealist. Although Marx began with the same kind of humanism the parting of the ways with Feuerbach only meant a more specific form of humanism, a philosophy in which the focus of attention changed to man's daily and social life of labour. But he was critical of those forms of materialism which eliminated the distinctly human, including the moral, the aesthetic and the cultural. Thus although in *The Holy Family* he expressed admiration for the considerable achievements of French 'mechanical natural science', in the Third Thesis on Feuerbach he rejected the application of a mechanistic model to the human sphere and in the Paris Manuscripts he rejected the materialism of 'crude and thoughtless communism'. The true materialists of the nineteenth century were those medical scientists like Ernst Brücke and his colleague Émil du Bois-Reymond who were determined to end the old 'vitalist' approach to physiology. 'Brücke and I pledged a solemn oath to put into power this truth: no other forces than the common physical-chemical ones are active within the organism.'[1] This turned out to be not so much science as ideology, as Frederick Gregory has noted. 'Their denials to the contrary, the scientific materialists were certainly metaphysicians by twentieth-century standards.'[2] Such medical materialism was incompatible with religion, but then it was deliberately designed to eliminate many other things as well. It was not scientific, and as a dehumanizing ideology was contrary to everything to which Marx committed his life. I have shown in Chapter 3 that his materialism was not necessarily the rejection of everything religious. Now in this chapter we must investigate how it was that his philosophy as it developed included fundamentally religious elements.

As already indicated, this possibility seems to fly in the face of Marx's increasingly materialist development. In *The German Ideology* he was clear that Old and Young Hegelians were in fundamental agreement in their premises. Even the latter, who were critical of the present order, assumed that the problem lay in 'the illusions of consciousness' and consequently that all that was required was a new interpretation of the world, a new consciousness (5.30). Marx began from very different and materialist premises. The starting point is empirical and not merely contemplative. Man is distinguished from all other species by labour, by the fact that in producing the means of subsistence man actually produces his own material life. But this labour is not always the same: the mode of production changes and develops. This is intrinsic to the process.

> This mode of production must not be considered simply as being the reproduction of the physical existence of the individuals. Rather it is a definite form of activity of these individuals, a definite form of expressing their life, a definite *mode of life* on their part. As individuals express their life, so they are. What they are, therefore, coincides with their production, both with *what* they produce and with *how* they produce. Hence what individuals are depends on the material conditions of their production (5.31–2).

The mode of production therefore determines not only the lives of individuals, but also social and political relations within society and external relations with other nations.

This is the opposite of what we are led to believe. We think that mental creations come before and are independent of such material conditions, that life, including work and other activities and relationships, is a product of consciousness. This, the premise of the old philosophy, is a common ideological assumption. But it is an inversion and misrepresentation of the actual order. 'It is not consciousness that determines life, but life that determines consciousness' (5.37). Like many of Marx's assertions this is not so much a statement of fact as a prescription of how things should be. All too often life is determined by consciousness, by false consciousness. The contradictions of this false consciousness are disguised from us, or explained away. To escape from such ideological distortions we must allow our daily experience to determine how we view and understand the natural and social world around us.

However, an important corollary attaches to this position. If actual life produces consciousness, then emancipation cannot be effected simply at the level of consciousness. This would bring about only a different understanding of the world. It can only be brought about by a change in the mode of production. Real liberation for the slave, Marx claims, is brought about by the steam-engine; real liberation for the serf is brought about by agriculture (5.38). But with the division of material and mental labour consciousness can emancipate itself from the world and proceed to 'the formation of "pure" theory, theology, philosophy, morality . . .' (5.45).

In the treatment of the division of labour and the mode of production Marx develops a materialistic perspective which finally frees him from the pseudo-materialism of Feuerbach. Within the premises of idealism – but only within these parameters – Feuerbach stood Hegel on his head. But this no longer describes Marx's relationship to Hegel. Both Feuerbach and Hegel were agreed that consciousness produces life, but from a materialist perspective this order inevitably produces ideology. At the time Marx began the exercise in clarification in *The German Ideology* Feuerbach had even described himself as 'a communal man, a communist' (quoted 5.592 note 26), but as befitted a religious thinker he still took the view that man's existence could be reconciled to his essence by a change in consciousness and an act of will.

(b) Historical materialism

The emerging materialism of *The German Ideology* relates everything to material conditions: consciousness, self-understanding, social and political relations all arise, or should arise, from the circumstances of labour, which in turn are determined by the mode of production of the period. Changes in these areas of life are brought about not by purely mental processes, but by changes in the mode of production. The question therefore arises whether these various modes of production are related to each other. History which is conceived without reference to modes of production is not materialist; materialism which does not deal with changes in the modes of production is not truly historical. We have already referred to his criticism of Feuerbach in this respect. 'As far as Feuerbach is a materialist he does not deal with history, and as far as he considers history he is not a materialist.'

Historians characterize the past in a variety of ways: the Hellenistic age, the Roman Empire, the Middle Ages, the Crusades, the Renaissance, the Reformation, the Enlightenment. We should not expect Marx to use such categories. For materialism, life is not determined by ideas, nor is history. Instead, Marx refers to historical periods by the division of labour or the forms of property associated with them: tribal property, ancient communal and state property, feudal or estate property. The history of each period, the social, economic and political relations which constituted it, arose directly from the distinctive mode of production of the time. 'Feudalism' on this view did not 'produce' serfdom, as if some Hegelian Idea was expressing itself in historical conditions. Rather, the possession of land as property and the conditions of labour on the land characteristic of the period gave rise to certain relations between classes which we now designate as 'feudal'. By such a materialist approach to history Marx intended to demystify 'the connection of the social and political structure with production' (5. 35). History is no longer 'produced' by ideas which are taken to be characteristic of the epoch. Marx approved of what he considered in his own time to be 'the first attempts to give the writing of history a materialistic basis' (5.42), works in which commerce and industry are given a central place. In the Moscow edition the reader is referred to the work of the Edinburgh moral philosopher Adam Ferguson, who was born in the same year as Adam Smith. However, the claim that the life of an epoch is determined by its mode of production is original to Marx.

> This conception of history thus relies on expounding the real process of production – starting from the material production of life itself – and comprehending the form of intercourse connected with and created by this mode of production, i.e., civil society in its various stages, as the basis of all history; describing it in its action as the state, and also explaining how all the different theoretical products and forms of consciousness, religion, philosophy, morality, etc., etc., arise from it, and tracing the process of formation from the basis . . . (5.53).

Historical materialism therefore presents a new understanding of each epoch. Previously it was assumed that ideas explained practice, but on this view the formation of ideas is explained by reference to material practice. The importance of this reversal can be seen when we recall the production of ideological systems and their promotion of the interests of the ruling class. An ideology disguises the true basis on which all other social relations are established. It is also a distraction, since the impression is given that in order to change these relations it is only necessary to change the ideology, to reinterpret the world. It might be thought that the Eleventh Thesis on Feuerbach expresses irritation at those who talk about change instead of getting on with the job. Not so. The distinction is not between thought and action, but between the false and the real basis of society. According to Marx the real basis is the mode of production and only when it is replaced can there be any fundamental change in the social world built upon it. Naturally such revolutionary change will take place only in face of the fierce opposition of that class whose interests are best served by the existing relations. Hitherto the philosophers and ideologists have neither understood nor wanted to understand the base or its relationship to the superstructure.

If the writing of *The German Ideology* marked the final break with all forms of Hegelian philosophy, it is interesting to see how Marx's self-understanding changed at the same time. In the same year, 1846 P. J. Proudhon published *Système des Contradictions Économiques, ou Philosophie de la Misère*. By the spring of 1847 Marx was writing a reply, also in French, the title for which indicates that however his position had changed, he had not lost the old ironic style. Instead of *The Philosophy of Poverty*, Marx's work revealed *The Poverty of Philosophy*. He continued to ring the changes in the Foreword as he introduced M. Proudhon: 'In France, he has the right to be a bad economist, because he is reputed to be a good German philosopher. In Germany, he had the right to be a bad philosopher, because he is reputed to be one of the ablest French economists. Being both German and an economist at the same time, we desire to protest against this double error' (6.109). Between 1846 and 1847 there has been a reversal in self-consciousness: Monsieur Charles Marx, the French writer, is now an economist. And this precisely when he was expelled from France and moved to Brussels.

For those who wish to know Proudhon's position it would be as well to read his own work: Marx was not a sympathetic expositor of the views of those with whom he disagreed. From his new position of historical materialism Marx makes several specific criticisms. The first is that Proudhon is no materialist: he reproduces the old Hegelian reversal. He quotes Proudhorn to the effect that 'in civilization as in the universe, everything has existed, has acted, from eternity . . . *This applies to the whole of social economy* (6.171). Marx concludes that what Hegel did for religion and law, Proudhon has done for political economy. Actual productive relations are seen as but the incarnation of principles and categories which already existed. The second criticism is, naturally, that Proudhon is not a historical materialist. His approach is counter to history. It is not that ideals in the form of economic categories produce social relations which then lead to economic forces. Rather, productive forces produce certain social relations, in the context of which ideas arise. But as usual Marx in the course of criticism develops his own thinking. 'There is a continual movement of growth in productive forces, of destruction in social relations, of formation in ideas; the only immutable thing is the abstraction of movement – *mors immortalis*' (6.166). There is not only a sequence of epochs, each characterized by its mode of production, there is a movement within history which can be traced not through ideas or social relations, but through the succession of production relations. Thirdly, Proudhon presents a view of history which is in essence religious. If man ought to seek the good and equitable within each economic system, he is swimming with the tide of history: 'Equality is the *primordial intention*, the *mystical tendency*, the *providential aim* that the social genius had constantly before its eyes as it whirls in the circle of economic contradictions' (6.173). And finally, Proudhon presents history as a series of contradictions, but these are conceived of only in moral terms. He begins from an acceptance of the dominant economic relations of the epoch and seeks to ameliorate them. In this Proudhon, who is often thought of as an anarchist, was judged by Marx to be the ideologist of bourgeois interests. Like many before him, far from going beyond Hegel, he had lost the historical dynamic of the dialectic. Indeed we might pause at this point to reflect that although Marx was one of the first to criticize Hegel, and perhaps the the most incisive of his critics, yet at the same time it was he who understood Hegel's real and lasting contribution. Without Hegel Marx could not have achieved his new position. As George Lichtheim comments, 'the originality of Marx's achievement lies in the fact that in some sense he went on being a Hegelian.'[3]

In contrast to Proudhon's idealism Marx returns to his earlier themes. Contradictions cannot be overcome by changes in consciousness. But here again he goes beyond his previous position, in two respects. It is not simply that the contradictions cannot be overcome through moral judgments. They can of course only be overcome by the creation of a new society, when the oppressed class emancipates itself. But Marx also goes beyond this point. 'For the oppressed class to be able to emancipate itself it is necessary that the productive powers already acquired and the existing social relations should no longer be capable of existing side by side. Of all the instruments of production, the greatest productive power is the revolutionary class itself' [6. 211] This means that the oppressed class while it can emancipate itself, cannot do so on its own initiative, but only when the new mode of production has already emerged within the old society.

Although we are tracing the development of Marx's historical materialism through a series of books and essays, we have already noted that the circumstances of his life should not be forgotten. While living in Brussels he worked with Engels to set up the Communist League. At its Second Congress in London at the end of 1847 Marx was asked to draw up a programme for the League. Marx and Engels collaborated on this and by the end of January 1848 they had completed what was to become their most famous work, a twenty-four page pamphlet *The Manifesto of the Communist Party*.

The striking feature of the *Manifesto* is its focus on class struggle and the necessity of a communist revolution. Once again the situation of nineteenth-century Europe is generalized. 'The history of all hitherto existing society is the history of class struggles' (6.482). The crisis deepens and the classes now concentrate into two, the bourgeoisie and the proletariat. For Marx this further illuminates the movement which he has identified within history. The transition from one epoch to another takes place by revolution: the bourgeoisie were the new revolutionary class which brought feudalism to an end. However, by its nature this new class has not established a stable order. If social relations arise from economic relations, the basis of bourgeois society is free trade. 'In one word, for exploitation, veiled by religious and political illusions, it has substituted naked, shameless, direct, brutal exploitation' (6.487). And herein lies the danger. The characteristic of this epoch is that the bourgeoisie are 'constantly revolutionizing the instruments of production' (6.487). Marx compares this situation to that of the sorcerer who can no longer control the powers which he has set in train. These productive forces appeared within feudal society and eventually could not be contained by the institutions of that epoch. They destroyed the former basis of society, substituting free trade and also the social and political relations which expressed it. But the same forces continue within bourgeois society and Marx can detect the first signs of the emergence of the next epoch. In the development of capitalism Marx does not fail to see yet another irony: the most productive system in history has succeeded in producing not only commodities, but a new dispossessed and exploited class, the proletariat. 'What the bourgeoisie, therefore, produces, above all, is its own gravediggers. Its fall and the victory of the proletariat are equally inevitable' (6.496).

We have already noted that in this new account of history, epochs are not sequential, but consequential. One epoch leads directly to another. The bourgeoisie are not simply the obstacle to the next epoch, communism, but as a revolutionary class they have been instrumental in bringing history to its present level. On this view it is not possible to move from feudalism to communism. Since capitalism has been the link, it is also a necessary stage. Capitalism has revolutionized society in fundamental ways. By its development of communications it 'draws all, even the most barbarian, nations into civilization' (6.488). Because of its impact, which is irresistible, 'it creates a world after its own image' (6.488).

We might pause again at this point. Arguably in the last forty years Marxism has had more impact on the under-developed countries of the Third World than on the developed. But this is not at all what historical materialism predicts. According to Marx, communism can only come about after capitalism, even through capitalism. The class which leads the revolution is to be the urban, industrialized protelariat. Peasants are incapable of such a revolution.

> The bourgeoisie has subjected the country to the rule of the town. It has created enormous cities, has greatly increased the urban population as compared with the rural, and has thus rescued a considerable part of the population from the idiocy of rural life. (6.488).

How many peasants who have been provided with edited editions of the *Manifesto* realize that in it they are described as idiots? Historical materialism works both ways. The next epoch, the communist phase, will come about 'inevitably'. But this historical necessity means that all previous epochs must take their place in that sequence and cannot be omitted. Why? Because the revolution is not simply a political revolution. In dealing with Proudhon Marx made it clear that the revolution can only take place when the new production forces can no longer be contained by existing social relations. In the *Manifesto* he tells us that capitalism is necessary in preparing society for communism. If the USSR and the Peoples Republic of China now appear to be introducing an element of capitalism, this does not mean that they have abandoned the goal of creating a communist society. The development may be providing confirmation of Marx's doctrine, since in both societies the attempt was made to move directly from feudalism to communism, by-passing the necessary phase of capitalism. Either under-developed countries cannot become truly communist, or if they can, historical materialism is descredited. To this point we shall return in Chapter 12.

Returning to the *Manifesto*, if the communist revolution is to follow the historical pattern, then it will not simply be one class replacing the ruling class and controlling the means of production. Nor will it maintain the existing form of property. 'The distinguishing feature of Communism is not the abolition of property generally, but the abolition of bourgeois property' (6.498). The supposed human right of property is for Marx but another example of making into eternal laws relations which arise from and are only valid within their own historical epochs. The end of bourgeois society and with it the end of classes and class antagonisms will lead to 'an association in which the free development of each is the condition for the development of all' (6.506).

The *Manifesto* ends with the anticipation of a bourgeois revolution in Germany, to be immediately followed by a proletarian revolution (in that order but presumably necessarily involving both stages). Therefore the famous words with which it ends, 'Workers of the world unite', were first published in German. Germany did not respond immediately, but in the same month, February 1848, revolution occurred in France. The Provisional Government invited Marx to return, which was fortuitous, since in March he was arrested in Brussels and expelled from Belgium. But Germany had responded, to the French example if not to the *Manifesto*, and in April Marx returned to Cologne. In December he was arrested, tried and acquitted on charges of organizing the revolution in the city. How embarrassing for Marx to be publicly exonerated from having any influence whatsoever in instigating a revolution! In May 1849 he was expelled from Germany. He returned to Paris, but with the collapse of the revolution he was expelled from there in July. In August he and his family arrived in London. It is a tribute to English imperviousness to ideas that he was never considered to be a threat to the political life of the nation, and was allowed to live in London till his death in 1883.

It is hardly surprising, therefore, that the decade following the publication of the *Manifesto*, though politically intense and fraught, was not conducive to the production of substantial literary works. It was not till the middle of 1858 that Marx was able to begin the next and final phase of his development with the preparation of the book published in the next year as *Zur Kritik der Politischen Oekonomie*. Although it was written in London, sixty years passed before an English edition appeared. This was in part because although it was originally planned as the first half of a longer study, it became the basis for *Capital*, volume 1, Part One, 'Commodities and Money'. Indeed some of the obscurities in the early section of *Capital* arise because Marx simply refers the reader to the earlier work.

(c) Base and superstructure

In his *Contribution to the Critique of Political Economy*, published in 1859, few of the familiar themes from Marx's early writings appear. He can refer to gold in the terms in which he exposed the reversal of consciousness which is embodied in money. 'The servant becomes the master. The mere underling becomes the god of commodities' (29.359). Sellers and buyers become creditors and debtors, and with a little pun on the terms *der Gläubige* and *der Gläubiger* Marx tells us that 'the former believer becomes a creditor, and turns from religion to jurisprudence' (29.373). But for the most part he can leave behind all discussions of religion, philosophy and morality. In the light of his discovery these are secondary to the economic base from which they arise. Marx's task was therefore to pursue historical materialism in the sphere of political economy. Although he takes up the same issues as bourgeois economists, the characteristic difference in his treatment is that commodity, labour, value, money are not viewed as fixed entities, but rather as historically transient in character. In the Preparatory Materials, which were omitted from the book when its original scope was limited, Marx deals with 'The Transformation of Money into Capital' in the context of the dialectical movement within history. 'The exposition of the general concept of capital does not make it an incarnation of some eternal ideas, but shows how in actual reality, merely as a necessary form, it has yet to flow into the labour creating exchange value, into production resting on exchange value' (29.505).

As indicated, the book was gathered up into the more extensive treatment of *Capital*, although there are purists who consider that its treatment of money is not overtaken. The Preface, however, has come to be valued on its own account, somewhat like the case of the Introduction to the *Contribution to the Critique of Hegel's Philosophy of Right*.

In the Preface Marx returned to the theme of the relationship between the base and superstructure. He describes it as 'a guiding thread' in his studies of political economy. In the following passage he conveniently summarizes the position which I have already described in this chapter including the themes of materialism, historical materialism, and the relationship between consciousness and life.

In the social production of their existence, men inevitably enter into definite relations, which are independent of their will, namely relations of production appropriate to a given stage in the development of their material forces of production. The totality of these relations of production constitutes the economic structure of society, the real foundation, on which arises a legal and political superstructure and to which correspond definite forms of social consciousness. The mode of production of material life conditions the general process of social, political and intellectual life. It is not the conscious-

97

ness of men that determines their existence, but their social existence that determines their consciousness (29.262).

The social relations which arise from the base are not devised by men. They come about because of the mode of production of the time and not through any conscious decision of those whose lives are determined by them. This is historical materialism in the sense in which we have already examined it. Changes in modes of production form a definite sequence. There are stages in the development of productive forces. There is not only a vertical relationship within the history of an epoch; there is a horizontal relationship between the bases of successive epochs. But in addition to that, since these stages represent a development of the productive forces, we should understand that by some criterion, for example economic efficiency, the sequence of modes of production is not only successive, but progressive. The fundamental structure of society is not to be defined in terms of any idealistic form: it is economic. From an economic base arises an economic structure. The legal, social, political, and educational institutions of that society correspond to the characteristic of that particular base. They are what the mode of production produces. It also determines the consciousness specific to that society. However, because the productive forces are also part of a progressive development, in the long term the situation always becomes unstable.

> At a certain stage of development, the material productive forces of society come into conflict with the existing relations of production or – this merely expresses the same thing in legal terms – with the property relations within the framework of which they have operated hitherto. From forms of development of the productive forces these relations turn into their fetters. Then begins an era of social revolution (29.262).

This position is familiar from our previous discussions of *The German Ideology* and the *Manifesto*. We shall further consider the content of this passage directly, but there is a feature which at the outset might strike us as very odd indeed. It describes a situation, indeed what is envisaged is a succession of such situations, from which there is a surprising omission: man. It is like a landscape from primordial times before man has appeared in history. Alternatively it is like a post-apocalyptic time after the disappearance of the human race. The paragraph describes forces and the relationship between forces. It describes property and its relationship to production. We hear of conflict, fetters and even revolution, but in completely impersonal terms.

What is at stake here? Unfortunately we have now entered an area of intense debate among Marxists, and by 'Marxists' I do not necessarily mean those whose overriding concern is to establish what Marx himself said. For many Marxists that is not nearly as important as what they consider to be true Marxism. The sky over this particular Preface is dark with fowls coming home to roost. We have already noted that Marx can be regarded as one of the founders of the modern social sciences. The question which must now be raised is whether he has contributed, or at least whether he claimed to have contributed, to the natural sciences. Without entering into the philosophy of science we can say that there is a qualitative difference between man and nature, and that there is a corresponding difference between the social and natural sciences. Of course there are aspects of individual and societal life which can be investigated scientifically, but not necessarily the most important aspects. In short, the decisive element is human freedom. This means that the social sciences cannot proceed by the methods of the natural sciences. For example it is not possible simply at will (or budget) to reproduce social situations for measurement exactly. And it is not possible to predict future behaviour exactly. Is it simply by chance that Marx describes historical materialism without reference to human behaviour, or rather is he claiming that historical materialism lies within the field of the material, natural, sciences? In short, is historical materialism an interpretative theory arising within the social sciences, or is it a scientific law propounded within the natural sciences?

This, then, is the dilemma for Marxists, who are much given to describing Marxism as 'scientific'. If historical materialism states a natural law, human history is a determinate environment from which human freedom is eliminated. But if historical materialism is less than that, if it is an interpretative theory, then Marx is reduced to the ranks. He belongs with Feuerbach *et hoc genus omne*, a philosopher who merely interprets the world. Surely Marx does not attempt to eliminate human freedom from his account: but if he retains it can he still keep his badge, can he still be given the titles of scientist and materialist? The dilemma is acknowledged by Lezek Kolakowski in his discussion of *The German Ideology*

Marx, then, cannot be regarded as maintaining that history is an anonymous process in which conscious intention and thoughts are a mere by-product or causal accretion. Yet there is room for controversy over his theory even if we accept that thoughts, feelings, intentions, and the human will are a necessary condition of the historical process. For this view is compatible with strict determi-

99

nation on the basis that although 'subjective' factors are necessary causal links, they are themselves entirely due to non-subjective factors; thoughts and feelings, on this assumption, have an auxiliary role in history but not an originating one. In short, even if we do not interpret Marx's position as one of economic determination, there is still room for argument as to the role of free action in the historical process.[4]

I have headed this section 'Base and superstructure', since this is the short way in which the issue is often described. Kolakowski attempts to be objective and fair, acknowledging that there are grounds for saying that Marx's theory compromises human freedom, if it does not actually eliminate it. Once again the issue is considered to be human freedom. But even Kolakowski is in danger of getting the subject the wrong way round. The question is not whether human freedom is significant in human history. There is no internally consistent position which can argue against this fact. There is a danger that the issue will simply be approached as an example of the traditional philosophical question of free-will and determinism. The issue, however, is ontological, not epistemological. What is at stake is whether Marx can establish an objective structure within history which exists independently of human freedom, will and intention. Some Marxist writers are concerned to deny that he does this, considering that this would make his position untenable. My point is that if Marx does not establish this structure, then he has established nothing at all. It is not a matter of placing him on one side or the other in the great epistemological debate between libertarians and determinists. Marx's originality is that he has completely by-passed that debate to concentrate on a much more profound issue.

Some Marxists, who consider the matter to be epistemological, find Marx's theory embarrassing. They try to save him from himself, as if he blundered into an untenable position. They try to save face. My own view is that we should take Marx at face value. He knew perfectly well what he was saying, and to save him from that is to destroy the only form in which historical materialism could conceivably be significant. If historical materialism is correct, then Marx has made a quite extraordinary breakthrough, but only if historical materialism has uncovered an objective structure independent of human consciousness and intention.

All that having been said, it might be assumed that Marx is confused, confusing and ambiguous about the matter. On the contrary, he is perfectly clear. Historical materialism is a natural law, as we can see if we look again at the Preface.

The changes in the economic foundation lead sooner or later to the transformation of the whole immense superstructure. In studying such transformations it is always necessary to distinguish between the material transformation of the economic conditions of production, which can be determined with the precision of natural science, and the legal, political, religious, artistic or philosophic – in short ideological – forms in which men become conscious of this conflict and fight it out (29.262).

An important distinction is made here between the base and the superstructure. The latter is governed by human consciousness, intention and will, and is therefore open to ideological interpretation and misinterpretation, such that men can be mistaken in how they read the situation and the nature of the conflict. In contrast the base, the new mode of production and its relation to the previous mode of production do not belong to this sphere. They can be analysed as if they were the proper subjects of a natural science. Far from misrepresenting Marx, if there is no distinction between the base and the superstructure in this respect, then historical materialism is not material in any important sense and he is still a disciple of Feuerbach. And who would wish that upon him?

I have been arguing that historical materialism must be historical determinism, at least as far as the base is concerned, if it is to have any significance. I have argued that this does not misrepresent Marx: he clearly knew what was at stake. Historical materialism must identify an objective structure, which is independent of human consciousness, will and intention, and can therefore be studied scientifically. We are claiming that this is not his weakness, but his strength. It could be a false hypothesis, but if proved correct it would be a discovery of extraordinary importance for the human race. *Capital*, like the *Contribution to the Critique of Political Economy*, represents the application of historical materialism in the economic sphere. Or rather it was a movement in the opposite direction, the attempt to confirm empirically the existence of historical materialism as a law already existing within history.

Thus in the Preface to the first edition of *Capital* Marx refers to 'the natural laws of capitalist production'. 'It is a question of these laws themselves, of their tendencies winning their way through and working themselves out with iron necessity.'[5] This must be science, or pseudoscience, since it is not good historiography. We have already seen that the law of development traced by historical materialism entails that every epoch must be gone through. Men have no choice in the matter. 'Even when a society has begun to track down the natural laws of its

101

movement – and it is the ultimate aim of this work to reveal the economic law of motion of modern society – it can neither leap over the natural phases of its development nor remove them by decree.'[6] Marx clearly considers that this natural science has no space for human freedom or decision. 'My standpoint, from which the development of the economic formation of society is viewed as a process of natural history, can less than any other make the individual responsible for relations whose creature he remains, socially speaking, however much he may subjectively raise himself above them.'[7] Regardless of human freedom within the superstructure, Marx is clear that the base is a sphere in which the laws of natural science operate. However, the model is the natural science of biology, not physics or chemistry. This is made clear in the Preface to the second edition of *Capital*, in a long extract which Marx includes from a Russian review of his work.

Those who wish to deny that Marx thought of his work as scientific in a quite literal sense do him a grave disservice. I therefore close with confirmation by Engels, Marx's closest friend and long time collaborator, who presumably knew what Marx meant and also what was at stake. Two examples illustrate the point.

In the spring of 1852 Marx published *The Eighteenth Brumaire of Louis Bonaparte*, a study of the recent revolutionary upheavals in France. In 1885, two years after the death of Marx, the third German edition was published, to which Engels contributed a brief Preface. It is worth quoting in full the claims Engels makes for this 'work of genius':

It was precisely Marx who had first discovered the great law of motion of history, the law according to which all historical struggles, whether they proceed in the political, religious, philosophical, or some other ideological domain, are in fact only the more or less clear expression of struggles of social classes, and that the existence of and thereby the collisions, too, between these classes are in turn conditioned by the degree of development of their economic position, by the mode of their production and of their exchange determined by it. This law, which has the same significance for history as the law of the transformation of energy has for natural science – this law gave him here, too, the key to an understanding of the history of the Second French Republic. He put his law to the test on these historical events, and even after thirty-three years we must still say that it has stood the test brilliantly.[8]

Engels in this passage is prepared to extend the parallel beyond biology to physics, but in any case it is not possible to drive a wedge between Marx and Engels here. If Engels calls historical materialism

102

a law of natural science that is precisely what Marx himself called it in the last quotation given above from the Preface.

The second example concerns the prefaces to *The Communist Manifesto*. In the Preface to the English translation published in 1888, after the death of Marx, Engels referred to the 'fundamental proposition' which forms the nucleus of the *Manifesto*.

> That proposition is: that in every historical epoch, the prevailing mode of economic production and exchange, and the social organization necessarily following from it, form the basis upon which is built up, and from which alone can be explained the political and intellectual history of that epoch . . .[9]

In the Preface to the German edition published in 1883 Engels stated the fundamental proposition and then went on to make this generous attribution 'this basic thought belongs solely and exclusively to Marx',[10] but in the English preface he claims that coincidentally he and Marx approached the same position independently. 'This proposition which, in my opinion, is destined to do for history what Darwin's theory has done for biology, we, both of us, had been gradually approaching for some years before 1845.'[11] Whether it belonged exclusively to Marx, or whether they both arrived at it independently is not as fascinating as the parenthetic remark that historical materialism is destined to do for history what the theory of evolution has done for biology. What could that possibly mean except that historical materialism is a scientific hypothesis which will eventually be vindicated by cumulative evidence? As we have just seen, in his Preface to *The Eighteenth Brumaire* Engels refers to the law of motion of history as if it had been constantly tested against history like a hypothesis. And once again, it is not possible to drive a wedge between Marx and Engels here. If Engels compares historical materialism to the theory of evolution it is because Marx had already enthusiastically made the connection. Darwin published his work *On the Origin of Species by Means of Natural Selection* in 1859 and it was the end of the following year before Marx read it, but when he did, he saw immediately the connection with his own work. In a letter to Engels dated 19 December 1860 he refers to his recent illness and the books which he has been reading during that time, and specifically to Darwin's *Natural Selection*. 'Although developed in the crude English fashion, this is the book which, in the field of natural history, provides the basis of our views' (41.232). Nor was this a passing observation: he later sent Darwin a copy of *Capital*.[12] What Darwin made of it I am not in a position to report.

(d)   Meaning in history

It is perfectly clear, therefore, that Marx considered historical materialism to be a law of natural science. What is not immediately clear is why he was interested in formulating it. We know of mountaineers who can give no reason for climbing Everest, or more often failing to climb it, other than that it is there. We do not ask scientists why they made a particular discovery, since a question beginning with 'Why?' tends to induce in scientists a sense of vertigo or an anxiety attack. But Marx was no scientist – nor mountaineer. He would only be interested in a natural law of historical motion if it could be related to his life-long moral concerns. The connection requires a context.

Although secularization was a major issue in the period after the Second World War, for example in the field of sociology of religion, the impact of secularization was already experienced in the first half of the nineteenth century. It might be said that Hegel's system was fundamentally a secular restatement and development of the Christian religion. Feuerbach's mission, to turn men from contemplation of another world, back to their real lives in this world, was a secular goal, and his reversal of subject and predicate, his reappropriation of the divine attributes as the human attributes of the species might be taken as a project in secularization. As we noted in discussing Feuerbach's second use of the dialectic, this was very important for many of his contemporaries since it provided a way of appropriating the cultural richness of religion in an age of alienation from institutional religious forms.

If Feuerbach therefore addressed the need of individuals who wished to preserve their religious roots, others perceived that the loss of religion had much more extensive implications. This new development in European culture was described by Nietzsche as 'the death of God'. The origin of this phrase goes back to Luther, but it was Hegel – of course – who gave it its modern meaning when in the *Phenomenology* he dealt with the 'unhappy consciousness'. 'It is consciousness of the loss of everything of significance in this certainty itself, and of the loss even of this knowledge or certainty of self – the loss of substance as well as of self; it is the bitter pain which finds expression in the cruel words, "God is dead".'[13] But Nietzsche was also a dialectical thinker, and his treatment of the subject is very different, as can be seen in the following passage from *The Joyful Wisdom* (1882) entitled 'What our cheerfulness signifies'. He points to its consequences.

> In the main, however, one may say that the event is far too great, too remote, too much beyond most people's powers of apprehension, for one to suppose that so much as the report of it could have reached

them; not to speak of many who already knew what had taken place, and what must all collapse now that this belief had been undermined – because so much was built upon it, so much rested on it, and had become one with it: for example, our entire European morality.[14]

Nietzsche saw more clearly than anyone else what had become one with the Christian religion, what elements of modern society and culture rested upon assumptions which were valid only for believers. He is sometimes called a nihilist, because he did not hold Christian beliefs or subscribe to Christian moral judgments, but this is entirely unjustified. His particular concern was for values, moral and aesthetic, but he would not continue to associate himself with a previous system of values when he could no longer assent to its fundamental premises. In fact he had an alternative set of values, what he called 'the noble values', and these he set out in *The Antichrist*, the first volume of his *magnum opus*, *The Revaluation of All Values*. His problem was how to justify them. Where could he discover a basis for his system which was independent of the Christian religion, and indeed the whole philosophical and cultural tradition which had 'become one with it'? Walter Kaufmann points to the answer with a neat little historical reference. 'Nietzsche was aroused from his dogmatic slumbers by Darwin, as Kant had been by Hume a century earlier . . .'[15] Morality was to be based on nature, on an understanding of man as part of the natural, material world. But because Nietzsche was such a rigorously honest philosopher, he would not smuggle back into his system elements which could only be justified on religious premises. From Darwin he took the view that there is progress in human history, in natural, material terms. But what he would not include was any teleological dimension. He saw quite clearly that the idea of meaning in history arose from the biblical faith. History was not going anywhere: it was not an inherently meaningful process. 'The goal of humanity cannot lie in the end but only in its highest specimens.'[16]

I hope that the point of this slight digression will now be clear. In the nineteenth century secularization forced many to look for new ways to continue cherished beliefs. These beliefs rested on Christian faith, and the secular writers related to Christianity in a variety of ways. Hegel, far from rejecting Christianity, considered himself a good Lutheran who had reconciled philosophy and religion at a higher level. Feuerbach was fulsome in his praise of religion and its continuing value. Nietzsche occupied a place at the other end of the spectrum. He not only rejected the religious beliefs which had been the foundations of life and culture, he rejected everything which had been built thereon. He was the most consistent secular thinker in this respect.

Obviously the question arises as to where Marx is located on this spectrum. At the outset we reviewed the religious influences on his early life, and we have noted that his economic works are full of examples of righteous anger. Marx did not reject the moral values of biblical religion, however critical he might have been of the practices of Christians who departed from their own avowed standards. Nor did he make any attempt, as did Nietzsche, to base his moral values on new premises. In the best traditions of religion and morality, he did not feel the need to justify the decision to dedicate his life in the service of the oppressed. On the spectrum I have described, Marx stood at the end close to biblical religion so far as morality was concerned. But what of the other issue, teleology, meaning and purpose in history? Nietzsche was clear that although there was progress in evolutionary history in material terms, this could not be used to justify the belief that human history was progressing towards a moral goal. History does not incarnate moral values. On this Nietzsche departed from Christianity, and exposed all those philosophers who halted between two ways. Hegel, for example, not only continued the Christian belief that human history has a moral purpose: he went far beyond the wildest claims of theologians in presenting history as the progressive incarnation of Spirit. Although Feuerbach was so much influenced by Hegel, yet by comparison he was little concerned with the sweep of human history. Darwin came at the right time for Nietzsche, but Darwinism, especially social Darwinism, was very important to those who wished to continue the fundamentally religious belief that there is meaning in history, that history has a moral significance. Those who could no longer justify that belief on religious grounds relocated it on social Darwinism. But as Nietzsche saw, there is no basis in Darwin's theory for such a belief.

What, then, of Marx? The two main influences on his early life had been Christianity and Hegelian philosophy. Even after he broke with each in turn, he continued with the moral values which both shared. Did he also continue with the teleological view of history which both shared? The answer is clearly, Yes. We have already noted the eschatological and even christological form of his conception of the proletarian revolution. But it might be said that that was only a step from capitalism to communism, not extensive enough to be called a new view of the broad sweep of human history. Yet Marx did conceive of history in the broad sweep as moving in a certain direction. In the Preface to *A Contribution to the Critique of Political Economy* appears one of his most famous assertions. 'In broad outline the Asiatic, ancient, feudal, and modern bourgeois modes of production may be designated as epochs marking progress in the economic development of society'

(29.263). It is for this reason that Engels' claim is so appropriate, that historical materialism 'is destined to do for history what Darwin's theory has done for biology'. Historical materialism contains three elements which are problematic for the writers to whom we have been referring, but more than that in reconciling the three it provides the elusive solution. First of all, following the rejection of a religious or philosophical foundation, it provides a natural basis for understanding human (societal) life, a base in the material world independent of the will of man. In the second place it traces, if sketchily, the sequence of transitions between historical epochs, each characterized by a different mode of production. But there is a third element, unique to historical materialism. This sequence which takes place in the material world, under the laws of a natural science, is progressive, not simply in economic but in moral terms. This is inevitable when we consider that Marx was above all a moral philosopher and a man with a moral vocation. He would not have been interested in a theory which explained material change unless it could be related to his great moral and righteous crusade.

Historical materialism therefore offers an account of history which contrasts and competes with the accounts offered by Christianity and Hegel. In the case of the biblical faith, God guides history towards his goal. Its teleology is eschatology; the goal lies in the end. In Hegel history is the progressive incarnation of the Spirit, through which its self-consciousness is being achieved to higher and higher levels. The process itself is controlled by inner teleology. Marx rejects both religion and idealist philosophy. But if this study has underlined anything, it is that criticism more often than not continues to operate within the premises of the rejected position. Later in this chapter we shall argue that while Marx criticized Christianity, he did not break with it at the most fundamental level. For the moment it is not difficult to show that his criticism of Hegel was anything but a total rejection of the system. We have already noted that Marx was critical of Proudhon for his failure to understand the dialectics of history. Marx was one of the first critics of Hegel, and behind him came lesser men who tried to make their reputations by maligning the master. It was not simply contrariness which led Marx at that point to declare himself on the side of Hegel against this rabble. In 1873, in the Preface to the Second Edition of *Capital*, he was able to point to his debt to Hegel.

I therefore openly avowed myself the pupil of that mighty thinker, and even, here and there in the chapter on the theory of value, coquetted with the mode of expression peculiar to him. The mystification which the dialectic suffers in Hegel's hands by no means prevents him from being the first to present its general forms of motion in a comprehensive and conscious manner. With him it is standing on its head. It must be inverted in order to discover the rational kernel within the mystical shell.[17]

There was a shell, but Marx could not have proceeded with his own philosophy if he had not discovered the rational kernel within. In the rationale of *Capital* Marx was indebted to Hegel. It is hardly surprising that when Engels reviewed the *Contribution to the Critique of Political Economy* a few months after publication in 1859 he was able to identify the Hegelian element. 'What distinguished Hegel's mode of thinking from that of all other philosophers was the exceptional historical sense underlying it.' 'He was the first to try to demonstrate that there is development, an intrinsic coherence in history . . .' (16.474). And this is what Marx claimed, that there is an intrinsic coherence in history. Not extrinsic, as theology claimed. Not alienated, as idealism claimed. But for all his criticism of the mystical and the mystified, Marx shared this premise with religion and philosophy.

Nietzsche saw the premise very clearly and rejected it. In respect of the idea of meaning and purpose in history Marx did not free himself from the religious premise. Nor could he. His whole life and vocation were based on the assumption that it is possible to achieve at last something like a secular version of the Kingdom of God on earth. For Marx, if life is to have any meaning at all, such a moral goal must be attainable. To do for history what Darwin did for biology meant uncovering the real, objective, structure of history which involves man, affects man, but which is independent of his will. Nietzsche borrowed from Darwin, but understood that it is not possible to extract a teleology from a biological process. Marx looked for teleology, but as a moral philosopher sought it not in nature but in history. He was much encouraged by Darwin's work because of the historical dimension, the conflict and contradictions through which progress took place. Not materialism, but historical materialism. This is clear in a comment which Marx made in a letter to Ferdinand Lassalle in January 1861, a few weeks after he read Darwin.

> Darwin's work is most important and suits my purpose in that it provides a basis in natural science for the historical class struggle. One does, of course, have to put up with the clumsy English style of argument. Despite all shortcomings, it is here that, for the first time, 'teleology' in natural science is not only dealt a mortal blow but its rational meaning is empirically explained (41.246–7).

If we overlook the pretentiousness of a man who knew nothing at all about science taking it upon himself to criticize the research method of a world-famous scholar, we see that the significance of Darwin's work for Marx is not that it has done away with all forms of teleology, but rather it has discredited teleology in its purely material mode, just as he himself had attempted to discredit it in its mystical and mystified modes. No such conclusion can be legitimately drawn from Darwin's work, but it was what Marx needed – and of course ideas arise from needs, do they not?

This materialist teleology is a radical departure both from Christianity and the Hegelian philosophy of history. And yet what matters how radical the alternative answer, when it is still an answer to a question first set by religion, a question which has no meaning apart from the religious premises? Anyone seeking an alternative to religion could look to Nietzsche. But anyone seeking merely an alternative form of religion need look no further than Marx.

(e) The necessity of Hegel

I have distinguished between two different aspects of historical materialism. The emphasis in the first might fall on the material. Historical materialism reviews various epochs in (mainly European) history and relates the social superstructure and ideological formations to the material base, the division of labour, the form of property and the mode of production. In its second aspect the emphasis falls on the historical. The epochs are linked in sequence, so that it is possible to rewrite world history in terms of a progression from one mode of production to the next, and the consequent changes in the superstructure. If we refer to this latter aspect of historical materialism as a theory of history, then it marks an important division in Marx's work.

Marx was one of the founding fathers of the modern social sciences, and his work has been applied in sociology, political theory, history, moral philosophy, psychology, religious studies and literary criticism. His analyses of the formation of consciousness and social institutions have been suggestive, as have his accounts of the place and function of money in modern society, the subjective essence of labour and private property, the nature of ideology, and the relationship of base and superstructure. These studies are available to anyone to use as appropriate, and they are now frequently used by people who know and care nothing of Marx himself. He has slipped quietly into European intellectual history.

Such is not the case with regard to historical materialism considered now as a theory of history. As already indicated, if it were true, it would be one of the most extraordinary discoveries in human history, even more important than Darwin's theory of biological history. Yet it is asserted in the most perfunctory manner. 'In broad outline Asiatic, ancient, feudal, and modern bourgeois modes of production can be designated as progressive epochs in the economic formation of society.' They can be 'designated'. Was there one mode of production which characterized the whole of Asia?[18] And did it lead directly to an 'ancient' mode? Did primitive communal life and slavery lead directly to European feudalism? Even if the epochs could be 'designated', is this the same as being demonstrated to be progressive epochs? Can such a world-shaking conclusion be drawn without any attempted proof? Darwin dedicated a large part of his adult life to the painstaking task of collecting data from around the world. In the best scientific tradition the initial study of the data suggested a hypothesis: years of careful study confirmed it. Historical materialism is asserted simply from a gesture towards the history of the world. It needs no more than an indication in 'broad outline'.

Previously I discussed at length whether historical materialism should be regarded as a law of natural science, or merely an interpretative theory. But now another question arises. Even if it purports to be a natural law, whence does it come? 'Designating' is not at all the same thing as investigating: it is a movement in the opposite direction. It raises the suspicion that historical materialism did not arise from the painstaking scrutiny of the plethora of historical data, a process which would be tedious and frustrating. Tedious because of the quantity of material relevant to the task, frustrating because of its ambiguous nature. A more direct and satisfying approach would be to assert a hypothesis which derived from elsewhere. In his review of Marx's book, *Contribution to a Critique of Political Economy*, Engels seems to be attempting to deal with this issue, claiming that Marx could have chosen either starting point. 'Even after the determination of the method, the critique of political economy could still be arranged in two ways – historically or logically' (16.475). Engels maintains that it was for practical reasons that the historical approach was set aside.

The logical method of approach was therefore the most suitable. This, however, is indeed nothing but the historical method, only stripped of the historical form and of interfering contingencies. The point where this history begins must also be the starting point of the train of thought, and its further progress will be simply the reflection, in abstract and theoretically consistent form, of the course of history, a correct reflection, but corrected in accordance with the laws provided by the actual course of history, since each moment can be examined at the stage of development where it reaches its full maturity, its classical form (16.475).

Far from allaying our suspicions, this assurance makes things worse. The source of historical materialism is not historical/empirical studies of the data. It derives from a much more available source, what Engels calls 'logic': it is a materialistic version of the Hegelian philosophy of history. Engels claims that 'Marx was and is the only one who could undertake the work of extracting from the Hegelian logic the kernel containing Hegel's real discoveries in this field, and of establishing the dialectical method, divested of its idealist wrappings, in the simple form in which it becomes the only correct mode of the development of thought' (16.474–5).

A good deal of ink has been spilt by Marxists on Marx's relationship to Hegel. It has become something of a dogma to declare that Marx utterly rejected Absolute Idealism. This would mean that historical materialism was derived from some completely different source. And yet in this last quotation Engels tells us what in any case we already knew, that historical materialism is a particular appropriation of Hegel's philosophy of history. Those who come across historical materialism for the first time might have mixed reactions to it. In the first place it seems a quite extraordinary conception, the product of a some highly creative and original thinking. But in the second place it might lack credibility: it is not self-evident and appears frankly an unlikely scenario. However, reactions to historical materialism in Marx's own time would in fact be entirely the reverse. That is to say it would not be extraordinary at all, and far from being original would be recognized as a variation on Hegel's thought. And given the all-pervasiveness of Hegel's philosophy, it might seem quite reasonable. Elements in it which are problematic today might simply be assumed by Marx without comment. For example, if historical materialism is approached from the perspective of what in our time we are pleased to call a scientific standpoint, then the relationship between human freedom and natural necessity is an insuperable problem. However, since Hegel had reconciled necessity and freedom, anyone approaching historical materialism from its Hegelian premises would not see this as an issue.

In Chapter 2 I provided a brief introduction to some of the central themes in Hegel's philosophy, to clarify the ongoing debate among the Young Hegelians. I should now take time briefly to say something specifically about his understanding of the movement of history. It will become clear that Marx was indebted to Hegel not simply in the broad sweep, but also on specific details.

We have already seen that in Hegel's ontology history is the manifestation of the Idea: 'and Spirit, the rational necessitated will of that conductor, is and has been the director of the events of World History'.[19] In claiming that only the actual is rational, Hegel was using language in a very specific way: what exists is actual in so far as it manifests the rational. Similarly, what is actual is necessary, not in the normal sense in which objects of scientific study are governed by causal necessity. He is not dealing with the contingent or the merely 'fortuitous'. This necessity reflects the extent to which the actual expresses its rational essence.[20] It exhibits a certain kind of order, design or purpose, but not one imposed from outside. Hegel therefore distinguishes two different kinds of teleology. There is a design or end which is external to the thing itself, the causal necessity of the sciences. But there is also 'inner design', an idea of immanent teleology which Hegel takes over from Aristotle.[21] In this case the thing manifests the Idea, 'which posits the external reality necessary for its realization, and then develops this full realization in the external reality'.[22] It can then be understood to exist in and for itself and not simply in relation to a field. 'The End therefore in its efficiency does not pass over, but retains itself, i.e. it carries into effect itself only, and is at the end what it was in the beginning or primordial state.'[23]

Although there is a parallel between philosophy and religion in this matter, Providence is normally counted as external teleology. Yet the position is more subtle than might appear. Hegel is often prepared to identify God and *Geist*. Thus, as Taylor says, God 'is the subject which is at the same time the rational structure of the whole. Hence necessity is his trade mark, not a limitation on him.'[24] This can be more clearly illustrated in two texts which Grace Jantzen has brought together. The first is from the Collect for Peace. 'O God, who art the author of peace and lover of concord, in knowledge of whom standeth our eternal life, whose service is perfect freedom . . .' The second is from R. G. Collingwood: 'Perfect freedom is reserved for the man who lives by his own work, and in that work does what he wants to do.'[25] In the light of these quotations we can see why Hegel claims that 'this truth of necessity, therefore is Freedom . . .'[26] History as the manifestation of the Idea embodies freedom precisely in its necessity rather than in its contingency.

History is therefore directed by immanent Reason; it 'is none other than the progress of the consciousness of Freedom; a progress whose development according to the necessity of its nature, it is our business to investigate'.[27] As I noted in Chapter 2 it is by the cunning of reason that the end achieved is its end, not the ends which men plan or desire or intend. But history is not a single movement; it can be represented as a series of epochs. Each stage begins when Spirit has achieved a higher level of self-consciousness, a new level of freedom. This becomes embodied in the institutions appropriate to the new epoch.

However, since this is only a provisional representation, eventually the contradiction between consciousness and its external forms becomes unbearable and in the ensuing crisis a higher level of consciousness appears. Those embodiments which at the outset were the new expression of freedom eventually become obstacles to the next stage: the negations must themselves be negated in order that the next positive stage can be achieved.[28] J. N. Findlay stresses the dynamic dimension of the dialectic. 'Nowhere does it merely elicit what some firm basis entails: everywhere does it rather overturn its basis as involving incompleteness or conflict, and then progresses by a leap to something more harmonious and complete.'[29] And Hegel says of the dialectical nature of the idea 'that it assumes successive forms which it successively transcends . . .'.[30] But as we have seen, it is not possible to dispense with an epoch: 'Here is Rhodes, now jump.' No one can leap over his own time and place: the achievement of one epoch is the necessary foundation for the next.

Hegel therefore presents us with a view of history as a series of epochs, each following necessarily upon the other. They can be designated as that of 'Objective Spirit', the world of the Greek city state and the early Roman Empire; the 'Self-estranged Spirit', the period of feudal Europe; and 'Spirit certain of itself', the period ushered in by the Enlightenment and the French Revolution.[31] It is historical necessity, but it arises from ontological necessity. Within each epoch there is a relationship between the rational cause and its actual manifestations. The epochs proceed without regard to human plans or intentions, but because the finite spirits and Spirit itself are of the same nature,[32] history is moving in a direction which leads also to the self-realization of man.

According to Engels, Marx was the only person who could discern the kernel within the shell. It is a suggestive metaphor, one also used by Schleiermacher to distinguish religion itself from what he calls its 'trappings'. But considered more closely the metaphor is not at all apt. The strength, and for his followers the hypnotic attraction, of Hegel's system is that it is all of a piece. It is quite obvious that Marx took over the whole system, rejecting only a few points. Yet, as we shall see, he was not the first apprentice to discover that without these pieces the system could not be made to work.

The basis of Marx's criticisms of each of the Young Hegelians could be expressed by saying that far from superseding the master, they reverted to a previous position, one which he had envisaged and specifically rejected. Inevitably this was true also of Marx. He accepted Hegel's philosophy of history in the main. He too believed that history can only be understood according to the dialectic. It can be designated as falling into a series of epochs. He also took over the theory of transition by contradiction and the negation of the negation. The crisis was not now one of consciousness; nevertheless it arose from the incapacity of the manifestations, the superstructure, to express the next phase in the development of the base. And of course Marx believed that it was not possible to leap over an epoch. Just as for Hegel the conceptual powers of each epoch are the necessary foundations for the realization of the next phase, so for Marx there can be no revolution in society before the new mode of production appears. History is therefore proceeding, not by the intention of men, but in a direction which is progressively achieving human self-realization. Small wonder that he preferred to develop historical materialism from 'logic'. He would have needed better than 20/20 vision to discern it by looking at the data.

In fact it is difficult at first to see what Marx has not taken from Hegel. But of course he has rejected the Idea; in common with Feuerbach he has substituted man for God. That is all. Yet in the *Phenomenology* Hegel deduces absolute knowledge from the world, concluding that it is not possible to understand reality without acknowledging the Idea. Every previous stage – consciousness, self-consciousness, reason, spirit and religion – breaks down into contradiction and requires its supersession. It is not possible simply to take the kernel without the shell. In fact we might as well say that Marx attempted to take the shell without the kernel. Or to revert to our more mechanistic metaphor, without immanent reason the system will not run. Marx desperately wants history to exhibit inner teleology, but he rejects both providence and Spirit.

It is at this stage that he takes a fatal step. I do not think that Marx had his own words in mind at this point, but it is as if he applied his theory from the *German Ideology* that consciousness should be determined by social being. It is as if he extrapolated it from the individual to historical epochs. How would it work? We have seen that on this view ideology controls the lives of men. False consciousness makes them think that history is governed by the development of ideas. But is this not true of Hegel's philosophy of history, that historical epochs are controlled by the development of consciousness, and that consciousness then determines the way in which freedom is embodied? If Marx were to apply his theory at a macro level, then he should be maintaining that life, labour, comes first and determines consciousness and the institutions of the superstructure. I do not think Marx consciously applied his theory of ideology in this way, but it approximates to the result. He is in effect identifying the Hegelian philosophy of history as a reversal of reality on the largest possible scale. For Hegel consciousness determines life. For Marx, life, work, the mode of production, governs consciousness.

Unfortunately for Marx, in the course of this reversal something disappears, namely necessity. Necessity (as we have seen) is integral to Hegel's view of history, a necessity which far from negating freedom is the very basis of freedom. Marx now has a model of history, but it does not work, at least it does not work necessarily. As I have already noted, the critical point is the transition from one epoch to another: this is the heart of historical materialism as a theory of history. It is here that by sleight of hand, or possibly a category mistake, that Marx substitutes one kind of necessity for another. He takes to describing the movement as a natural law and since natural laws entail causal necessity, so historical materialism includes necessity. But this is not to supersede Hegel. It is a reversion to the Enlightenment, a position which Hegel regarded as useful, valuable, but in the end inadequate. As Taylor puts it, summing up the discussion of law in the *Phenomenology*, law is 'a way of conceiving the necessary relatedness underlying phenomena. As such it fails. Of course, it may be perfectly valid as a tool of empirical science. All we know is that it cannot be the final word and stopping point of our quest for a valid ontology.'[33] Earlier I distinguished between an epistemological and an ontological approach to necessity. Marx's position is an embarrassment to his followers because he has reverted to the terms of the debate posed by the Enlightenment. What he was attempting to do was to solve the ontological problem he had created for himself. He wanted the inner teleology found in religion and in philosophy, but having rejected its ontological foundation, either as God or *Geist*, he ended up with what he called the 'iron necessity' of natural laws. That is a poor foundation for humanism and an unlikely basis for a historical movement which is supposed to achieve human self-realization.

But there is a second respect in which Marx fails to supersede Hegel. He follows Feuerbach in substituting man for God, but this does not fully manifest *Geist*. Religion represents Spirit in an immediate form, and as such is not the final stage. 'Spirit as a whole and the moments distinguished in it fall within the sphere of figurative thinking, and within the form of objectivity.'[34] By substituting man for God, Marx fails to establish inner teleology. Providence is external teleology, operating upon the material world from outside. In making man the active being in history Marx reverts to the Enlightenment opposition of man and nature. Man acts upon the world to make it useful to him and to conform to his design or plan. But this is a very limited exercise. It is external, but it hardly deserves the name 'teleology'. It does not even achieve Marx's own purpose, since the epochs of history are specifically not directed by human intention. So there is still something missing in Marx's appropriation of Hegel. The substitution of man for God does not provide Marx with the inner teleology he seeks, because Hegel had already established that neither religion nor the Enlightenment could overcome the dualism between Spirit (whether divine or human) and the material world. Inevitably the question arises: if historical materialism is so blatantly inconsistent, why was Marx so committed to it?

(f) Ideological faith

Marx claimed that historical materialism was scientific, a natural law of motion, comparable to evolution in biology. It is not clear why he made this claim. At the outset it seems either absurd or at least meaningless: how could the complex relationships of social history ever be the subject of a natural science? But I have already noted that Marx described this movement in impersonal terms, as if the phenomenon was not after all human activity, but the outcome of natural forces. Yet how could social history be conceived of in other than human terms? That idea is borrowed from Hegel: history involves human beings, but it is not their story. It is the saga of the ages through which Spirit has externalized itself into the material, to overcome its alienation and return in full consciousness of itself. The Hegelian kernel of the dialectic is not human. Nor, of course, is it nature. However, since Marx has reverted to the dualism of Enlightenment thinking, yet if the dynamic history is not located in the sphere of the human, it must be found in the only alternative: nature. 'Nature' is not conceived of narrowly, but refers to the whole of non-human reality. The law of historical motion is therefore part of the sphere of nature and therefore a fit subject for scientific investigation. The law of historical determinism affects humans, but it neither originates with men nor can it be altered by them.

Along these lines it might be possible to understand how a law of history could be regarded as scientific. But of course it will not do. There are no laws of history: history is a social science and has to cope with the variables to which we have already referred, arising from the exercise of human freedom. Historical materialism does not arise from a scientific approach to historical data. It is a materialization of Hegel's philosophy of history. As such it is not even good historiography. Marx claimed it was scientific, Engels claimed it was historical, but it was neither. Alternatively, Engels said it was logical, but, as we have seen, it is not even a consistent appropriation of Hegel's position.

It is not science, or history, or philosophy. We seem to be running out of ways to describe it. Two further categories remain, and we shall look at them in turn. If we cannot understand historical materialism through the categories of science, history or philosophy, we must attempt to understand it instead in relation to the further categories of ideology and religion.

The idea that there is a movement in history which, independently of human intention, achieves humane goals, comes to Marx from Hegel, who in turn received it from the Christian religion. It did not arise from the investigation of data: it is not scientific in the terms of the natural or the social sciences. It is therefore an interpretation of the world, which is constructed independently of experience, and that means by Marx's own definition that it is an ideology. Of course selected data could be brought forward to support the thesis, but that could not disguise the fact that it had not originated from detailed historical investigation. Marx himself did not care to become involved in such tedious research, nor have his supporters cared to fill in the great gaps left in his 'broad outline'. Nor have the intervening decades provided automatic confirmation of the theory. Every hiccup in the SE 100, Dow-Jones or Nikkai averages has been interpreted by Marxists as signs of the times, the final incapacity of 'late capitalism' to contain its contradictions. The parallel between such apocalyptic predictions and the eschatological prophecies of religious sects has its own significance, to which we shall return.

In the best ideological tradition Marx was already convinced that there must be meaning and direction in history, and his moral crusade required it. All he needed was an alternative justification for it. The course of history must lead to a humane and moral goal, the end of alienation and exploitation. The idea that it must be so came from religion; the dialectic of how it is coming about came from philosophy. With a snip here and a tuck there the new creation was brought before the public: few looked and fewer still bought it. There were continuing doubts about whether it fitted.

If historical materialism had arisen from data, as a scientific hypothesis, then even if Marx was not equipped to gather the data, others could by this time have filled in the details. In similar fashion, the course of world history after the death of Marx could be sifted for data to confirm the theory. The prior data has not been constructed into a demonstration of the hypothesis; the subsequent data has at the very least failed to confirm the hypothesis. Yet historical materialism is alive and well in the hearts and minds of Marxists. It is not a scientific hypothesis: it was impervious to facts when first formulated and is incorrigible by facts now. It is in fact an ideology, more specifically an ideological faith. We have already described an ideology as a picture of reality, a world-view which purports to explain all relationships, and which bestows meaning and value on those who live within it. The term 'Marxist' should properly be applied not to those who simply use Marx's critical social analyses in an *ad hoc* manner, but to those who accept historical materialism in its ideological form.

It may seen unlikely at first sight that Marx could fall into the trap of constructing yet another ideology. It was he, after all, who had first analysed the phenomenon. But on closer inspection it is yet another of Marx's own internal contradictions. In *The German Ideology* we were told that 'Life is not determined by consciousness, but consciousness by life.' This is a prescriptive statement. All too often life is determined by the consciousness, or false consciousness, which is given to us by the ideology of the ruling class. Marx is advocating a critical break: consciousness should be determined by life, by actual experience, by the material conditions of labour. But was Marx's own consciousness was so formed? For example he was not a worker, a proletarian. He was never employed in a factory or on a building site. Earlier we saw that Marx traced the origins of ideology to the division of labour which allowed mental labour to be divided off from other forms. But this describes Marx himself as a philosopher. In his own terms we should expect his understanding of life to be determined by his philosophy, by consciousness and therefore by ideology. This is an important issue, though not unique to Marx. Philosophers have often constructed theories which are supposed to describe how things function, except that their own work contradicts the theory. Thus logical positivism devised rules for determining which kinds of statements are meaningful: except that their own rules failed the test. Thus Marx is describing how consciousness should be formed: except that it does not describe his own work. His theory of historical materialism did not arise from the experience of labour within the circumstances determined by the particular mode of production of the time. Rather it arose entirely within the superstructure, the realm that Marx designated as that of ideological production. I believe that Marx may have been aware of this contradiction, and for this reason sought to make his case an exception. This can be seen in two stages.

The first comes early, in the Introduction to the *Contribution to the Critique of Hegel's Philosophy of Right*. As Marx began to develop his critical philosophy he seeks to justify this apparently unpractical activity. 'The weapon of criticism cannot, of course, replace the criticism of weapons, material force must be overthrown by material force, but theory also becomes a material force as soon as it has gripped the masses' (3.182). Marx claims that although his work is critical theory, it can clarify and so contribute to the revolutionary activity of the masses. The Fabian Society was founded in the year that Marx died, but is he not here exhibiting one of its characteristic features: the leadership of the unassuming élite? The fact that Marx wishes to put his theory to good use in helping the poor does not extricate it or him from the ideological sphere in which it was developed. This leads to a second aspect of the contradiction: Marx, and indeed all his colleagues at that time, belonged to the middle class. By birth, family, education, training and culture they were better connected with the oppressors than with the exploited. Marx could not deny this fact, and no doubt others would not allow him to ignore it. Why did Marx write for capitalist newspapers? Why did he accept money from Engels, money which came from the exploitation of the mill workers in Manchester? The reason was quite simple. Marx had to have time to continue his work in the British Museum. Working like a proletarian would have interfered with this programme. When therefore he of all people sent out the call, 'Workers of the world unite!' there must have been not a few actual workers who advised him in proletarian terms what to do with his *Manifesto*. Marx had to justify not only his theory but himself. This he attempted in the *Manifesto* itself in a passage which is written in the most general terms, but is in fact autobiographical.

Finally, in times when the class struggle nears the decisive hour, the process of dissolution going on within the ruling class, in fact within the whole range of old society, assumes such a violent, glaring character, that a small section of the ruling class cuts itself adrift, and joins the revolutionary class, the class that holds the future in its hands. Just as, therefore, at an earlier period, a section of the nobility went over to the bourgeoisie, so now a portion of the bourgeoisie goes over to the proletariat, and in particular, a portion of the bourgeois ideologists, who have raised themselves to the level of comprehending theoretically the historical movement as a whole (6.494).

Marx identifies himself as a bourgeois ideologist who has betrayed his class. Has he come to join them as a worker? Certainly not. His contribution is to present them with a theory which will assist the revolution. But here is the contradiction, since Marx did not develop the theory within the experience of the proletariat. He brought with him in his defection a theory which he had devised from the resources of the ruling class. The process by which the ideology of historical materialism was formulated far from illustrating the theory itself, contradicts it.

There is, however, another internal contradiction. In *The German Ideology* Marx described the circumstances of the production of an ideology. It expresses and promotes the interests of the ruling class.

119

By contrast, historical materialism is the ideology of the oppressed class. In the preface to his doctoral dissertation Marx expressed admiration for Prometheus, who stole fire from the gods to bring comfort to men, at considerable cost to himself. We can now see that Marx was himself a Promethean figure. He brought an ideology from the ruling class, to give hope to working men, at considerable cost to himself. Marx saw clearly that the oppressed class required such an ideology and that they could not provide one for themselves. The ideology of the ruling class taught them that what is real is rational and what is rational is real: what is is what ought to be and it will continue to be so. What the exploited class needed was assurance that what is would not continue for ever. In dealing with the controversial question of the relationship of base and superstructure I said that even Kolakowski had fallen into an inversion. Philosophers after Hume and Kant assume that the issue is human freedom and determinism: how can human freedom be defended? But this is itself a bourgeois approach to a bourgeois issue. In the eighteenth century 'freedom' was the freedom of the new middle class, the entrepreneurial class, to trade without undue constraint: *laissez faire, laissez aller, laissez passer*. But to the exploited classes such freedoms are as relevant as a law permitting everyone to drive a Rolls-Royce. Such a spirited defence of the freedoms of power and privilege was not what was required in the circumstances which Marx faced. The exploited class in his day were confronted by the freedom of the ruling class to preserve the present order of things indefinitely. What they needed to hear was that there is a force in history which is stronger than the ruling class, which will achieve a utopian goal, and that this force cannot be defeated even by all the freedoms which the rulers can exercise. They needed to be assured in ideological terms what in former times religion had proclaimed, that God's will will be done and that the gates of hell will not prevail against it. It is enough that the proletariat take the side of this historic force: that is sufficient freedom for them. What is all-important is that the freedom of its opponents will delay but not finally defeat the revolution. The gift of this latter-day Prometheus, this renegade from the ruling class, this self-styled bourgeois ideologist, was nothing so insignificant as a scientific hypothesis: it was a living faith, it was good news to the poor. Marxists, as befits those who stand squarely within the western religious tradition, are people of a book (*Capital*), who are united by faith (historical materialism) and hope (the utopian vision) and assurance (the ultimate victory of the revolution): the suffering of their lives is as nothing compared to the true life for those to come. Their faith is unswerving in face of opposition. No plans of men can defeat the moral purpose of history. That this does not misrepresent Marx's position can be illustrated from the examples given in our final section.

(g) Marx's fetish

In Chapter 1 I described Marx's conversion to the Hegelian system, or rather to Hegelism, as a life-philosophy. I said that he was then what he continued to be, a man of faith. One of my friends is a Catholic priest in a diocese where the cathedral is now a suburban church. He has been left in charge of the old building, in the unfashionable part of town. I have often thought how proud of him his family must be: he has done awfully well, he has his own cathedral now. Would Marx's family have been proud of him? No longer just another Hegelian: he has his own ideology now. How much more proud would they have been if they had suspected that he had his own religion! Marx was not a Christian, nor overtly religious, but I noted at the outset certain religious themes which were important for him throughout his life. He never questioned or rejected them, though he could not justify them in his own terms. In the following examples we see Marx the man of ideological faith, a faith which has certain distinctly religious elements within it.

In June 1847 there was held in London the First Congress of the Communist League, the successor to the League of the Just. Marx was unable to attend, but Engels prepared a draft programme for the League. The document, 'Draft of a Communist Confession of Faith', was first published only twenty years ago, in 1969. It is in the form of a catechism:

Question 1: Are you a Communist?
Answer: Yes.
Question 2: What is the aim of the Communists?
Answer: To organize society in such a way that every member of it can develop and use his capabilities and powers in complete freedom and without thereby infringing the basic conditions of this society (6.96).

The catechetical form was not uncommon in socialist circles, but under the circumstances it seems not at all inappropriate. While it pre-dates the more extensive statements of historical materialism, it includes elements which transcend facts and exhibit faith in the theory. For example, the Answer to Question 14 includes an assertion which was later to appear in the Preface to the *Contribution to the Critique of Political Economy*. 'We are also aware that revolutions are not made deliberately and arbitrarily, but that everywhere and at all times they are the necessary consequence of circumstances which are not in

121

any way whatever dependent either on the will or on the leadership of individual parties or of whole classes.' (6.102) As we have seen, proletarians when they first heard this view would not display any bourgeois anxiety about human freedom, rather, they would take great comfort from this assurance that not even the freedom of the ruling class can prevent the revolution which will bring such relations of exploitation to an end. That this is the inevitable course of history is an affirmation of faith, and its origins lie in primitive Christianity. We have seen that historical materialism does not destroy Hegelian philosophy: it rescues the kernel from the shell. Historical materialism is Hegelian philosophy of history in other terms. And does it destroy religion? Hardly.

Question 22: Do Communists reject the existing religions?
Answer: All religions which have existed hitherto were expressions of historical stages of development of individual peoples or groups of peoples. But communism is that stage of historical development which makes all existing religions superfluous and supersedes them (6.103).

Historical materialism arises from religion and Hegelian idealism, and attempts to supersede them. But as we have seen frequently in previous chapters both in religion and philosophy, critics who attempt to go beyond must first basically accept. In this case there is what Wittgenstein might have called a family resemblance among Christianity, Absolute Idealism and historical materialism. The Hegelian dialectic can be illustrated in the sequence of Judaism, its encounter with its contradiction, Hellenism, and outcome of their clash, Christianity. We might say that Hegel's dialectic was, appropriately, itself an illustration of such a sequence. (In this case the formulation of the theory would not be an exception to the theory itself.) Aristotelian *entelechy* and its contradiction, the Christian *telos*, are united creatively in Hegel's idealist philosophy of history. In this case the balance has been tipped against the materialist element in Aristotle and in favour of the idealist element in Christianity. An alternative reading of the same process would preserve the idealist element of historical purpose, but root this more directly in the materialist world. Historical materialism, far from being the rejection of Hegelianism would be a variation on its fundamental premises.

I have spent a good deal of time on Marx's relationship to Hegel. I must now return to my original theme of the relationship between Marx and Christianity. I begin with a historical reference. In the early centuries the Christian church suffered sporadic but at times horrific persecution. To those living within such periods it would have been easy to argue that the facts were against them. They should give up their religion: their suffering contradicted their proclamation of Christ's victory over the powers of evil. But their faith carried them through: events were given a very different interpretation. As Tertullian wrote at the beginning of the third century: 'We multiply whenever we are mown down by you; the blood of Christians is seed.'[35] Paul also suffered many reversals in his life as an apostle. In his letters addressed to the small Christian communities located in the cities of the Roman Empire he is sometimes elated when things turn out well, downcast at least for a time when things go against him. But as for all men of faith, defeat is but a set-back, there is no doubt about the eventual victory. 'And we know that all things work together for good to them that love God . . .'[36] Despite the evidence of experience, faith does not lose hope.

There is a general parallel between Marxist faith and Christian faith at this point. Indeed it is more than a general parallel, as can be seen in the following example which arose from a campaign in the American Civil War. Whatever the real causes of the conflict, Marx, like many others, thought of it in moral terms: he and Engels often referred to it as the 'pro-slavery rebellion'.[37] In 1863 Marx reflected on the defeat suffered by the Union army as the Confederate army advanced into Maryland. Apart from its military significance, as a defeat for Lincoln, whom Marx greatly admired, it was a setback for the cause of democracy. To those directly involved it was not at all clear at that point which way the conflict would go, and an outside observer who was concerned about human values and decency might have wondered whether any progress could ever be made. That, however, was not Marx's reaction. He took the long view, expressed in a most extraordinary aphorism. 'Reason nevertheless prevails in world history' (19.249). This is not the voice of pragmatism but the confession of faith. It closely parallels Paul's statement. Indeed it is the third of the four points to which I referred in Chapter 1, continuing religious influences on Marx's thought: despite everything man is sustained by faith.

The same sentiments were already expressed in 1854 during the period in which Marx was writing articles for the New York *Daily Tribune*. In an article on 'The English Middle Class' he declared his faith that 'though temporary defeat may await the working class, great social and economical laws are in operation which must eventually insure their triumph' [13.665]. Nor was it something later overcome. In 1895, some twelve years after the death of Marx, Engels could sum up the position which he held to the end of his life:

According to Marx's views all history up to now, as far as the great events are concerned, has come about unconsciously – that is, the events and their further consequences have not been intended. The ordinary actors in history have either wanted to achieve something different, or else what they achieved has led to quite different unforeseeable consequences.[38]

This is historical materialism as an ideological faith: history is proceeding in a rational direction. That is to say, in spite of appearances to the contrary, the goal for which Marx and his friends worked is nearer now than when they first believed. They have worked very hard, and endured a great deal of abuse and suffering. And yet such progress as has been made does not depend on them. 'Reason nevertheless prevails in world history.' The rational structure of the world, as uncovered by historical materialism, directs history, and this progress is not dependent on men, those who oppose it or even those who seek to promote it. This was not a new idea for Marx. It is the last of the four points to which I drew attention in Chapter 1, that from his earliest days Marx knew that it is not by human intention that history is directed. Indeed Marx can allude from time to time to a not dissimilar point made by Adam Smith, who was so influential on his development. In *The German Ideology* Marx refers to that principle which relates supply and demand, which according to Smith 'hovers over the earth like the fate of the ancients and with invisible hand allots fortune and misfortune to men . . .' (5.48). In *Capital*, in a discussion of Adam Ferguson and Adam Smith, he can also refer to the idea of 'an invisible bond uniting various branches of trade'.[39]

As we have seen, Engels claims that he and Marx arrived at historical materialism about the same time. They shared the common faith, as can be seen in this letter written in 1892. 'Actually there is nothing in history which does not serve human progress in one way or another, though often by a terribly circuitous route.'[40] These are surely the sentiments of ideological faith. It is incorrigible by any facts or situations. A scientific hypothesis is of course constantly correctible by new data, but not an ideological faith. Earlier when quoting from the preface to *A Contribution to the Critique of Political Economy* I referred to the impersonal way in which the relationship between the base and superstructure could be described. In the ideological faith this impersonalism is in large part overcome. To be sure it is not God who directs history, but at least it is reason. It is not impersonal material forces, but reason, which historically in European thought has been the common element linking God and man. I have drawn attention to the close parallel between Marx's position and that of Paul, but since neither Marx nor Engels expressed themselves in religious language, it is not surprising that the parallel is even closer with Hegel, the secularizer of Christian faith and hope. In 1889 Engels speaks of the hope which arises from his ideological faith. Once again we hear that although men must work hard to change the world, the outcome is not determined by human intention. 'And in face of all these disputes I had little hope that things would turn out alright, that immanent reason, which little by little is evolving to consciousness of itself in this history, would be victorious as soon as this.'[41] In the *Logic* Hegel had envisaged the same situation, although he was prepared on this occasion to use religious language. 'God lets men do as they please with their particular passions and interests; but the result is the accomplishment of – not their plans but his, and these differ decidedly from the ends primarily sought by those whom he employs.'[42] In 1856 at a public lecture in London Marx expressed his ideological faith in Hegelian terms. 'On our part, we do not mistake the shape of the shrewd Spirit that continually manifests himself in all these contradictions' (14.656). This is an expression of faith, and I believe there is an intriguing parallel between it, Hegel's cunning of reason, and Adam Smith's invisible hand.

Adam Smith was a moral philosopher, and one of the most prominent influences on his thought was Stoicism. In *The Theory of Moral Sentiments* he writes of their doctrine of Providence and their belief that 'every single event ought to be regarded, as making a necessary part of the plan of the universe, and as tending to promote the general happiness of the whole . . .'.[43] As men act to pursue their own interests, a natural harmony is achieved. It is not by their intention, and in this they are deceived.[44] This 'deception' recurs in *The Wealth of Nations* in which the natural harmony is transferred to the field of economic relations. The entrepreneur 'intends only his own gain, and he is in this, as in many other cases, led by an invisible hand to promote an end which was no part of his intention'.[45] Both of these themes are repeated in Hegel. For Providence and the natural harmony we have the cunning of reason, to which I referred in Chapter 2, which remains in the background while allowing others to serve its will. In the *Phenomenology* Hegel describes the individual's activity and declares that 'the extent to which he looks after his own interests is the measure with which he must also serve the purpose of others.'[46] Marx's shrewd spirit, Hegel's cunning of reason, and Smith's invisible hand have two things in common. The first is that they apparently explain how moral goals are brought out of immoral or amoral situations. On closer inspection they are devices which are necessary precisely because there is no connection between the goals and the situations, no matter how

125

much human beings would wish it otherwise. The second is that they originate in a doctrine of Providence, in religious faith in the final cause of the universe.

In the case of Marx's shrewd spirit, the fact that Hegelian terms are used to express an ideological faith should not obscure the fundamentally religious origins of that faith. Devotees of a particular faith, ideological or religious, are naturally anxious to make claims for its originality even when parallels with other faith are all too evident. On the relationship between ideological and religious faith, there is an instructive parallel from an unexpected quarter. In his epoch-making *Commentary on Romans*, Karl Barth distinguished Christianity from religion. Christianity is the truth, God's disclosure of himself in Christ. Religion by comparison is man's pathetic, misguided and benighted search for the truth. Anyone who is familiar with this move, by which Christianity is not only distinguished from all other religions, but is placed beyond their criticism, will recognize the same move on behalf of Marx, carried out by Althusser in an article entitled 'On the Materialistic Dialectic'. 'This article proposes the term *Theory* (with a capital T) to designate Marxist "philosophy" (dialectical materialism) – and reserves the term *philosophy* for *ideological* philosophies.'[47] This is the more ironic, since Marx specifically referred to this ploy among theologians in his criticism of Proudhon (6.174).

In the early years Marx made a considerable investment of time and effort in analysing the ills of society and the obstacles to the achievement of communism. As a man of faith and commitment he needed the assurance that his efforts and those of his colleagues would not be forever thwarted, that evil and injustice would not for ever hold the oppressed in thrawl. That moral imperative predated his discovery of historical materialism. And the ethical rightness of his social vision was transferred to become the empirical correctness of historical materialism. Marxism as a faith is defended because of its ethical imperative, long after it has been discredited on empirical grounds.

I began this Part by reviewing Marx's early relations with religion before going on to his various critiques. As we saw, the most challenging is that religion is a reversal of reality. He began with Feuerbach's projection model. A mental construct is projected away from man and gains objective form over against him. Forgetting that he is its creator, he allows it to act back and control his life. Marx was able to take this reversal model, originally identified in religion, and apply it to every other form of festishism in modern society. Hegel had introduced the term 'fetish' in his discussion of African religion, to refer to material objects which were regarded as endowed with supernatural power and consequently treated with awe.[48] In *Capital* Marx used the term to illuminate the problem of commodities by reference to 'the misty realms of religion'.

> There the products of the human brain appear as autonomous figures endowed with a life of their own, which enter into relations both with each other and with the human race. So it is in the world of commodities with the products of men's hands. I call this the fetishism which attaches itself to the products of labour as soon as they are produced as commodities, and is therefore inseparable from the production of commodities.[49]

And here unfortunately we encounter yet another internal contradiction, one which further illustrates our earlier discussion of theories which condemn their authors. A historical parallel might illustrate. Albert Schweitzer, in his monumental analysis *The Quest of the Historical Jesus*, with considerable insight exposed the ways in which so many before him had composed pictures of Jesus in their own image, only to fall into the very trap himself. Schweitzer, who started out as a critic of all forms of the movement, ended up as yet another example of it. Unfortunately the same must be said of Marx. Historical materialism is not part of the natural or material world. It is a mental construction, which has gained objective status in the world, at least the world of Marxists. Forgetting its human origins, it has been allowed to act back on men, to govern their lives. Historical materialism in Marx's own terms is a religious movement. As an ideology it is both faith and fetish.

PART TWO

Marx and Liberation Theology

6

Redemption and Revolution

(c) Theology and social being

In an encyclopedia which allowed only one sentence to the subject, it would not be wrong to say that liberation theology began in 1969 and that its founder was Gustavo Gutierrez. However, all social movements have roots, and in order to understand our subject it is necessary to say something about its prehistory. Liberation theology emerged first of all in Latin America out of the interaction of two movements. Viewed in intellectual terms they are theology and philosophy: the new theology stimulated by the Second Vatican Council and the new Marxism of the post-Stalinist era. However, having just made such a detailed study of Marx it would be surprising if we accepted as a matter of course that new movements arise simply from the availability of ideas. After all, the same theology and the same philosophy were present in Europe without producing liberation theology. If consciousness is produced by social being, then a more adequate explanation of the rise of this movement would have to begin not with the purely intellectual forms of theology and philosophy, but with their social expressions. We should therefore say that in Latin America liberation theology arose from the creative interraction of two social movements: the ecclesial situation brought about by the Council and the presence in the continent of the Cuban revolution. The combination did not exist anywhere else in the world, but the resultant movement itself became a social factor in the production of related forms of liberation theology elsewhere.

As indicated at the outset, I shall not be concerned to provide an exposition of the main themes of liberation theology. Such a project has not as yet been undertaken, and it is even possible that it might be worth doing. But since liberation theology has arisen out of a creative interaction of Christianity and Marxism, we shall focus attention on the way and extent to which Marx's thought has been appropriated. To begin with we shall consider the prehistory of the movement, examples in which Christian theology and revolutionary praxis have coincided without producing an integrated liberation theology.

(b)   Cuba and unredeemed America

Whatever happened to Cuba? In recent years Cuba is only mentioned in international affairs either because of the heroic services of its sons in the assistance of emergent countries or the equally devastating services of its daughters on the volley-ball courts of the world. But of Cuba itself we hear little. In 1961 my wife and I left Glasgow, the number one target for nuclear attack in Europe, to live in New York. A few months later the Cuban missile crisis went to red alert, and we found ourselves at the centre of one of the main targets for a nuclear attack on America. President Kennedy, representing the hopes of liberals everywhere, brought the world closer to final destruction than President Reagan ever did. The New York business community of course took the matter in its stride. Not a moment to lose: get a fall-out shelter now for your back yard. Easy credit terms over twenty-five years. Straight out of the American Surrealist School of Business. By coincidence, as I write this, Mikhail Gorbachev has just arrived in Havana for a meeting with Fidel Castro. At sixty-two Castro is the older of the two, but whereas Gorbachev was born after the Russian Revolution and has progressed to the Presidency via the bureaucratic ladder, Castro was not yet thirty when he embarked on the revolutionary guerrilla war which was to topple the Batista regime. In many respects, such as democratic reforms, new-style elections, the easing out of the old guard, stimulation of the market economy, but including appearance – clean-shaven, trilby hat and expensive suits which actually fit – Gorbachev has more in common with President George Bush.

Our subject, however, is not the reality of the Cuban revolution as it celebrates its thirtieth anniversary, but rather the perception of the Cuban revolution in its early years and the impact which this perception made throughout Latin America.

Andy Warhol said that in the future everyone would be famous for fifteen minutes: he did not say they would be admired or remembered. By contrast there is a small band of charismatic people who are known throughout the world simply by a single name, and among them is Ernesto Che Guevara. The reality of the Cuban revolution is inconceivable without Fidel Castro, but its perception is largely connected with Che. He was a man of faith driven by a sense of mission: motivated by love he sacrificed his life for others. A tough revolutionary, commander of the Second Column, he preserved his humanity and integrity; in his commitment to Cuba he never lost his internationalist vision.

He was born in Buenos Aires, Argentina, in 1928. His internationalism went back through both sides of his family, being of Irish and Spanish descent. From an early age he suffered from asthma and failed the draft: he was not fit enough for the Argentinian army. His concern for the exploited and oppressed, especially the Indians, emerged in his student days as he toured his own country, Chile and Peru. In 1953 he graduated from medical school and set out to assist in what had to be done in Central America. Ten years later in a letter he describes his credentials. 'I was born in Argentina, I fought in Cuba, and I began to be a revolutionary in Guatemala.'[1] He died as a guerrilla commander in Bolivia in 1967: captured by the army in an ambush, shot in a prison cell.

He had spent time working in a leper colony in Bolivia before travelling to Peru, Ecuador and Costa Rica. In December 1953 he was in Guatemala and it was there that he met Hilda Gadea, whom he married. She was a Peruvian exile well connected with revolutionary movements in Central America. It was she who introduced Guevara to the 26 July Movement, the date on which Fidel Castro had led an unsuccessful attack on the Moncada Barracks in Santiago, in Cuba.[2] Although Guevara was a committed humanitarian, he specifically refused to join the Guatemalan Communist Party. However, because of his experience at the time of the American invasion of Guatemala in 1954 he was already committed to revolutionary struggle when in the summer of 1955 he met Fidel Castro in Mexico. In November of the following year he was one of the eighty-two who set out on the eirenically named *Granma*, to take the struggle to Cuba. Three days after they landed, the army struck and only twelve of the insurgents survived. Yet two years later, in January 1959, Fidel Castro was Prime Minister of the Provisional Government. The war was over: the revolution just begun. Guevara made a good deal of this distinction, and to it we shall return.[3]

In North America the revolution was represented in the most extreme rhetoric of the Cold War; worse since it was in America's back yard. Those of us who have a genuine affection for America are distressed by its double standards. It will having nothing less than democracy and justice at home, and yet apparently it will enlist as an ally abroad any tyrannical and corrupt régime in order to protect and further American interests. If only America knew what its true interests were! The defeat of the Batista régime was somehow regarded as an unfriendly act towards America. But the same defeat was of great interest to the people of other countries in the area who had régimes not at all unlike that of Batista, régimes also regarded by America as allies. The eyes of the Americas were upon Cuba. At one time, more than three centuries ago all eyes had been upon America itself, as it set out to establish a new democracy. As John Winthrop, the governor of the Massachusetts Bay colony, declared in the religious sentiments of the Puritans: '. . . we must consider that we shall be a City upon a Hill, the eyes of all people are upon us.'[4] In the early years of the revolution Guevara saw Cuba in a similar situation and he expressed himself in religious terms which are not unfamiliar.

> We are now in a situation in which we are much more than simple instruments of one nation; we constitute at this moment the hope of unredeemed America. Today all eyes – those of the powerful oppressors and those of the hopeful – are fixed on us.[5]

We can hardly read this without recalling the imagery by which Marx described the proletarian revolution: redemption through sacrifical suffering. During the struggle the Batista regime forcibly moved thousands of peasant families out of the Sierra Maestra as a punishment for assisting the guerrillas. After much hardship many of them returned and some even decided to join the struggle and 'proceed resolutely along the road to their redemption'.[6] In the Manichaean terminology of the Cold War, America stood for freedom and spiritual values, while the communists were materialists. What then was at stake in Cuba? Guevara expresses it in the most natural terms: 'the struggle of a people to redeem itself'.[7] Who in the spiritual West would think to describe a social movement in such terms? Who would understand what was meant? But its meaning was perfectly clear throughout Latin America.

I have been present when Marxists have sought to compare the leaders of our two faiths unfavourably. But I have poured scorn on that reversal of reality. If Marx had fallen in a hail of bullets in the front line of a revolutionary march it might have been more credible. But Marx, so far as I know, never put himself in physical danger at any time for the sake of the cause. By comparison Jesus of Nazareth was arrested by the Jewish authorities, and sentenced to death by the imperial power, the Romans. He died by crucifixion, the prescribed form of execution for dangerous enemies of the state. I have therefore often scoffed at the idea that Marx was an example either to workers or to revolutionaries. Not so with Che Guevara, who suffered hardship and risked his life for a moral cause. And when that cause was established and he could have lived the rest of his life in Cuba as one of the fathers of the revolution, his internationalism called him on again.

As he said in a letter to Castro, on the eve of his departure to assist the revolution in Bolivia, a decision which would lead to his death: 'other nations of the world call for my modest efforts.'[8] When Marx finds he must describe the revolution as redemption we are intrigued; when Guevara so describes it we are challenged. When Marx uses the term he takes over its religious meaning; when Guevara uses it, religious people must ask whether they have ever fully understood its implications. In a tribute to his dead comrade Castro says quite simply: 'His blood was shed in Bolivia, for the redemption of the exploited and the oppressed.'[9] 'It is man himself, his fellow man, the redemption of his fellow man, that constitutes the objective of the revolutionary.'[10]

We can therefore see why the Cuban revolution, rather than Marxist revolutionary theory, became one of the roots of liberation theology. Those who look only to Marxist philosophy often ask how it could have any impact on Christians. As usual this is to get things the wrong way round. We might rather ask if what Guevara stood for was actually Marxism. It seems to bear little resemblance to the philosophy I have analysed in Part One. At the end of his life, less than a decade after victory, Guevara thought of himself and his work as Marxist. This is clear in a letter which he wrote to his parents before going to Bolivia.

> Nothing has changed in essence, except that I am much more aware, my Marxism has taken root and become purified. I believe in the armed struggle as the only solution for these people who fight to free themselves, and I am consistent with my beliefs.[11]

But this reflected the second phase of his development, after the end of the war. For the moment we shall concentrate on the first phase, during which, while there are broadly Marxist elements in his ideology, there are also elements which contradict Marx's doctrines.

If we look first of all at those aspects which are compatible with Marxism, we see that Guevara is a man of conviction, a man of faith in a cause. It is a moral crusade which purifies his life. But why does a man who wishes only for a normal, peaceful life become involved in guerrilla warfare? He is motivated as a 'social reformer',[12] taking up arms on behalf of the exploited and oppressed. Guevara could express this in terms which even surprised himself. 'Let me say, with the risk of appearing ridiculous, that the true revolutionary is guided by strong feelings of love.'[13] But the sacred cause requires a higher quality of love. 'Our vanguard revolutionaries must idealize their love for the people, for the most hallowed causes, and make it one and indivisible. They cannot descend, with small doses of daily affection, to the terrain where ordinary men put their love into practice.'[14] Thus although

Guevara begins with a Marxist theme, he is prepared to express it in religious terms. As we have seen, Marx not only rejected religion, as an obstacle to human emancipation, but constantly used religion to illustrate the negative elements in other institutions. But just as the French communards had a very different experience of religion, so Guevara does not attack religion. He rarely mentions it, and never identifies it as belonging to the ruling and exploitative classes. Thus he is able to use religious terminology in a positive way to identify what is required of the revolutionary in his relationship to the people he seeks to serve. The revolutionary is 'a true priest of the reform', a 'guiding angel'. Because so much depends on him as he acts for the people, the guerrilla must drink no alcohol, and must abstain from sexual relations: he is 'an ascetic'.[15] Less flatteringly, the furtiveness and deviousness of the guerrilla's work means that he is 'the Jesuit of warfare'.[16]

What is at stake here is the theme of the quotation from the letter to his parents. The Marxist must become aware; his consciousness must be raised, but not simply at a theoretical level. He must internalize the revolution and become one with it in his life and his relationships so that there is no contradiction between the values and goals he aspires to and the life he leads to achieve them. Precisely because there is no rejection of religion here, it is an even greater challenge to the Christian life. Although Guevara rarely mentions religion, it would seem that it was allowed to play its normal role in the life of the guerrillas even when they were in the field. This emerges in an incident in which revolutionary justice is meted out to the leader of a gang who, while pretending to be guerrillas, were simply brigands. Chang not only faced death with composure and serenity, but asked for the last rites to be administered by Father Sardiñas. Guevara simply remarks that the priest did not happen to be there at the time. A few days later a similar incident took place, and the priest was there. Father Sardiñas was a priest who joined the guerrillas, except that he did not bear arms. A second illustration of the relationship between priests and guerrillas can be deduced from a book which Guevara wrote just a year after the defeat of Batista. It looks like a textbook on how to wage a guerrilla war, but naturally and indeed properly it is a summary of the lessons which they had learned during their recent campaigns. In the use of civilians both as couriers and spies he specifically includes 'clergymen'.[17] Since this is experience and not theory, we must assume that some clergymen actually did function in this way.

Thus although there are elements in Guevara's position which are compatible with Marx – though not necessarily inspired by Marx – there are other elements which are not. One of the most important is the matter of 'epochs' which we discussed in relation both to Hegel and to Marx. Guevara remains entirely at the level of the 'superstructure'. He shows no interest in, or awareness of the 'base'. Thus he rejects the 'dogma' of when and in what circumstances the revolution can proceed.[18] For him it is when all the normal democratic means have been tried and been demonstrated to be ineffectual. The people have then no alternative. If anything, Guevara is closer to Hegel than to Marx: the crisis is provoked when the consciousness of freedom cannot be contained or expressed by the existing institutions of the state. There is no mention of the mode of production, and this leads us to the most important difference between Guevara and Marx.

We have seen that both for Hegel and for Marx, though for different reasons, it is not possible to jump over an epoch. And for Marx this means that every society has to go through the same sequence, culminating in feudalism, capitalism and then communism. More than that, it is the virtue of capitalism that it rescues peasants from the idiocy of the rural life. According to Marx what Cuba requires – if it has indeed reached the end of the epoch – is a bourgeois revolution which will introduce a capitalist epoch. This in turn will produce a proletariat, the class which will wage the revolutionary war to bring about communism. But Guevara specifically rejects attempts elsewhere in Latin America to introduce 'national capitalism'.[19] He draws attention to the early failure of Mao when he began with industrial workers, and to his success in the Long March when he associated himself with the peasants and the issue of agrarian reform. Cuba is therefore compared to China, North Vietnam and Algeria. The objective of the revolutionary struggle will be agrarian reform, to satisfy 'the age-old hunger of the peasant for the land on which he works or wishes to work.'[20] And this is the struggle for communism. As I suggested in Part One, the failure (or aggravated disappointment) of the Cuban revolution cannot be attributed to its adherence to Marxism, but rather to its failure to follow Marx's clear teaching on the subject. It is not possible to move directly from feudalism to communism, not even via state capitalism.

There is a further point which raises doubts about whether Guevara was a Marxist, as distinct from a revolutionary. His reminiscences of the war are amazingly frank. Indeed the continual ineptitude recorded would suggest there is ample material here for a TV series: 'Carry On Castro'. According to Guevara's account, these weaknesses of planning and discipline continued right to the final victory. Perhaps he could after all have borrowed from Hegel the idea that the victory came about by the cunning of reason rather than the actions of men. At the beginning of the guerrilla war he was regarded as the doctor, but he tells us that he knew virtually nothing about medicine. Thereafter he was responsible for ideological instruction. But did he know any more about that subject? Or rather had it anything to do with Marxism? For example, he advocates that each man should carry one book, which could be shared round. This ensures that various subjects will be covered, but the subjects are 'good biographies of past heroes, histories or economic geographies, preferably of the country, and works of general character that will serve to raise the cultural level of the soldiers'.[21] Clearly in this adult education movement no one is expected to carry anything from verbose and boring old Marx and Engels. Almost the same list of subjects is recommended when Guevara advises on what should be taught in youth indoctrination classes. In an interview six months after the end of the war, Guevara acknowledges his debt not to Marx but to Mao. They studied Mao in the field, using mimeographed copies of his work. Clearly the situation in the Sierra Maestra was much closer to that of rural China.[22] This stage in his development thus stands in marked contrast to his position a few years later. We must therefore doubt how ideologically sound he was, compared to his intention in 1964 'to approach Marxism with the seriousness that this monumental doctrine deserves'.[23]

There is one final respect in which the Cuban revolution is reminiscent of Marx's own position. Although the situation of the peasants may require a revolution, they themselves cannot organize it. Yes, the 'initiators' and 'directors' of the guerrilla war are not peasants.[24] Led by a lawyer and a doctor, they are from other classes, and included university graduates and people of middle-class backgrounds as well as privileged urban leaders. Here indeed are Marx's bourgeois ideologists. The peasants must have been much relieved that in fact they knew little of ideology but were rather imbued with great moral courage and fortitude. The eyes of 'unredeemed (Latin) America' were upon them. They were humanists and communists, but whether they were Marxists is open to doubt.

All that was soon to change. The war had been to bring about an agrarian revolution, and six months after victory the Land Reform Law was passed, leading to conflict with the USA. But the future lay with industrialization, with the production of wealth and the satisfaction of needs. Guevara was appointed president of the Cuban National Bank and became involved in economic planning and the development of international trade, including new credits with the USSR. Two years later, in 1961, he was appointed Minister of Industries. In this context Guevara developed a very much more orthodox form of Marxism, even Marxist-Leninism. He was conscious of the division to which I have already drawn attention. 'In fact the Cuban Revolution must be separated into two absolutely different stages: that of armed action until January 1, 1959, and the political, economic, and social transformation since then.'[25] It is now in the second phase that Marx is their guide: they follow the 'laws of Marxism'.[26] But this was so much rhetoric. In a speech in Havana in 1960 he claimed that if the Cuban Revolution looked to others to be Marxist, it was not because it slavishly followed Marx, but rather 'because it discovered by its own means the path that Marx pointed out'.[27] There is a parallel here with Castro, who in this was influenced by Guevara. Although in 1967, in retrospect, Castro could say that it was inevitable that a true socialist should be a Marxist, yet at the end of the war, when concrete programmes had to be undertaken, he was satisfied with neither option of capitalism or communism. Like that other pupil of a Jesuit college, Castro distinguished his position from the alternatives by calling it 'humanism'.[28]

On closer inspection Guevara was very selective in what he took from Marx. It soon became clear to him that Cuba was not going to have the capital for a programme of rapid industrialization. He was in a situation which had confronted not Marx, but Trotsky. How can a pre-industrial socialist country industrialize? The solution was for advanced socialist countries to assist the emerging ones. When this aid was not forthcoming Guevara criticized the USSR, in March 1965. A few weeks later he wrote the letter to Castro to which we have already referred, announcing in effect that he was resigning as an ideologist and returning to being a guerrilla. In November 1966 he contacted his new guerrilla group in Bolivia. As was his custom he wrote up a diary of the campaign. Like the *Reminiscences of the Cuban Revolutionary War*, the *Bolivian Diary* is a catalogue of ineptitude bordering on the absurd. However, while the first is intriguing, in view of the success of the outcome, the second, although simply written, is now read with pathos. It was not possible to recreate the situation of the Sierra Maestra. The peasants never trusted the guerrillas, and far from supporting them, constantly informed the army of their movements. Often without medication for his asthma, Guevara describes himself latterly as a human wreck'.[29] Few of his group exhibited that integration of mind, heart and hand which he had advocated in Cuba. However, Guevara to the end never lost hope, nor did he lose faith in the ideal: 'This type of struggle gives us the opportunity to turn ourselves into revolutionaries, the highest state of the human species, but it also allows us to graduate as men . . . .'.[30]

The eyes of unredeemed America were on Cuba and then Bolivia, on the humanist revolutionary who was willing to give his life for the cause of justice. Ironically, in the life and teaching of Guevara they saw little to advocate ideological Marxism. His own socialism recalls rather that of Marx in the Paris Manuscripts, the condemnation of all that diminishes man, the vision of a society in which every human potential can be fulfilled, the life dedicated to 'creating a new man'.[31] And if this is redemption, achieved by the shedding of blood, where does religion stand in relation to it?

(c)   The revolutionary as priest

On 3 October 1965 Fidel Castro made public the letter in which Che Guevara declared his intention to become a guerrilla again. Two weeks later Camilo Torres told his mother that he would not be home, bade farewell to his friends in Bogota and travelled to the mountains, to become a guerrilla in the Colombian Army of National Liberation. Four months later he was dead, killed in an ambush on a military patrol in Santander province. Had he thrown away his life in a futile gesture? No, the impact of his death far outweighed everything he had done in his life. Had he turned his back on his vocation? No. 'I took off my cassock to be more truly a priest.'[32] Had he betrayed his religion? No. 'The Catholic who is not a revolutionary is living in mortal sin.'[33] But how did it come to this, that a priest should see it as his Christian duty to become a guerrilla?

The eyes of Latin America were on Cuba, but as Marx would have expected, what they saw was in large measure determined by where they stood. One of my former colleagues was born and educated in India. In recounting to me how he came to be a Marxist, he told me that Marxism had liberated him from religion. Few Marxists in Britain enter the ideology at this point. With them it is more likely to be via Marx's class analysis or his account of alienated labour. For Torres Marxism was the ideology (he called it a *Weltanschauung*) best equipped to guide the revolution which was necessary to end the exploitation of the peasants and to establish a new economic, political and social order. It did not liberate him from religion, since he was a committed Christian, but it did raise the problem of reconciling the necessity of the revolution with the traditional teaching of the Catholic church and indeed with the place of the church in Colombian society. In arguing that he did not achieve that reconciliation, I am in no way criticizing his courage, integrity or costly sacrifice.

Camilo Torres Restrepo was born in Bogota in 1929 and by this time we are not amazed to learn that his father was a wealthy professional man, his mother descended from one of Colombia's most aristocratic families.[34] That part of the story seems strangely familiar. In his early years, he lived in Belgium and Barcelona before returning to Bogota. He attended two religious schools, but by the time he entered university to study law he was living a rather wild life. However, he admired the new-style, socially progressive French Dominicans he encountered, and it was very much against his mother's wishes that he joined the order. After ordination he went to Louvain to study social science. There is some speculation about his exposure to Marxism at this time, but although his mother says that he visited East Europe,[35] his writings show no influence of ideological Marxism. He returned to the National University in Bogata as a lecturer and chaplain. As John Gerassi puts it, he 'threw himself into the struggle of his countrymen for liberation – first as a sociologist, then as a politician, finally as a revolutionary, and always, in his own eyes at least, as a priest'.[36]

His writings and addresses at this time were mainly analyses of some aspect or other of Colombian life. For example, two chapters have survived of his doctoral dissertation, written in 1958. One is on the pre-industrial history of the city of Bogota, the other a detailed study of the standard of living within the city. The latter covers topics including levels of domestic spending, wages, diet and consumption of milk and meat, all based on the comparison of social classes. In 1960 he declared his position on the need for land reform. There is another empirical study, published in 1961, on radio schools and cultural changes, including many tables of statistical material. These empirical studies on many aspects of life made him increasingly aware of dangerous tensions building up within society. 'The discontent could lead to a violent revolutionary situation, as often happens when perceived needs find no pacific outlet or hope of solution.'[37]

In 1962 he came into conflict with the authorities. He supported the students' strike, and was required by the archbishop to resign from his work both as a lecturer and chaplain. For the next two years he concentrated on the need for land reform and also on issues of social welfare. Working largely outside ecclesiastical circles he came to apply the categories of the social sciences to the church itself. In 1963 he wrote a long article on 'Social Change and Rural Violence in Colombia' in which he noted that the peasants were increasingly rejecting priests who failed to show solidarity with them. He was also critical of the fact that although the church still had the potential to bring about change, it continued the identification of its interests with those of the ruling class.[38] By 1964 he concluded that 'in economic planning Marxists have held the first place'.[39] As in Cuba, they are to be the leaders of the revolution, both in the guerrilla war and in the post-war reconstruction of society. However, he was critical of current examples of Marxist dogmatism, considering that in the early stages 'planning in socialistic countries was the result more of needs than of a policy premeditated by Marxist experts'.[40] In particular he condemned party members who, even in Cuba, 'diverge from the revolutionary struggles that are not in keeping with these schemes.'[41]

Torres would not accept that the situation should be resolved into the convenient opposition of Christianity and communism. He could see too many people in society who were committed to similar values and goals. He therefore conceived of a United Front, in which all groups could participate, and in May 1965 published a 'Platform of the United Front of the Colombian People'. Its main features are land reform, democracy and socialist planning: it is a reformist document, free from ideological jargon. In a document calculated to enlist the broadest support, this has its own significance: an earlier draft had been circulated widely among various revolutionary groups. In these situations some factions try to insert their own code-words, like dogs marking their territory. When I agreed to contribute a chapter to a book on education some years ago, the general guidelines circulated by the editor included a request to avoid such phrases as 'running-dogs of the imperialist powers' and 'lackeys of the capitalist class'. I was able to comply with this suggestion without compromising what I wanted to say or unduly restricting my vocabulary or prose style, but I did wonder who else was contributing.

Not surprisingly Torres came under pressure from Cardinal Concha. He decided that because he could not give up his commitment to the revolution, he must apply to be returned to the lay state – or, as he puts it in a letter to the Cardinal Archbishop, 'reduction to the lay state'.[42] This detail is worth noting since, as we shall see, revolutionary social attitudes in Latin America have frequently co-existed with reactionary theological attitudes.

Since we now know what was to happen within the year, we must view the enthusiasm and optimism which Torres displayed over the next few busy months with real sadness. We are all familiar with that 'realism' which saves men from taking a stand on any issue, which prevents them from defending any value or advocating any cause. By comparison anyone who suffers for his beliefs is regarded as 'naive'. For Christians at least, the answer to such realism, often cowardly and always dehumanizing, is given in the cross. Nevertheless there is a suspicion of *political* naivety about Torres. On his laicization in June, 1965, he issued a statement to the press. He had worked as a priest to rally support for the revolution within the church and outside, but it had not been forthcoming. Did he actually think that revolution was a good cause which people would publicly support? At another level, the Vicar General of the Archdiocese Medellin suggested that Torres was mentally unstable, on account of his family tensions.[43] I find this

Freudian reductionism distasteful, but there is no doubt that Dona Isabel Restrepo de Torres was a formidable influence on her son's life, as noted by his friend Gustavo Gutierrez.[44] Therefore although I find offensive all portrayals of Torres as naive and immature, yet his reaction to the lack of popular response to his message appears almost like pique. 'In the absence of a massive response, I have resolved to join the revolution myself, thus carrying out part of my work of teaching men to love God by loving each other.'[45]

Over the next few months he threw himself into this work with great energy, exhibiting considerable skills as an organizer and communicator. There are his letters which were smuggled to Fabio Vaquez, commander-in-chief of the Army of National Liberation, reporting on his efforts to rally support for the United Front. In July 1965 he seemed to believe that it would be possible to seize power without bloodshed or armed struggle. And there is a series of articles in the movement's newspaper, *Frente Unido*, in which he addressed each social and political group in turn. But for all the support he claimed, it was not enough for a peaceful transition, and in October he slipped away secretly to join the armed struggle. His last article, 'Message to Colombians from the Mountains', was written in January 1966, five weeks before his death. Perhaps by that time his optimism had waned: 'What else are we waiting for, Colombians?'[46]

There are many points of comparison between Camilo Torres and Che Guevara. They shared concerns for the plight of the peasants, the need for agrarian reform, the necessity of revolution – reluctantly by armed struggle – and the creation of a new order in which the new man might appear. Neither was motivated by Marxism as an ideology. It would seem that Guevara became alienated from a form of socialism which was being constricted by Marxism as a dogmatic system. And we have seen that Torres was aware of and critical of these developments within Cuba. It is when we come to basic motivation that we see a specific difference between the two. Guevara was a humanist, Torres a Christian. Although that would not have divided them in practice, it did mean that the reconciliation of Christian responsibility and revolutionary struggle was an issue for Torres throughout his adult life.

The issue was not raised initially at a theoretical level. Rather, from his days as a student of sociology in Louvain and under the influence of the Dominicans Torres began to form a more social view of religion, as it emerges from what he calls the 'long lethargy of individualism'.[47] We can examine three different, though of course related, ways in which he attempts to deal with the problem.

The reconciliation which he seeks is first of all that of understanding society and social needs, and the Great Commandment of love. The former, understanding society and its needs, is increasingly influenced by Marxist categories, but religion is always the practical love of the neighbour. Indeed in his writings Torres seems to say little more about religion than that. Now of course if Christianity had always been at least as much as the Great Commandment, the history of the world would have been very different, but most Christians would expect a priest to say more than that. This is one of the reasons why I have placed Torres in the prehistory of liberation theology. In 1964 he read a paper at an international conference in Louvain, entitled 'Revolution: Christian Imperative'. Everlasting life is the life of the Kingdom of God, and that life is manifested in love for the neighbour. But that love is now expressed through a new understanding of society, and that includes the recognition of the necessity of revolution. In seeking to fulfil the Great Commandment Christians will need to learn from Marxists, whom, as we have already noted, Torres considered to be better equipped both to lead the struggle and the phase of economic planning. Yet in 'Communism and the Church', an interview given in 1965, he still distinguished commitment to ideological Marxism from a pragmatic use of Marxism. 'Communism holds a philosophical system incompatible with Christianity, although in its socio-economic aspirations most of its postulates do not conflict with Christian faith.'[48] The most important division in society as he sees it is not between Christians and Communists, but between those who have faith but do not love, and those who love, even when they have no (Christian) faith.[49] For Christians who know what is going on around them, 'the revolution is not only permissible but obligatory'.[50]

The second context in which Torres attempts to reconcile Christian responsibility and revolutionary struggle is through the relationship of the supernatural and the natural. Although his understanding of society is becoming more sophisticated, his theology seems not just traditional but undeveloped. This is illustrated in a lecture delivered in 1963. 'There are two objective realities – the natural and the supernatural. There are objective supernatural realities which we perceive by faith. Objective symbols of the supernatural include miracles and sacraments.'[51] It is by grace that man's natural life is raised to the supernatural level. The Christian's life is 'meritorious' because he has received grace; the non-Christian's life is not meritorious because he lacks grace. Although his dogmatics teacher might have been delighted with this assertion, it is altogether out of step with Torres' experience of co-operation between Marxists and Christians. He looks to 'the integrated man', who combines the material and spiritual, the natural and the supernatural, in love for his neighbour.[52] And is this integrated man so very different from Guevara's new man? In the Louvain lecture to which we have alluded, Torres could discuss good works. 'To become supernatural, they must necessarily be performed by someone in the state of grace, and this requires that the person have faith, even if it is only implicit.'[53] No, liberation theology has not yet appeared.

The third context in which Torres attempts to reconcile Christian responsibility and revolutionary struggle is that of the priesthood. We have already noted that he holds a very traditional view, and it reinforces my previous point. 'The mission of the priest as such is exclusively supernatural.'[54] Entailed in this mission is obedience and submission to the bishop. This pure doctrine has to be set beside the 'Last Clarification', in which Torres accused the cardinal of having gone back in his public statement on a private agreement they had reached.[55]

Apparently in applying for laicization Torres thought that when he had assisted in bringing the revolution to pass, he could revert to being a priest again. We have already noted a certain naivety in his appreciation of situations.[56] According to Marx the exploited masses must be roused to emancipate themselves, but the initiative is taken by representatives of the middle class who associate themselves with the masses. For Guevara the initiative is taken by the guerrilla. For Torres it is taken by the priest.

> When circumstances prevent men from actively consecrating their lives to Christ, it is the priest's duty to combat these circumstances even if he must forfeit the right to officiate at Eucharistic rites, which have meaning only if Christians are so consecrated.[57]

This is a very convoluted argument. He is speaking about the revolution. Laymen who are prevented from consecrating their lives to Christ must rely on the priest to so change things that it is possible for them to do this. However, since the Cardinal Archbishop considers that this is no part of the priest's role, the priest must become a layman in order to do for laymen what they cannot do for themselves. Torres must therefore make a metaphysical distinction between being a priest in some essential way, while not being a priest 'in the external aspects' of religion. Yet he sees that the priesthood is defined in terms of celebrating the mass. The position is even less satisfactory, since soon afterwards in 'Crossroads of the Church in Latin America' he drew attention to the tendency of the Catholic church to concentrate on externals, a tendency which he refers to as 'fetishism'.[58]

In an 'Address to Union Delegates' in July 1965, Torres claims that although he comes from the bourgeois class they should not exclude him from those who unite to bring about the revolution. He goes on to speak of his dual vocation: 'my vocation as priest and my vocation as revolutionary'.[59] I am somehow reminded of the conversation between Tarrou and Rieux in Camus' play *The Plague*. Tarrou says that he would like to become a saint. Rieux, the doctor, who has made the most important practical contribution to the people of the town during their suffering, is a non-believer. 'Heroism and sanctity don't really appeal to me, I imagine. What interests me is – being a man.'[60] For Torres it is not enough to be a man, not even a man like Guevara, not even the new socialist man, not even a Christian man. He must be more than man: he must be a priest. The following passage is worth having before us. It is sincere and moving, but its ontology of priesthood provides no basis for a theology of liberation.

> I have given up the duties and privileges of the clergy, but I have not ceased to be a priest. I believe that I have given myself to the revolution out of love for my fellow man. I have ceased to say Mass to practise love for my fellow man in the temporal, economic, and social spheres. When my fellow man has nothing against me, when he has carried out the revolution, then I will return to offering Mass, God permitting. I think that in this way I follow Christ's injunction: 'Therefore, if thou art offering thy gift at the altar, and there rememberest that thy brother has anything against thee, leave thy gift before the altar and go first to be reconciled to thy brother, and then come and offer thy gift' (Matthew v, 23–4). After the revolution we Colombians will be aware that we are establishing a system oriented towards the love of our neighbour. The struggle is long; let us begin now.[61]

Go first and be reconciled to your neighbour: the example of Camilo Torres marks an important advance in the relationship between religion and revolution, but it is not yet liberation theology.

(d) The spiral of violence

When I joined the Iona Community in 1961 there was a fierce though non-violent debate about pacifism, and whether it should be a condition of membership. Several of the most impressive arguments for the position came from men who had been combatants in World War II – and of course the Leader, the Very Reverend the Lord Macleod of Fuinary who had served in World War I. It was a debate about Christian realism. Were the pacifists who had been there, had experienced war and only just survived it naive in their refusal to countenance its use ever again? Or were the others, who certainly did not want war, even more naive in thinking that it is possible to counter evil by evil means, without giving evil itself the victory? In the end pacifism did not become a condition of membership, but I recall a contribution which summed up the dilemma for me. One of the members had been a pacifist right up to the last moment, to the outbreak of war. He then volunteered and became a fighter pilot for the course of the war, before returning to his role as a parish minister. This course of action did not solve the moral problem: it was a symptom of it. Yet, like the expression of real suffering, it arose from the most acute awareness of the dilemma.

For all the violence endemic to Latin America, violence is only a problem for some people. Unfortunately for many of those who perpetrate it violence is no problem at all, certainly not a moral problem. Guevara was prepared to engage in revolutionary war to bring violence to an end, to initiate the revolution of the new man. Indeed in the *Bolivian Diary* he mentions incidents in which he released soldiers whom the group had captured. He took their weapons, and sent them off 'with a severe warning about the rules of war'.[62] Camilo Torres saw the violence of the state and would not leave it to others to take the necessary steps to end it. He would not preserve his moral purity at their expense. Would he have been morally pure to leave it to them? Guevara saw the guerrilla as a man who acts on behalf of others to bring about a good which they are not capable of achieving for themselves. As we have seen, he could call this a priestly role. Torres saw it as the continuation of his priestly vocation by other means. We turn now to consider a third figure, Helder Camara, archbishop of Recife in north-east Brazil. If he takes the pacifist, non-violent side, it is not because he feels the problem less acutely than the other two. Nor is he prepared to allow his own rejection of violence to be used to condemn them. He describes himself as 'a pilgrim of peace', declaring that he 'would prefer a thousand times to be killed than to kill', but that does not mean that he takes sides against those who have laid down their lives in revolutionary struggle. 'In my opinion, the memory of Camilo Torres and Che Guevara merits as much respect as that of Martin Luther King. I accuse the real authors of violence: all those who, whether on the right of the left, weaken justice and prevent peace.'[63]

Helder Camara was born in 1909,[64] in the coastal town of Fortaleza, some 250 miles north of Recife. His father was a journalist, and for a time owned a newspaper in the town. His mother was a teacher, and ran the primary school which Helder attended before going on to seminary. Although he is recognized throughout the world as a humble, modest, ascetic figure, apparently an innocent abroad, in fact he spent most of his adult life in educational or ecclesiastical posts which insulated him from daily contact with the poor and oppressed.

147

He was never a parish priest, and through his contacts in Rome, for example with Monsignor Montini (later Paul VI), he looked to be in the fast lane for a cardinal's hat.

Ordained in 1931, Camara did not look like a future champion of the peasants. Indeed he was one of the founders of the 'October Legion', a Brazilian fascist movement. As Brazil approached the elections of 1934 which were to give it a new constitution, many looked to the example of Portugal, the former colonial power, where Antonio Salazar had established a fascist dictatorship in 1933, the same year in which Hitler and National Socialism came to power in Germany. Mussolini, who, backed by his black shirts, had become dictator in Italy, was to intervene in the Spanish Civil War on the side of Franco in 1936, the same year in which he formed the Berlin-Rome Axis. In the 1930s European fascism, with its themes of national unity, spiritual rebirth and anti-communism, was attractive to many Brazilian patriots.

No one challenged the young priest with getting involved in politics: indeed he was encouraged by his bishop to accept the invitation by the fascists to become their education officer in his home province of Ceara. After the election, again with episcopal blessing, he was appointed as Minister for Education for the province. In 1936, at the age of twenty-seven, he moved to the capital, Rio de Janeiro, to become an education expert in the federal Ministry of Education. By this time Camara felt that he was not fulfilling his priestly vocation, but as he turned towards ecclesiastical work again, he was drawn into becoming an adviser to the papal nuncio in Rio. It was at this point that he conceived of the idea of an episcopal conference, serviced by its own secretariat. In 1950 on a visit to Rome he was able to put the proposal to Montini, and in 1952 the first National Conference of the Bishops of Brazil met, with Camara as its secretary-general. The pope created similar conferences for the other countries of the continent, and in 1955 the first meeting was held of the Episcopal Conference of Latin America (CELAM). Camara was given the task of organizing it, as well as the International Eucharistic Congress in Rio. Neither through his political nor ecclesiastical activities did Camara look likely to dedicate his life to work among the poor, yet this was soon to happen.

Increasingly in the 1960s Camara became concerned about injustice, and felt that he would not be free to pursue his concern until he moved away from Rio and his patron and namesake Cardinal Camara. In 1964, while Camara was in Rome for the Council, and after a certain amount of behind-the-scenes discussion, a not entirely suitable diocese was chosen for him. At 1 p.m. his appointment to the diocese of São Luis do Maranháo was announced. Later that afternoon news arrived of the death of the Archbiship of Recife. Camara recalls appearing the following day before the pope. 'He was sad, but he remarked that God knew how to derive good from sorrow, and he saw in this a sign of Providence that called me to Recife.'[65] Thus it was that by the providence of God Camara was named Archbishop of Recife in March 1964. On 1 April, in the name of 'God and country', a coup d'état brought down the progressive government of President João Goulart and 'brought to power the most reactionary and backward military factions in Brazil'.[66] Which of these actions was by the hand of God would soon be an issue which divided the country – and the church.

Twelve days after the coup Camara addressed his new diocese, as a man returning to his own people, as a pastor open to all, and as a bishop, a father in God speaking out clearly and with passionate concern about the injustice, poverty and misery imposed upon the weak, the poor and the defenceless. He condemned the attitudes of greed and indifference, attitudes among the wealthy which he would later characterize as 'the mentality of medieval barons',[67] but the evils to which he pointed were deeply ingrained in the fabric of society.

> Let us not think that the problem is limited to certain slight reforms and let us not confuse the good and indispensible notion of order, the goal of all human progress with caricatures of it which are responsible for the persistence of structures which everyone recognizes cannot be preserved.[68]

This was to be one of the recurring themes in his sermons and speeches. In an interview given in Rome in November 1963, during the first session of the Council, he had already claimed that 'the so-called "social order" in the under-developed countries is nothing but a cumulus of stratified injustices'.[69] Violence is already there in the very order of society, there in the legal system which protects and promotes injustice, there in the power of the police and military who when coercion and threats fail are brought in to impose silence and submission. Camara exposes this violence and calls it by its name. By comparison, although he personally would not seek or expect to achieve the ends of justice and peace through violence, he can well understand those who are driven to it. There are those who turn to violence, not as brigands for their own ends, but in defence of the poor and oppressed, those who can speak of 'a liberating violence, of a redemptive violence'.[70] His fear is that violence from one source intensifies violence from the other side, dragging the world down into 'a spiral of violence'.[71]

Camara, as already noted, is full of admiration for the witness of the late Martin Luther King, 'the black apostle of non-violence'.[72] He has also shown a keen interest in the possible application of Gandhi's moral weapon of non-violence, used so effectively in political campaigns both in South Africa and India.[73] 1968 was an important year in this respect. Symbolically, it was the twentieth anniversary of the violent assassination of Gandhi.[74] It saw the assassination of Martin Luther King. It was also the year of the second meeting of CELAM. Camara brought these things together in a challenge to his fellow Brazilian clergy to commit themselves to 'Moral Pressure for Liberation'. CELAM met in Medellín, Colombia, in September 1968, and at the beginning of October was launched 'Action, Justice and Peace'.

But is Camara's message religious? Indeed is it Christian? Those who oppose him point to his use of the term 'liberation' as evidence that he has joined the Marxists. In calling for agrarian reform is he not attacking the private property of landowners, a basic proposition of communism? He has certainly refused to perpetuate the tradition by which the church sided with the ruling class. The movement for 'Action, Justice and Peace' was opposed by that of 'Family, Tradition, Property'. Camara's reply to his critics is to take as his motto the words of the Good Shepherd, who seeks out the poor and the needy, 'I came that they may have life, and have it abundantly'.[75] There can be no doubt about the depth and constancy of the archbishop's spirituality, but in the address given at the opening of the new regional seminary he issued a warning:

> To persist in pure spiritual evangelizing would be to give, within a short time, the idea that religion is a theory separated from life and incapable of touching it or modifying its absurdities. Among other things, it would support the view that religion, the great estranged and the great alienator, is the opium of the people.[76]

His great concern is for development. Abundant life must not be so spiritualized that Christ appears to care nothing for the misery, the squalor and the despair of the poor. It must not be abundance for the Western world at the expense of the Third World. Nor through internal colonialism can abundant life be for a minority within a country without consideration for the vast majority. Thus development which includes material provision is a moral matter. But development is also a religious matter. The life of the developed countries cannot be the model for the rest of the world. A culture which leads directly towards atheism and religious insensitivity does not yet exhibit the full dimensions of development. In the 1980s the New Right, both in the USA and the UK, condemned welfarism and the dependency culture, but twenty years before that Camara had anticipated this attitude. He called it the 'assistance mentality',[77] the assumption that all problems, including structural injustice, can be coped with through charity intended to aleviate the sufferings of the defenceless.

The abundant life is therefore neither narrowly spiritual nor narrowly material. As a moral and religious matter it is a challenge to bring about 'humanism in the fullest sense'.[78] The north-eastern province of Brazil is the largest under-developed region of the Western hemisphere. That it is in the largely affluent Western hemisphere raises even more acutely the moral dimension. But in the context of integral development Camara can even speak of 'the redemption of the north-east'.[79] He is neither a materialist nor a humanist. He certainly calls people of all faiths and ideologies, and none, to join in this great work, but he himself is entirely motivated by faith in Jesus Christ. 'Just open your eyes and see: the Good Shepherd bears on his shoulders the underdeveloped world.'[80]

Having given a broad indication of the scope of Camara's concerns, we must now turn to two matters specific to our interests. The first concerns his relationship to Marxism and the second his possible contribution to liberation theology.

There is a tendency in theological discussions to omit reference to the non-theological context in which issues arise. Thus throughout the Christian world the name of Medellín recalls the optimism of the second meeting of CELAM. For the secular world Medellín is the headquarters of the Colombian cocaine syndicate. When we turn to the question of Camara's relationship to Marxism we should not think of it as a theoretical matter. In 1968 Camara called for a pact on 'Moral Pressure for Liberation'. This has to be seen in the context of the outbreak that year of guerrilla warfare in Brazil. Unlike Guevara, who had no historical links with the Left, Carlos Marighela had been one of the central figures in the Communist Party of Brazil for more than forty years, latterly running the party in São Paulo. But he responded to the call to revolution which went out from Havana after the Tricontinental Conference in January 1966. The following year, against the orders of the Party, he attended the meeting in Havana of OLAS, the Organization for Latin American Solidarity.[81] Marighela and Mario Alves left the party and the following year set up the Revolutionary Communist Party of Brazil. That year, 1968, the year Camara wished to associate with the movement for peace, saw the beginning of the revolutionary struggle. What might strike us about Camara's pact for 'Moral Pressure for Liberation' is the apparently revolutionary term 'Liberation'. However, in view of the creation of the ALN (Action for National Liberation), the stress must lie rather on the fact that Camara's call was to 'moral pressure'. Far from being revolutionary it sounds completely ineffectual. Camara, ever faithful to Giovanni Montini, by that time Paul VI – the pilgrim for peace – was not allying himself with Marighela, but dissociating himself from the way of violence.

Although in his integralist period Camara was anti-communist, his statements of the 1960s express a balanced view on the subject. He deals with communism and the real enemy, communism and dialogue. First of all, he is concerned that too much is conceded. There is an anti-communism which sees its foe in every sermon about injustice, every lecture about development. Not only is this silly, it is dangerous: 'it makes communist propaganda when it identifies communism with every courageous and intelligent act in defence of truth and justice'.[82] It is like those who would defend the truth of Christianity against historical criticism by handing over to its opponents human reason, the concern for data, the rules of evidence. In this case everything with which communists are concerned is quickly ceded to them. They therefore stand for justice, equity, the defence of the oppressed, the aid of the poor. Christianity by contrast is identified with those things which the communists oppose. This is a poor bargain, but it mistakes the enemy. The enemy is not communism but the very injustice and state violence which communists oppose. Anti-communism gets into the absurd position of 'maintaining injustices because tackling them "might open the door to communism" '.[83] Is this not an offer to vindicate Marx's criticism of religion for him? No rationally devised policy could more successfully give the victory to communism, but more important, such attitudes completely distort and betray the entirely legitimate concerns of Christians for social justice.

In the first place, therefore, Camara does not make anti-communism the foundation of Christian social action. Linked to this is the new situation created by Vatican II. Dialogue replaces condemnation. Some of course are more Catholic than the pope, but it is a time for exploration of how people of good will can work together for common goals. It must be said, however, that Camara does not seem much inclined to spend time in such dialogue with Marxism. It would seem that he has his hands full working within the church. To this point we shall return in examining his theology. Having refused to demonize communism, his attitude is fairly predictable. He praises Marxist social criticism and rejects Marxist humanism or atheism. He holds in regard people of good will but of no faith, 'who wander in darkness, especially when they are atheist in name but Christian in deed'.[84] Such a patronizing view bristles with problems. He warns against falling under 'the Marxist spell',[85] which so affects workers and university people. But there is no analysis of why Marxism is attractive to those who find religion not so much irrelevant as itself part of the problem.

Therefore although Camara does not regard anti-communism as a legitimate or adequate basis for Christian social action, yet he has a rather traditional view of the relationship between Christianity and Marxism. Thus we hear that if Marx could only see the social action of Christians today, he would not have made his famous criticism of religion.[86] Yet, as we have seen, this view of Marxism as a moral system altogether ignores its ontological criticism of religion. Camara's main criticism of Marxism concerns its atheism, its ignoring of the transcendent. But the question of the reality of the religious transcendent is never discussed.

In two respects Camara goes beyond the traditional view of Christianity and Marxism. The first is his tendency to pronounce a plague on both houses, capitalism as well as communism. He can refer to 'the equally inhuman character of the capitalist investment policy',[87] and hold up the USA as 'a living demonstration of the internal contradiction of the capitalist system'.[88] But the USSR and China can be as ruthless imperial powers as the USA. He therefore advocates neither capitalism nor socialism. If he has a third way it is 'personalist socialization'.[89] Whatever this is, we can be sure it is not evidence of the undue acceptance of Marxism. But there is one further respect in which Camara goes beyond what might have been expected, and this is in his call for the normalization of relations with Cuba. There are two reasons for this. The first is already familiar: the makers of the Cuban revolution were motivated by a hatred of injustice and a love of the people. Why should they be forced into the arms of the USSR on this account? The second reason is somewhat familiar: the policy of isolation mystifies what is actually happening in Cuba and perpetuates the notion that it is somehow a model of development for Latin America as a whole.

In all this we can see that the ex-fascist, the bureaucrat and ecclesiastical administrator is less anti-communist than might be expected, but Marxism plays no part at all in defining his position or promoting his work. As we turn finally to look at his theology, we shall not find any attempt to integrate it with Marxist themes.

It might be worth digressing here briefly. I have been discussing Camara's writings which date from the 1960s in order to see how he might have influenced the emergence of liberation theology. A decade later, because of liberation theology, the relationship between Marx and theology had emerged as an important issue. In 1974 the University of Chicago chose to celebrate the seven-hundredth anniversary of the death of Thomas Aquinas. Among those from around the world invited to contribute to the occasion Helder Camara might at first seem a surprise choice. However, no sooner had he begun his lecture than its relevance became clear. Thomas had displayed great courage, as well as powers of intellect, in undertaking a detailed examination of the works of Aristotle. In the first place these works, and their exposition, were under papal ban during the first half of the thirteenth century. But beyond that, Aristotle was a materialist philosopher, whose system was founded on principles not only incompatible with Christianity, but revered throughout the Muslim world. Camara in effect was calling on present-day Christians to undertake an equally thorough and critical examination of the anti-Christian, materialist system of Karl Marx. 'But when someone, philosopher or not, irresistibly attracts millions of human beings, when he inspires the life and death of a great part of mankind, and makes the powerful of the earth tremble with hate and fear, that man deserves to be studied.'[90] The project is exciting, but Camara hardly begins to indicate what is involved. Indeed he tells his audience probably more about Aristotle and Aquinas than they wanted to know, and less about Marx and Christianity today. In view of the parallel, he might have included an observation made by the Cambridge mediaeval scholar Dom David Knowles, that 'Aquinas stood the system of Aristotle on its head'.[91] We might ask whether Christians should do to Marx what Marx did to Hegel!

Not surprisingly Camara identifies atheism as the main feature of Marx's criticism of religion: the existence of God diminishes man and weakens human responsibility for changing the world. But as we have seen in Part One, this is not the most important aspect of Marx's critical philosophy for religion. Alternatively, Camara attempts to incorporate Marx. He tells his audience that Marx's view 'that the relationships of production generate class struggle, exploitation, tensions, rebellion, ideologies, and superstructures, that this view is 'a neglected Christian truth'. In Part One I presented historical materialism as a variation on Hegel, and of course Hegel was deeply influenced by Aristotle. But Camara is implying that historical materialism is all there already in Aquinas. I have already drawn attention to this kind of imperialism and triumphalism which only guarantees that nothing new can be learned. Returning to our main discussion, we should not expect Marxist themes to have any decisive or incisive place in Camara's theology.

William Temple, Archbishop of Canterbury during World War II, is credited with having a considerable influence on the moral development of the British people at that time, and the subsequent creation of the welfare state. For my own part I have always been more impressed that anyone born in Castle Howard should have held such socialist views at all, and that holding them he should have become Primate of

All England. Helder Camara was not appointed to the diocese of Recife in spite of his position on social questions, nor because of them, but rather (as we have seen) because of his reputation as an ecclesiastical organizer and his friendship with Paul VI. Thus in the discussions concerning the building of the regional seminary, to which I have already referred, Camara could say to Cardinal Garrone: 'Any desire of Rome is a command for me.'[92] In the light of the confrontation between Cardinal Ratzinger and the Brazilian Franciscan Leonardo Boff, such an unquestioned submission to Rome would seem to distance Camara from liberation theology.

Camara's world-wide reputation is based on his criticisms of capitalism, socialism and materialism, his denunciations of the powerful rulers of Brazil, and of the even more powerful directors of multi-national companies, his unmasking of attitudes of greed and indifference. Indeed what has he not criticized with perception and courage, except the papacy, the church and its theology? This trinity has a privileged status in his eyes which it certainly does not in liberation theology. The radicalism of his social criticism is not matched by any criticism of religious institutions or attitudes.

He recalls that as a seminary student dogmatics was his best subject. We might conclude that he has not felt it necessary to question received positions. This, as already indicated, goes together with his submission to the pope. José de Broucker has written a very perceptive and sympathetic account of Camara's position, but even he notes the lack of response when ecclesiastical or theological matters are raised. I include a long quotation which illustrates this point.

> When one talks to him about the pope, about the Council, or the Synod, the Curia, CELAM, or the Conference of Brazilian Bishops, of the assembly of the continental bishops at Medellín, one elicits from him only words of praise; everything and everyone concerned are sufficiently good and are reason for hope and faith, if not enthusiasm. Moreover, it is the same thing when one talks to him about the seminaries that are emptying, the priests who are secularizing themselves, the nuns who are becoming impatient, the theologians who are putting everything in question, the laymen who occupy cathedrals, the tensions, the disputers, the conflicts. In all this he finds merely reasons for hope.[93]

We shall return to this point in later chapters, for it is of fundamental importance not so much for our discussion of Camara as of liberation theology. How is it that a church and a theology which cannot learn from developments in the modern world are well equipped to direct the future development of that same world?

If the Pope will not tolerate discussion of married clergy, then Camara will not discuss the matter either, no matter how pressing the problem. The Council decided that deacons could be married men. Camara did not ordain any, awaiting a simplified rite. The rite was simplified, but still he did not ordain. And of course there is the subject of birth control. He does not discuss the principles involved: it is enough that Paul VI has issued an encyclical on the matter. It has always seemed to me there are issues to be discussed, even within the Catholic circle. It is interesting to see how sexual matters are given a centrality that they do not have in the Protestant churches. And there is also the confidence with which absolutes are asserted. 'Thou shalt not kill.' That is surely an absolute command? But no, it is treated more subtly through casuistry. But there are other absolutes. 'But you are not to be called rabbi, for you have one teacher, and you are all brethren. And call no man your father on earth, for you have one Father, who is in heaven.'[94] That is surely an absolute command from the Lord. Apparently clear absolutes need not be observed, but when it comes to sexual matters then absolutes are defined where metaphysicians fear to tread. If the foetus can only be recognized as a human being, then abortion can be forbidden absolutely: after all, 'Thou shalt not kill.' But as we have just noted, killing has never been absolutely rejected even where its meaning was perfectly clear. The encyclical *Humanae Vitae* was a flag which, when run up, settled no moral issues. But it did identify those loyal to the pope. Camara did not question it. He claimed that the issue of birth control 'is too delicate to be resolved from without'.[95] Does that mean it must be decided by the loving couple within Christian marriage? No, the 'within' refers to within the magisterium of the church. In the real world, although Rome has spoken the matter has not been settled. On practical matters Camara will co-operate with Marxists and others, but he is not interested in an internal dialogue with Marxism. And it would seem that he need have no further interest in theology, ancient or modern. *Roma locuta est, causa finita est.*

(e) Marginal Marx

In reviewing those social movements which might be thought to give rise to liberation theology I drew two conclusions, one which could have been anticipated, the other which is more surprising. The first conclusion is something of a tautology: the theology which immediately precedes liberation theology is not an example of liberation theology. I noted that the theology of Camilo Torres is altogether unreconstructed. It shows no influence of the main themes of Marx's critical philosophy, though as a sociologist Torres must have been acquainted with the system. Nor is there any attempt to respond, positively or negatively, to the Marxist critiques of religion.

When we turned to Helder Camara the situation was similar. During the 1960s, when the Marxist-Christian dialogue was much in evidence in Europe, Camara held to the line that while it was possible to cooperate with men of good will, there was no point in discussing faith with atheism. And as we saw, even when later he specifically raised the question of a Christian examination of Marx's thought, comparable to Aquinas' work on Aristotle, he had no appreciation of the relevant dimensions of Marx's work. Liberation theology does not begin with the revolutionary activity of Torres nor with the non-violent commitment of Camara.

The second conclusion, however, is more surprising, namely that Marxism was not important in revolutionary praxis. This came out clearly in our study of Guevara, both in the Cuban revolutionary war and in the Bolivian campaign. The importance of the Cuban example was humanism, self-sacrifice and basic socialist values such as justice and equity. As we saw, Marx was not important for Castro or Guevara during the guerrilla war. Since in important respects they ignored basic Marxist principles, the success of the revolution did not legitimize Marxism in Latin America.

At several points in the *Bolivian Diary* Guevara mentions Régis Debray, who was at that time being interrogated in a Bolivian jail. Debray had been a student of Louis Althusser, and in 1961 visited Cuba and observed the transformations taking place under the revolutionary government. In 1965 he returned for an extended visit, and was able to spend a good deal of time with those who had directed the guerrilla war. His book, *Revolution in the Revolution*, published in 1967, was described as the first 'comprehensive and authoritative presentation of the revolutionary thought of Fidel Castro and Che Guevara'.[96] He presents the Cuban revolution as a third way, for it does not follow the examples of the USSR or China. In fact it suggests that no revolutionary theory can in advance dictate how the revolution shall be effected. The danger is that the present is viewed in the light of models from the past. This guarantees both distortion and failure. In view of our studies in Part One it would suggest that neither is it possible to jump backwards over history. But this revolution in the revolution is a threat to the 'hallowed principles of organization, apparently essential to Marxist theory'.[97] He quotes Guevara's dismissal of the attempt by non-revolutionary communist parties to control developments. 'The Manichaeism of the Party (no revolution outside the Party) finds its reflection in the anti-party Manichaeism (no revolution in the Party): both are quietist'.[98] The revolution cannot be brought about by the bourgeois party members in the city, with their theory which is never put into practice. In the revolution 'the political word is abruptly made flesh'.[99] The Cuban guerrilla war was certainly not fought by applying principles taken from Marx.

Some of the same themes appeared about that time in the campaign initiated by Carlos Marighela in Brazil, whom I have already mentioned. Although he had been an orthodox member of the communist party, he was disillusioned by the non-revolutionary attitudes of its leaders. We hear again the criticism of that attitude which 'sticks religiously to the old-fashioned theoretical canons'.[100] It is revealing that although he can refer to the classical tradition of Marxist-Leninism to which for so long he was committed, he can associate it with the 'Castro-Guevara theory'.[101] He claims to be inspired by the heroic example of Guevara, and we see in his writings the difficult transition which he has made from orthodox Marxism, which referred to situations in Europe, to this new revolutionary praxis which is determined by the very different circumstances of Brazil. As I have noted earlier, one of the differences was the central place given to agrarian reform and therefore the peasants, rather than the urban proletariat. Miguel Arraes, writing from exile, points out that urbanization in Brazil (or the Third World more generally) is not the same as in Europe during the Industrial Revolution. There has been a great exodus from the country towards the towns, but since industry has not been able to absorb these people they live physically, economically and politically outside the city. They are the marginals who suffer in double measure the loss of the old social order and denial of entry into the new.[102] For this reason one of the themes running through Marighela's work is the Cuban emphasis on the rural setting of the revolution. He cannot turn his back on the city, or the workers, but increasingly he sees that in Brazil there must be an alliance of the proletariat and the peasants. There is an ironic parallel with Guevara when in his *Handbook of Urban Guerrilla Warfare* he includes a reading list of some seven titles, plus a periodical. Also like Guevara, Marighela does not see religion as a tool of oppression. He addresses his appeal to various groups, including the clergy and bishops. In a list of fifteen promises he makes to the people the second is 'Liberty of Artistic expression and religion'.[103]

There is, then, a curious agreement in the sources which we have examined. Marx was not determinative for dedicated revolutionaries, nor was he inescapable for prophetic Christians. At this stage Marx is like a marginal, existing somewhere between two worlds, participating in neither.

(f) Conciliar developments

At the beginning of this chapter I indicated that there were two sources of liberation and theology. The first was the Cuban revolution. As we have discovered, in the general perception of this movement Guevara was more important than Marx. The second source was the new ecclesial situation created by the Second Vatican Council. To this, and to parallel developments in the World Council of Churches, we now turn more briefly.

We ended our discussion of Camara by drawing attention to his essentially conservative position, especially with respect to the magisterium. 'Rome has spoken: the matter is decided.' But in the 1960s what Rome said concerning contraception and celibacy was very different from what it was saying on justice and peace. As we have seen, Camara is concerned for integral development, for that fullness of life which is both material and spiritual, individual and social. In this he stands in the tradition of Pope John XXIII and the encyclical *Pacem in Terris*, issued in April 1963. The subject of this letter is less peace on earth than the divine order, the observation of which is the basis for peace. It is an order which envisages 'the proper development of life'.[104] In the liberal tradition it asserts various rights: security, information, religious liberty, the family, work, a working wage, private property, assembly and association, freedom of movement. This is not a Marxist agenda, and indeed following Hegel's distinction, Marx claimed that this approach leads to 'civil society', an essentially bourgeois form of association. Nevertheless when read in a Third World context it marks a considerable advance on what Camara describes as feudal relations and mediaeval attitudes.

A more radical line is taken with regard to government. All authority is of God, and therefore if the civil authorities attempt to legislate in any way contrary to God's order, 'neither the laws made nor the authorizations granted can be binding on the consciences of the citizens, since God has more right to be obeyed than men'.[105] This is a statement of the moral and religious obligation to civil disobedience. 'This means that, if any government does not acknowledge the rights of man or violates them, it not only fails its duty, but its orders completely lack juridical force.'[106] What conclusions are to be drawn from this statement? It is potentially revolutionary. Although it is without any Marxist influence whatsoever, it is, as we shall see, more radical than a good deal of liberation theology. It was certainly too radical for much of the Catholic church. The military coup in Brazil which brought Castello Branco to power took place a year almost to the day after the encyclical was published. Two days after the coup, on 3 April 1964 the USA sent its congratulations, confirming for many the involvement of the CIA. To this was added a public statement of support by twenty-four Brazilian bishops, referring to the fall of the progressive Goulart government and claiming that 'the country had been saved from the abyss it had been heading for'.[107] However, encyclical watchers are well prepared for compensation. Thus *Pacem in Terris* ends with the rejection of violence and revolution: if such strategies are incapable of establishing God's order the conclusion would seem to be that they are against God's will.

Although John XXIII's teaching was useful to the church in Latin America, it did not constitute a systematic basis for a fundamental critique of the existing social order. Indeed, although John XXIII called the Second Vatican Council, it was not through his influence that more radical voices in the church were strengthened. On 25 December 1961 he convoked the Council, claiming that councils were called when the troubles of the world were acute. The tone is triumphalist: the church will assist the world in its time of crisis. In October 1962 in his opening address the same note is struck. The main concern of the council is to be doctrine: the only concession is that the way in which doctrine is stated in the modern world has to be examined. It was during the first session of the Council that this uncritical, triumphalist position was challenged. The case for a more open and honest dialogue with the modern world was put by the Belgian primate, Cardinal Suenens. The point was taken up next day by another leader of the progressives, Cardinal Giovanni Montini.[108] Six months later, on the death of John XXIII, Montini was elected pope and took the name Paul VI. He presided over the remaining three sessions, including the fourth and final session in which was published *Gaudium et Spes*, the 'Pastoral Constitution of the Church in the Modern World'.

It may be that Paul VI would not have convoked a council, but it was he who accelerated the movement of *aggiornamento*. The Catholic church took giant steps to catch up with developments in the modern world. But more importantly, in the context of our subject, he directed the attention and concern of Christians towards the great social issues of the day. He set up the Commission for Justice and Peace, and on Easter Day 1967 he issued the encyclical *Populorum Progressio*. It is with this document that we encounter analyses and value judgments which would have greatly encouraged the humanist, socialist Marx.

The Council was ecumenical in two senses. It called to Rome bishops from every continent, including representatives of the Third World. Although at first they were reticent in their contributions to its deliberations, their presence directed attention outwards, beyond Europe. When the pope spoke on the subject of progress, his concern was not simply for the rich and powerful nations of the northern hemisphere, but for the peoples of the world and especially those who could not speak out for themselves.

Human progress, we are told, is 'the great social problem of today'.[109] The church cannot avoid it, since the church was founded 'to set up the Kingdom of Heaven, right down here on earth'.[110] God's will for mankind is humanism, though not in some narrow or restricted and materialist form. But if it is to be described as 'a higher humanism', certainly not a 'Godless humanism', it is not a narrowly spiritual form which ignores the real needs of the poor and oppressed. The encyclical therefore refers specifically to poverty, to inequality, to hunger, to the widening gap between rich and poor. In face of such a crisis certain lesser goods must be reviewed. 'Even the right to private property, and the right to free enterprise, must yield to justice.'[111] The encyclical becomes quite specific. 'From time to time the good of all demands that private property should be taken over by the state.'[112] Money cannot be allowed to move freely out of the country if this impoverishes the people. The profit motive must not be the foundation of industry. Unbridled freedom which admits of no social obligation 'leads to the tyranny of wealth'.[113] Capitalism too often breeds misery and injustice, and the conditions of modern work 'can dehumanize the worker'.[114] How often did we encounter these themes in our study of Marx! Yet the encyclical warns that while conditions of despair drive men towards revolution and violence, these solutions bring worse problems in their wake. The encyclical turns from injustice and dehumanization within countries, to the global situation in which whole regions of the world suffer misery, malnutrition and despair. Progress there depends on initiatives from the rich nations, not only in taxes and aid, but also in the terms of trade. A World Fund could be set up from reductions in military expenditure.[115]

Although the encyclical deals with very specific economic and social issues, it is throughout a religious document. The integral development for which it calls is to lead to that fullness of life for which people were created by God. That life cannot be achieved while the world is organized on an unjust basis. Failure to repent will lead to the judgment of God and the wrath of the oppressed. 'Development is now the name for peace.'

Many biblical, especially gospel, passages are quoted in the encyclical. They stress the special place of the poor, the Christian vocation to help the neighbour, the responsibility to feed the hungry. Marx would have approved of these sentiments, but they cannot be attributed to his influence. However, we have already identified other elements in the encyclical which are not biblical and do go back to

Marx's philosophy. This is true of the curtailment of private property and its appropriation by the state for the common good, the restriction of free enterprise, the control on the movement of capital, the dehumanizing conditions of labour, the production of misery by capitalism. There can be no doubt that these are Marxist themes. They are clearly accepted here as part of a moral argument, and certainly do not imply that Paul VI shared the Marxist ideological faith. We are therefore led to an unexpected and even paradoxical conclusion. At the outset we claimed that the roots of liberation theology lie in Cuba and the post-conciliar church. What emerges is an intriguing reversal. From the Cuban revolution, specifically the example of Che Guevara, comes a new and deepened understanding of redemption. It challenges the old doctrinal order in the name of contemporary experience in Latin America. At the same time the value of Marx's critical philosophy is demonstrated not by the revolution, but by the papacy. It challenges the old accommodation of religion and the interests of the ruling class. It is not wrong to say that liberation theology combines theology and Marxism, or at least elements from Marx's philosophy. But it is quite wrong to see the process as one by which Marxism, already in Latin America, was added to theology brought from Europe. The stimulus to use Marx's critical philosophy in the service of God's demand for justice and peace came to Latin America from the pope himself.

7

The Influence of Marx on Liberation
Theology

(a)   An ecumenical theology of liberation

In the last chapter I claimed that Vatican II was ecumenical in two
respects. The first was in the original meaning of the term, since
it drew representatives from throughout the world. But it was also
ecumenical in the modern meaning of the word, since a number of
distinguished Christians were invited from other churches as observers.
In one sense this was a bold step; in another it was merely recognizing
the fact that in a variety of fields Catholics were already participating
unofficially with Protestant and Orthodox Christians. In contrast to
the lack of progress on matters internal to the churches, there was
a good deal of co-operation and agreement on matters outside the
ecclesiastical sphere. A good example of this was the series of meetings
which took place throughout Europe during the 1950s and 1960s as
part of the ongoing Marxist-Christian dialogue. There was also the
parallel development of political theology by Jürgen Moltmann and
Johannes Metz. The parallel thinking extended to developments in the
World Council of Churches and the Vatican. In 1966 the WCC sponsored an important consultation in Geneva under the title 'Church and
Society'. The report was published as *Christians in the Technical and
Social Revolution of Our Time*.[1] There was enough common ground
that in 1968 a joint body was set up called SODEPAX. The Committee
on Society, Development and Peace was a co-operative venture by the
Pontifical Commission Justice and Peace and the WCC. Its main areas
of concern were justice, development and peace, and its task was to
focus attention on the problems of international social injustice. In
November 1969 it held a conference at Cartigny, Switzerland, on
'Theology of Development'. One of the papers, later published as *In*

163

Search of A Theology of Development, was entitled 'The Meaning of Development: Notes on a Theology of Liberation'. It was the first time I had come across the phrase 'theology of liberation', and the first time I encountered the name of the author, Gustavo Gutierrez Merino.

Most of the papers given at Cartigny were by Europeans, but in addition to Gutierrez Latin America was well represented by Rubem Alves. Gutierrez, a young theologian from Peru, had been a consultant to the Second Episcopal Conference of Latin America, CELAM, which met at Medellín in 1968. Alves, a Presbyterian from Brazil, was Professor of Theology at the University of Campinas, São Paulo, and secretary of ISAL, Church and Society in Latin America. His paper, 'Theology and the Liberation of Man', and that of Gutierrez, were the only ones to attempt to move beyond development to liberation. The theology of liberation has been ecumenical from the outset, in the two senses already indicated. It emerged simultaneously in different churches, so that contributors seemed to have more in common with each other than with most of those belonging to their ecclesial communities. They represented a new generation and their ecumenism was natural and dynamic, not formal and constrained. Gutierrez recalls a phrase which aptly describes traditional ecumenism: 'a marriage between old people'.[2] Many of the participants had pursued graduate studies in Europe and the USA, but Gutierrez and Alves came to Cartigny not to learn from their old teachers, but to dialogue, and to challenge even the most progressive theologians of Europe and North America with a new movement taking place in Latin America.

During the subsequent two decades dozens of books have been published in the field of liberation theology. As already indicated, it is not my intention to provide a history of the movement, an account of its main features, or even a summary of the works of its main contributors. My objective is more limited in scope, but arguably more fundamental in its critical analysis. I shall examine the place of Marx in liberation theology, making use of the extensive examination of Marx's criticism of religion undertaken in Part One above. This will be a suitably dialectical process, since I shall consider not only how liberation theologians have made use of Marx, but also what aspects they have deliberately avoided using.

(b)   A theology provoked by Marxism

In this chapter we shall consider passages in liberation theology which indicate the influence of Marx. This is an imprecise concept. I shall not attempt to show any direct or conscious borrowing from Marx. It will be enough to say that such statements can be made because

Marx's critical philosophy is available for use without any ideological commitment. For example, in the Cartigny paper Gutierrez begins by setting aside the term 'development', which at the time was used enthusiastically by social scientists, politicians, agencies and church leaders. The aspirations of the Third World are for a society founded on 'justice and brotherhood'. He claims that the term 'development' is inadequate to express these longings. 'The word "liberation" seems more precise and potentially richer, as well as more suitable for theological reflection.'[3] Gutierrez is not using the term in the way in which it would be used among Marxists, but it is a term available to him both challenging and relevant because of the influence of Marx's thought. But in addition, it is because of Marx that he senses the inadequacy of development. Despite attempts to extend its scope by speaking of integral development, or development as the new name for peace, the term tends to suggest material and economic growth. Development can take place while alienation continues or intensifies. Marx's suspicion then enters: whose interests are best served by development, those of the Third World, or of the First? This is an example of what I shall call the influence of Marx. In subsequent chapters we shall consider the deliberate and conscious use of Marx's philosophy.

A second example is Gutierrez' claim that such matters as the need for justice and brotherhood call in question the church's 'practice'. As in the first example there are two aspects here. The term 'practice' is available through Marx's analysis of praxis. Gutierrez means more than simply the way in which the church does things. But beyond that he is referring to a reversal which reflects the influence of Marx. He acknowledges that he is only able to speak of the Catholic tradition, but previously when problems arose in society the church turned to the resources of fundamental doctrine for the answer. Today experience brings the tradition into question. Gutierrez says no more, but this reading of the situation shows the influence of Marx's view of praxis, the relationship between theory and action. More ominously there is the hint that the church, far from graciously providing the answer, is part of the problem.

With regard to the first example, expressed in *Populorum Progressio* as having more to be more, Gutierrez can refer to Marx's Paris Manuscripts in which a similar sentiment is expressed during the discussion of private property. On the second example he quotes the Eleventh Thesis on Feuerbach. Both of these references come in the footnotes, and suggest that Gutierrez did not consciously move from Marx to the current situation, but rather that he recognizes that his thinking has already incorporated such themes from Marx.

A third example of the general influence of Marx concerns the

3. movement of history. It might be objected that the idea that there is direction in history comes from biblical religion. And yet this has not been a feature of Christian faith down through the centuries. It is a modern discovery, or recovery. It also runs counter to the scientific world-view, in which even evolution is irrelevant to moral and religious values. It is also out of fashion in philosophy which stands in the tradition of Descartes and Kant. In the face of these modern trends why should there be a new expectation among the poor of the Third World that things can change? For Gutierrez the new outlook is in large part due to the renewed influence of the tradition of Hegel and Marx. He specifically mentions the master/slave relation, but extends it to international relations. The aspirations of the Third World are not articulated through the term development, but rather through liberation.

> The liberation of man in the course of history entails not only improved living conditions, a radical transformation of structures, and a social revolution, but much more: the continual creation of a new manner of being human, a permanent cultural revolution.[4]

Once again it is in the footnotes that Gutierrez draws the specific parallels. This hope for the future need not now be specifically related to Marx: it is in the air. Marx raised the matter of justice out of the liberal context of individual rights and gave it a historic, utopian setting. Gutierrez sees this influence channelled through the works of Bloch and Moltmann.

4. A fourth example of the influence of Marx arises in the discussion of salvation. If Christian faith is about human salvation, and liberation is about the freeing of men and women from whatever constricts and diminishes them, then the question is inevitably posed as to the relationship of salvation and liberation. Traditionally the two spheres were quite separate: outside the church, no salvation. This division between the spheres of the church and of the secular was also reflected in the roles of the priests and the laity. At this point Gutierrez seems to be struggling with an as-yet unresolved complex of issues. He would not necessarily express it in these terms, but it is as if inside the church there is a traditional confidence about what constitutes sin, and how salvation from sin is to be brought about. At the same time God is more concerned with what is happening to his world, to men and women and children who are oppressed and suffering, dehumanized and denied that fullness of life to which they are called. If inside the church there is a need for salvation, outside there is a need for liberation. But are the two completely different? Or should we say that 'participation in the task of liberating man is already, in a way, a work

of salvation'.[5] So far so good, but it is not enough to extend the present understanding of salvation beyond the confines of the church. Gutierrez does not make this point, but it might be worth exploring the parallel here with the distinction made by (Hegel and) Marx between civil and political society. Civil society is concerned with individual rights; political society is characterized by fully human social relations. There is a danger that sin is conceived only in terms of individual behaviour, which leaves the structures of oppression untouched. There is the further danger that the church would then not be contributing to the establishing of political society, a vision in Marx's work which corresponds to the kingdom of God. Just as development has become too narrow a concept and liberation is more adequate, might we not say that sin has become too narrowly conceived? It is of some significance that in the heading to this section Gutierrez can use the term 'alienation'. This would complete the parallel of sin/salvation, alienation/liberation. Nothing is taken directly from Marx, but the perception of the whole complex now owes a great deal to his philosophy.

A fifth example emerges as Gutierrez probes the issue of that from which Latin America needs to be liberated. The model of development suggests that all the countries of the world are on the same historic road, but at different stages. Thus Third World countries need only to follow the example of those now considered developed. The metaphor begins to break down when we realize that the as yet under-developed countries are not pursuing their goal independently. Through investment and trade the developed countries are intervening in the process. While this interaction was regarded in the decade of the 1950s as of great assistance to the Third World, the following decade saw considerable disillusionment. Third World countries have not been enabled to develop according to the model of the West. Rather, they have been incorporated into the continued development of already developed economies. Thus instead of becoming mature and independent, they have become unstable and dependent. Colonialism and imperialism, while being eschewed politically and morally, have been reasserted through economics. Thus at the outset it was assumed that development would liberate people from suffering and misery, but now it is seen that this process merely intensifies the oppression. Liberation must now include liberation from domination by developed capitalist economies such as the USA. Gutierrez acknowledges that most of those who are aware of this situation and are active in challenging it 'are more or less inspired by Marxism'.[6] What he does not acknowledge is that his awareness of the complexities of the situation also derives from the Marxist tradition. But before leaving this matter, there is one further point which might be examined.

Although Gutierrez is happy to subsume the analysis and the (sometimes violent) resistance under 'Marxism', it will be recalled that the examples we discussed earlier, including Guevara and Marighela, cannot be so described without qualification. It is therefore interesting that Gutierrez now rejects the idea that under-developed countries are simply at an earlier stage in someone else's history. In a footnote, once again, he quotes Theotonio dos Santos with approval: 'a society cannot move towards previous stages of existing societies. All societies move together and in parallel towards a new society.'[7] This is not Marxism: it is the exact opposite of the point that Marx makes about the necessary achievements of Western capitalism. Whether he is aware of it or not, at this point Gutierrez, while accepting Marx's social analysis, rejects his historical materialism. His vision is determined by religious and not ideological faith.

Having considered the influence of Marx in a social context, we must now ask to what extent Gutierrez has been influenced specifically by Marx's criticism of religion. In Part One we considered Marx and religion under four headings: religion as reconciliation with evil and injustice, religion as reversal of reality, religion as ideology, and historical materialism as a faith. Has Gutierrez been influenced by Marx's thought under the headings of 1. Reconciliation, 2. Reversal, 3. Ideology and 4. Historical consciousness?

1. One of the main themes running through the Cartigny lecture is that Christians must now take the side of the oppressed. This could be misunderstood at a superficial level as a call to forsake religion and turn to politics. But this is quite the opposite of his position. He is identifying the struggle against injustice as the very work of Christ.

> All the dynamic forms of human history, the struggle against all that depersonalizes man, the social inequalities, misery, exploitation, have their origin, are transformed and achieve fulfilment in Christ's work of salvation.[8]

If this call is heard, then religion will no longer be guilty of reconciliation with evil. It will neither legitimize the evil order of a fallen world, nor will it encourage the victims of oppression to accept their lot in this world for the sake of supposed rewards in a world to come.

3. Turning to theology, Gutierrez is prepared to admit that it has in the past served an ideological function. First, because of its extremely rational and dogmatic form, it has become a pre-established picture of reality to which actual life is expected to conform, an account of the world which is incorrigible by contemporary experience. Secondly, it

has often discouraged Christians from getting involved in political matters, as if their duty lay in another, spiritual, sphere. In both of these ways theology has acted as an ideology which, whether by intention or by default, furthered the interest of the ruling classes. Gutierrez is aware of this function, and entirely rejects it. 'Christian theology is being provoked by Marxism and is turning toward reflection upon the meaning of the transformation of this world.'[9]

4. Although I have reviewed five topics in which it is clear that Gutierrez had been influenced by Marx's critical social philosophy, there is no evidence to show that Gutierrez accepts historical materialism, considered as an ideological faith. The only possible area of doubt might be his view of history as a history of human liberation, and yet, as we have seen, his position – as illustrated in the quotation from dos Santos – is entirely at odds with Marxism.

Observant readers will have noted that reference to 2. is omitted. Gutierrez has not responded, consciously or unconsciously, to Marx's criticism of religion as the reversal of reality. This is neither a misprint nor a mistake and is of fundamental importance to the argument of this book. We shall take the matter further in Part Three.

(c)   The new theological epoch

'There is one thing stronger than armies, an idea whose hour has come.'[10] On Hegel's view of history we are familiar with epochs in which the new reality can no longer be contained within the institutions, customs and thought-forms of the day, and finally bursts through; sometimes violently, but always with a release of creative energy. Whatever the material base, in Marx's terms, the catalyst is often an idea, a phrase which captures the imagination and enables people both to articulate the contradictions of experience and to move beyond them. For the church in Latin America such was the impact of the phrase 'theology of liberation'. At Cartigny in 1969 Gutierrez was struggling with the contradictions and inadequacies of the given situation. The theology of development had superseded the theology of revolution, but it was still itself part of the problem.[11] The sub-title of the lecture, 'Notes on a theology of liberation', opened the way to the necessary breakthrough. In 1971 Gutierrez published the first full-length study on the subject. A Theology of Liberation marks the transition to a new theological epoch.

The book has become a classic of modern theology: that is to say, it is not read as much as it should be, and its contents are largely taken for granted. The fact that most theology is still being pursued within a previous epoch may be disappointing, but it cannot be surprising. However, it is not my task to repeat or summarize the contents of this important book. My interest is much more specific, namely to identify the influence of Marx's thought on the theology of liberation, and to assess the extent to which it has addressed Marx's various criticisms of religion. Nor is this alien to Gutierrez' own understanding of his work, for he claims that

> contemporary theology does in fact find itself in direct and fruitful confrontation with Marxism, and it is to a large extent due to Marxism's influence that theological thought, searching for its own sources, has begun to reflect on the meaning of the transformation of this world and the action of man in history.[12]

But our interests are twofold: not simply how Marx has influenced liberation theology, but what aspects of Marx, which should be taken into account, have been ignored by liberation theology.

Not surprisingly, Gutierrez spends some time clarifying the understanding of liberation. He associates it with Hegel's view of history, the movement from awareness of freedom to the achievement of freedom. Marx carried this analysis into the transformation of the external world of labour, and Freud dealt with the obstacles to its achievement in the inner life of the individual. But Gutierrez preserves the Hegelian-Marxist dynamic: liberation is not a condition once achieved, the overcoming of external constraints. The goal is 'the continuous creation, never ending, of a new way to be a man, a *permanent cultural revolution*'.[13] If this is liberation, then a theology of liberation will reflect on the will of God and the work of Christ in this context. 'For freedom Christ has set us free.'[14] We might say that this is not the legitimation of the bourgeois freedom of civil society, but the establishment of that gracious freedom for others which belongs to the kingdom of God. Gutierrez has already referred to Hegel's analysis of the master-slave relationship, in which eventually the next step in freedom comes not from the sphere of the master but the experience of the slave. So liberation theology does not view the process of the creation of the new man from the perspective of the developed nations, but from the perspective of the poor, the victims, the underside of history, those whom Christ calls blessed. In this provisional indication of the nature of liberation theology it will be clear that while Marx is not its source, his thought has provided a context in which theology can reflect systematically on its new situation and role.

If in earlier centuries religion determined social relations, attitudes and consciousness, the new situation for theology is that it must operate within a humanistic context which it does not control. It must take into account the aspirations of the mass of the population who are no longer prepared to allow small groups to pursue their narrow interests. Nor can theology stand apart from or above the struggle and issue reformist calls based simply on general moral principles. Gutierrez believes that this was still the position of the Council and papal encyclicals up to and including *Populorum Progressio*. But when Gutierrez moves beyond this reformist moral hectoring, broadly Marxist assumptions appear. Theology, if relevant to the struggle, must deal with such matters as the building of a just society 'on new relationships of production', the ending of domination by 'some social classes', and the ending of 'low-cost conciliation'.

> Social praxis makes demands which may seem difficult or disturbing to those who wish to achieve – or maintain – low-cost conciliation. Such a conciliation can be only a justifying ideology for profound disorder, a device for the few to keep living off the poverty of the many.[15]

Liberation theology, as orthopraxis, arises from the experience of living within this situation, not from alienated reflection upon it from outside. *A Theology of Liberation* is not a new work, but a more extensive treatment of the themes from the Cartigny lecture. It includes the same criticism of developmentism, the 'ideology of modernization', economic and cultural forms of imperialism and colonialism. Dependency is placed in the broader context of 'the worldwide class struggle'. In addition to these general points, capitalism is more specifically criticized, both at national level and at that of the multi-national companies. At the same time there is a more positive advocacy of socialism as 'the most fruitful and far-reaching approach' to the issues.[16] yet Gutierrez adopts the now familiar position that there are many forms of socialism and that it must be a form appropriate to Latin America. The Cuban revolution has played 'a catalytic role'. 'With certain qualifications, this revolution serves as a dividing point for the recent political history of Latin America.'[17] He refers to the claim by Fidel Castro that Cuba has its 'own way of interpreting socialism'. He also quotes with approval the Marxist writer J.C. Mariategui (who is turn seems to be borrowing from Benedetto Croce) that historical materialism is above all 'a method for the historical interpretation of society'.[18] Gutierrez, when describing the condition of liberation theology, is therefore drawing a parallel with the required social theory. Both must arise from within the situation. Latin America, if it is to be rid of dependence, must not be subjected to a form of dogmatism – whether ideological or theological – imposed from Europe. He quotes Guevara's admission that revolutionaries are not well-equipped to develop 'a new human being'. It would seem that

Gutierrez is therefore drawing a further parallel between the Latin American form of socialism and liberation theology. They can both contribute to the same goal. But there is one important proviso. One of the reasons for the failure of revolutionary campaigns in Latin America has been that the groups did not take the trouble to work with the peasants and the marginals: they were making the revolution on behalf of the oppressed. But both Hegel in his analysis of the liberation of the slave and, more recently, Paulo Freire in *The Pedagogy of the Oppressed*, condemn this approach as counter-productive. For Gutierrez, unless the oppressed are enabled to take the initiative, dependency by definition will continue, if in a different form. Liberation theology is therefore much influenced by Marx's thought, but it is certainly not dependent on it. I should also point out that Marxism here seems to be restricted to what I called Marx's critical philosophy, his social analysis. In the quotation from Mariategui, Gutierrez seems to be rejecting historical materialism in its full ideological form.

As we shall see, Gutierrez is never dismissive of the Christian dogmatic tradition. It is a continual source of wisdom, reflecting the experience of past generations. That is its strength, and weakness, for it is always in danger of becoming distorted into a body of prescriptive knowledge regarded as authoritative even in completely unforseen situations. It will be recalled that for Hegel philosophy is a secondary activity: wisdom comes from reflection on the past, from our new perspective. 'The owl of Minerva spreads its wings only with the falling of the dusk.' Gutierrez claims that the new theology 'rises only at sundown'. 'Theology does not produce pastoral activity; rather it reflects on it.'[19] A theology which, even while not setting aside the tradition, arises from social praxis, will produce a transformation of doctrine, practice and ecclesial forms. This is the agenda for the rest of Gutierrez' work, and indeed the agenda posed for all who participate in liberation theology.

Thus biblical doctrines are given a new context; partly Hegelian, partly Marxist. The work of God is seen both in creation and in history. Because of sin, re-creation is required, but the God of salvation is the God of liberation. Exodus is treated at length, as has now become customary in liberation theology, though its problematic aspects are ignored. In Egypt the slaves worked in conditions of alienated labour. God responds to this need by calling Moses.

Only the *mediation of this self-creation* – first revealed by the liberation from Egypt – allows us to rise above poetic expressions and general categories and to understand in a profound and synthesizing way the relationship between creation and salvation so vigorously proclaimed by the Bible. The Exodus experience is paradigmatic.[20]

Oh really? Or is it not in important respects rather the opposite? First, in terms of conscientization, there is no evidence in the Exodus account that the Hebrews took any initiative in the analysis and transformation of their situation. But secondly, there is a moral issue. Were there no poor and oppressed Egyptians when the Hebrews lived in slavery? Is it entirely in order that their firstborn were killed so that the Hebrews might go free? How many brave liberation theologians who flourish Exodus like a weapon have read the small print?

> At midnight the Lord smote all the first-born in the land of Egypt, from the first-born of Pharaoh who sat on his throne to the first-born of the captive who was in the dungeon, and all the first-born cattle.[21]

And is this the revelation of the work of salvation which comes to perfect fulfilment in Jesus Christ, that innocent children should be struck down? The children not only of Pharaoh, but of those languishing in his dungeons, some of whom might well have been his fierce critics? Is such slaughter paradigmatic of how the God of the Christians deals with his creatures? And how does it compare with those words of Helder Camara which I have already quoted: 'I would prefer a thousand times to be killed than to kill.' But liberation theologians are also scientific scholars, and no doubt would assure us that the plagues did not happen exactly as retold. But if the plagues did not happen like that, then neither did the Exodus. Beware of proving too much.

In demonstrating how liberation theology arises from social praxis, Gutierrez chooses to illustrate from Exodus. But is this the experience of the poor in history, or on the contrary is this paradigm an ideology laid on them from a previous time and place? This particular owl has been up and about since daybreak. A second example follows from this: Christ comes as liberator. Sin must not be understood in some narrow individualistic and private sense, as if it were not embodied also in the institutions and economic relations of society. Salvation therefore runs along 'the social injustice-justice axis, or, in concrete terms, the oppression-liberation axis'.[22] Where concern for salvation for the individual from the consequences of private sins might lead to a turning away from the social world, in liberation theology the quest for salvation involves a rejection of the existing order. 'This rejection does not produce an escapist attitude, but rather a will to revolution.'[23] In Latin America in the 1960s this claim might have to be spelt out, but at least this radical view of liberation uncovers the presence of alienation in all aspects of societal life. And how is this expressed in correspondingly radical terms by the new liberation theology? 'This radical liberation is the gift which Christ offers us. By his death and resurrection he redeems man from sin and all its consequences . . .'[24] We have already seen that when Guevara speaks of redemption he gives it a new depth, but is Gutierrez here not simply repeating the traditional dogmatic formulation of the efficacy of the death of Christ? And does it arise from the social praxis of the oppressed in Latin America today, or from the religious presuppositions of the first century?

Gutierrez is perfectly clear about the need for change in society, but despite his agenda his theology seems remarkably unliberated. By a radical appropriation of Marxist critical theory this Moses of ortho-praxis has brought liberation theology to the very frontiers of a new epoch but, like Moses, he does not himself enter the promised land.

(d) The underside of history

The criticism of the development model of the 1960s was that it did not encourage or enable poor countries to follow the historic path of the rich nations. Rather, the under-developed countries were set up to contribute to the further expansion of the developed economies. The poverty of the Third World countries was further highlighted by the increasing gap between rich and poor, and in many cases poverty increased in real terms. In these circumstances the economic situation becomes a moral and religious issue. From the world of technology the cries of the poor are excluded, as the Brazilian writer Alceu Amoroso Lima points out.

> Suffering starts to dehumanize us from the moment we stop being aware of it. It has crossed the sensitivity-barrier, as planes cross the sound-barrier. And as the sound-barrier is really silence, so the sensitivity-barrier is indifference.[25]

The way out of this situation is for the poor to break through this sound barrier, to gain the power of speech. According to Gutierrez, 'the theology of liberation represents *the right of the poor to think*'.[26] Not that the poor themselves write books on theology. Just as for Hegel philosophy should reflect on what is happening, so Gutierrez describes theology as a 'second act', the reflection on the situation which leads to further action. There have been attempts by the poor to raise their voices, even in recent history, but the movements have failed. There were, for example, the 'peasants' leagues in Brazil, under the leadership of the lawyer Francisco Julião. In 1963 in the north-east they were reputed to have the support of 500,000 peasants. The main centre was Recife, when Miguel Arraes was governor.[27] The movement did not survive the 1964 coup. Nor, although centred on Recife, did it influence the theology of the archbishop. However, the relationship between theologians and the *comunidades eclesiales de base* is much closer. Their experiences in the base communities have changed their approach to theology, affecting both method and content.

It is appropriate now to say something about the influence of the poor on the form and content of liberation theology. But once again I must point out that this is not an exposition of liberation theology. Our interest is in the extent to which liberation theology has responded to Marx's criticisms of religion. In dealing with the central point about the place of the poor in liberation theology we can see a movement which might have taken place under the influence of Marx. But more intriguing is the parallel with Marx's life. The liberation theologians are not peasants. Many of them come from middle-class families and they have benefitted from the best education available in Latin America, Europe and the USA. The parallel is therefore with Marx who forsook his class and joined himself to the proletariat. His hopes for the future lay with this class, and his analysis of history was from their perspective. The liberation theologians seem to have made a similar choice, crossing that line which in the Third World clearly marks the boundary between rich and poor, powerful and weak, articulate and silent, the actors and those acted-upon. Gutierrez, who in other respects is highly critical of European theology, is much taken with a passage from one of Bonhoeffer's prison letters.

> We have learned to see the great events of the history of the world from beneath – from the viewpoint of the useless, the suspect, the abused, the powerless, the oppressed, the despised. In a word, from the view-point of the suffering.[28]

Bonhoeffer was executed before he could pursue theology from this new perspective: the mantle has fallen upon the liberation theologians. They have committed themselves to the poor, to the life of the poor, and from that perspective they write a very different kind of theology. Not surprisingly it is no longer susceptible to Marx's criticism that religion is reconciliation with injustice and an ideological legitimation of the structures of oppression.

The change of perspective is clear in the theology of Gutierrez. Sin, which from a traditional perspective was often narrowed down to aspects of individual (sexual) behaviour, is given a new context. 'To sin – not to love, not to know, God – is to create relationships of injustice, to make an option for oppression and against liberation.'[29] For traditional theology God became man. Some attempted to avoid impersonalism by insisting he became a man. But is this not still to avoid the fundamental reality? 'Jesus Christ is precisely *God become poor*.'[30] For many communicants the reception of the body of Christ in the eucharist is a moment of sacred isolation from the world. For Gutierrez the very opposite is the case. 'The celebration of the Lord's Supper presupposes a communion and solidarity with the poor in history. Without this solidarity, it is impossible to comprehend the death and resurrection of the Servant of God.'[31]

Religion so understood and practised cannot be described as reconciliation with injustice. It overcomes the alienation assumed in the designation of religion as an opiate. There can be no reconciliation with injustice, because God has taken sides. He has pitched his tent with the poor; he has taken the side of the oppressed. This was the message of the second episcopal conference, at Medellín in 1968. A decade later the preparatory documents appeared for the third conference, to be held in Puebla. There was a real danger that the new perspective would be lost. Gutierrez was influential in making sure that the perspective of the underside of history was maintained, 'the preferential/non-exclusive option for the poor'.[32] If the effect of an opiate is to cloud consciousness and weaken resistance, theology of liberation describes a religion which is characterized by militancy. The examples given in the previous paragraph represent what Gutierrez calls 'a *militant* reading' of the Bible. Those who take the side of the poor do not work instead of them, but are committed to 'militant cooperation with them in their struggles'.[33] The new theology arises not from reflection upon the social struggle, but from involvement in it. 'The theology of liberation is rooted in a revolutionary militancy.'[34]

And if religion so understood and practised cannot be described as reconciliation with injustice, it certainly cannot function as an ideological legitimation of the interests of the ruling class, Marx's third criticism of religion. We can see the clear influence of Marx himself in a passage dealing with militancy.

> In the immensity and complexity of the social process that must crush a system of oppression and lead to a classless society, ideological struggle too has an important place. Hence it is that the communication of the message as reread from the point of view of the poor and oppressed, and from the point of view of militant cooperation with them in their struggle, will have the function of unmasking all intent and effort to make the gospel play the role of justifying a situation at odds with what the Bible calls 'justice and right'.[35]

There are echoes here in almost every phrase of Marx's critique of ideology. Theory, in this case theology, cannot replace the struggle,

but it becomes a weapon in that struggle when it develops the consciousness of the people. Liberation theology has an important part to
play in exposing and nullifying that form of theology which does act
as an ideology of the ruling class, an ideology which pictures God on
the side of the rich and powerful makers of history. The new theology
unmasks the function of the old. But from this preferential but non-
exclusive perspective, it is important to say that liberation theology
does not become simply the legitimation of some other system: it 'has
no intention of being a revolutionary Christian ideology'.[36]

The material discussed in this section comes from essays published
throughout the 1970s. It shows the clear influence of Marx's thought
on Gutierrez, though I must repeat that this does not mean that Marx
is his inspiration. The influence declines in the next decade, and is
little evidenced in *We Drink From Our Own Wells: The Spiritual
Journey of a People* (1983) or *On Job: God-Talk and the Suffering of
the Innocent* (1986). But before we end this discussion I must take up
two further points.

The first is the absence of Marx's second critique of religion, religion
as an inversion of reality. The first and third critiques are comprehensively answered, as we have seen, yet the second is not even addressed.
It might be suggested that an argument from omission is not very
significant. The matter apparently did not arise. Even so, it would be
surprising if Marx were so influential in three out of four points and
ignored in the remaining one. But what if Gutierrez chose to enter
this further area, and still failed to deal with it? I have already drawn
attention to his attachment to the quotation from Bonhoeffer about
viewing history 'from beneath'. The essay in which it is quoted,
'Theology from the Underside of History', was first published in 1977,
and the passage appears at the end, after an extended discussion of
'theology and the modern spirit'. Gutierrez goes on to indicate that
this spirit represents many things, including the bourgeois revolutions
of England, the USA and France. There is Rousseau, civil society and
the rights of man. It also includes the Enlightenment, with the advances
in the sciences and the autonomy of human reason over against all
forms of external authority. Descartes and Hume must be mentioned
on epistemology. Eventually this brief check-list in the history of ideas
and institutions reaches a section entitled 'the new critique of religion'.
Ten pages are perhaps not enough for such a complicated subject, but
at least we can be sure that if only the main participants are able to
appear, there is one critic who is unavoidable. Since, having read Part
One above, we reckon ourselves to be tolerably well-informed on
the subject, we await with scarcely controllable anticipation for the
confrontation: Gutierrez and Marx. We wait. And wait.

First up are Machiavelli and Montaigne on the social function of religion. Bayle on religious tolerance rates more than Weber on capitalism. But at last when Feuerbach's name is called we know that the climax is near. Yet no, the father of German materialism is not allowed to utter a sentence. Instead, Kant makes an appearance to defend morality and faith. He is followed by Schleiermacher himself, the father of modern theology. We are told that modern liberal theology combines Schleiermacher and Hegel. At the name of the master hope springs momentarily, but we are confronted with Tillich, Barth and Bultmann as they criticize liberal theology. We are now reconciled to the fact that Marx is not going to be mentioned as a nineteenth-century figure. But perhaps if we press on we shall meet him second time round, when he is rediscovered in the twentieth century. There is an extensive discussion of Bonhoeffer, followed by something on Vatican II and its recognition of the existence of atheism. Hope revives with the mention of Metz and Moltmann and political theology, but there is no mention of its Marxist, neo-Marxist or revisionist roots. By way of conclusion we are told that 'political theology seeks to face up to the questions of the modern story of freedom, enlightenment, and a Marxist critique of religion'.[37] But of that Marxist critique we hear not a word, either from the nineteenth or from the twentieth centuries.

The story then passes to the non-European world, and eventually in discussing Latin America we are informed of the nature of the struggle:

> This is why the popular movement is also the locus of encounter of the social sciences and Marxist analysis with theology – an encounter, to be sure, involving criticism of theology, and an encounter undertaken within the dynamics of a concrete historical movement that transcends individuality, dogmatisms, and transitory enthusiasms.[38]

We have already noted the importance of Marxist social analysis for theology, but in addition there are Marx's various criticisms of religion. It would seem odd if his analysis was accepted largely without qualification and his criticism of religion ignored. Gutierrez goes on immediately to relate the criticism of religion to injustice and to ideology, the first and third of Marx's critiques. When I therefore say that Gutierrez deliberately avoids addressing himself to the ontological critique, it is because he provided several occasions on which it would have been appropriate, but failed to take advantage of them. Indeed he seems to admit as much when he dismisses the question of 'how to speak of God in an adult world' as an 'old question'.[39] It is certainly an issue raised in Europe forty-five years ago, but since Gutierrez steadfastly refuses to face Marx's ontological critique of religion, it will always lie not behind him, but ahead of him, yet to be confronted.

This, then, is the first of my two concluding points: the failure to address Marx's second critique of religion. The second and final point arises from a parallel which I drew earlier between the life of Marx and the careers of liberation theologians. Like Marx, they have forsaken the middle class, the class of their birth or at least of their adoption. As he joined himself to the proletariat, they have made their lives with the poor. In the case of Marx this step led to great cost and suffering to himself and to his family. In the case of the liberation theologians, to personal cost there is often to be added deliberate misrepresentation by church and state, and even physical risk. Nevertheless, given the parallel, the same question has to be faced. In the *Manifesto* Marx seems to be describing himself when he writes of 'a portion of the bourgeois ideologists' who forsake their class and join the revolutionary class. In discussing this movement I raised the question whether Marx brought any luggage with him. Did he arrive simply with a clear mind, to begin the construction of a philosophy which derived entirely from the experience of the working class? The answer is clearly, No. He brought with him a form of bourgeois philosophy, a variation on Hegel's idealism. Adopting the perspective of the underside of history, Marx's philosophy is a very radical revision of Hegel's philosophy, but it never ceased to be just that. The comparable question will now be clear. Liberation theologians did not enter the base communities empty-handed. They brought with them orthodox, even conservative, forms of Christian theology. The issue is whether I can repeat, *mutatis mutandis*, my previous comment. That is to say: adopting the perspective of the underside of history, liberation theology is a very radical revision of traditional orthodox theology, but it has never ceased to be just that. Nor can it be, as long as Marx's second, ontological, criticism of religion is deliberately avoided.

(e) The owl of theology

In this chapter we are examining the influence which Marx's thought has had on the emergence of liberation theology. I make no apology for concentrating on the work of Gustavo Gutierrez: he might justifiably be regarded as the founder of the movement. However, it would have been possible to illustrate the points from other writers. I am certainly not implying that his work is unique in this sense, though no doubt careless reviewers of this book will confidently make this criticism. In section (*b*) I was able to illustrate Marx's influence in five different areas of social criticism. Thereafter I noted how Gutierrez had responded to Marx's thought as set out in Part One of this study: that is, the three critiques of religion plus historical materialism as a faith. We saw that he rejected historical materialism as a faith, and accepted the first and third critiques. But on the second criticism, religion as a reversal of reality, he has nothing to say.

Some might say that in the rambling, programmatic Cartigny essay this omission is not significant. However, the same pattern emerges in the full-length study, *A Theology of Liberation*. We have already noted that through the quotation from Mariategui Gutierrez restricts Marxism to social criticism and rejects it as an ideological faith. He also accepts the first criticism of Marx, namely religion as reconciliation with evil. This was illustrated in the quotation concerning 'low-cost conciliation'. Towards the end of the book he declares that 'the Latin American Church must make the prophetic *denunciation* of every dehumanizing situation, which is contrary to brotherhood, justice, and liberty'.[40] He also accepts the third criticism, that religion can function as an ideology. Liberation theology must be critical theology. As such it will not only cease to function as an ideological legitimation of the interests of the ruling classes, but will perform a therapeutic function for Christians, 'preserving them from fetishisms and idolatry'. 'Understood in this way, theology has a necessary and permanent role in the liberation from every form of religious alienation . . .'[41] Indeed he can even put down an early marker against 'the danger of oversimplifying the Gospel message and making it a "revolutionary ideology" '.[42] The ideological captivity of the church can take place from the left as well as the right.

But as in the previous section what we do not have is a single example of Gutierrez accepting or even addressing himself to Marx's second criticism of religion, that it is a reversal of reality. Why should Marx, who is so influential in other respects, be totally ignored here? A Marxist answer would of course be 'interest'. In accepting the first and third critiques it is hoped that theology will be purified, and enhanced. But the second, the ontological criticism, threatens to undermine the premises of theology, and it is simply and silently set aside.

This is the emerging pattern, but it also includes another element. Now that liberation theology has been enlightened by Marx's social philosophy and purified by his moral criticism, why does it still cling to models and repeat doctrines from a tradition which is so alien to experience in the modern world? We must conclude that theology cannot make the required leap on the basis of social and moral criticism. So long as the ontological criticism is ignored, theology will continue to be an ideology, a Procrustean system which does not arise from experience. Until this challenge is faced, the owl of theology will spread its wings before the dawning of the working day.

8

The Use of Marx in Liberation Theology

(a) Hermeneutical spiral

In the previous chapter I examined the influence which Marx's thought
has had on the emergence of liberation theology. In this chapter we
proceed to a further stage, namely the conscious use of Marx by
liberation theologians. It would have been possible to include Gutierrez also in this category, though I believe this would not be a comprehensive way of approaching his work. I maintained that even although
Gutierrez was only influenced by Marx, he should not have avoided
Marx's second criticism of religion, religion as an inversion of reality.
He certainly addressed the other two criticisms and declared himself
on historical materialism as a faith. If it is true that Gutierrez should
have consciously taken up the second criticism, then this must be true
a fortiori of those who make a more conscious use of Marx's critical
philosophy. Surely those who consciously make use of Marx must face
the whole range of his challenge. If his work is so valuable as to be
inescapable, then such a central element as his ontological criticism
cannot be ignored.

We might reasonably expect that anyone dealing with Marx and
theological method would incorporate the full range of his criticisms
of religion. It is therefore appropriate that we now turn to the work
of the Uruguayan Jesuit theologian Juan Luis Segundo. The reversal
of terms in the title of his book *Liberation of Theology* prepares us
for his judgment that after a decade of liberation theology it was
necessary to address the issues of epistemology and method.

As we have seen, liberation theology is written from a very different
perspective from more traditional theology. As important as the fact
that this is so is the significance of the fact. Segundo is not unique in
this respect, but following training in Uruguay he pursued graduate

studies in Louvain before going on to receive his doctorate at the Sorbonne. Clearly he could write from the perspective of traditional Catholic theology, but does not. In the eyes of some critics this is tantamount to saying that he gives up Catholic theology for local theology, absolute theology for relative theology, theology of the centre for peripheral theology. But on reflection this is not the way to describe the difference between the two theologies. It is not that one is timeless and culture-free, the other rooted in the experience of a specific people. Rather, both reflect the perspectives of their authors. Traditional theology is European: indeed it is for the most part European of a previous age. It is not even rooted in contemporary experience. But as we have seen, any system of ideas which exists independently of experience is an ideology. And no one who is familiar with Marx could stop at this point. Does traditional theology, as an ideology, serve the interests of the ruling class? The ruling class here might refer to a class within Europe, but on a larger scale it could refer to the North against the South, the First World against the Third. And of course it could refer to the ruling class within the church, bishops against priests, clergy against laity, men against women. For this reason we must go beyond the fact that liberation theology is written from the underside to examine the significance that this is so. It is in this context that Segundo takes up the issues of epistemology and method.

To say that liberation theology is written from a certain perspective might give a rather static impression. By contrast Marx favoured the more dynamic Hegelian model of the dialectic. We can identify four stages in this movement.

(a) We live in a situation interpreted for us by the ideology of the ruling class. Life is determined by (false) consciousness.

(b) In certain circumstances our experience may contradict this picture of reality to such a degree that we become suspicious of it.

(c) We come to trust our experience, and revise our picture of reality. This is the movement from false consciousness to true consciousness.

(d) This new understanding then informs our actions: praxis changes the world.

In this dialectical movement each stage is the basis for the next, and is superseded by it. It goes beyond the Hegelian triad because it is revolutionary: it supersedes interpretation with action. However, I should add that the movement continues: the new consciousness becomes the base for the next sequence.

Segundo beings his discussion of epistemology and method with what he calls 'the hermeneutical circle'. It, too, has four stages, clearly indebted to Marx's dialectic. 'Circle' is an inappropriate model, since only if the process failed should we return to the point from which we started. 'Spiral' might be a better model, incorporating circular and linear motion. In any case, his four points describe a movement which is said to be characteristic of liberation theology.

1. Our way of experiencing reality leads to ideological suspicion.
2. Our ideological suspicion is applied to the whole ideological superstructure in general, and theology in particular.
3. We experience theological reality in a new way, and become suspicious about the adequacy of current biblical interpretation.
4. We reach a new heremeutical position for dealing with the Scriptures.[1]

There are three fundamental problems with Segundo's approach.

In the first place, although this framework looks to be worked out in detail, it begs fundamental issues. The analysis is derived from Marx and yet immediately departs from Marx without any justification. Anyone using terms such as 'ideological superstructure' must be assumed to be using Marx's theories both of ideology and of the relationship between base and superstructure until further notice. In 2. theology is part of the ideological superstructure, as Marx indicated. But in 3. there is something called 'theological reality', which for Marx's theory is a contradiction in terms. I have argued in Part One that theology will always remain part of the ideology until it has addressed Marx's second critique. Whether Segundo does this remains to be seen: even already the signs are not promising.

The second problem with Segundo's approach arises when he seeks to use this model on other forms of theology. The proposition is that liberation theology follows this model and traditional theology does not. He will therefore apply the model to examples of traditional theology to test the thesis. And what are these traditional theologies? In broad outline (!) we might designate the following as candidates: patristic, mediaeval, Reformation, liberal Protestant, neo-Thomist, neo-orthodox. Instead, the traditional theologies are represented by Harvey Cox, Karl Marx, Max Weber and James Cone! A significant test for the model might have been Athanasius, Aquinas, Schleiermacher and Barth. But what is the model testing by substituting Cox, Marx, Weber and Cone? Alternatively, if liberation theology is being distinguished from all other forms, why not run political theology through the machine and deal with the theologies of Metz and Moltmann?

The writers selected in this arbitrary way are not theologians. (I should have no objection to describing Cone as a theologian, but many see his work as christology.) Applying the model to their work would prove very little (with the possible exception of Cone). But there is a third problem. Segundo does not actually apply his own model properly. Our interest naturally is in his treatment of Marx, but I can illustrate this briefly with reference to Cox.

The fact that Cox is chosen as the first example, or indeed chosen at all, probably owes less to his contribution to theology than to the fact that *Liberation of Theology* represents an expanded version of lectures given at the Harvard Divinity School (where Cox was teaching) in 1974. However, *The Secular City* presented an important challenge to traditional theological assumptions and it should have been possible for Segundo to apply his model to it. He identifies the various stages as follows:

(i) Cox adopts the pragmatic approach to problems characteristic of the technopolis.

(ii) Secularization and urbanization provide a new ideological way of viewing reality, including theological reality.

(iii) The new theological reality enables Cox to establish a new theology of revolutionary social change.

(iv) According to Segundo, Cox never reaches the fourth stage. He never really attempts an interpretation of the Bible which would be meaningful for pragmatic man. He was not committed to the experience of pragmatic man.

It seems to me that if there is one thing even more eccentric than the choice of Harvey Cox in the first place, it is this presentation of his position. If this is how the model is to be applied, the result is more damaging to the model than to *The Secular City*. How might Cox's position be represented in terms of Segundo's own model?

1. When Harvey Cox was a student he moved from his home town of Malvern, Pennsylvania to the city of Philadelphia. He made the move with some misgivings, since he knew what everyone else knows, that rural life is more wholesome than city life. To his surprise and relief he discovered that the reality was quite different from the picture (ideology).

2. This led him to question the ideological picture, including the part of religion in its formation.

3. He came to question traditional interpretations of the Bible, for example the identification of city with sin, rural with righteous. At this stage Cox's other concern takes over, namely secularization. He sees that the process is not irreligious, but rather the culmination of a movement with its roots in the Bible.

4. From this new perspective, the perspective of people like himself who are committed to the urban-secular life, he is able to gain new insights from the Bible.[2]

If Cox's work is to be criticized, it is because he does not gain any new insights; rather, he falls into an uncritical legitimation of the characteristics of modern urban-secular life. If he fails, it is in this area, rather than the pragmatism identified by Segundo.

I have thought it appropriate to deal briefly with the application of the Segundo model to Cox, because it prepares us for a comparable misrepresentation of Marx. It should have been easy to apply the model to Marx's work, since Marx is the inspiration of Segundo's model, but as I have already hinted, there are inconsistencies in the model which become important in this case. Segundo's analysis is particularly interesting for our purposes, since he specifically deals with Marx and religion.

1. Marx takes the side of the proletariat in the class struggle. The world must be changed in their favour.

2. Historical materialism is a theory which enables Marx to understand reality. It relates ideas, including religious ideas, to the mode of production.

3. The interpretation of scripture current in any age is that which derives from the perspective of the ruling class. Segundo claims that Marx suggests that it is possible for the proletariat to discover a more faithful interpretation of scripture, which will assist them in the struggle.

4. But as with Cox, the fourth step is not taken. Marx does not go on to discover the 'spiritualized' form of actual social relations. Rather, he dismisses religion as 'an autonomous ahistorical monolith'.[3]

On this view Marx should have gone on to enquire how religion could be changed so that it could contribute to the ending of 'real suffering'. Segundo complains that 'Marx does not seem to have shown any interest in trying to find out whether distortion had crept into the Christian message and whether a new interpretation favoring the class struggle of the proletariat might be possible or even necessary'.[4] His criticism is that Marx should have been committed to change theology, just as he was committed to change the world. But it is surely entirely inappropriate to blame Marx for not conforming to a model which is inconsistent with his own position.

There are several further problems, specific to Segundo's treatment of Marx. The first is that he does not begin at the beginning in dealing with what he calls the relationship of Marx's thought with religion. It will be recalled that religion occupies a central place in Marx's thought. 'The criticism of religion is the premise of all criticism.' It is the first example of the inversion of reality. It is of some significance, therefore, that Segundo omits this stage, and thereby in common with other liberation theologians avoids Marx's second criticism of religion.

The second problem follows from this. In Part One we noted that it would be possible to provide a materialist account of religion, but that Marx does not attempt to provide one. To this we shall return in Part Three. Religion exists and can be analysed in various ways. Theology is but one approach to it, but on Marx's view theology is an inherently ideological mode. It must therefore serve the interests of the ruling class.

The third problem follows in turn. There can be no question of blaming Marx for not proceeding to transform theology into a weapon of the class struggle, this time on the side of the proletariat. Such a move in the realm of ideas would be comparable to advising the working class how to become capitalists.

This illustrates the fourth problem, namely that there is a confusion in the application of the model. It purports to be describing a hermeneutical movement in Marx's thought, but on closer inspection it is an attempt to set Marx up as the basis for liberation theology. That is to say, the example expresses Segundo's interests rather than those of Marx. This explains Segundo's attempt to introduce into the third stage the realignment of theology from being an instrument favouring the ruling class, to a weapon of use to the working class. But by avoiding Marx's second criticism of religion he has committed the cardinal sin of the reformist: he has introduced into the camp of the proletariat a Trojan horse which carries within it the continuing presence of the ruling ideology.

A final problem concerns Segundo's insistence that the movement round the hermeneutical circle must exhibit 'partiality',[5] that is, commitment to a type or class of people. He claims to derive this from Mannheim, but in the latter's analysis such 'interest' is no guarantee of achieving true consciousness. It is for this reason that Segundo begins his treatment of Marx with the Eleventh Thesis on Feuerbach and the commitment to the proletariat, rather than with the critique of religion as inversion of reality. There is an instructive point which emerges in Segundo's fourth example, the early work of James Cone. He notes Cone's partiality, his taking the side of American blacks, and goes out of his way to avoid any criticism of Cone. Although at that point in his Harvard lectures he speaks of the real danger of death which attends liberation theologians, did he perhaps take fright at the idea of criticizing the leading advocate of black theology? By comparison the South African theologian Allan Boesak has no such fears. 'Cone's mistake is that he has taken Black Theology out of the framework of the theology of liberation, thereby making his own situation (being black in America) and his own movement (liberation from white racism) the ultimate criterion for all theology.'[6] The theme of 'partiality' echoes Medellín in God's bias towards the poor. But God's partiality cannot justify all forms of taking sides. In *Black Theology and Black Power*,[7] Cone's interests lie with the Black Power movement. It is quite astonishing that Segundo declares that he will not comment on Cone's new insights into the scriptures. It is as though relating the Bible to a contemporary situation is in itself a virtue. In reality it is quite clear that Cone is offering a religious legitimation of the ideology of Black Power. God's partiality and man's ideological interest must be clearly distinguished. The fact that Segundo's model does not require him to make this distinction demonstrates that it is of little practical significance.

The model is therefore highly problematic and, as we have seen in the case of Cox, Segundo does not necessarily use it well. This is true also in the case of Marx. If we were to use Segundo's model to represent Marx's treatment of religion it would have to take a different course.

(i) As we grow up, society communicates to us in a variety of ways that what is real is rational, and yet eventually our experience contradicts this view.

(ii) Historical materialism exposes the ideology of the age. What exists arises not from the implementation of ideas or ideals, but from relations brought about by the mode of production. Theology is part of this ideological superstructure and as such it is an inversion of reality.

(iii) Despite what Segundo claims, Marx does not offer us a new way of experiencing 'theological reality' at this stage. Instead he uncovers the way in which biblical texts have been interpreted to suit the interests of the ruling class.

(iv) At this stage in Part One we came to the conclusion that although Marx was not sufficiently interested to perform this function, it would be possible to offer a historical materialist account of religion.

To this we shall return in Part Three. But for the moment I must say that Segundo has entirely missed the point of Marx's criticism. Following Feuerbach, Marx dismissed theology as an ideological product, the expression of the inversion of reality characteristic of human thinking. While it is possible to conceive of a historical materialist understanding of religion, it does not follow from this that it could sustain as its superstructure a form of the old traditional metaphysical theology. At this point Segundo is making the same assumption as Gutierrez, namely that it is possible to accept Marx's first and third criticisms of religion without regard to the second. They assume that this can be done in such a way that theology no longer performs an ideological function on behalf of the ruling class and against the interests of the proletariat/the poor. But as we saw in Part One, any variation on theology which continues the historic idealist tradition is inherently ideological.

(b)   Theologies of explanation and change

Liberation theology has attracted attention because it deals with poverty, suffering, capitalism, international trade. But then so do many other forms of theology. And it also deals with very traditional subjects including ecclesiology, liturgy, spirituality. Liberation theology is distinguished from other theologies by its perspective, by its starting-point, by its method. The subjects are not in themselves distinctive but their treatment is. Segundo has consciously used Marx in tracing out the necessary sequence round the hermeneutical circle. We turn now to the Jesuit theologian from El Salvador, Jon Sobrino, who uses Marx in identifying the necessary epistemological break. Once again, the aim is not to provide an exposition of Sobrino's work, but to examine whether he exposes his position to the full range of Marx's criticism of religion.

When feminist theology first appeared its exponents contrasted it with male theology. It was not static but dynamic; not concerned with the past but with the future. In fact these themes were characteristic of the theology of hope, a theology first formulated by male theologians. As a rule of thumb those aspects of theology that were progressive and humanizing were placed in a (shopping) bag marked 'feminist theology', while everything that was left was designated as 'male theology'. From time to time I have had the same impression on reading liberation theology, when for example it claims Carlos Marx as one of its own. In Part One we noted that few could have had a more Jewish upbringing than Marx, but we also saw that above all he was a European, who openly taught that the whole world must follow the pattern of Europe. Marx's thought reached Latin America via European theology, both Protestant and Catholic. We are examining how that critical thought has been (selectively) appropriated.

In an essay 'Theological Understanding in European and Latin American Theology', written in 1975, Sobrino focusses on the 'epistemological break' in relation to theology and its context.[8] Does theology arise from conceptual problems, or in confrontation with social reality? Whose 'interests' does theology serve? Throughout the history of Christianity, all theologies have been concerned with a disparity. There is man, society, the world, as they are and as they should be. The analysis has taken many different forms, and therefore what constitutes good news has correspondingly changed. But this is the proclamation, that in Christ God has redeemed the world, has offered liberation. Sobrino does not trace the history of this process from the beginning; he proposes to start with the dawn of the modern world, the European Enlightenment. Or rather he confusingly distinguishes two phases of the Englightenment, as if there was one in the eighteenth and a second in the nineteenth century. Theology has been characterized correspondingly by two different analyses and therefore two different forms of liberation. These contrasting approaches can be exemplified by Kant and Marx. They have in turn produced two very different approaches to liberation, two different forms of theology. Well, you can guess whom we get stuck with! European theology stands in the tradition of Kant. Really? All of it? And why the Enlightenment? We have had many other important movements in European history during the two centuries since Hume awakened Kant from his dogmatic slumbers. If we are to be denied Marx, could we at least have Scheleiermacher and Hegel, both of who were extremely critical of the Enlightenment? But no, we must make do with Kant. Denied Heidegger, we must play the hand dealt to us; without Bloch, we must proceed without hope.

According to Sobrino, European theology has responded to the challenge of the Enlightenment in two ways. The first is that it offers an explanation of the world. In the age of reason, man was offered liberation from error, from superstitition, from arbitrary external control. The sciences would liberate man from ignorance about the world; philosophy based on science would liberate the mind from confusion. External control by arbitrary political and economic domination would be ended in new rational social conditions. Morality would be placed on an autonomous basis. And of course religion would be brought before the bar of human reason. It would be discredited and dismissed unless it could demonstrate the validity of its sources in face of historical criticism; its dogmas must be shown to be at least compatible with the advances of reason in all other fields.

This picture hardly seems to correspond to Sobrino's claim that theology comes to liberate. It appears, rather, that reason comes to liberate man from religion. But as we have already discovered, Latin American theologians have no sympathy for the idea that theology might be inherently an obstacle to human liberation. This is Marx's view, but not theirs. Sobrino, therefore, like Segundo before him, fails to use the model which he has set up. Reason liberates man from error, but it also liberates theology from its errors. It is purified by this process. Sobrino does not elaborate this point, but this is the effect of the confrontation with the natural sciences. Theology emerged more specifically religious when it ceased to act as alternative science.

As Sobrino presents his case – or as it could be presented if he had taken the time – theology after Kant has responded to the challenge of the Enlightenment. It has accepted the emerging modern view of reality, and has reformed itself in the light of the advances in the natural and historical sciences. But since we know that European theology is being set up for a fall, there is somehow an implied criticism of these admirable developments. It is as if the motivation was simply to conform to the world. Yet as we saw in Part One, Strauss rejected a rationalist approach to the Gospels, just as Bultmann rejected a shallow enlightenment. Sobrino refers in passing to Protestant theologians who stand in the Kantian tradition. But as we have seen, Schleiermacher, the first to be mentioned, was extremely critical of the Enlightenment, especially of reducing religion to a 'knowing' or a 'doing'. The history of religions movement is represented as seeking to show the harmony of Christianity with other world religions. But this was neither the intention nor the effect of this movement. This dismissive remark probably owes something to a parochial lack of interest among Latin American theologians in world religions, because of their specific situation. The quick survey ends with Barth, who while not above criticism certainly cannot be accused of attempting to bring theology into harmony with the ethos of the day. If Sobrino is really giving European theology these characteristics of responding positively to the developments of the natural and historical sciences, then we must be grateful and delighted. Does that mean Latin American theology does not share these concerns? Perhaps Bonino, Dussel and others would decline to be included in this scheme of things. All this can hardly be represented as theology providing an explanation of the world. Rather it accepts – on good grounds – the explanations which the modern natural, historical and social sciences provide in their respective fields. At most theology attempts to reconstruct a religious world view which is in large part informed by the new knowledge.

But now we come to Sobrino's main point. Does this kind of European theology liberate, or does it co-exist with a non-liberated world? Yet this is a rather pretentious starting point. It was Enlightenment reason which first of all liberated theology from a web of ignorance and error endemic in the ancient world-view. And with regard to the liberation of millions of people from genetically transmitted disorders or contagious diseases, that emancipation from suffering and misery was brought about by medical sciences, and not by theology. We must display some humility and acknowledge that theology cannot liberate people from all that constrains them or dehumanizes them, nor need it pretend to do so. But Sobrino's question is an implied criticism. Is European theology so alienated from reality that it exists without challenging that reality? We can say that it is not so alienated from reality as it was before it was liberated by the modern sciences. But Sobrino's point concerns only the moral issue. Is it merely an intellectual construct, an explanation of the world as it is? And beyond that as an intellectual construct, is it (unwittingly) an ideology promoting the interests of the ruling classes? This was Marx's view, but he did not pretend to relate it to Kant. But Sobrino cannot afford to agree with Marx here, since Marx claimed that all theology was ideological.

And if the answer were, Yes, a good deal of European theology is ideology, what conclusion could be drawn? Would it be a condemnation of theology which responded to the Enlightenment? Hardly, since theology has always performed the function of acting as an ideology for the ruling classes. But if the Enlightenment has led to a better understanding of reality, how could such theology be inherently ideological, since ideology leads only to false consciousness? But Sobrino would like to draw another conclusion, which if truth be told really has nothing to do with the Enlightenment at all. He would like to represent European theology as avoiding criticism of an evil world. And of those he has arbitrarily mentioned, would that be true of Barth, whose neo-orthodoxy arose directly from his rejection of the religious legitimation of the Kaiser's war policy, and developed in opposition to National Socialism in Germany? In Britain there is a long tradition of Christian socialism, which runs from F. D. Maurice in the 1840s to the present Bishop of Durham. It began through Ludlow's involvement with the Paris communards, and was effected in the co-operative movement. Its more recent exponent incurred the wrath of the government for defending the distress and suffering of the poorest families during the long-running miners' strike of 1985. This, too, is European theology which has been emancipated by the Enlightenment but which is certainly not alienated from a non-liberated world. And it is of some significance that Sobrino deals with Pannenburg, but not Moltmann, whose theology has developed with his social and political experiences, for example being a prisoner of war in the 1940s, and being involved with Marxist activists in the ferment of the late 1960s. In Europe there is no one theology, nor do these theologies perform the same function. Some are no doubt ideologies of the ruling class. Some are not. But we must press on to see whether Sobrino is able to face the question which should be inescapable for anyone who uses Marx, namely whether liberation theology is also an ideology of the ruling class.

At this point Sobrino turns to liberation theology. Having demonstrated beyond all reasonable doubt that European theology is an ideology with its roots in the tradition of Kant, he now turns with relief to that third world figure who owned nothing to Kant, namely Karl Marx. An intriguing scenario, in view of the fact that Marx was a disciple of Hegel, who in turn was deeply critical of Kant. But there is no mystery. In the best tradition of inversion, Sobrino did not begin from a careful analysis of the history of European theology before drawing his conclusion. Rather he begins from Marx's Eleventh Thesis on Feuerbach, which divides the world. If there are some people who merely interpret the world and some who work towards changing it, who could this be but Europeans and Latin Americans respectively? Once the roles are assigned it takes but a few flourishes in the direction of the nineteenth century to establish the point conclusively. European theologians have explained the world, in various ways, the point of Latin American theology is to change it.

Hence the epistemological break found in Latin American theology, according to Sobrino. He describes European theology as characterized by continuity, analogy, by the accommodation of religion to culture. But is this the case? Modern theology begins with Schleiermacher, who pointed to the experience of the Infinite in the finite, but nevertheless asserted the discontinuity of the two. (On this he was criticized, of course, by Hegel.) The next most important source of modern theology is Kierkegaard, whose insistence on 'the infinite qualitative distinction between God and man' was fundamental for Barth's position. This theme of contradiction is carried into the political, as exemplified by Moltmann's chilling dictum: 'Peace with God means conflict with the world.'[9] How can Sobrino maintain that the epistemological break is absent from European theology, but central to Latin American theology? By a little bit of cultural imperialism: 'a positive influence of the theology of liberation is discernible in Moltmann's book *The Crucified God*.'[10] If there is anything good in European theology, which would contradict the scheme, it must come from Latin America!

If European theology is supposd to explain the world, it has not done a very good job of it. But at the same time we may doubt whether liberation theology has changed the world. Of course brave and honest men and women in Latin America, some of them Christian, have challenged the existing order and in some instances have managed to change it to some extent. But I have already advocated humility in such matters. Is liberation theology a theology which liberates, or is it theological reflection on a liberating movement? The fact that it is reflection on a real movement does not guarantee that it is not itself an ideology. It is being radically changed in the light of experience, but it does not initially arise from that experience. In the Eleventh Thesis on Feuerbach Marx distinguishes between interpretative theories of reality which are brought to the world and those which arise out of engagement with the world. Unfortunately for Sobrino liberation theology still belongs to the former category. It is an interpretative theory which originated neither in Latin America nor in the twentieth century. In Marx's terms, no matter how it is reconstructed to express contemporary experience, that experience must be fitted in a Procrustean way within a system which is in essence pre-Enlightenment. No theology can decide where it stands in relation to reality: reality decides that in spite of all pretentious claims.

We have seen that in spite of Sobrino's claim, European theology can hardly be characterized as attempting to explain the world. But he also makes the claim that it performs a second function. At the outset he described a situation in which developments within European culture produced a crisis for theology. Now he is referring to a very different situation, one in which there is a crisis in European culture, a crisis of meaning. But just as in the earlier discussion he at once departed from his own model, so again he immediately ignores his own terms of reference. It is true that post-Enlightenment European culture has faced a crisis, or series of crises, concerning an autonomous basis for meaning and value. Feuerbach simply continued to affirm religious values while rejecting their metaphysical basis. Marx continued to affirm meaning in history while rejecting its religious basis. Nietzsche was the most consistent of the critics of religion when in face of the loss of religious faith he rejected both Christian values and also the idea of externally bestowed meaning in history. The secular culture which he predicted and in large part exemplified appeared in Europe only in the 1950s. Modern secular theology was the attempt to express theologically the experience of this new culture, and for some the experience of the death of God. Sobrino is saying that European theology has attempted to provide meaning in a situation without meaning. And this is not only true but has been good news to many. But this is not the situation which he describes. Once again everything is reduced to morality. The situation without meaning is subtly changed into the situation of injustice. European theology is therefore accused of attempting to provide meaning (i.e. justification) for an unjust situation. But this is an unworthy blurring of important distinctions. If we reverted to Segundo's example, Harvey Cox, we should have to distinguish between *The Secular City*, which attempts to disclose the religious significance of secular urban life, and *God's Revolution*, which maintains a prophetic criticism of Western social and political life. Sobrino therefore sets up another no-win situation. European theology is said to be concerned with the crisis in meaning for the subject, while Latin American theology is concerned with the crisis in reality. This is simply an assertion that European experience is not real, not compared with Latin American theology.

> European theology is trying (admittedly in goodwill) to reconcile the wretched state of the real world at the level of theological thought, but it is not trying to liberate the real world from its wretched state.[11]

Although European theology has addressed itself to experience and in some cases has been radically transformed in the process, this whole movement is simply rejected because the experience in question is not the experience of Latin America. But it will be – and to this point we shall return in Part Three.

(c) Epistemological presuppositions

In this chapter we are considering the conscious use of Marx in liberation theology. If Marx were used only peripherally to illustrate a point which could be justified on other grounds, then the implications of his work more generally could be ignored. However, when as in the case of Sobrino liberation theology is characterized by its relationship to Marx, then the situation is different. He specifically refers to the Eleventh Thesis on Feuerbach as he accuses European theology of being an ideology of the ruling class. It is not difficult to show that this is not true of all European theology, especially in the modern period. But that is not the issue for our specific study. Any theologian who wishes to make use of Marx, especially in the context of ideology, must surely begin by demonstrating why it is that his own theology escapes Marx's general condemnation of all theology as ideology. Nor can this criticism be pushed aside simply by saying that liberation theology takes the side of the poor, or even that it is done by theologians who share the life of the poor. Marx's criticism is more fundamental that that: theology by its nature as theology is ideology. Once again we find that Marx's first and third criticisms are accepted, on the grounds that liberation theology does not seek reconciliation with injustice, nor does it seek to promote the interests of the ruling class as an in-house ideology. But equally there is no consideration of Marx's second criticism, that theology by its nature is an inversion of reality. Sobrino writes as if Marx were unknown in Europe, yet ironically it

195

is European theology which has addressed this second criticism, while Latin American theology has simply ignored it.

A writer who comes close to considering the issue is the Brazilian theologian, Clodovis Boff. In 1976 he defended his doctoral dissertation in Louvain. It has since been published under the title *Theology and Praxis: Epistemological Foundations*. It reflects the need at that time to stop and consider important methodological questions which the early contributors to liberation theology could not undertake as they developed the field. Adolphe Gesché was Boff's dissertation supervisor, and makes the following observation about the work.

> Clodovis Boff's book is not a theology of liberation, or a political theology, or a theology of praxis. It is a critical reflection bearing on the epistemological *presuppositions* in terms of which any such theology, present or future, will indeed be *theology* – and not, for example, ideology or exhortation.[12]

As an extensive discussion of the relationship of theology and politics it presents a critique of other forms of theology, including European political theology, uncovering their assumptions and presuppositions. In the process the correct relationship emerges; not surprisingly it is close to the approach of liberation theology.

Sobrino, in the essay I have just discussed, brings forward a further point to distinguish European and Latin American theologies. The former is related to philosophy, the latter to the social sciences. European theology responds to the challenges of philosophy, but also uses the categories of various philosophical systems to elaborate its own position. Thus it offers an interpretation of the world which is largely incorrigible by actual experience. This is Sobrino's view, which seems to be in some respects contradicted by the fact that the philosophies used have been – when first appropriated – the most comprehensive, secular, non-Christian compendia of human knowledge, for example Plato and Aristotle in the ancient world, Hegel, Whitehead and Heidegger in the modern period. However that may be, Sobrino contrasts this with the use which Latin American theology makes of the social sciences. This corresponds to his view that liberation theology does not wish to interpret the world, but to change it. In order to change the real world it is necessary to understand the nature of existing relations, the forces which create and maintain them, and the processes by which they might be challenged and changed. It is often said that there are more economic theories than economists, and there are certainly many conflicting positions located in what is loosely referred to as the social sciences. The Adam Smith Institute, the neo-liberal think-tank, lies untapped by Latin American theologians, but of course

Marx is constantly used. Indeed although Boff's work is to track down and drag out into the glare of critical scrutiny all theological presuppositions and assumptions, he simply presupposes Marx's social theories without further comment. He is, however, critical of those who polarize Marx's distinction between interpretation and action. As we saw in Part One, Marx was certainly not recommending praxis divorced from theory. Boff condemns such 'theoricide'.[13]

Boff, unlike Segundo or Sobrino, seems to be aware that to seek to relate theology to social reality through the use of Marx's philosophy raises the question of Marx's criticism of theology. We therefore approach the section on 'Marx's Critique of Theology' with anticipation: here is a liberation theologian actually addressing the issue. But no, the section, which occupies two pages in a work some four-hundred pages, is highly circumscribed. Boff declares that he will restrict his discussion to Marx's criticism of the Hegelian theologians Bruno Bauer and David Strauss. Hence in a book about presuppositions he presupposes Marx and then immediately presupposes that Marx was only criticizing one kind of theology. Thus Boff is not after all facing the force of Marx's critique of all theology: he is simply assuming that liberation theology escapes censure.

If we were to adopt Sobrino's terms here, Boff is assuming that Marx's criticism applies to those theological systems which are related to philosophy. They are in double jeopardy, since they are alienated intellectual constructions which function as ideologies when they interpret and thus justify an alienated world. Boff presents Marx's criticism as the exposing and reversal of such inversion. Thus as we saw in Chapter 3, 'the criticism of theology is transformed into the criticism of politics'. Sacred perspectives are replaced by secular perspectives. Only in this way can actual problems be addressed, and real change effected. Boff also refers to the 'de-theologizing' process adopted by Marx in his essay 'On the Jewish Question'. He transforms the religious issue into a secular issue. Boff's conclusion to this all too brief discussion of a historical debate is that *since Marx it is no longer permissible to theologize as before with regard to social problems*.[14] But this conclusion does not at all follow from the passages cited. If Marx has transformed all theological issues into non-theological issues, what is the place and role of theology? Boff's position is that 'theology is theology of the nontheological'.[15] But far from clarifying the relationship, this begs further questions. On closer inspection Marx does not transform all theological issues into non-theological issues. He regains secular control of some issues, so that they can be properly understood and dealt with. But other theological issues are simply declared to be non-issues, the 'products of men's minds'. When Marx is finished, it is quite clear what a non-theological issue is, but what is a theological issue? Boff is clear that there must be a difference between theology and the social sciences, but the manner in which he alludes to the difference is not at all reassuring.

> In sum: the text of a theological reading with respect to the political is prepared and furnished by the sciences of the social. Theology receives its text from these sciences, and practices upon it a reading in conformity with its own proper code, in such a way as to extract from it a characteristically, properly, theological meaning. Consequently, it must be denied that the sociological and the theological subsist in the same continuum. A qualitative transition is at play, which may be called an *epistemological breach* or rupture.[16]

Here we are confronted with further presuppositions. There is a rather touching assumption that social analyses will provide social facts, but apart from that, these facts are to be reviewed now within theology's 'own proper code'. Since such a code comes neither from the base nor the superstructure, its origins must be a matter of suspicion – in a Marxist sense. Likewise there are presuppositions lurking in the identification of 'a qualitative transition' between sociology and theology. On what non-metaphysical grounds can it be claimed that these disciplines do not 'subsist in the same continuum'? This is a very different epistemological break from the one encountered in Sobrino. Although the theological view of the non-theological has changed, there is no evidence that the presuppositions of theology itself have been challenged by Marx's critique. Marx's criticism of theology does not apply simply to Hegelian theology, but to all theology.

Boff, as we have just noted, takes a tough line with regard to other people's theologies: 'Since Marx it is no longer permissible to theologize as before with regard to social problems.' But apparently his own theology is protected against Marx. Theology is certainly not part of the mode of production, and yet 'it cannot allow itself to be measured by the yardstick of Marxism and accept the place Marxism assigns to it, a place in the superstructure'.[17] Boff seems perfectly clear on where the line is to be drawn between the acceptable scientific Marx and the unacceptable totalitarian, atheistic Marx. With regard to Marxism, theology 'is obligated to distinguish between its *hypothetico-scientific* aspect (historical materialism), which theology is bound to respect, and its *philosophico-metaphysical* aspect (dialectical materialism), which theology can only criticize and reject'.[18] And yet the relationship between base and superstructure is fundamental to Marx's historical materialism, whether or not one goes on to accept his account of successive epochs. Relevant here is his reversal of Fernando Belo's project, *A Materialist Reading of The Gospel of Mark*. Boff, in contrast, would prefer 'a Markan reading of Marx'.[19] He would like theology to be a protected area, beyond the competence of Marxism to comment. But this is to ignore the fact that theology is itself a social issue.

(d) Unavoidable historical mediation

It is difficult to avoid the impression that some liberation theologians relish the fact that their use of Marx will be shocking to many in the churches, and offensive to those concerned with traditional ways and good order. The more abrasive and uncritical the use of Marx, the better. Those who are offended are by that very fact identified as reactionaries. Nothing could be further from the position of the Argentinian Methodist theologian José Míguez Bonino. He is prepared to defend the use of Marx, but he is sensitive to the criticism that liberation theologians have become Marxist Christians, and like the German Christians before them have allowed the faith to be subverted by an alien ideology. He notes that the 'theology of liberation has not yet become sufficiently aware of the weight of this risk and consequently has not yet developed adequate safeguards against it'.[20] Nevertheless Marx has been of fundamental importance in the development of the new theology. If liberation theologians are saying things which are different from the tradition it is not because they have replaced Christian dogmas with Marxist dogmas. Their relationship to the truth has changed. And if they now find that 'the knowledge is disclosed in the doing',[21] then this was the constant theme of both Old and New Testaments long before it emerged as Marx's epistemology. Their theology arises from the struggle to be obedient. Marx's contribution has not been to the content of theology, but to the sociology of knowledge which has encouraged them to suspect that European Christianity does not represent absolute truth, but took the shape it did because of its own interests.

If the epistemology has changed, under the influence of Marx, so too has the approach to verifiability. Previously truth was regarded as absolute and timeless. It could therefore be verified through the use of the most contemporary form of philosophy. But now verification comes through praxis. God makes himself known through a series of historical actions, and as recounted in the Bible these are events of economic and political as well as moral significance. The truth of Christianity is confirmed in the economic and political sphere, and in decided how to act, Marx's analysis has proved invaluable. The practical significance of this is, for example, 'that a position taken at one point in history may acquire in a different setting an ideological connotation'.[22] The fact that it now serves an ideological interest may well be disguised from those holding the position. It is along these and similar lines that Bonino distinguishes Christianity from Marxism and justifies the use of Marx.

> Our assumption of Marxism has nothing to do with a supposedly abstract or eternal theory or with dogmatic formulae – a view which is not absent in certain Marxist circles – but with a scientific analysis and a number of verifiable hypotheses in relation to conditions obtaining in certain historical moments and places and which, properly modified, corrected, and supplemented, provide an adequate means to grasp our own historical situation . . . [23]

Bonino recognizes the sincerity of those who feel that they cannot use Marx at all, but he finds that without its rigorous, scientific analysis such people end up with merely ethical guidelines which are inevitably reformist. At the other extreme there are some who embrace Marxism in its ideological form 'with a sort of religious fervor'. They do indeed surrender the historical content of the faith. But Bonino can accept Marxist analysis within the limits indicated. It arose in historical circumstances, and it too has to be corrected and developed in the light of praxis. 'But it seems to many of us that it has proved, and still proves to be, the best instrument available for an effective and rational realization of human possibilities in historical life.'[24] It is 'the *unavoidable historical mediation* of Christian obedience'.[25]

Bonino goes on to discuss the importance of Marx's analysis of class struggle, and its relationship to the biblical teaching on 'the poor'. An issue closely related to this is ecclesiology and the question of the true church. There is a review of Marx's position on revolutionary violence, and the institutionalized violence of the state. This is followed by a discussion of the eschatological and utopian aspects of Marx's philosophy and their relationship to the Kingdom. There is also an exploration of the meaning of salvation in relation to liberation. However, it is not my purpose to expound Bonino's position in detail but to examine the extent to which he deals with Marx's critique of religion. We must therefore go on to enquire where the criticism of religion lies in Bonino's division between the scientific analysis and the metaphysical hypothesis.

Those who have worked with (non-dogmatic) Marxists in specific situations may well have experienced a disconcerting reversal. Marxists have inherited a method, a point of view, a perspective, an explanatory ideology, and they are free to act through it – and upon it. Christians in the same situation might well adopt much of the scientific method and explanatory ideology, but they also have an inheritance. 'For freedom Christ has set us free', says Paul,[26] but the question is whether the Christian religion has not become a new bondage or constraint. Yet this point does not occur to Bonino, or to any of the other liberation theologians. We have already noted that when it comes to aspects of the tradition he can raise the possibility 'that a position taken in one point in history may acquire in a different setting an ideological connotation'. But anyone who is using Marx's scientific analysis must surely come to terms with the fact that it includes the judgment that whatever function Christianity originally performed within Palestine or the Roman Empire, religion is inherently ideological. Nor can the criticism of religion be relegated to the metaphysical hypothesis of historical materialism. Bonino details the elements in Marx's analysis which are vital to Christian praxis. They are 'the social (collective) appropriation of the means of production, the suppression of a classist society, the de-alienation of work, the suppression of a slave consciousness, and the reinstallation of man as an agent of his own history'.[27] Yet these are the very forms of secular criticism which, as we saw in Part One, are raised up on the foundation of Marx's criticism of religion. The criticism of religion is the premise of each of these subsequent elements in his analysis. And let us be quite clear that this particular criticism of religion, the premise of all other forms of criticism, is Marx's second criticism, his ontological criticism, not his moral or ideological criticisms. Bonino is on record as basing Christian praxis on Marx's critical social philosophy, yet he ignores the premise of that philosophy – the criticism of religion as a reversal of reality, as inherently ideological. Every social institution can expect to bear the full weight of Marxist analysis, except religion, the very institution with which Marx began his philosophy and without which it could not have been developed.

9

Marxist Liberation Theology

(a) Faith and dialectics

So far I have examined the work of liberation theologians who have been influenced by Marx, or who have consciously made use of Marx in a selective way. I have observed that it is surprising that none of them has felt it necessary to deal with the implications of Marx's second, ontological, criticism of religion. Although implausible, it would still be possible to argue that since Marx is more illustrative than inherent in their work this is not crucial. I proceed now to writers whose relation to Marx is even closer. In Chapter 5 I made a distinction between those who merely use Marx's critical philosophy for the purposes of social analysis, and those who accept his ideology of historical materialism. In this chapter the liberation theologians whose work I shall examine begin from premises taken from Marx without which their entire positions could not have been developed and could not be sustained. They may use Marx inconsistently, but they all accept historical materialism in some form. Although their positions are distinctive they belong together, since in contrast to those we have already discussed the balance has shifted. In this chapter I shall be dealing not with liberation theology which makes use of Marx, but with Marxism expressed in a theological mode. My immediate interest it not to evaluate this change of emphasis, but rather to point out that surely no one this committed to Marx's philosophy could afford to ignore his criticism of religion, especially his ontological criticism.

Few Western theologians use Marx's philosophy in their work. It is not just that it would be improper, or would compromise the theologian's image amongst his or her social peers. On the contrary, it might be thought rather daring to be seen to take a swipe at this dead dog. At most, Marx might be mentioned in passing to illustrate a point

202

which could have been justified on other grounds. Or with a Pavlovian reaction, any chance use of words such as 'opiate' or 'materialism' could suddenly produce Marx's name on the page or screen. By contrast I have been examining the works of Latin American theologians whose positions actually depend on their conscious use of Marx's philosophy. Where a European theologian might prefer to draw an essentially Marxist conclusion without reference to Marx, lest the point be rejected simply by association with his name, Latin American theologians, at least liberation theologians, seem to expect that associating their positions with Marxist analysis will somehow gain them immediate support.

In most instances a crude word-count of the occurrence of Marx's name would distinguish European and Latin American theologians. Yet in a small number of cases this approach would be quite misleading. A few theologians have so internalized Marx's philosophy that for them it is no longer necessary to mention him at each stage. Thus José Porfirio Miranda begins his study of *Marx and the Bible* with the assurance that it is not his intention 'to find parallels between the Bible and Marx, but rather simply to understand the Bible'.[1] A word count would show that Bultmann and von Rad are each referred to over fifty times, while in the main exegetical chapters Marx is mentioned only ten times. Miranda was born in Mexico and studied theology and economics in Frankfurt. Because of his experience in Christian social action with working class groups he undertook further study in two areas. One was Marxism, and as we shall later see, he is very well read indeed in this area. But significantly he also pursued further studies at the Biblical Institute in Rome. Although familiar with contemporary critical biblical scholarship, he now reads the Bible from a perspective opened up by Marx.

Miranda's use of Marx is, if anything, more consistent in this sense than that of the theologians we have already discussed. We might present it in three phases. The first phase is his use of Marx's analysis of social and economic relations. The sub-title of *Marx and the Bible* is 'A critique of the philosophy of oppression'. He identifies capitalism with exploitation and oppression, but that is because it is a specific form of a philosophy which has been the basis of European society since the great days of ancient Greece. Behind modern attitudes of scientific research, technological control, entrepreneurial attack and private interest lies a philosophy which by its nature dehumanizes and oppresses. Miranda's starting point is therefore Marx's First Thesis on Feuerbach.

The chief defect of all previous materialism (that of Feuerbach included) is that things (*Gegenstand*), reality, sensuousness are conceived only in the form of the *object, or of contemplation*, but not as *sensuous human activity, practice*, not subjectively.

Marx and the Bible begins with the rejection of private ownership of the means of production, not simply because of its abuses, but as such and as a basis for society. And yet Miranda considers that Marxism is in danger of underestimating Marx's real discovery.

> But if Marxism does not recognize that capitalism is the consummation and the deepening of the oppression which was inherent to human civilization since biblical times, then it is denying dialectics and attributing the birth of capitalism to exterior causes, exactly as metaphysics and mechanistic humanism would do it.[2]

In this joining of faith and dialectics Miranda thus passes from the first to the second phase of his own development.

In this second phase Marx is neither accepted nor rejected. What could he be but superseded? Capitalism is understood neither as a chance development nor a more efficient stage in an economic sequence. It is the historical form, expression or manifestation of an underlying philosophy which is the subject of the Bible itself. It is for this reason that although Miranda could not have formed his perspective on the Bible without Marx, once he has formed it, Marx is no longer the subject of his study. The main chapters of the book expound the Bible from this new perspective. The author appeals to his readers to judge whether this approach uncovers the true message of the Bible. He neither calls on us to accept Marx, nor does he advocate his view by appealing to the authority of Marx: 'I am not reducing the Bible to Marx nor Marx to the Bible.'[3] Marx disappears from the discussion: he is not competent to participate. The use of Marx is more deeply embedded in the argument than could be judged simply from the incidence of references to him.

From his new perspective Miranda understands the second commandment in a particular sense. The philosophy which lies behind capitalism, and which lies at the heart of European civilization, is an objectifying approach to the self, to others, to the world – and to God. The philosophy of oppression is the philosophy which makes an object, an image out of God. The God who is revealed in the commandments is set aside.

> And man has many resources at his disposal to cause this command to come to an end. He need only objectify God in some way. At that moment God is no longer God. Man has made him into an idol; God no longer commands man.[4]

Marx need no longer be mentioned, but Miranda is following his lead as he claims that the biblical position is more radical than the traditional alternatives. 'The antithesis between materialism and idealism is totally irrelevant in the matter, for both philosophies are constructed by prescinding from my concrete existence.'[5]

It is not my purpose to provide an exposition of Miranda's work, but rather to discover how a theologian who consciously uses Marx deals with his various criticisms of religion. However, we might take time to briefly see how this use of Marx affects Miranda's reading of the Bible.

Miranda is saying that Marx, at the end of a long process of European history, has discovered that the characteristic features of capitalism lead to alienation from reality. But he is claiming that the position towards which Marx struggles was already central to the Bible even before European civilization began. In the European intellectual tradition the existence of God can be debated, the attributes of God established and the law of God proclaimed in an objective way. Through a withdrawal into the interior life God can be encountered in a subjective way. But according to Miranda these are the ways to the gods, or images: the Bible declares that Yahweh cannot be approached by these routes. Jeremiah proclaims the word of God to the new king, challenging him with the record of Josiah, his father.

> Did not your father eat and drink
> and do justice and righteousness?
> Then it was well with him.
> He judged the cause of the poor and needy;
> then it was well
> Is not this to know me?
> says the Lord.[6]

Knowledge of God comes through establishing justice; God is to be sought in defending the needy. As Miranda summarizes it, 'To know Yahweh is to achieve justice for the poor.'[7] Knowledge of God does not come through a 'religious' sphere, through religious actions, intentions or attitudes. The radical nature of the divine transcendence is not that God exists in another ontological dimension inaccessible to human beings, but that God cannot be objectified, cannot be approached except through the quest for justice.

Nor does Miranda avoid the implications of radical transcendence for the whole complex liturgical tradition. He refers to the anti-cultic denunciations found in the eighth-century prophets, of which the following passage from Amos is typical.

I hate, I despise your feasts
and I take no delight in your solemn assemblies.
Even though you offer me your burnt offerings
and cereal offerings
I will not accept them,
and the peace offerings of your fatted beasts
I will not look upon.
Take away from me the noise of your songs;
to the melody of your harps I will not listen.
But let justice roll down like waters,
and righteousness like an everflowing stream.[8]

These are not alternative routes to God, cultic worship or social justice. It is not a matter of individual disposition, whether we seek God by one route or the other. Worse than that, the prophets denounce any attempt to find God by the cultic route. Only an idol or image can be approached in this way. *'The question is not whether someone is seeking God or not, but whether he is seeking him where God himself said that he is.'*[9] Nothing could be further from the Western philosophical tradition which discusses the possible existence of God beyond the world, or the mystical tradition which seeks God apart from the world.

Nor can a wedge be driven between the tradition of the prophets and the teaching of Jesus and the practice of the early church. In answer to the question put by the lawyer Jesus summarizes the basis of 'all the law and the prophets'.[10] The first of the great commandments of Jesus is taken from Deuteronomy 6.5: 'And you shall love the Lord your God with all your heart, and with all your soul, and with all your might.' The second great commandment is from Leviticus 19.18: 'You shall love your neighbour as yourself.' But these are not the alternative routes again. 'No one has ever seen God; if we love one another, God abides in us and his love is perfected in us.'[11] The same commandment lies behind the celebration of the Lord's Supper. It can be called by many religious names which allow it to be interpreted within the Western ontological tradition, but Paul is quite clear that if it is not an occasion in which people are united in love with their neighbours, then it is not of God, and they 'come together to be condemned'.[12]

I have taken time to illustrate Miranda's reading of the Bible, since it arises from a perspective derived in the first instance from Marx. Marx is not mentioned, nor need he be. Yet in two important respects his influence is clear. The first is ontological, and arises from Marx's First Thesis on Feuerbach, as we have seen. Marx was critical of Hegelian idealism and some forms of materialism. Miranda, as already quoted, is consistently critical of idealism and materialism because they both arise from a common European ontological tradition which stands in contrast to the biblical tradition, what he calls 'the Western absolutization of the ontological point of view'.[13] For Miranda, the biblical position is more fundamental and consistently radical than Marx's. He does not elaborate the point, but it may be that his position could be described by drawing a parallel between his rejection of idealism and materialism and his rejection of alienated verticalism and reductionist horizontalism.

The second influence of Marx is epistemological. Miranda might well have quoted the Second Thesis on Feuerbach.

> The question whether objective truth can be attributed to human thinking is not a question of theory, but is a *practical question*. Man must prove the truth, i.e., the reality and power, the this-worldliness of his thinking in practice. The dispute over the reality or non-reality of thinking which is isolated from practice is a purely *scholastic* question.

Miranda has applied this to the knowledge of God. The philosophical and cultic approaches do not stand as alternatives to the ethical. In theological courses pride of place has gone to the rigorously demanding disciplines of philosophy of religion and dogmatics. Ethics has been practical theology, and therefore somehow compromised. But Miranda follows Marx here in his interpretation of the Bible. The knowledge of God can be reached only through the commitment to justice. Any other 'knowledge' is simply scholastic, in the pejorative sense.

With this we enter the third phase of Miranda's development. Having begun with Marx, and superseded Marx, he finally defends Marx. This might seem strange, since his position is now independent of Marx, and more consistently radical. We might approach this matter by recalling that when Jesus was questioned by his opponents he linked his mission to that of John the Baptist. 'Was the baptism of John from heaven or from men?'[14] The ministry of Jesus was not identical with that of John, but the reasons which prevented some people from responding to the preaching of John would prevent them from hearing Jesus. I intend no offence in using this as a point of entry into Miranda's defence of Marx. In fact it is not so much a defence of Marx as a proclamation of communism. In what he calls his 'manifesto', entitled *Communism in the Bible*, Miranda says that a Christian claim to be anti-communist 'without doubt constitutes the greatest scandal of our century'.[15] In a century which tragically has not been short of 'scandals' this is an extreme position, but Miranda makes the point because it is in his view fundamental to understanding the Bible, and responding to it. Once again we see that Marx only recalls Christians to their biblical roots. Allow me to illustrate.

I have always been fascinated by the debate about ecclesiastical organization, or rather the 'interests' which are disguised behind it. It is a contrast of absolute and relative. On the one hand there is the absolute claim that whatever form of organization was adopted in the early church is binding on the church subsequently. On the other hand there is the relativity of our historical sources for the period in which bishops, presbyters and deacons emerged. Church leaders are therefore prepared to make absolute claims on behalf of relative knowledge. Why should that be? What interests are being defended? The differences between episcopalians and presbyterians are not nearly as important as what they have in common in accepting this procedure. But what is more fascinating is the juxtaposition of another absolute and relative. This is the case of what Troeltsch called the 'primitive Christianity of the Book of Acts' and Lenin referred to as 'primitive Christianity with its democratic revolutionary spirit'.[16] In this case the absolute refers to our historical knowledge (in so far as there can be such a thing) and the relative refers to the relative indifference which church leaders and scholars have displayed towards the phenomenon.[17]

> And all who believed were together and had all things in common; and they sold their possessions and goods and distributed them to all, as any had need.[18]

This is one of the first decisions which the apostles took when they had to start taking initiatives after the ascension of Jesus. It clearly corresponds both to their experience of living in community with Jesus during his ministry, and to his teaching on the Kingdom of God. Possessed by the Spirit of God, 'no one said that any of the things which he possessed was his own, but they had everything in common'.[19] Why should the teaching and example of the apostles, taken to be so authoritive in other matters, but set aside by the churches without any qualms or questions? What interests are served by this conspiracy of silence?

These thoughts might provide a context in which to understand Miranda's suspicion of those who reject communism for the sake of Christianity.

> In fact, the definition Marx borrowed from Louis Blanc, 'From each one according to his capacities, to each one according to his needs', is inspired by, if not directly copied from, Luke's formulation eighteen centuries earlier. There is no clearer demonstration of the brainwashing to which the establishment keeps us subjected than the

officially promulgated conception of Christianity as anti-communist.[20]

As we saw in Chapter 1, Marx was influenced by biblical religion at a fundamental level. Why should communism be given over to a movement with its origins in the nineteenth century, especially if this means ignoring its presence in the New Testament?

Is communism to be attributed to Marx, so that Jesus and Christianity stand on the opposite side? The danger here is two-fold. In the first place this once again fails to bring out the fact that the Bible is more radical than Marx. Communism comes originally from the Bible, long before Marx. But secondly, there are the motives and interests of those who wish to defend Christianity against communism. Is it really because they wish to defend true Christianity, or is it because they truly wish to defend their own interests? In the post-World War II era we have had many instances in Africa and in Latin America of oppressive, totalitarian, capitalist regimes which represent themselves as defenders of Christianity, against communism. Miranda is therefore suspicious of those who wish to discredit and denounce Marx in the name of supporting and promoting Christian values. Just as the question of the existence of God has no place in the epistemology of the Bible, so the enemy is not atheism but injustice. Miranda does not defend Marx in order to be thought 'modern' or 'fashionable'. Neither he nor those with whom he works have any interest in this direction. 'In the name of my Latin American brothers and sisters I here formally declare that we are shameless conservatives.'[21] Others have sought to conform Christianity to the interests of the ruling class, but his concern is simply to understand and proclaim the message of salvation in Jesus Christ, a message which cannot be rarified into something narrowly spiritual: 'For I was hungry and you gave me food, I was thirsty and you gave me drink, I was a stranger and you welcomed me.'[22] For Miranda, Marx becomes something of a stalking horse or even litmus test. Those who violently reject Marx are likely to reject the message that God can only be found in seeking justice for the poor.

For Miranda there are too many convergencies between Marx and the Bible to be ignored.

This leads us to suspect that between faith and dialectical thinking there is a common denominator considerably more serious than western positivistic scientists disparagingly are accustomed to believe, those who claim to discredit authentic Marxism by saying that it is not science but faith. Both faith and dialectical thinking (of Hegel and Marx) accuse the 'wisdom of the world' of total superficiality, indeed of blindness, in its knowledge of reality.[23]

My purpose is not to expound Miranda's position but to illustrate his use of Marx in the development of a new (or very old) perspective on the Bible. Neither in *Marx and the Bible* nor in *Communism in the Bible* does he address himself to Marx's criticisms of religion. This could be misleading, since it is actually Marx's criticism of Western ontology and epistemology which leads him to his reinterpretation of the Bible. This is of particular interest to us, for I have maintained that liberation theologians have entirely ignored Marx's ontological criticism of religion. Since Miranda accepts Marx's general critique of Western ontology, it would have been interesting to see him deal with its application to religion. His concern is with regaining the fundamental understanding of the Bible. But how would this be applied to Christianity in the modern world? The ambiguity remains, since Miranda sees himself among the liberation theologians, and their 'shameless conservatism' has not yet taken onboard Marx's criticism.

Although, as we have seen, Miranda can distance himself from Marx, he comes close to accepting something which approximates to a biblical form of historical materialism. Since God is known only in justice, his wrath can be known in injustice. This is the theme of the curse of Adam in Genesis 3.17, and Romans 1 in which God gives men up to their wickedness.

> But what God's intervention does is precisely to set in motion the immanent horizontal causality of human history itself. What the biblical authors want to highlight is precisely the immanence of this mechanism, the causal link intrinsic to history, by which a certain type of event brings certain other types with it.[24]

We have heard a great deal from biblical scholars this century about salvation history. They seem reluctant to show how this history continues after the closure of the New Testament canon. Miranda not only indicates how salvation history continues but preserves its dialectic by presenting us with something which might be called a history of salvation and damnation.

(b)   Religious capitalism

My second example is that of the Brazilian Franciscan, Leonardo Boff (brother of Clodovis Boff, whose work was discussed in Chapter 8). There is a *prima facie* case for viewing him as a Marxist liberation theologian, since that was the basis on which he was silenced by The Sacred Congregation for the Doctrine of the Faith, a body previously known as The Inquisition. Just as I have not attempted a simple exposition of liberation theology, so now I shall not rehearse the controversy over the silencing of Leonardo Boff. The background details are now in the public domain.[25] September 1984 saw the publication of an 'Instruction on Certain Aspects of the "Theology of Liberation" '. It had been signed in Rome on 6 August by Cardinal Joseph Ratzinger and Archbishop Alberto Bovone, respectively prefect and secretary of the Congregation for the Doctrine of the Faith, and approved by the Pope. The authors recognized the importance of the theme of liberation in contemporary theology, and promised to treat it more fully and positively in a subsequent document.[26]

> The immediate purpose of the document was more limited and negative: to draw the attention of pastors, theologians, and all the faithful to the deviations, and risks of deviation, damaging to the faith and to Christian living, that are brought about by certain forms of liberation theology, which use, in an insufficiently critical manner, concepts borrowed from various currents of Marxist thought.[27]

From our study so far it will be clear that it is not possible to generalize about the use of Marxist analysis by liberation theologians. The implication is that Latin American theologians have fallen into an unconsidered use of Marx. This is clearly not the case, and Segundo responded with a very detailed analysis and criticism of the Instruction.[28]

Although he is not mentioned by name, it is generally agreed that the immediate subject of criticism was Leonardo Boff. In May 1984 Boff received a letter from Cardinal Ratzinger summoning him to Rome to answer questions concerning his book *Church, Charism and Power*, first published in Portuguese in 1981. He arrived in Rome on the 2nd September, and on the following day, by what has been described as complete coincidence, the Instruction was published. Since my purpose is not simple exposition, Ratzinger's criticisms of liberation theology in general, or Boff in particular, need not detain us. Ratzinger criticized liberation theology for being too Marxist. My criticism has been that it is not Marxist enough. Or rather that liberation theology, far from using Marx's philosophy 'in an insufficiently critical manner', has not cared or dared to apply it in a sufficiently careful and comprehensive manner.

Although there have been some very fine monographs on liberation theology, it is difficult to resist the conclusion that in some cases publishers have said to famous and best-selling authors, 'Surely you must have something that we could publish!' *Church, Charism and Power* was not so much written as thrown together, and that by someone whose aim was suspect. While there are chapters which deal with basic ecclesial communities, other occasional papers which have been included have nothing to do with liberation theology. And finally there is at least one chapter which looks to have come from Boff's doctoral dissertation written in München a decade earlier. This now seems ironic, since the work, entitled 'The Church as Sacrament in the Horizon of World Experience', was submitted in 1971 to none other than Professor Joseph Ratzinger, who judged it to be outstanding.[29]

Marx is hardly mentioned in the whole book and there are long passages and even chapters which are entirely uncontroversial. At first sight it is not easy to see why it should have aroused such antagonism. And yet the answer is there in the sub-title: 'Liberation Theology and the Institutional Church'. Boff was silenced not for what he said in favour of Marx, but on account of his outspoken criticism of the Roman hierarchy. And yet if his work is not consistently Marxist, there is a specific area in which he accepts the fundamental premise of historical materialism.

As usual I shall not attempt to expound Boff's work in detail; rather, I shall indicate where he bases his position on Marx and examine the extent to which he addresses himself to Marx's criticisms of religion. Boff is a well-trained and well-read scholar; his works are replete with references to Latin American literature and to European sources, both contemporary and historical. Marx is hardly ever mentioned, or quoted. Yet I can illustrate five of Marx's premises which are fundamental to *Church, Charism and Power*.

The first is class division. Although this is a widely used model we should remember that it is not characteristic of other ideologies, such as liberalism or fascism. It is not welcomed by the Roman hierarchy, in whose view the church transcends all social division. Many traditional discussions of the church have been highly idealized theological treatises which have paid little attention to the actual situation of the church. But the church as an institution exists in a class society, and by intention or default is located on one side or the other. Since the time of Constantine (Boff prefers Theodosius) the hierarchy, with honourable exceptions – which were just that – has taken the side of the ruling class. The laity have identified with their own social classes, and in modern Europe the working class has often been alienated from the church altogether. The church has prided itself in being above such social divisions, but as we have already observed, to be even-handed in an unequal society is to take the side of the powerful.

The second premise taken from Marx is that social being determines consciousness. The social location of the church, at least the hierarchy who define and control its life, is within the ruling class, and that in turn determines not only the outlook of the hierarchy, but the form and structure of the institution. Hierarchical government was borrowed from the very efficient example of the Roman empire. But as a political structure it was intended to ensure that power was transmitted one way, from top to bottom, and that control of ideas and actions was exercised according to patterns established without consultation. By taking over a system of administration explicitly established to perform these functions the church therefore became such an institution itself: social being determined consciousness.

> The faithful in the church occupy objectively different social positions according to their social class. They perceive reality in a way that corresponds to their social condition, and so they interpret and live the gospel message out of the needs, interests, and behaviour of their particular class.[30]

With this mention of interest we pass to the third premise borrowed from Marx, namely the relationship between ideology and interest. It is the intention of the ruling class to promote its ideas, its picture of the world and social relations. In order for this picture to seem natural and therefore beyond question the ruling class enlists the aid of religion. This would not be possible if religion were prophetically critical of the picture, but since the hierarchy have already been located within the ruling class they are more likely to identify with the interests of that class. And as we have seen, this is not simply opportunism or cynicism – at least not entirely – since the consciousness of the hierarchy has been determined by their social being, which is shared with the ruling class.

If Boff had taken over only these Marxist premises, then his work would have been no more critical than that of other liberation theologians. But he went on to adopt further premises which arguably indicate an acceptance of historical materialism.

In the period immediately after Vatican II there were many strident criticisms of the church by priests, some of them theological teachers. The denunciations were essentially negative, often a last communication prior to leaving the priesthood and the church. Did they fall or were they pushed? No doubt the Curia would bear up rather well in face of a decision by Leonardo Boff to leave the church, but that is not his intention. He describes himself as 'loyally disobedient'.[31] But unlike the isolated criticisms of the post-Vatican II period to which I have referred, Boff's criticisms arise not from a theory, but from experience. He is not contrasting the Roman church with an ideal, but with an existing reality. The basic ecclesial communities are not outside the church; they are not a new church, but a renewed church.

The phrase 'church of the poor' is used by Boff, Sobrino and others, but in the light of what has been said this expression has important ramifications. The church for the poor would be the hierarchically structured church taking up the cause of the poor in particular respects. Thus a cardinal might take the opportunity to discuss a particular matter with the state president while attending a banquet: the church acts for or on behalf of the poor. And yet although the specific issue might be resolved in the short term, this way of proceeding reinforces the existing control of society by the ruling class, reconfirms the parallel structure of the church, and provides continuing religious legitimation of the former by the latter. The poor are still absent from the feast: their lives are still manipulated even by those who wish to help them. The very act of assistance perpetuates the circumstances which oppress them. The intolerable is made tolerable. That is the negative side.

On the positive side, the church of the poor is the church which exists on the other side of the line drawn in a class society. We have already quoted Boff when he claims that the social being of the poor leads them to experience reality in a different way, and to experience and live the gospel in correspondingly different ways. Thus the church of the poor does not experience the present order of things as reasonable, natural or just. They do not assume that the interests of the church are the same as those of the rulers. When they read the Gospels they are confronted by Jesus of Nazareth, a poor man who was never incorporated by the rich and powerful. He openly criticized them and was murdered through the joint action of foreign imperialists and those nationals who had thrown in their lot with them.

When Boff criticizes what he calls Roman Catholicism, with the emphasis on Roman, he does so not because of a fine ideal which he has formed in his mind, but because he has already experienced a very different ecclesial reality. In the base communities there is no hierarchy: they are essentially democratic. The core of these groups is usually a number of families. The initiatives come from the laity, and women often have leadership roles. In the process of conscientization, as the people become more aware of their situation and its causes, there is a danger that the groups become political, or merely political. Boff is clear that just as there must be personal conversion as well as structural change, so underlying the political involvement of the groups there must be maintained the quest for perfection in the Christian life, the mystical and the liturgical.[32] Priests, religious, bishops and even cardinals have joined base communities, but without introducing the old hierarchical values and relationships. Their presence is welcome, but it does

demand a redefinition of the roles of bishop and priest while allowing for new ministries and a new style of religious life incarnated in the life of the people. The hierarchy is functional and is not an onto-logical establishment of classes of Christians.[33]

Boff began by insisting that the church must be understood as an institution located within a class society. He is critical of its traditional identification with the ruling class. This criticism is not new, but as we have seen it cannot be met simply by the hierarchical church becoming a church for or on behalf of the poor. Nevertheless it is unlikely that Boff would have become a subject of examination by The Congregation for the Doctrine of the Faith had he stopped at this point. His most abrasive criticism is not simply that the church exists within a class society, and is divided along the lines of social and economic class. Rather, his criticism is that the church is itself a class society. Whereas up till now he has been applying Marxist premises to society at large, and noting how they affect the church within that society, now he applies these and subsequent premises to the church *as* a class society.

The church is therefore a class society, in which there is a ruling class consisting of the pope, cardinals, and bishops. There is the oppressed class of the laity, with women as always subject to further domination and discrimination. There is a middle class of priests and religious whose roots are often in the oppressed class, but who have come to identify with the ruling class. Social being determines consciousness. The laity become dependent on the ruling class, indeed this becomes a virtue. Boff quotes Pius X.

> Only the college of pastors have the right and authority to lead and govern. The masses have no right or authority except that of being governed, like an obedient flock that follows the Shepherd.[34]

People become sheep. Indeed this is a source of alienation in societies in which many lay people are highly educated decision-makers. For the religious middle-class obedience is a virtue: the more arbitrary the treatment, the greater the virtue of submission. And of course the ruling class, if not in this case born to rule, soon learns to adopt the command mode.

> It is strange to see that the Church institution has developed into exactly that which Christ did not want it to be; from the will for power, hierarchies of teachers, doctors, fathers, fathers of fathers, and servants of servants have all arisen.[35]

Class society, social being, and of course the ideology and interest of the hierarchy. As we have previously noted, ideologies tend to be conservative; they are intended to preserve the interest of the ruling class against change. Change must be managed so that it is seen as a development and extension of the existing order. And if it is in flat contradiction to the tradition or the life and ministry of Jesus, that is why ideologists are employed to explain and interpret the facts. And in the final analysis there is always the fundamental law of ideology: those who suffer under it are most fervent in their defence of it. If they do not have the historical training to know better, neither do they wish their secure picture to be undermined.

If the church is itself an example of a class society, then Marx's analysis of secular society can be applied to the church. But there are two further premises which Boff takes from Marx. The first of these, in fact our fourth premise from Marx, concerns the division of labour. As we saw, Marx took this concept from Adam Smith, but he saw in it a further source of human alienation. According to Boff there is a division of labour within the church, and the present division lies at the heart of the problem. In the Preface to his book he makes this clear. 'The grassroots are asking for a new structure, a new ecclesial division of labour and of religious power.' The division of labour is not in itself a bad thing, but it becomes a source of power and injustice in society when the production of certain goods and services is artificially controlled. The situation lends itself to abuse when production is the monopoly of one group. It is not difficult to see how this model can be applied to the church.

> The bishops and priests receive all religious 'capital', produce the religious 'goods', and the people consume them. This is a monarchical model, common in the history of the Church.[36]

The Roman church which Boff is now criticizing can be characterized as operating a system of monopoly religious capitalism. The hierarchy controls the means of religious production. We might say that the church is a multinational religious corporation, with its headquarters in Rome, and branch offices throughout the world. Only those who have been licensed by Rome can produce the religious goods. For those who wish the real thing, it is obtainable only through a Roman franchise. Boff does not pursue the metaphor, but we might say also that what constitutes 'the real thing' is determined by the ideology to which I have already referred. Whether it is the real thing, and whether it is available only on the terms offered, is not questioned by those who live within the ideology. Indeed one of the reasons why Boff does not pursue the metaphor is because in this area his own position is fundamentally conservative: the head office in Rome does not realize just how effective was his ideological formation.

According to Boff, the church adopted in turn the means of production characteristic of the ancient world, the feudal world, and now the modern capitalist world. In each case, but particularly in monopoly religious capitalism, the control of the means of production gives the religious ruling class power over the rest of the church.

> The group that holds the means of symbolic production develops a corresponding theology that justifies, reinforces, and socializes its power by attributing divine origin to its historical exercise of power.[37]

The ideas of the ruling class become the ruling ideas. Arising from the division of labour the church becomes a society in which there is a gross imbalance of power. Anyone who exposes or challenges this situation, observes Boff rather prophetically, is silenced. The Inquisition, predecessor of the Congregation for the Doctrine of the Faith, was concerned with heresy, not sin. Indeed where would monopoly religious capitalism be without sin! The continuation of sin is the premise of this supply-side economy. But heresy is another matter. The heretic, literally the one who does not believe what the majority believe, raises questions about the legitimacy of the whole system: he draws attention to the taken-for-granted.

We are therefore presented with two forms of the church: one old, the other new; one totalitarian, the other democratic; one which mirrors the communities of the ancient world, the feudal world and the capitalist world, the other which has characteristics reminiscent of the Jesus community and the Pauline churches. Clearly one form must be replaced by the other: the model of the basic ecclesial communities must overtake the pyramid model of the hierarchical, monarchical church. This is an understandable but altogether naive reaction to the situation, and Boff does not fall into the trap. He began with the assertion that the church must be understood as a social institution. Only within the old idealized theological circle would it be possible to conceive of a transition from one model to another effected simply by moral judgment. On the basis of everything that has been said, the church's form, structure, theology and relationships are not determined simply by ideas or ideals. Boff would have been better placed than most to attribute the ills of the church to the incompetence, bad faith or wickedness of those who run it. How much easier the problem would have been if this were indeed the case.

> There are violations of human rights within the Church itself. These are not those abuses that are the result of individual abuses of power which are temporal in nature; we refer to those that are the result of a certain way of understanding and organizing the reality of the ecclesial structure – a somewhat permanent state of affairs.[38]

217

How simple it would have been if a few ecclesiastical civil servants could be sacked – or promoted! The implication would have been that fundamentally the structures are sound. But Boff will not take this way out. He goes out of his way to claim that 'the majority of those in authority in the Church are men of good faith, clear conscience, impeccable personal character'.[39] The conclusion is therefore that these violations of human rights occur not when the machinery is being misused, but when it is being operated properly.

How, then, can the transition be made from one model to the other, when it cannot be effected by a change of ideas? It is with this that we come to the fifth and final premise which Boff takes from Marx, a premise which seems to indicate his acceptance of the ideology of historical materialism.

In Chapter 5 I discussed Marx's materialism, and his view that since social being determines consciousness, and the mode of production determines social being, liberation can only be effected through a change in the mode of production. It might be useful to have before us again the famous passage from the Preface to the *Contribution to the Critique of Political Economy*.

> In the social production of their existence, men inevitably enter into definite relations, which are independent of their will, namely relations of production appropriate to a given stage in the development of their material forces of production. The totality of these relations of production constitutes the economic structure of society, the real foundation, on which arises a legal and political superstructure and to which correspond definite forms of social consciousness. The mode of production of material life constitutes the general process of social, political and intellectual life. It is not the consciousness of men that determines their existence, but their social existence that determines their consciousness.

It is in the light of this passage that we should read Boff's analysis of the church in a class society. The church is a social institution and must therefore be assumed to be subject to the same processes as other institutions.

> The religious-ecclesiastical realm is a part of the social realm which influences it in a dialectical manner. A premise taken here – and it is far too difficult to prove here – is that the organization of a society revolves around its means of production.[40]

And what is this premise which is too difficult to prove here? It is the premise of historical materialism, as set out in the above quotation from the Preface to the *Contribution to a Critique of Political Economy*.

The church is part of the superstructure of society, and therefore part of that sphere which cannot be fundamentally changed until the base is changed, the mode of production characteristic of the epoch. But in addition, when the church is considered as itself a class society, there can be no fundamental change in relationships or structures within it until there is a change in the mode of religious production. This is the final premise which Boff takes from Marx, that the 'organization is infrastructural, and the rest of society is built upon it'.[41] The base determines the superstructure, so that 'the means of production determines which religious-ecclesiastical activities are impossible, undesirable, intolerable, acceptable, necessary, and primary; that is, it determines the characteristics of the Church'.[42] As Marx points out in the above quotation, the relationship between base and superstructure is not brought about by human intentionality, nor are its effects what human beings intend. Boff takes over this aspect of the premise. 'Such a class structure limits and determines all activity within society, independent of an individual's intentions, and this also includes religious-ecclesiastical activity.'[43] When it is recalled that on several occasions Boff refers to the church's relations to the successive epochs of ancient, feudal and capitalist modes of production, another aspect of the Preface, we should have to say that it looks as if he espouses historical materialism in its ideological form. For this reason Cardinal Ratzinger may have been correct about Boff, intuitively, though without citing the most important evidence.

I have already suggested that Boff is a good deal less radical than first appears, and I must also say he is a good deal less consistent in his use of Marx than might appear from this study. There are several passages in which he retreats from Marx's position that the base determines the superstructure. His position is not fully developed. For example, we have been dealing with class analysis at two levels. First of all the church has been viewed as an institution within a class society. Second, the church has been examined as an example of a class society. Boff does not develop these two discussions fully in the light of the premise from the Preface. In the case of the church within a class society, if the premise is accepted, then no new form of the church could appear until the mode of production within society has changed. I noted in Part One that this entails going beyond capitalism. Since no capitalist country has become socialist it is not surprising that the church has not fundamentally changed. Boff rejects capitalism as an unbalanced basis of social relationships, and claims that 'a democratic and socialist society would seem to offer better objective conditions for a fuller expression of the Church's catholicity'.[44] He seems to believe that this is emerging in the basic ecclesial communities. But since these communities are formed among either the marginalized in the *favelas*, or the peasants in the country, it is clear that they cannot be achieving basic socialism – not in Marx's terms. Are they, contrary to Marx's explicit teaching and specific contemporary examples, going to jump over history and move directly from feudalism to socialism? And is liberation theology, the theology of this pre-industrial, pre-capitalist, pre-urban society, the next phase in world theology, or is it the theology of a previous epoch?

But there is a further point which Boff does not explore. What happens if the premise from the Preface is applied not to the church in a class society but to the church as a class society? The mode of production now is monopoly religious capitalism. Marx, following Hegel, believed that when existing institutions could no longer contain the progressive forces of the next epoch, then a new mode of production would appear, with revolutionary effect. Earlier I asked how the new form of the church could overtake the old. Certainly not at the level of ideas. The ownership and control of the means of religious production are being challenged in Latin America, but the question still remains whether for all that the mode of production is not exactly the same.

Leonardo Boff goes as far as any liberation theologian I have discussed in his acceptance of Marxist premises, and yet he does not mention Marx's criticisms of religion. There is an implicit acceptance of Marx's first and third criticisms, but as usual no mention is made of the ontological critique. We might have expected that anyone who accepted the premise of the relationship between the base and super-structure would have to justify the assumption of the integrity of an essentially conservative theology.

(c)   Halo of the revolution

Elsewhere I have examined in some detail the criticisms of Boff's *Church, Charism and Power* made in Cardinal Ratzinger's 'Instruction on Certain Aspects of the "Theology of Liberation" '.[45] Even by 1984 it was impossible to suppress the theology of liberation. It was not the product of a few mad monks or unfrocked priests. Given its support among the Latin American hierarchy, there was no alternative but to adopt the Vatican fall-back position of incorporation. If the theme of liberation cannot be eliminated, then it must be espoused. Liberation did you say, we speak of little else in Rome. New? On the contrary, it has been central to the history of Catholic theology, just as it is central to both Old and New Testaments. The Instruction therefore attempts to define liberation from a Roman perspective, and denounce it in its Marxist form. It is for this reason that terminology can come very close. Ratzinger can speak of 'Christ, our Liberator', in the knowledge that in 1972 Leonardo Boff had produced *Jesus Cristo Libertador*. The issue was not whether Christ is liberator, but in what sense this is to be understood.

In fact there is nothing in the original version of *Jesus Christ Liberator* to which a liberal historical-critical scholar like Joseph Ratzinger could take exception. Its non-political character can be seen in the three-page discussion headed. 'The Kingdom of God Implies a Revolution of the Human World', much of which is taken up with consideration of the law, and of the Pharisees. It is a study by a Catholic theologian of the issues given prominence in the 1950s and 1960s by Rudolph Bultmann and his school. The sub-title is 'A Critical Christology of Our Time', and it can be understood entirely in the context of the renewed discussion about the historical Jesus. I have already alluded to the tragic case of Albert Schweitzer, who, having drawn attention to the series of pictures of Jesus created in the 'quest of the historical Jesus', *Von Reimarus Zu Wrede*, eventually fell into the trap of adding another to the collection. In the course of the quest there have been many examples of writers who by-passed the traditional metaphysical christology, offering a picture of the historical Jesus in which his values, vision and motivation coincided with those of the author. Thus over a century ago Renan advocated the Romantic view of religion by presenting Jesus as an essentially Romantic figure. Earlier in this century Glover presented Jesus as a liberal ethical teacher. More recently the process has been politicized. Twenty years ago the black activist Albert Cleage, pastor of the Church of the Black Madonna, in Detroit, proclaimed Jesus as a black messiah. Anyone familiar with this literature must therefore wonder whether Boff has not simply added yet another portrait to the gallery, Jesus the liberator.[46]

To the English translation, published in 1978, Boff added an Epilogue, 'A Christological View from the Periphery'. If the Saviour is saviour in a particular situation, then in the circumstances of Latin America, Christ must be proclaimed as liberator. And if that seems politically committed, then we should remember that theology is never composed in a neutral environment. Like everything else it serves the interests of its authors. 'Every Christology is partisan and committed.'[47] Traditionally these interests have been those of the ruling class, even in the studies which have purported to be 'apolitical'. It is not whether to be committed, but which cause to serve.

A Christology that proclaims Jesus Christ as the Liberator seeks to be committed to the economic, social, and political liberation of those groups that are oppressed and dominated.[48]

But this is not an arbitrary taking of sides. It is not that liberation theologians were committed to liberation, and decided to employ the name of Jesus as a weapon. It was in Christ that they found the motivation to work for liberation.

This last statement seems particularly naive. All authors of the lives of Jesus have made the same claim, that amazingly they discovered in contemporary social consciousness exactly that for which Jesus stood. This particular characteristic whether a Romantic approach to religion, or the perspective of *négritude*, apparently lay dormant for almost 2,000 years, and the fact that it is now recognized is apparently quite independent of contemporary social consciousness. (Hegel, we have learnt nothing!). But the situation is, if anything, worse. Having begun with the brash assertion that all theology serves an ideological purpose, Boff now finds it necessary to retreat from this position, for of course that would mean what Marx's second criticism asserts that theology is inherently ideological. Boff not only wishes to avoid this conclusion; he never discusses it. Now he wishes to protect theology, to erect a barrier within which theology can be neutral.

Christology enjoys autonomy in elaborating its discourse in line with its own methodology. It has its own mode of theoretical praxis, and it does not have to justify itself before some outside tribunal. It possesses its own inner laws and the criteria to determine its own internal truth.[49]

This would mean that theology, and here christology, is not after all part of the superstructure, but entirely independent of it and of the base. This is indeed what Marx thought, and he called it illusion and fantasy. Even so, he did not believe that illusions and fantasies are created without reference to interests.

Yet Boff insists on the necessity of critical social theory. Before elaborating this point he gives two cheers for a movement which, although lacking in theory, intuitively seeks those texts and incidents in the Gospels which associate Jesus with the Latin American reality of the poor and oppressed. Gone is the picture of the downtrodden Christ of popular piety, and of course equally the image of the glorious monarchy, modelled on the kings of Spain and Portugal. Gone too is the image of the sorrowing Virgin, who personifies the submission and domination of women. (Perhaps in both cases we should say 'going' or 'should go' rather than 'gone'.) Boff is describing individuals or groups who, lacking in political theory, are guided by a naive reading of the Gospels. It is a start, but it is not a sophisticated enough basis for the required social revolution.

Just as it suited Marx to reduce class interests in society to basically two, the bourgeois and the proletariat, so Boff reduces interests to those of 'the dominant classes' and 'the dominated classes'. He characterizes their associated utopian theories as 'functionalist' and 'dialectical' respectively. The former is the approach of capitalism, development and technology. The latter is the approach of socialism, struggle and contradictions. Theology which reaches beyond the intuitive stage will make use of social theory, but which one? Not surprisingly Boff advocates 'the revolutionary and Marxist tradition'. What is more surprising is the instrument by which the choice is made.

> Faith will guide our choice toward the socio-analytical framework that is best at discovering the mechanisms that generate injustice, that offers us suitable means for overcoming them, and that does most to foster the notions of brotherhood and participation.[50]

Faith, not reason, decides between two social theories. But the argument, or assertion, is circular. The goal described is not Christianity, but socialism. Christian faith will tell us which social theory best leads to socialism. At no point is there any indication that Christianity knows anything on its own account. Apparently theology is built on the foundations provided by social theory. In the last chapter we discussed presuppositions in liberation theology. We have now arrived at the same point again. 'Thus liberation Christology presupposes an option for the dialectical approach to social analysis and for the revolutionary "project" of the dominated.'[51] This raises the familiar question. What does theology, in this case christology, add to social analysis?

Boff addresses this issue in a brief summary of points indicatintg 'The Liberative Relevance of the Historical Jesus'. Unfortunately the points included involve no social theory whatsoever, and are reminiscent of the intuitive approach. For example, Latin American liberative christology stresses the historical Jesus over the Christ of faith, 'because it sees a structural similarity between the situations in Jesus' day and those in our own time.'[52] Renan found a remarkable similarity between the outlook of Jesus and that of modern Romantics. Cleage found a remarkable similarity between the mission of Jesus and aims of Black Power. And now Boff finds a remarkable similarity between the social structures of Palestine in the time of Jesus and contemporary Latin America. These parallels are understandable among poor people with little formal education and no knowledge of theology. Numerous examples are to be found in the collections made by Ernesto Cardenal during meetings of local people on the island of Solentiname, Nicaragua. Thus the Old Testament judges are *caudillos*; the Herods are like the Somozas; Jesus is born in a situation of terror and repression (Herod and the magi); in dialogue with the Pharisees Jesus practises conscientization; Satan tempts him to developmentalism.[53] But this intuitive approach is not yet christology. Boff accepts Marxist analysis applied to society, but he does not apply it to theology or religion. His christology is really a Latin American contribution to the pictues of the historical Jesus. In a situation in which liberation is required he provides a legitimizing figure of Jesus Christ Liberator.

One of those critical of Boff's approach is Hugo Assmann. He too has been in conflict with authority, but it may be significant that this has been with the civil and political authorities. He was exiled from his native Brazil, and also from Uruguay, Bolivia and Chile, before going on to teach theology in Costa Rica. He has no sympathy with those who are critical of liberation theology because it is contextual: to insist on theological absolutes is to prescind from history and to ignore what God is saying through contemporary experience. But he has sympathy for a very different kind of criticism, which doubts whether it is possible to resolve christological conflicts through increasingly more detailed historical critical exegesis of Bible and tradition. 'The conflict of differing christologies cannot be analysed or resolved outside the dialectic of socio-political conflicts.'[54] This was Boff's intention at the outset, but he did not carry it through in practice.

Assmann is critical of the picture of Christ among those whom he calls 'reactionaries' and the use to which this Christ is put, but at least they do not make the mistake of the 'metaphysical left', who ignore the continuing importance of religion in society. Alternatively, some of the revolutionaries follow the examples of Engels and Kautsky and leap over history backwards to express admiration for the Christ of primitive Christianity, a procedure which Assmann observes to be 'neither very historical nor materialistic'.[55]

There seems to be no resolution of the problem at the level of ideas, not even through detailed exegesis, but Assmann takes as the motto for his essay words of Paul in a conflict situation in the early church:

> But I will come to you soon, if the Lord wills, and I will find out not the talk of those arrogant people but their power. For the Kingdom of God does not consist in talk but in power.[56]

What is the power of these various images of Christ? For some the power of Christ is in the inner life of the individual, a secret work that leaves the world unchanged. For others it is an eschatological power which will be manifest in the distant future. But is this power real power in the world, or is it no different from talk about power? For liberation theology the power of Christ is a real power in history, exercised on the side of the poor and the oppressed. Against those images which consciously or unconsciously serve the interests of the ruling class, the Christ comes as liberator, now, in concrete situations – and is known as such.

Although we started off with Boff's christology, the subject of this section is Hugo Assmann. I became aware of his work first when I heard him speak at a conference in 1973. He was introduced as a theologian, but what struck me was his allegiance to Marxism. Not that I was much impressed by either side of his work. His theology, such as it was, seemed very unreconstructed. As for his Marxism, I thought he must have got it off a cereal packet. But in this section, as elsewhere, I am not so much concerned to expound or evaluate his theology as to examine the extent to which his commitment to Marxism leads him to take seriously Marx's criticisms of religion. At the point we have now reached in the essay Assmann is obviously entering a crucial state in the argument. He will not rest content with christology which is simply an alienated ahistorical conception. He is not saying that the real is rational, but he comes close to saying that the real is at least historical, and if it does not register on some scale in human history, it is not real. Like other liberation theologians he is concerned to be true to the social sciences – or at least to one specific tradition.

> Can we assume, for example, that the historical dialectics of Christ's liberative power at work here and now shares in the dialectics of the 'economic project'? For the Christian who is also a Marxist in many respects, this is a real dilemma. For Marxism asserts that the economic factor, or the material structure of society to put it more broadly, is the determining factor in the 'last instance', though this notion remains rather mysterious and unexplained.[57]

The liberation theologian can be as radical as he likes when he insists to his theological colleagues that Christianity is a historical religion. But when he turns to address his colleagues in the social sciences he is then required to explain or illustrate how the power of Christ affects human history. This is an issue of fundamental importance to 'the Christian who is also a Marxist in many respects'. It is not clear what Assmann has in mind at this point, but perhaps he should say that a liberation christology would have to avoid the reifications of traditional theology, in which the Work of Christ is effected outside human history and apart from human praxis. However, we have already noted how traditional are liberation theologians on such doctrines. He certainly rejects ecclesiastical 'Yalta pacts', by which there is division of the world; a peaceful co-existence between Christ's power and the powers of the ruling classes. But is this all that can be said? In the eighteenth century the Boyle Lectureship was endowed to answer those who doubted the existence of God. Anthony Collins, an atheist of the period, declared that it was one thing to reject atheism as a matter of course, quite a different thing to offer to answer it. And of course worst of all was to offer a proof and then fail to provide it. Assmann has declared, in the best Marxist tradition, that what does not exist effectively within human history does not exist, but he than fails to demonstrate what would count as the power of Christ in historical, concrete situations. What conclusion is then to be drawn? Is the situation not even more damaging that that of the dogmatic, ahistorical tradition? An alternative way of interpreting Assmann's difficulty is to say that he has not faced Marx's second criticism of religion, that theology is inherently a reversal of reality.

In 1973 Assmann had already raised these issues in *Teologiá desde la Praxis de la Liberación*.[58] He further clarifies in what respects he is a Christian who is also a Marxist, but he does not solve the problem he has set for himself. Given the inconsistent attention paid to Marx by the Latin American theologians we have discussed, it seems self-congratulatory of Assmann to claim that 'another error of the European theologians is to take too little notice of Marx in their reworking of the relationship between theory and practice.'[59] The criticism is made more specific.

> But there is no point in a political theology that fails to rise to the dialectical challenge of openly naming the components of the infra- and super-structures of power, and the implications of stategic and tactical attacks on them.[60]

Theology cannot be political theology (or theology at all?) unless its relationship to the infra-structure is uncovered. As we shall see in a moment, 'infra-structure' for Assmann is synonymous with 'base'. Does this mean that Assmann accepts historical materialism, that the superstructure arises from and is in some sense determined by the base? The answer must be Yes, given the following two claims.

The first looks very much like a theological form of historical materialism (just as historical materialism looks like a form of the theology of providence).

> In the light of basic theological principles like this, we must now have to examine the implications of the fact that faith must be understood as the historical unfolding of the process of liberation of man; unfolding in the sense of the truth of faith 'becoming true'; liberating efficacy as an intregral component of faith; efficacy and

gratuitiousness; what can be measured and what cannot in the historical efficacy of love.[61]

History is here understood in terms very similar to historical materialism; and liberation of man is being achieved through a historical movement which while it involves man is independent of him (gratuitious). The second claim which seems to confirm Assmann's acceptance of historical materialism concerns a situation internal to the church. He is dealing with the relationship of the base and the superstructure, but just as Boff could apply his theory to the church as a class society, so Assmann now applies it to explain the form of theology which arises from a certain ecclesiastical base. He is discussing the tendency to 'verbal magic', to 'presence through the word', devoid of follow-up action.

The roots of this inclination to a mere verbal debauch are probably to be found in the material base (infrastructure) which, historically, conditioned the ideological superstructure of the Church – the understanding of power that conditioned the notion of the efficacy of the word, seen at its height in the *ex opere operato* of sacramentalism removed from its real historical preconditions, for example.[62]

It is interesting to see Assmann apply Marx's theory of base and superstructure to a theology which he is quite prepared to designate as an ideology. It would have been more interesting if he had indicated the stages by which Latin American theology had moved to a new mode of production which produced a very different theological superstructure and it would have been most interesting of all had he faced Marx's proposition that theology as part of the superstructure is an ideology regardless of what mode of production forms the base.

In these passages Assmann has further clarified the extent to which he is a Christian and a Marxist. But what he does not do is present us with a Marxist interpretation of religion and theology. Instead, like Boff, he seeks a waiver, an exemption, in the case of Christianity.

Taking this historical situation as the starting-point for reflection on the Christian faith does not mean that the concept of liberation has to be restricted to the economic plane, but it is on this plane that the priorities become dramatically obvious.[63]

He wishes theology to be applied to the economic sphere: it must not be narrowed down in such a way as to omit the political, economic or historical dimensions. But at the same time he does not offer us a Marxist account of religion to show what is the relationship between theory and practice. But that is where we came in: that was his criticism of European theology.

Although Assmann seems to be aware of the problems, his reluctance to make a consistent application of Marxist analysis leads to ambiguity. Theology cannot undertake the social analysis he requires. Thus it must be the 'second word' behind the social sciences. This metaphor recalls Hegel's view that philosophy is secondary, coming after the event. But if theology in turn comes behind social philosophy, is it still in touch with the situation in any real sense? The relationship of liberation theology to the revolution is not clarified, except that 'it must take sides and place itself at the service of groups recognized as being in the van of the process of liberation, just as the social sciences are doing.'[64] But is this any more than exchanging one form of dependence for another? Assmann does not seem hopeful there. He bravely rejects the 'fundamentalism of the Left' which pulls texts out of the Bible to serve as instant legitimations. But he can see no possibility of an independent contribution to the struggle from existing ecclesiastical structures or theological forms.[65]

Assmann does not disguise the problem. Unlike traditional theology he insists that liberation theology must begin not simply with its own resources, but with those of the social sciences. This is a common theme among liberation theologians, as we have seen, but it is Assmann who applies to it the question about the emperor's clothes. Theology formerly offered its own analysis of a situation, apart from the social sciences. But now, if theology begins with and accepts the analysis of the social sciences, what remains to be said? 'What makes this sort of inquiry theological?'[66]

All credit to Assmann, for he knows very well that such is the place of religion in the cultural life of Latin America that a theological interpretation of the situation can always be added. His honest question is whether this is not simply 'theological adornment'?[67] The phrase cannot but recall Marx's first sustained critique of religion. How embarrassing it would be if liberation theology turned out to be no more than the 'halo' of the revolution, its 'aroma', its 'spiritual *point d'honneur*'. And yet this danger remains as long as Marx's criticisms of religion are not squarely faced.

(d)   Christians for Socialism

Some of the problems raised by Assmann had already been experienced in a very practical way in Chile. Although all liberation theologians accept the goal of socialism, they are very critical of the totalitarian systems of Eastern Europe, and of dehumanizing dogmatic Marxism. It was therefore with considerable interest that in 1970 the new movement viewed the election of Salvador Allende as President of Chile. Here was a Marxist elected democratically through the support of the broad coalition of the Popular Front. In April 1971 a group of Chilean priests met in Santiago to consider 'Christian participation in the task of developing and implementing socialism in Chile'. At the end of their discussions they issued a now-famous 'Declaration of The Eighty'. We are now coming to the end of a sequence of three chapters in which we have examined a spectrum of positions in which Christianity and Marxism are related. We began with Gutierrez, in whose work Christianity is mildly influenced by Marxism. We end with the Chilean Declaration in which some would say Marxism is but mildly influenced by Christianity. In the works we have examined Marxism peeps through liberation theology to varying degrees. In the Declaration it is possible to see theology peeping through. But whether such statements represent merely a 'theological adornment' is a matter of dispute. In previous sections we have considered how Marxism impinges on liberation theology, but since there is scarcely any theology here and since the document is relatively brief, it is more convenient simply to reprint it in full.[68] There is no difficulty in identifying Marxist presuppositions, terminology and analysis. What is more difficult is to determine whether the obligatory theological interventions add anything or change the Marxist position in any way.

DECLARATION OF THE EIGHTY

We are a group of 80 priests who live and work with people of the working class. We came together to analyse the present situation of Chile as it begins to develop and implement socialism.

The working class is still subject to exploitation and its attendent conditions, i.e. malnutrition, lack of housing, unemployment, and limited possibilities for further education and cultural development. The cause of this situation is specific and clear. It is the capitalist system, resulting from a domination by foreign imperialism and maintained by the ruling classes in this country.

This system is characterized by private ownership of the means of production and by every growing inequality in the distribution of income. It turns the worker into a mere cog in the production system, stimulates an irrational distribution of economic resources, and causes an improper transferral of surplus goods to foreign lands. The result is stagnation, which prevents our country from escaping its situation of underdevelopment.

Such a situation cannot be tolerated any longer. It is clear to us that the working masses found great hope in the accession of the People's Government to power and in this respect they were not mistaken.

Socialism, which is characterized by social appropriation of the means of production, paves the way for a new economy which makes possible autonomous development at a more accelerated pace and which overcomes the division of society into antagonistic classes. But socialism is not just a new economy. It should also generate new values which will pave the way for a society that evinces more fellowship and brotherhood. In this society the worker will shoulder his proper role with new dignity.

We feel committed to the process that is now under way and we want to contribute to its success. The underlying reason for our commitment is our faith in Jesus Christ, which takes on a depth and vitality and concrete shape in accordance with historical circumstances. To be a Christian is to be in solidarity, in fellowship, with other human beings. And at this moment in Chile fellowship means participation in the historical project that its people have set for themselves.

As Christians we do not see any incompatibility between Christianity and socialism. Quite the contrary is true. As the Cardinal of Santiago said last November: 'There are more evangelical values in socialism than there are in capitalism.' The fact is that socialism offers new hope that man can be more complete, and hence more evangelical; i.e., more conformed to Jesus Christ, who came to liberate us from any and every sort of bondage.

Thus it is necessary to destroy the prejudice and mistrust that exist between Christians and Marxists.

To Marxists we say that authentic religion is not the opiate of the people. It is, on the contrary, a liberating stimulus to revivify and renew the world constantly. To Christians we offer a reminder that our God committed himself personally to the history of human beings. And we say that at this present moment loving one's neighbour basically means struggling to make this world resemble as closely as possible the future world that we hope for and that we are already in the process of constructing.

We are not unaware of the difficulties and the suspicions on both sides. In large measure they have been caused by past historical circumstances that no longer prevail in Chile today. There is a long road ahead for both Christians and Marxists. But the evolution that has taken place in Christian and Marxist circles permits them to engage in a joint effort on behalf of the historical project that the country has set for itself.

This collaboration will be facilitated to the extent that two things are done: 1. to the extent that Marxism presents itself more and more as an instrument for analysing and transforming society; 2. to the extent that we Christians proceed to purify our faith of everything that prevents us from shouldering real and effective commitment.

Hence we support the measures aimed at social appropriation of the means of production: e.g., the nationalization of mineral resources, the socialization of banks and monopoly industries, the expansion and acceleration of agrarian reform, and so forth.

We feel that much sacrifice will be entailed in the implementation of socialism, that it will involve a constructive and united effort if we are to overcome our underdevelopment and to create a new society. Obviously enough this will provoke strong resistance from those who will be deprived of their special privileges. Hence the mobilization of the people is absolutely necessary. With some concern we note that this mobilization has not been achieved as had been hoped.

We also believe that it is indispensable to lay the foundations for the creation of a new culture. This new culture must not be the mirror image of capitalist concerns and interests: it must be the real-life expression of the genuine values of our people. Only then can we see the emergence of the New Man, who will create a societal life that is truly one of fellowship and solidarity.

We note that there are large groups of workers who are in favor of the changes taking place and who are benefiting from them, but who are not actively involving themselves in the process that has already been initiated. The union of all workers, whatever their party loyalty may be, is crucial at this juncture. Our country is being offered a unique opportunity to replace the existing system of dependent capitalism and to promote the cause of the laboring class throughout Latin America.

Lack of class consciousness among these workers is being encouraged and fostered by the ruling groups, primarily through the communications media and party activities. They are inculcating suspicions and fears, which ultimately lead to resistance and passivity.

We must recognize and admit that not everything being done is necessarily positive and effective. But at the same time we insist that criticism should be formulated from within the revolutionary process, not from outside it.

It is a time full of risk, but also a time full of hope. We priests, like each and every Christian, must do what we can to make our own modest contribution. That is why we have come together to reflect and to prepare ourselves in this workshop on the participation of Christians in the implementation of socialism.

Not surprisingly, the Declaration attracted hostile criticisms from 'outside the revolutionary process.' Of more interest were the fraternal criticisms made by those who themselves were in favour of a new socialist society, and of Christians participating in the process. An immediate response from within Santiago came from Beltrán Villegas, who raised the point we have already encountered. If the eighty had said that as Christians they had decided to proceed in a certain way that would have been admirable. But according to Villegas the order is reversed in the Declaration. Instead of faith leading to a political option, to the political option is 'added a dose of theological merit'.[69] The absolute character which belongs to faith is transferred to the political option which is by nature relative. His second criticism concerns the place given to class struggle. 'The Marxist evaluation of the proletarian class as the exclusive bearer of humanity's future does not at all dovetail with the gospel's blessing on the poor.'[70] As we have seen, liberation theologians are hopeful that the church of the poor will provide a real alternative to the church of the powerful, and in this way make a fundamental contribution to the revolution, but this is not at all the same thing as the dictatorship of the proletariat. A third criticism concerns the fact that the eighty are priests. In a more specific manner than the first criticism, they are legitimizing their political option by designating it not simply Christian, but the option chosen by priests. Villegas deems this to be 'the sin of clericalism'.[71] This is a particularly sensitive point among those advocating the church of the people. This final point was also noted by the bishops of Chile a few days later, at their annual convocation.

Throughout Part Two our focus of attention has not been on a general exposition of liberation theology, but on its use of Marxism and in particular how it responds to Marx's various criticisms of religion. I have already drawn attention to the failure of those who rely heavily on Marx's analysis of social institutions to take seriously his analysis of the social institution of religion. In the case of the Declaration the silence is even more astonishing. There are few references to Christianity, faith or theology in the Declaration, but Marx's first and third criticisms are recalled. Authentic religion (i.e. the religion of the eighty) 'is not the opiate of the people'. This corresponds to Marx's first criticism. The signatories go on to say that it is the responsibility of progressive Christians to proceed 'to purify our faith of everything that prevents us from shouldering real and effective commitment'. If this means preventing religion from supporting the ideology of the ruling class, then this refers to Marx's third criticism. But of his second criticism there is no sign whatever. Marx said that religion inverts reality, and that it predisposes people to accept the inverted reality of other social institutions. He did not make any exception for 'authentic religion'; it is by nature ideological. This may or may not be true, but those who base their entire social philosophy on Marx must surely make some response to that criticism if their intention is to harmonize Marxism and Christianity.

Arising from the Declaration it was decided to hold the First Latin American Convention of Christians for Socialism. In December 1971 priests from Argentina, Brazil, Bolivia and Peru met in Santiago, Chile with members of the Chilean secretariat of Christians for Socialism to plan the meeting and draw up a draft agenda for the convention. In this document three stages were envisaged:

1. An analysis of the phase in the revolutionary process reached in each country. 'It will be viewed primarily in terms of *the emergence of the proletariat and the mobilization of the people.*'[72] The 'Christian element' will be examined, as it is committed to the 'implementation of socialism through the rise of the proletariat to power'.[73] The phrase 'Christian element' presumably replaces the 'church' in order to dissociate progressive Christians from historical and contemporary ecclesial doctrines and practices when these are reactionary.

2. The examination of the contribution – positive and negative – of the Christian element must be carried through scientifically.

> To do this we feel we cannot prescind from the posture of historical materialism. That is, we must situate ourselves on the material and this-worldly terrain of history and have recourse to Marxism as an analytical tool – while remaining cognizant of the fact that Marxism, too, is part of a historical process still going on and that it is not a dogmatics.[74]

Naturally religion's part in the process cannot be judged on theological terms, since theology is part of the ideological superstructure. 'The ideological character of Christianity in its sociological manifestations – and we mean this in the pejorative sense of the word 'ideological' – can only be unveiled through *an analysis of the functions it performs within the framework of the modes of production and other socio-*

economic formations.'[75] Only then will it be possible to understand 'how the pristine dynamism of Christianity in favour of liberation has been castrated so frequently.[76] But surely this is to depart from historical materialism and to contradict the very method which it purports to accept. Anyone who insists on being 'situated on the material and this-worldly terrain of history' must accept the judgment that religion is part of the ideological superstructure – not just the worst of religion, but also the best. On this view there is no 'pristine' Christianity which escapes from being an ideology. To harbour this assumption is simply the pathetic refusal to allow Marx to criticize all aspects of religion, not just those which belong to the religion of the ruling class.

3. Beyond the merely tactical contribution which the Christian element can make to the revolution, the Convention is to seek the long-term strategic contribution. This can only arise from praxis, from the long-term commitment to the revolutionary struggle. 'It cannot be verified by superficial and forced presentations of the "specific contribution of Christians", which are wont to crop up in dialogue between Christians and Marxists.'[77] And if their Christianity is as well-founded as their grasp of Marxism, we may well fear for the future of both. Is the Christian contribution to arise after the acceptance of Marxism? As we saw in the criticism of the Declaration, unless Christians bring something absolute to the struggle which is at the level of faith, of conviction, of certainty, then they will have nothing to contribute but the 'adornment' of Marxism. But more relevant to our enquiry is the fact that Christians for Socialism have not faced Marx's criticism that religion even in its progressive forms is still ideology. The document goes on to warn about tactical allies: 'it often happens that groups which seem to be progressive or even leftist end up as strategic enemies of an authentic revolutionary process in the long run.'[78] Exactly.

10

The Evaluation of Marx in Liberation
Theology

(a) The unsubstitutability of Marx

In the previous three chapters we have considered examples of
liberation theology increasingly committed to and inextricably linked
with Marx's scientific analysis and historical materialist ideology. At
each stage I have expressed surprise that theologians who find it possible and even necessary to defend Marx in order to expound their
own positions, can completely ignore the fact that Marx criticized
religion, not simply bad examples of religion, but religion in itself. It
has been increasingly difficult to argue that it is possible to elaborate
the method and reinterpretation of theology found in Latin America
while ignoring this basic fact. It would seem that the last opportunity
would come among writers who pause from the construction of liberation theology to turn their attention specifically to an evaluation of
Marx from a Christian perspective. So that I do not have to first outline the general position of the theologians in this chapter I shall
illustrate from some of those already dealt with in the previous
chapters.

In 1974 José Míguez Bonino was the first to deliver the newly
sponsored London Lecture in Contemporary Christianity. Two years
later he published a more extensive treatment of his subject under the
title *Christians and Marxists: The Mutual Challenge to Revolution.*
Bonino justified the book, which might otherwise have been taken for
a contribution to the European Marxist-Christian dialogue, on the
grounds that he was writing from a specifically Latin American perspective. He did not believe that the necessary correlation of Christianity
and Marxism could be brought about through 'theoretical discussion'.
By this time we know what this means: in Latin America there is no

theory without praxis, while in Europe it is simply theory and no praxis. If I feel it necessary to intervene it is not simply in self-defence, but because there is a fundamental issue at stake.

From his writings, and from the fact that we both did our graduate work in the same seminary, I believe Bonino to be essentially fair and honest in his evaluations of particular scholars and movements, but I do wonder if his comment here is not simply a knee-jerk reaction. I have never put in my diary: 'Attend meeting of the Marxist-Christian dialogue'. My involvement in such discussions, both in Africa and in England, has been in the midst of specific social and political conflicts. In the course of these movements we have discovered that some of us were primarily motivated by Christian faith, others by Marxism. In the situation we have met to challenge each other and also to learn from one another. We should certainly not have had these meetings had we not proved ourselves to one another in the conflict itself. To this extent I agree with Bonino that the correlation does not arise from a 'theoretical discussion', but perhaps I can in turn direct a question towards him. This little digression is in part an attempt to vindicate myself and other Europeans with similar experiences, but it raises the further point that when the 'theoretical discussion' does take place, the questions must be asked by Marxists. So far in our study the liberation theologians have selected only those criticisms of religion to which they wished to respond. Marxists, however, might well raise further issues, issues critical not simply of European theology or the theology of Latin America's colonial period, but of liberation theology itself. The 'challenge to revolution' in this sense must be 'mutual'.

Bonino begins with two theses which arise from the situation in Latin America in the present time.

It is my thesis that, as Christians, confronted by the inhuman conditions of existence prevailing in the continent, they have tried to make their Christian faith historically relevant, they have been increasingly compelled to seek an analysis and historical programme for their Christian obedience. At this point, the dynamics of the historical process, both in its objective conditions and its theoretical development, have led them, through the failure of several remedial and reformist alternatives, to discover the unsubstitutable relevance of Marxism.[1]

We have already encountered this position in previous chapters. Through bitter experience Christians have discovered that charitable actions have not changed the structures which produce and maintain oppression. Even while treating the symptoms, it is love's responsibility to go beyond or behind these surface conditions to confront the causes.

And Bonino tells us that they have discovered that it is through Marxist analysis and only through it that Christian love can begin to take this further step of obedience. If in this first thesis Marxism makes a contribution to Christian responsibility, there is a second thesis which describes the Christian contribution to the Marxist revolution.

> The Latin American revolutionary is confronted with a state of consciousness in the masses (particularly but not exclusively in the rural population) in which the slave relationship of traditional society, the cultural alienation imposed by imperialism and the magical forms of folk-religion have produced a lag in the revolutionary consciousness in relation to the demands of the objective situation. In the effort to change this situation, the Marxist revolutionary has found himself side by side with a number of active revolutionary Christians and has discovered, in the new movement within the Christian fold, the potential motivating and mobilizing power of the Christian faith for revolutionary change.[2]

In Chapter 6 I drew attention to the fact that in Latin America Marxist revolutionary groups seldom troubled to make contact with the masses. The situation described by Bonino is one in which Marxists with the appropriate ('unsubstitutable') analysis make common cause with progressive Christian groups which are well connected with the grass-roots. At this point Bonino goes out of his way to make a brief reference to the theory of historical materialism set out in the Preface to Marx's *Contribution to a Critique of Political Economy*, the relationship between the base and the superstructure. Yet there are problems in this scenario to which Bonino does not refer. First, the suffering of the masses in this situation arises from the contradictions of feudalism, not capitalism. And if Marx is to be our guide, then if there is to be any change it will be because feudalism is about to be superseded by capitalism. Little wonder that Marxists, who are an epochal step ahead, have poor relations with the peasants. But secondly, if the feudal form of Catholicism is being replaced by a more progressive form of Catholicism, it means that one religious interpretation of the world is being replaced by another. At what stage does the Marxist raise the question of superseding this essentially ideological stage? Or to put it another way, how long can the compartmentalization continue, within which Marx's analysis is applied to the full range of social institutions, except religion? One man's revolution is another man's reform.

Bonino therefore turns away for the moment from revolutionary praxis to more theoretical questions, specifically the Marxist critique of religion. In Part One we saw that Marx formulated three very different criticisms. In the studies which we have so far completed, liberation theologians have been willing to accept the first and third, the opiate and ideological critiques. As they interpret them, neither of these criticisms rejects religion as such, merely its misrepresentations. We are not therefore much encouraged when Bonino tells us that the reason for embarking on this issue will be to determine 'to what extent the Marxist criticism of religion can help us to expose the shortcomings or betrayals in our obedience and to correct our attitudes'.[3] But what of the second criticism, which is not merely a corrective to bad practice or unbiblical attitudes? Will it be faced at last?

Bonino does indeed quote that famous starting point from the Introduction to the *Contribution to the Critique of Hegel's Philosophy of Right*. 'For Germany the criticism of religion is in the main complete, and criticism of religion is the premise of all criticism.' We are on familiar grounds. There is the criticism of the Prussian state which has taken upon itself a religious guise, the objections to the censorship laws, the division of man between egotistical and species being. There is the critique of money which has now become the universal value of all things. This is followed by the exposure of alienated labour, and the commodity fetishism of capitalism. It will be recalled that these are among the institutions which, according to Marx, exhibit the same reversal of reality first seen in religion. It is for this reason that the criticism of religion is the starting point for all criticism of secular institutions. Bonino is providing a very brief outline of Marx's argument, but it seems clear that he has no objection to Marx's findings so far as the secular sphere is concerned. What is not at all clear is whether he accepts that if Marx is correct in his analysis of the secular, he must also be justified in his critique of religion.

Instead he immediately turns to the first criticism, that religion reconciles man to the injustices of this world. Bonino certainly accepts this criticism, or rather is determined that religion should no longer perform this function. But he also recognizes that this is not original to Marx, and that it can be a distraction. As we saw in Chapter 3, Marx did not believe that the pursuit of atheism was the way to socialism; rather on the way to socialism, religion would become obsolete.

At this point Bonino contrasts the dogmatic anti-religious stance of the communist parties of the USSR and the Chinese People's Republic with the more pragmatic and 'non-sectarian' views of Palmiro Togliatti in Italy and Fidel Castro in Cuba. Bonino goes on to quote the French Marxist, Roger Garaudy, on the need for Marxism to correct its view of religion in the light of recent progressive examples. The question is raised whether atheism must be a dogma of Marxism. However, this approach entirely avoids the fundamental issue raised by the second criticism of religion. It is not whether atheism is a premise or not, but whether, if Marx is correct in his identification of the secular examples of reversal, he must therefore be correct in his identification of the reversal in the case of religion. As we saw in Chapter 2, it is not possible to say how Marx became an atheist. It seems to have coincided with his entry into the Doctors' Club. But his second criticism of religion is not an atheist denial of the existence of God. It is much more productive than that, since it is the premise of all forms of secular criticism. However, this argument must run in both directions. If his philosophy, accepted as 'unsubstitutable', rests on the premise of the criticism of religion as reversal, it is not possible to ignore this criticism – at least it should not be possible. But it happens and it happens once more in the case of Bonino. Among progressive Christians religion no longer operates as an opiate. On pragmatic grounds there may therefore be a case for allowing Christians into the Communist Party, but that has nothing to do with Marx's second criticism.

Christians and Marxists is a fascinating book. It is indeed written out of a specific involvement and not simply theoretical interest. It is suitably critical of Marxism, not simply when it conflicts with the central tenets of the Christian faith, but when it fails to do justice to human experience. One of the most exciting features of liberation theology is that it is written from a perspective which has now achieved independence from its European roots. It is particularly interesting to read criticisms that Marx was after all a very European thinker, whose philosophy is certainly not to be applied dogmatically throughout the world. But all this goes beyond our very specific enquiry. Although in his study of Marx Bonino comes close to our sources, he still avoids the fundamental challenge of Marx's criticism of all religion, including liberation theology.

It will be recalled that Bonino justified writing the book because of the relevance of the perspective of Latin America. With this in mind I can refer to two observations he makes in the course of the discussion. First, he accepts Marx's objections to religious socialism 'as a valid warning against the self-deception and confusion which so easily creep into a political programme of any sort when it is clothed in religious language.[4] In Chapter 4 I warned that so long as Marx's second criticism of religion is not faced, and accepted, religion will function in an ideological form. Of course Bonino intends that the acceptance of Marx's scientific analysis will close the door to such religious socialism. My point is that the door to the 'mystification of the struggle' will never be closed until the critique is faced. The second point concerns the function of religion in providing a false unity for man's still alienated world. In accepting Marx's third criticism Bonino is alive to the danger of religion functioning as an ideology. I could simply repeat my previous point, that according to Marx religion is inherently ideological, but there is another point that I have not made so far. What if Marxism works? What if the revolution is successful? What if alienation is overcome? Will liberation theologians have to pray that it does not work too well? But no, they already know that Marxism 'does not take seriously enough the depths of man's alienation'.[5] If the false unity which merely masks human alienation must be rejected, they expect to achieve a truly religious unity based on purified religion. The answer is that they know it is not going to work. They know something that Marx does not. But whether that religious knowledge is real or ideological can only be decided when Marx's criticism of religion has been fully faced.

(b)   Faith and ideology

It might seem that one of the main problems facing liberation theologians is that in Latin America until recently Christianity and Marxism have been regarded as incompatible. If anything, the problem has been more serious than that. It is not just that they represent two systems giving different answers to basic questions, but that they compete directly with one another. To the extent to which Christianity is true, Marxism is held to be false, and vice versa. In practice this is not always the case. Lawrence Bright's untimely death meant that he did not have the opportunity to engage in dialogue with liberation theologians, but Bonino quotes the English Dominican several times. 'One is Christian and Marxist because that's how things are.'[6] But how can it be so, and should it be so? The liberation theologians we have discussed have frequently distinguished Christian faith from Marx's scientific analysis, but that cannot be the answer. There is more to Marx than a neutral social theory. It is therefore necessary to carry out a more careful study of the relationship between the two. This is attempted by Juan Luis Segundo in *Faith and Ideologies*.

We saw in Part One that Marx was a man of faith, whose life was structured by his unswerving commitment to humane and humanizing values. It would be as unworthy as it would be impossible to deny to Marx this orientation of faith and values. And yet if he is allowed to occupy this space, religion cannot afford to cede it to him. Segundo therefore begins with the bold move of offering a phenomenological analysis of faith. At a stroke he breaks out of the familiar circle: faith is a religious virtue, in virtue of being religious. 'I am simply talking about an *anthropological* dimension, a dimension as universal as the human species itself, whether religion be involved or not.'[7] We might say that faith, so far from being peculiar to religion, is constitutive of being human. But I said of Marx that his life had been structured in the pursuit of certain values. Faith does not know the ways of the world or how to achieve the realization of its goals. This requires an understanding of social structures, a picture of social relations in their complexity: in a word, faith requires an ideology. 'While we are subjectively determined by the values we *choose*, we are objectively affected by the natural or artificial conditionings which we see or perceive (Greek *idein*), and which we are obliged to work with.'[8] Marx drew attention to the fact that the picture provided by an ideology is not always quite as objective as it claims to be. But then subjectively we may not be entirely honest even with ourselves about the values to which we claim to be committed. However, these distortions do not alter the difference between these two anthropological dimensions, faith and ideology.

What conclusions can be drawn from this phenomenological starting point? It is enough for Segundo that the old distinction between faith (=religion) and ideology (=atheism) is broken down. For him it is enough that he has demonstrated that in order to make (Christian) faith effective in the world it is necessary to enlist the aid of (Marxist) ideology. He has demonstrated phenomenologically what the other liberation theologians simply assert from experience. But it will not do. The subjective dimension is not simply faith, but faith/values. It is faith in certain values, or faith that these values must be preserved and promoted. And so far as Christian faith is concerned, it already has its own objective structure, namely the Bible, theology, the church, and liturgy. In other words, Christian faith already has its own ideology quite apart from Marxism. Segundo has not demonstrated too little, but too much. If religious faith is a particular instance of anthropological faith, systematic theology is a particular instance of anthropological ideology. Segundo's argument is confirmation, by a different route, of Marx's second criticism of religion: religion is ideological, not in its worst forms, but as such and inherently.

This is not exactly Segundo's conclusion, or rather he is hopeful that it need not be so, but he does recognize the problem with regard to Christianity.

> Rarely if ever does that term in the concrete refer solely to a faith. It is accompanied by, and fleshed out in, ideologies that are not specifically Christian. Indeed in some cases it may simply be replaced by such ideologies, as we shall see later.[9]

This is a recognition that Christian faith has always existed in ideological forms, but it suggests that this has come about when Christians have borrowed existing ideologies. This, of course, has happened, but it fails to grasp the point that the situation does not depend on such use of external systems. Segundo therefore avoids Marx's second criticism of religion; instead, he hints at the route by which he will seek to by-pass it. He will try to argue that Christian faith is not identical with the historical Christian religion. Although his approach is novel, the proposition is unfortunately very familiar. It recalls two movements in European history. First, it is a further addition to those pictures of the historical Jesus in which the author contrasts the 'real' concerns of the historical Jesus with the 'interests' the church's Christ. But secondly, in the best Barthian tradition Segundo is prepared to rubbish religion if only he can keep faith pure. He claims that both with regard to the Bible and to the phenomenology of religion it frequently happens that,

> the divine 'name' and the 'religion' associated with it do not at all designate the 'faith' which gives value-structure to life; instead they designate an 'instrument', a method, by which to attain values that have been fixed beforehand and that are independent of the god who is adopted and adored. In other words, perhaps in most instances with which we are acquainted, the religious realm is an instrumental, essentially 'ideological' realm as I defined that term in Chapter 1; it is definitely not the realm of 'faith' as I meant it.[10]

Although Segundo's phenomenological analyses of the anthropological dimensions of faith and ideology are useful, it is doubtful if the phenomenology of religion will serve his purpose. He mentions only the Dutch scholar, van der Leeuw, but there is a line which runs from Schleiermacher, whom we discussed in Chapter 2, through Otto and van der Leeuw, which maintains that the source from which religion arises cannot be expressed simply in terms of human values. Segundo would have been better served by the work of the leading contemporary scholar in this field, the Canadian, Harvard scholar Wilfred Cantwell Smith. In a series of original monographs over a period of almost thirty years Smith has developed his position. He not only distinguishes faith from religion, but now claims that the term 'religion' no longer serves its original purpose and should be replaced by the combination of 'faith' and 'cumulative tradition'.[11] Even so, it is doubtful if the phenomenology of religion, in any form, will identify the non-objectified, non-ideological core of religion in the terms which Segundo wishes to ascribe to Jesus. The quest of the historical Jesus is typified by claims of various kinds that Jesus's position was pre-religious. It is necessary to be highly selective and imaginative to argue such a case. These qualities are not lacking in the quest, nor in Segundo.

It will be recalled that Miranda interpreted the prophetic tradition as saying that there is no way to God through the cult. We must seek God where he says that he will be found, namely in the establishing of justice for the poor. Segundo applies this line of interpretation to the teaching of Jesus. 'The sabbath was made for man, not man for the sabbath.'[12] The sabbath is relative: human welfare is absolute. Jesus knows of human values by which religion must be judged. So also Jesus resolves the question of pure and impure meat into an ethical one. As the Markan redactor comments in parenthesis, 'Thus he declared all foods clean.'[13] In order that human values are preserved, even the commandments are criticized. 'In attacking the religion he found around him, the founder of Christianity was attacking the fact that it was an "ideology" rather than a "faith" – to use my terminology.'[14] This is the kind of selective exegesis which Albert Schweitzer exposed in the quest of the historical Jesus. He himself, following Johannes Weiss, accepted that the message of Jesus was inherently eschatological, proclaiming the immanent coming of the Kingdom of God, and the end of human history. But is this pure faith, with no religious objectification? Jesus also proclaimed the coming of the Son of Man, a figure found in apocalyptic Judaism. And even if we restrict ourselves to Mark, as Segundo tends to do, what are we to make of the 'stern charge' of Jesus to the leper whom he has just healed: 'Go, show yourself to the priest, and offer for your cleansing what Moses commanded, for a proof to the people.'[15] Nor is it possible to reduce this requirement to an ethical or secular action of primitive medicine or hygiene. What Moses required is set out in Leviticus 14, and it is about as obscurely cultic as a prescription could be, including as it does 'two living birds and cedar wood and scarlet stuff and hyssop', two male lambs and a one-year-old ewe lamb, together with 'a cereal offering of three tenths of an ephah of fine flour mixed with oil, and one log of oil'. In Leviticus this entirely non-functional rite, which includes the priest placing oil on the healed leper's right ear, right thumb and right large toe, is to make atonement to God. It is simply not possible to present the faith of Jesus prior to all religious (ideological) objectifications.

Segundo's problem is that the more he focusses on the human values of Jesus, the more he reduces Jesus to the role of ethical teacher. Far from being a radical move, this places Segundo among the nineteenth-century European liberals. For example, he does not want to say that Jesus reveals something religious, rather that 'Jesus was recognized as the revelation of God only by those people who *already* had those values'.[16] However, this begs several questions, and Segundo must therefore admit that Jesus was religious, by which he means that 'he did relate everything to God'.[17] For an aspiring phenomenologist this is not much of a definition, but it leads to a restatement of the problem: how does faith, in its anthropological sense, become *religious* faith?

Segundo proposes two conditions which must be met for faith to be religious faith. The first is transcendent data. This sounds as if he has reintroduced the whole metaphysical tradition of theology. In fact he restricts transcendent data to its utopian dimension. But once again the cost of reducing such religious concepts to ethical or secular dimensions is that it does not distinguish religious faith from anthropological faith. As Segundo admits, Marx also believed in such transcendent data. What then transforms anthropological faith, including transcendent data, into religious faith? The answer, when it comes, is far from hopeful: tradition. The second condition is 'adherence to a tradition of referential witnesses regarding the experiencing and acquisition of those data'.[18] Cardinal Ratzinger must have been delighted when news reached him of this second condition. But it will not do. It defines Christian faith as distinct from Marxist faith, or being a Buddhist or membership of the Masonic Order. But since there is no phenomenological analysis of religion, the distinction between religious and anthropological faith is not clarified.

Having distinguished (Christian) faith from (Marxist) ideology – at least to his own satisfaction – Segundo then turns to the conflict between the two. Yet he immediately reverts to a position which he had apparently rejected, the assumption that the criticism of religion arises from Marx's atheism. But I have already pointed out that Marx's second critique, that religion is a reversal of reality, is not simply atheism. It is the claim that religion is an objectified ideological formation. Atheism may or may not follow from that. Marx himself was an atheist, but at the end of Part One I left open the question whether a proper application of his own method might not produce a very different view of religion. But since Segundo is comparing faith and ideology, he by-passes the second critique of religion and moves directly to consider historical materialism as an ideology.

In Chapter 5 I identified the problems which Segundo raises concerning historical materialism as arising from typical bourgeois assumptions and interests. For example he claims that 'only the plane of consciousness could, voluntarily and initially, introduce changes in the economic process itself (i.e. in the mode of production) . . .'.[19] But not even the most liberal economist could take the view that some individuals decided to have an industrial revolution. Individuals and groups are free to act economically, within the parameters of the situation, which at the end of an epoch will present a conflict between two modes. Nor can Marx's own analysis be taken to undermine his argument. If Marx has indeed uncovered a fundamental law of historical motion, then that discovery itself divides history. That is to say, socialist countries have now attempted to change the superstructure of their societies by changing the mode of production. But this human initiative cannot be taken to disprove the very law on which it seeks to operate. That they should choose one kind of society over another depends on their faith/values. How they attempt to change society depends on their ideology, in Segundo's terms. In Hegel's terms the very discovery of the law of historical motion could only be made when human consciousness had reached a level which is conditional on (in that sense determined by) the process itself. Historical materialism may be true or false, but it cannot be fairly evaluated by a philosophy determined by the assumptions of the ideology of bourgeois liberalism.

As we have seen, Segundo wants to find a way of linking Christian faith to Marxist ideology. He therefore is not opposed to historical materialism as an ideology, but he rejects it in its dogmatic and metaphysical forms. This includes the rejection of any atheistic dismissal of religion. He specifically refers to the second criticism, that religion is 'an inverted consciousness'.[20] But as we have already noted, the second criticism does not arise from atheism, though it could in turn lead to atheism. Why religion is rejected in historical materialism has to be considered in relation to the formation of the second criticism. This Segundo does not care to do. Consequently in the conclusion to the book he describes popular Catholicism as a cultural movement which performs various functions magical as well as political, but he cannot find a way of discerning how the Christian tradition can be 'simultaneously normative and liberative as it passes through the ecclesial community'.[21]

(c) Atheism as an ally

For Segundo, ideology is not the enemy of faith, but can be its ally. For the Venezuelan Jesuit theologian Antonio Pérez-Esclarín, atheism can be of service in the purification of religion. In a previous age atheism was regarded as the main enemy of religion, but today Christianity everywhere is in the service of an idolatrous culture. 'The reign of idolatry is now firmly implanted in Christian civilization. The law of the golden calf now prevails in the name of God.'[22] Christianity, with its originally revolutionary message, is now a pallid shadow of its former self, 'living the life of a vegetable'.[23] Ironically, the term 'revolutionary' has become synonymous with atheism. Pérez-Esclarín therefore enlists the aid of atheism to expose the false and idolatrous basis of modern dehumanized culture, in order to regain the true God.

In Jesus Christ he becomes the very embodiment of liberation and guarantees definitive victory to all human beings, both atheists and believers, who are committed to constructing his utopian kingdom here and now on earth.[24]

The modern culture to which Pérez-Esclarín refers is that of a capitalist society characterized by consumerism, a society in which individuals understand themselves only in relation to the objects of their desires and convenience, in which they themselves are reduced to objects. It is paradoxical that materialism is usually assumed to be characteristic of communist societies which have legislated for atheism and against religion. Such societies do not display the materialism evident in capitalist societies, and indeed their stand may be against the religion which is quiescently part of the consumerist culture. Hence the paradox:

> In such a situation atheism may actually be the rejection of false notions of God. It may actually represent a real form of solid faith. On the other hand a self-satisfied faith devoid of any humanizing practice may actually serve as a cover for radical atheism.[25]

A neat little scheme, even if it is as unlikely as it is unrealistic. On the one hand the sharpest critiques of consumerism come from within the West, both from secular writers such as Herbert Marcuse and from Christian invididuals and communities. On the other hand, no one who is familiar with the life-style of the East European 'red bourgeoisie' can doubt that consumerist materialism is close to the heart of the communist world. But the real situation is not nearly so interesting as a paradoxical reversal. Pérez-Esclarín, therefore, from the perspective of liberation theology, joins forces with those who have denied the god who denies man. 'I am convinced that if people did feel the need to attack God in order to liberate humanity, it was precisely because people had totally lost sight of God as liberator.'[26]

He begins his dialogue with atheism with a brief study of Nietzsche. This goes beyond the scope of my study, but as we wait for Marx's turn the signs are not good. Nietzsche was the most radical critic of Christianity in the nineteenth century. Unlike Feuerbach and Marx, when he rejected Christian doctrine he also rejected Christian moral values. After the death of God, the end of religion, he was forced to begin again and find a new basis for very different moral and esthetic values. He did not seek to justify the old values in a new way. Hence his *magnum opus* was entitled *Revaluation of All Values*. As a rule of thumb Nietzsche rejected everything which Christianity affirmed, and posited the opposite. And so the first part of the major work was *The Antichrist*. The revaluation becomes 'the attempt undertaken with all resources, with all instincts, with all genius, to bring about the triumph of the *opposite* values, the *noble* values'.[27] In contrast to Marx he did not criticize Christians for failing to live up to their moral standards; he rejected the standards. If you wish to claim Nietzsche as an ally, then you must be prepared for the possibility that you form an alliance also with Wagner and the repudiation of the Christian Western tradition. Pérez-Esclarín does not honestly face these consequences. Instead he concludes, rather weakly, that 'at bottom, Nietzsche never was an atheist'.[28] And in this way the fearless liberation theologian dialogues with atheism.

Next up is Feuerbach, but there is no real discussion of his thought. His fundamental distinction between the 'true or anthropological essence of religion' and the 'false or theological essence of religion' is ignored. Hence his fine distinction concerning atheism is omitted. 'He who says no more of me than that I am an atheist, says and knows *nothing* of me'.[29] For all his faults Feuerbach's projection theory surely cannot be totally ignored either. It is a matter of observation that the Olympian gods personified aspects of Greek culture. And the attributes of Constantine were projected on to Christ in heaven.[30] When Pérez-Esclarín is confronted by an atheist (by whatever name) he retreats into declaring that Feuerbach's atheism was 'gratuitous'. That apparently settles everything.

Freud is also dismissed for the same reason, 'gratuitous' atheism. I need not conceal the fact that I find Freud's writings on religion to be unscientific and lacking in objectivity. They are marred by abusive and unworthy generalizations, but there is a case to answer, and no one who purports to be consorting with atheists can afford to treat them in such a cavalier manner. Pérez-Esclarín presents an inadequate account of Freud's anthropological theories of the origins of religion, without doubt the weakest and most speculative area of his treatment of religion. But there is no mention of the much more acute psycho-analytical observations, such as the essay on 'Obsessive Actions and Religious Practices', in which Freud notes the close parallel between what we might call performing a religious action, and performing an action religiously.

> In view of these similarities and analogies one might venture to regard obsessional neurosis as a pathological counterpart of the formation of a religion, and to describe that neurosis as an individual religiosity and religion as a universal obsessional neurosis.[31]

I have allowed myself a slight digression here to observe how Pérez-Esclarín actually deals with his new-found allies. Unfortunately it is similar to the way in which we have seen other liberation theologians deal with Marx. Like them, he is quite prepared to accept the validity of their criticism of religion when it concerns the dehumanizing practices of bad religion. What he is not prepared to consider seriously is any atheist criticism of what we have called religion as such, and certainly not any criticism of the very notion of a divine being. If the atheists are allies, full of insight and integrity with regard to their commitment to the liberation of man, why are they suddenly enemies, blinded by prejudice, when it comes to liberation from religion as such? There is in fact no sign that he is approaching the subject from the perspective of liberation theology, but if he is, then it could be seen as further confirmation of the suspicion that this kind of theology exhibits doctrinal fundamentalism.

We cannot therefore be hopeful as we turn to consider Pérez-Esclarín's dialogue with Marx. He presents Marx as a humanist, committed to the liberation of man. But at the same time Marx denied the existence of God, without ever giving the matter serious consideration. Marx assumed that the liberation of man required liberation from religion. We are presented with Marx's break with Feuerbach, his emphasis on the creative place of work in human life, and the place of the mode of production in social change. Capitalism and alienated labour are also mentioned. There is brief coverage of the ideological nature of religion, especially its function as the opiate of the people. Protestant Christianity is the appropriate religion of capitalism. When social conditions have been rectified there will be no further need of religion, and atheism will no longer be an issue.

As might be expected by this time, Pérez-Esclarín does not deal with Marx's critique of religion as a reversal of reality, the premise of all the forms of criticism which he mentions briefly. Instead he concentrates on only one issue, Marx's atheism. Although Marx warned against attempting to construct a philosophy on the basis of atheism, Pérez-Esclarín nevertheless makes this the decisive issue. The easiest way to dialogue with atheism is to say 'Me too!' You deny the god who diminishes man, but so do I. You oppose the god of a degenerate form of Christianity, but so do I. But Marx is wrong to think that this is the God of the Christians. Unfortunately Pérez-Esclarín deals with only the first of Marx's criticism of religion, and that the least dangerous. He concludes that 'modern atheism can clearly help to revitalize and purify authentic Christianity a great deal. It is paving the way for an encounter with the true and authentic God, the God who liberates us.'[32] He may well be right, but only when atheism is allowed to make more than a moral criticism. When we consider the complexity of historical materialism and its revolutionary impact on the history of the twentieth century, it hardly seems adequate to describe its founder in the following terms: 'Marx was the Good Samaritan of history.'[33]

(d) Marx the Christian humanist

A much more comprehensive discussion of Marx is to be found in José Miranda's study of *Marx Against the Marxists*.[34] As the title suggests, the situation is not without convolution or contradiction. Previously theologians felt a responsibility to answer Marx, to counter his criticism of religion. For them there was no distinction between Marx and Marxists. But liberation theologians have accepted Marx's position, including (for the most part) his criticisms of religion. They have attempted to demonstrate the continuity between the prophetic teaching of Jesus and the denunciation of injustice which characterizes Marx's work. Jesus took the side of the poor; Marx championed the cause of the oppressed. This happy reconciliation has not gone unchallenged. If the prodigal son has been rehabilitated, the elder brother has not been overjoyed. There are still theological Cold Warriors who consider Marxism to be a materialist, anti-humanist, determinist and amoral (if not downright immoral) system. It is therefore necessary for liberation theologians to show that Marxism should not be characterized in such ways: there is a family relationship between primitive Christianity and primitive Marxism. We must stress 'primitive' in both cases. Clearly Christianity as it has developed is one of Marx's main targets. But at the same time it must be acknowledged that Marxism as it has gained institutional expression has often been as materialist, anti-humanist, determinist and immoral as conservative theologians have claimed – indeed on closer inspection even more so. Liberation theologians are not the custodians of Marxist orthodoxy or neo-orthodoxy. If they wish to advocate Marx's teaching, then it may be necessary for them to dissociate Marx from at least some of his prominent and protective followers. During his own lifetime Marx discovered that certain French communists who held views very different from his own were calling themselves by his name. His response is a challenge to all who claim to be his followers. 'As for me, one thing I do know is that I am not a Marxist.'[35]

The purpose of *Marx Against the Marxists* will now be clear. The argument is in two stages. In the first stage Marx is defended against Marxists whose positions are substantially different from his. For example, there are the materialists who claim that the motive for the revolution is the satisfaction of material needs. Marx was perfectly clear on this point. 'To those proletarians who do not wish to be treated like garbage, courage, self-awareness, pride, and a sense of independence are more important than bread.'[36] Indeed capitalism will lead to higher living standards for the working class, and capitalists will expect the proletariat to accept the corresponding increase in exploitation as being an acceptable price. It is they who are the real materialists. Miranda is particularly critical of Althusser's 'fraudulent' misrepresentation of Marx. He claims that Althusser is a materialist who wishes to promote his views by claiming that they are Marx's views. Miranda is able to bring forward passages in which Althusser has manipulated the text to support his own materialism instead of Marx's humanism. This is particularly blatant, but it is common to claim that Marx was an anti-humanist materialist. 'When they talk about Marx, therefore, they must be talking about Groucho or one of the other Marx brothers . . .'[37]

Miranda also demonstrates that Marx's thought is guided by humanism, by the assumption that the most important objective is to enable men and women to live the truly human life. This is the basis of his criticism of capitalism, the moral judgment that under this system human relations are reducted to the animal relations of the survival of the fittest. Previously there were moral or moralistic criticisms of the evils of capitalism, but it was with Marx's understanding of the production of commodities, and the discovery of surplus value, that it was possible to see how these dehumanizing conditions were brought about and therefore how they could be brought to an end.

In Chapter 5 I discussed the vexed question of determinism. Once again it is the bourgeois economist who is the real determinist, referring to iron laws which cannot be broken, regardless of the misery they impose. Miranda is able to quote many important passages in Marx's writings where human freedom and initiative are not only given central place, but are regarded as more important than the mode of production in giving an account of historical events. Earlier I noted that Marx described historical materialism as a natural law. The existence of the laws of nature at first sight seems to threaten human freedom, but in fact knowledge of these laws enables human beings to use nature for their own ends. This is the basis of Marx's anti-reformism. Attempts to change a situation will not be significant unless the mode of production is also changed, but changes cannot be brought about without the exercise of human initiative.

Finally, Miranda feels it necessary to defend Marx against those Marxists who mock such concepts as moral conscience. To the bourgeois statement of equal rights Marx and Engels added equal obligations. I have already noted that Marx's life was characterized by self-sacrifice for the oppressed. The new order of mutual respect, honesty and integrity cannot be built upon foundations which deny the reality of these human virtues. I earlier drew attention to the fact that

Marx's vision for society was not a levelling down to a previous stage of civilization at which all established standards were lost.

> Marx himself was a gentleman of the old school. Is it an insignificant detail, for example, that he used a monocle all his adult life? He completely scorned popularity, felt an overwhelming sense of implacable moral responsibility, and the depth of that feeling made him a communist. The notion that he wanted to 'liberate' human beings from moral obligation is the sheerest nonsense propagated in recent times.[38]

Point taken, though whether the use of a monocle simply confirms the widespread view of Marx's myopia need not detain us.

This, then, is the first stage in the argument: Marx does not belong with the Marxists, at least with many of the most strident, from Lenin to Althusser. But there is a second stage. If Marx does not belong with the Marxists, *horrible dictu*, could he belong with the Christians? Cardinals might be as offended as commissars by the subtitle of the book, 'The Christian Humanism of Karl Marx'.

In Chapter 1 I examined the early influences on Marx's life, and specifically his school essays. There was undoubtedly a background of Christian humanism, but Miranda moves on to a comparison of the teaching of Jesus and Marx's economic analysis. In our earlier study of Marx we saw that he was acutely aware of alienating inversion, the personification of things and the reification of people. Institutions which have their origins in society come to exercise power over individuals. Miranda sees this as an echo of Jesus' warning that 'the sabbath was made for man, not man for the sabbath'.[39] But there is another such institution even more central to the teaching of Jesus, namely money. 'You cannot serve God and Mammon.'[40] Here we have not simply the personification of wealth, but its apotheosis, its glorification as a divine being in its own right. That is why this mere object, wealth, becomes idolatrous. We either live in a world in which God is Lord and the values of his kingdom hold sway, or we live in a world in which everything depends on wealth and the value which money bestows. On Marx's view there could hardly be a better definition of capitalism. But would it not be difficult to live in a world without wealth? Difficult is not the word for it. 'It is easier for a camel to go through the eye of needle than for a rich man to enter the kingdom of God.'[41]

Not surprisingly, as I have discussed earlier, the primitive Christian community was communist. Theirs was the kingdom of God. But according to Marx they did not know how to deal with the political consequences of their decision, and so the experiment failed. The rest is history, or church history.

Marx is also given to describing capitalism and the devotion to wealth by the biblical terms Moloch, Baal and Mammon. Miranda therefore regards the work of Marx as 'a commentary on Jesus Christ's denunciation of the worship of money'.[42] He reproduces a selection of quotation from Marx on the subject. 'Money is therefore the god among commodities.' 'The hoarder, therefore, makes a sacrifice of the lusts of the flesh to his gold fetish.' The god of Mammom 'proclaimed surplus-value making as the sole end and aim of humanity'.[43] In Chapter 5 I discussed the section of *Capital* entitled 'The Festishism of the Commodity and its Secret'. There Marx tells us that although the commodity at first sight looks to be a simple thing, its analysis involved 'metaphysical subtleties and theological niceties'.[44] Miranda takes up this point eagerly, as confirmation that Marx's criticism of capitalism is in effect a commentary on Jesus' criticism of the idolatry of Mammon. What he does not point out is that a few pages further on, Marx claims that for 'a society of commodity producers . . . Christianity with its religious cult of man in the abstract . . . is the most fitting form of religion'.[45] Miranda also refers to a passage in the next chapter of *Capital* in which Marx quotes the Vulgate text of the Apocalypse (17.13; 13.17). In fact, although they deal with the beast, and the second in particular with the beast's licensing of those who wish to buy and sell, the subject is the apotheosized Roman state, not money. This leads to my criticism of Miranda.

It will be recalled that it was through the criticism of inversion, first located in religion, that Marx uncovered the inversions in the state and money. Since the criticism of the state and of money depend on the 'premise' of the criticism of religion, anyone who accepts the first two is automatically committed to the last one, until further notice. Miranda has discovered that in the teaching of Jesus wealth can take a religious form, and I have just pointed out that John of Patmos taught that the state (in the person of the emperor) could also take on a religious form.[46] We might say that it takes one to recognize one: religious people are sensitive to institutions which aspire to being religious. But what conclusion are we to draw from all this? According to Miranda he has uncovered 'the gospel roots of Marx's thought'. That is interesting, too, but the conclusion which actually follows is that if it is by an inversion of reality that money becomes Mammon and Rome becomes the beast, this is possible because religion itself is an inversion of reality. This was Marx's second criticism of religion. What is surprising is not simply that Miranda fails to address the criticism or even mention it (this he shares with all the other liberation theologians), but rather that he should ignore it while dealing with the very inversion on which the whole of Marx's position depends.

The answer is as simple as it is depressingly familiar. 'Marx's attack on religion has frequently been interpreted as an attack on Christianity. But Christianity is not a religion . . .'[47] On the contrary, Marx had little else in mind. The situation recalls the scene in Henry Fielding's *Tom Jones* in which Mr Thwackum, the divine, offers his definition of religion.

> When I mention religion, I mean the Christian religion; and not only the Christian religion, but the Protestant religion; and not only the Protestant religion, but the Church of England.[48]

When Marx criticized religion, it was the Christian religion, and with regard to capitalism it was the Protestant religion, and especially the Prussian Lutheran Church. Marx was prepared to illustrate his criticism of the Christian religion from any period of its history. At the beginning of this section I said that the attempt would be made to associate primitive Marxism with primitive Christianity. This Miranda now seeks to do, to distinguish primitive Christianity from the entire history of the church. Whether this makes any sense theologically or even sociologically, we may doubt if it can solve the problem. Miranda requires the separation of Jesus from religion altogether, but as we saw earlier in this chapter, when discussing the work of Segundo, this cannot be done historically.

It is true that Marx and Engels often referred to Christianity with approval, regardless of the positivism – or sheer ignorance of sources – of some Marxists. I may say in passing that I have nothing but admiration for Miranda's encyclopaedic knowledge of the complete works of Marx-Engels. The way in which he rallies his material to illustrate points from the whole range of over forty volumes is quite astonishing. Such are his references to the parallels which Marx and Engels draw between their movement and Christianity. 'The persecutions of the governments against the International were like the persecutions of ancient Rome against the primitive Christians.' The solution to the Serbian problem envisaged by Marx was to erect 'a free and independent Christian state on the ruins of the Muslim Empire'. Engels, who undertook more research than Marx into religious subjects, could supplement primitive Christianity by references to the German Reformation. 'By the kingdom of God, Muenzer understood nothing less than a state of society without class differences, without private property, and without superimposed state powers opposed to the members of society.' Luther gave the people a powerful weapon, the Bible. 'Through the Bible, he contrasted feudal Christianity of his time with the simple Christianity of the first century.' 'Calvinism founded a republic in Holland, and active republican parties in

England, and above all, Scotland.'[49] But while such references are interesting and important in other contexts, they relate to Marx's first criticism of religion. Through these passages it is possible for Miranda to argue that Marx recognized that Christianity has not always and everywhere been the opiate of the people. Christianity is even seen as the source of socialism in specific periods, from the Book of Acts to Marx's older contemporary Wilhelm Weitling. But when all this has been duly noted it was *religious* socialism, not scientific socialism. It was based on an inversion of reality, not on historical materialism. At best one could say that the latter has superseded the former. But the former, Christian socialism, is not a continuing viable alternative in an age of capitalism. Like Segundo, Miranda would like to be able to extract aspects of primitive Christianity and join them to Marx's social analysis. But we should not allow Marx's occasional positive assessment of the courage and commitment of Christians to blind us to the fact that he regarded Christianity as founded on an inversion of reality. To attempt to avoid this fact by claiming that Christianity is not a religion (or was not a religion originally) is to set up a merely semantic distinction which cannot be sustained theologically or historically.

PART THREE

Beyond Liberation Theology

11

Marx and the Failure of Liberation Theology

(a)   Selective criticism

Liberation theology has been criticized for being too Marxist: in reality it is not Marxist enough. Its allegiance to Marx has been regarded as the basis of its success: in fact its resistance to Marx is the cause of its failure.

As we saw in Chapter 6, Marx occupies an ambiguous place in the development of Latin American liberation theology. In the terms of Marx's own philosophy the revolution in Latin America could not arise from Marxism: it must arise from the base, from the material conditions of the continent. Activists and commentators alike refer to the existing situation as largely feudal. As we saw in the case of Cuba, the initiative was not taken by an urban industrial proletariat; the revolution was essentially peasant-based. Despite Guevara's generous though unhistorical references to Marx, Marxism was not itself a factor in the process. The first order of business was not the public ownership of the means of production, as it would have been in the transition to communism, but rather land reform, as befits the transition from feudalism. Guevara was more influenced by Mao than Marx, and specifically compared the situations of Cuba and China, recalling that Mao succeeded only when he turned from the proletariat to the peasants. Within the framework of historical materialism we could say that the progressive forces of change could no longer be contained within the essentially feudal structures of society. It was only after the guerrilla war ended that Marxism was applied within Cuba. The importance of the Cuba revolution was its humanism, self-sacrifice and socialist values of justice and equity. But both Debray and Marighela indicated that orthodox Marxism was not the guiding principle.

Nor was there any specific use of Marx's philosophy in the theological movements immediately prior to the appearance of liberation theology. Although the self-sacrifice of Camilo Torres and the courageous witness of Helder Camara are in their different ways inspiring, neither attempted to produce a new form of theology, and neither attempted to incorporate Marx in any way. Torres believed Marxism to be incompatible with Christianity. Camara is conservative in things ecclesial, a loyal servant of the papacy. And yet while he holds what might now be called a 'Polish' view of Marxism, it was Paul VI who used the language of Marxism to describe the new agenda for change in Latin America.

Contrary to first impressions the revolution in society and the revolution in the church in Latin America were neither dependent on Marxism nor guided by it. And yet this is the context in which liberation theology arose, or emerged. We have examined the work of some of the leading figures in the movement and they have all self-effacingly claimed that they have only expressed what many have experienced. This should not be misunderstood, as if they were incapable of creating something on their own account. I have observed that they have all been trained to the highest levels of international scholarship. They could have continued to produce European theology at the frontiers of research. Instead, they have entered the very different world of the oppressed and have reflected theologically on that reality. This is the basis of liberation theology, its strength, its example and (if I may say so) its glory. It has been the most creative, exciting and challenging development in theology in modern times, second only to feminist theology.[1] Marx has therefore been introduced into an ongoing situation which did not depend on or arise from his thought. My criticism of liberation theology arises not from any doubts concerning the Christian commitment or moral integrity of the participants, but from the basis on which Marx has been used. Not that Marx has been used, but how. Or rather, not that Marx has been given free rein, but that he has been used only within limits.

The theologians we have discussed have called in Marx as a consultant: come over and help us. They have set him to work in the analysis of the ills of society. It is his position they have taken over in exposing capitalism with its attendant exploitation and alienation. But Marx having travelled so far, they have decided to get full mileage out of him by applying his analysis also to the church. Yet a moment's thought will suggest that this is not the best way to use a consultant, indeed it is even dangerous. It would be like telling a quantity surveyor that you want him to examine the roof of your house with great care, and the plumbing while he is about it, but he is prohibited from commenting on the state of the foundations.

No group of scholars met to set themselves the task of creating a new theology. 'Come, let us reason together and build a theology based on the work of one, Karl Marx. And men shall call it, liberation theology. And it was so.' But it was not so at all. To their credit those now called liberation theologians met not with other scholars, but with the poor and the marginalized. They prayed together and studied the word of God. And as Segundo suggests, to the substance of their faith, they added the form taken from Marxist analysis of their situation. Thus Marxism is used in a highly selective way, as the group – the ecclesial base community – requires. Admirable though this may be, it means inevitably that not everything that Marx has to say is heard. As we have seen, surprisingly little attention is paid to Marx's criticisms of religion. It is assumed that he must have been speaking about someone else's religion. His critique can be usefully applied to European religion, or to the religion of colonialism, or the religion of the ruling and exploitative classes. In other words it is assumed that the religion Marx was criticizing was that of the classes he was in any case criticizing on other grounds. And this is true, but not the whole truth. It is further assumed that Marx was only human (a claim which I should not wish to make too insensitively in the presence of Marxist friends). Thus he had a blind spot with regard to religion (the monocle again). We all have our aberrations. When questioned in an interview in 1871 about religion, Marx seemed to reduce the question of atheism to a private matter. 'On that point I cannot speak in the name of the society (i.e. the International). I myself am an atheist.'[2] But does this make the situation better – or worse? If the whole of his philosophy rests on the 'premise' of the criticism of religion, yet atheism is a personal matter, this means that the criticism is actually more fundamental than atheism, not less.

If only Marx's criticism of religion had been based on atheism, then it could have been ignored. The question of the existence or non-existence of the deity cannot in practice be settled by argument, one way or the other. In the present context we could describe it as a Mexican stand-off. On the assumption that the great man had an aberration about atheism, liberation theologians feel free to make use of other aspects of his philosophy. Indeed and shockingly they even apply his criticism of religion to the Curia and the Inquisition. And yet, as we have just noted, his criticism of religion is quite independent of atheism. This is why using Marx selectively is dangerous. It presumes that theologians know which words of Marx need to be heard and which can be ignored. But it does not take a phenomenologist to remind us that our unexamined assumptions are the greatest barriers to our understanding. Indeed intuitively we know that it is precisely what is protected by our unconsidered assumptions which most urgently requires critical examination. Adopting the attitude of the master of suspicion himself, we might ask whose interests are being served when theologians protect their own religion from scrutiny by the most acute social critic of the modern world. The Spanish theologian, Alfredo Fierro, offering fraternal criticism to liberation theology, comments on the harsh judgments made by Assmann, Richard, Alves and others on both society and church, judgments made by reference to traditional theological sources. 'But the fact that under the rubric of liberation theology we find proposals that are very conservative in terms of theology, though progressive in social terms, tends to undermine the critical capacity of that theology when taken in overall terms.'[3]

(b) Peasant theology

It transpires that what we are dealing with is not a Marxist reading of theology, but a theological reading of Marxism, a much less dangerous and much more amenable creature. Nor is this simply a little inversion of words in the Hegelian style, worthy of Marx himself. It discloses the true nature of liberation theology on the ground. Since we are continually reminded that liberation theology arises from the experience of the oppressed it would seem particularly appropriate to test out this thesis by examining a relatively recent work by one of those theologians whose earlier works I have already discussed.

In Chapter 8 we considered the sophisticated and scholarly work of Clodovis Boff, *Theology and Praxis: Epistemological Foundations*. This was his doctoral dissertation, submitted at the University of Louvain. It is mainly critical reflection on theology, not an example of theology itself. Something else must be added. Boff is a missionary priest and a professor of theology in the Catholic University of São Paulo. It is fundamental to liberation theology that the theologian is also a priest, the man of learning is also a man of the people, the intellectual is also a militant. It is therefore entirely consistent with this view that Boff should spend half of the year teaching theology in an urban university, and the rest of the year working with small communities of Christians in the Rio Branco area, some 1700 miles to the west, on the Bolivian border. *Feet-On-The-Ground-Theology* is an account of his work in this area. It is the record of 'A Brazilian Journey', literally as well as metaphorically.

The book is divided into two unequal parts. The main part concerns Boff's work with the *communidades eclesiales de base*, or rather with training courses for their lay leaders, but the first part describes a three-week missionary journey into the jungle, to visit very primitive groups of rubber-gatherers. These people are at the centre of the jungle, and the margin of Brazilian society, subject to every form of deprivation. Boff was born in the south, in Santa Caterina, a very European part of Brazil, and he shares the southerner's experience of being in the north: 'a strange and no doubt false feeling that it is all useless, even absurd.'[4] The rubber-gatherers have not reached this level of civilization. It will be a long time before they are able to form basic communities, or take steps to liberate themselves. Boff has no liberation theology for them, nor apparently does he gain any inspiration from them in this direction. They live in oppressive conditions but there is no Marxism, only 'Christianity pure and hard'.[5] But how pure is it? European Christianity has been brought to them, but such is the disparity of cultural levels, and the infrequency of visits by priests, that they are unsure of the words of the Lord's Prayer, and do not make the sign of the cross properly. Boff is told of a prayer for curing toothache, which involves the intervention of the saints and the Virgin Mary, and he copies it down like a recipe.

This part of the Brazilian journal makes for uncomfortable reading. Boff arrives among these primitive people like a being from another world. From *Theology and Praxis* one might have expected a liberation theologian to have two words, but he has only one. He wishes them to enter more fully into that mythological religious world from which all modern people are in practice entirely alienated. There is nothing of that other word, from Marx, no plans to liberate them from the 'idiocy' of the rural life. There is no hint of the crisis which will come when with the advent of a dentist the prayer for curing toothache will be obsolete. Immediately Boff returned to the city he went into hospital to be treated for vivax malaria. Some demons can only be cast out by penicillin. There is no thought of Marx's criticism of such religion. The only indication that Marxist consciousness has not been left behind entirely is that Boff recognizes that on his travels he tends to deal not with the rubber-gatherers but with the traders, thus repeating history. That is, as a representative of the church he is associating with that economic class which has some power and is therefore the closest thing to the bourgeoisie in the region.

The second part of the book deals with his work as in the Rio Branco area. The people are poor and oppressed, but they are at a more advanced stage than the rubber-gatherers and are capable of forming basic communities and taking political initiatives. But Boff warns against overly romantic views of such groups, especially making a 'fetish' of 'the people'.[6] Hardly any men participate in the communities, even although the leadership is predominantly male. However, one hopeful sign is the 'demachoizing' of the situation, whereby women who have natural leadership capacities are coming forward. But the grassroots communities reach only about 5% of the people. In fact the journal does not introduce us to the communities so much as to the lay leadership. Some of them are very impressive, and very eager to receive further training. Boff is called in as a consultant.

But as there was no liberation theology among the rubber-gatherers, there is surprisingly little among the base communities. Many people who spend their working lives in cities have enjoyed a vacation in a rural community. When our children were small we spent several summers on a farm in Dorset. It would be a foolish person who thought that such a life was easy or quaint. It can be hard and even soul-destroying. Yet part of the charm is to relax into the scene, to go native. This was my impression when reading the journal of Boff's time in Rio Branco. He left behind the modern world view of the city, and tried to share the life of the peasants. If he took a note of the prayer for curing toothache, now he is impressed by an old priest's prayer for making rain.[7] In his religious instruction he emphasizes the rosary, novenas, processions and Hail Marys.

If the theology is pre-modern, so also is the attitude towards Marxism. For Boff in Louvain, or São Paulo for that matter, Marxism is the exciting leading edge of modern critical thought. But now in Rio Branco, in the real world of the oppressed, the peasants are warned away from Marx. Not that they would have read any Marx, but perhaps rumour has reached them that he was on their side. But no, Marx is presented once again as an atheist, an enemy of Christianity, someone who knew nothing of religious experience.

That's the source of the basic philosophical or epistemological error of Marx's critique of religion: he thought he had found the essence of religion in the social and economic conditions surrounding it, not in its own irreducible experience. In doing so, Marx thought he had grasped the kernel of religion when he had scarcely touched the shell. And he came to the conclusion that religion was like an onion – it's outer peel; there's no inner core. If you keep peeling, it comes apart and there's nothing else. But when did Marx have a true religious experience or even study one?[8]

The peasants might not understand the basic philosophical or epistemological error, but they can be assured by someone who does that when it comes to religion Marx is suddenly an incompetent fool who knows nothing about the subject. How comforting it is to have a consultant on such matters!

But if Marx is easily disposed of when he criticizes religion, Marxism is also dismissed. In the heartland of Latin America the view of Marxism which is reinforced is not Cuban but Polish. In the privacy of their massive tomes liberation theologians can claim Marx as their own, but now among the people Marxism is presented as an alien system.

> The *de facto* socialism of Eastern Europe no longer represents a true alternative to capitalism, because it includes many of the same defects: authoritarianism, industrialism, consumerism – in short, materialism.[9]

Western capitalism will not do, and the socialisms of the USSR and China will not do either. And yet liberation theologians without exception have been critical of third-way alternatives. To update a familiar question: where, then is the positive possibility of a Latin American emancipation? The quotation continues:

> Who knows whether the peoples of Latin America, precisely because of their Christian tradition, might not be destined to inaugurate a model of a new society, one that would really be new, a valid alternative to the two other models, chained as they are to their patterns of gross materialism and truncated humanism. This is something Pope John Paul II seems to have intuited in his own way.

Let us sincerely hope that the poor are given more resources for this task than unreconstructed theology and traditional piety, now that they have been warned off Marxism. Not for three thousand years have oppressed people been required to build so extensively, making bricks without straw.

(c) Failing the people

Latin America will not replicate American capitalism. For some this may be a disappointment, for others a source of comfort, but the reason is simply that it would not suit American interests to have Latin America develop in this way. In Chapter 6 I noted that Latin America cannot develop industrially as Europe did in the eighteenth and nineteenth centuries, because unlike Europe at that time, it is developing in a world in which powerful industrial economies already exist. Nor will Latin America reproduce East European socialism. As I noted also in Chapter 6, it is ironic that Fidel Castro should be intent on preserving a social and political structure which Mikhail Gorbachev is attempting to dismantle. Whether the future of Latin America lies in the creation of a new third way, as envisaged by Boff, we may doubt. A movement which represents 5% of the (mainly peasant) population might exert some influence at the margins, but it is hardly likely to provide a new basis for the social and economic life of the continent.

In Chapter 5 I criticized historical materialism in its ideological form, motivated as it was by a quasi-religious faith. But it is possible to accept it as a useful and suggestive hypothesis for analysing current historical movements. In this chapter and the final one I shall proceed in this way. This will enable me to point to a further failure of liberation theologians. Many of them purport to accept historical materialism, but they have not located themselves within it. They have proposed analyses and courses of action which disregard its basic premises. Thus, if we were to adopt the perspective of historical materialism, we should have to say that the third way, as proposed by Boff and others cannot be brought about by a religious or moral movement. It would require a change in the mode of production before there could be fundamental change in the superstructure.

Within the superstructure, however, there will be significant cultural change. Despite what is said about the religiosity of Latin America, it is likely that even in this continent people will become increasingly secular. This is the unplanned but concerted effect of capitalism and socialism throughout the world. The secularization of consciousness is permeating all countries, and because of its image of modernity it is for the most part welcomed. The most notable resistance to it is to be seen in Iran, but the cost is so high in that country that the net effect elsewhere is further to enhance the image of the secular. To some the associations of being 'modern' and 'secular' are threatening and have to be derided. But whose interests does this attitude serve? Only the rich can choose poverty: only those who have been formed by the modern world can advocate a return to the old ways.

On which side of the line will religion fall as the new age dawns? At the beginning of this century the Catholic Church stood four-square *adversus modernitatem*, apparently opposed to every autonomous development which could not be controlled by the church. In spite of the much-heralded call to *aggiornamento* in Vatican II, will it end the century in the same position? In Latin America many Catholics undoubtedly will do just that, ably led by conservatives among the hierarchy.[10] They will be clear-sighted men of integrity and conviction who will know what is at stake and make their choice. I think they are wrong, but I have always admired conservatives more than liberals. I am more concerned about those who will support the conservative cause not by conviction but by confusion, and among them I number the liberation theologians. In this context the high-profile disagreement on ethical matters is not as important as the fundamental theological agreement. Because they have not faced Marx's second criticism of religion, liberation theologians are still on the conservative side of the ideological line.

In Chapter 3 we saw that the second criticism of religion, religion as an inversion of reality, is not the end for Marx but the beginning.

It is the premise of all other extensions of this criticism. Now that alienation has been unmasked in its religious form, it is possible to address the problem of alienation in its secular forms. It is at this point that we are confronted by the ambiguity of liberation theology, its halting between two ways. On the one hand, because of the sophistication of the writers, their level of critical awareness, they can follow Marx in the criticism of various secular forms of alienation: the state, money, commodity production and capitalism. But at this point they move in the reverse direction from Marx. Liberation theology, as theology, offers a religious interpretation of the secular. In *Theology and Praxis* Clodovis Boff described it as a theological reflection on the non-theological. By avoiding Marx's second critique, liberation theology does not follow him into an ideological criticism of the secular. Rather, it maintains a theological interpretation of the secular. This guarantees not an ideological *critique* of the secular, but an ideological *view* of the secular.

I deliberately moved on from *Theology and Praxis* to liberation theology in practice, *Feet-on-the-Ground-Theology*. Here the ambiguity clearly presents itself. Boff reflects on what is being achieved in the lay leadership training courses.

> What the church as such is doing is an initial 'priming'. In the area of conscientization, it provides an initial critical access to social reality. In the area of organization, it creates a whole mystique of unity. In BCCs (basic Christian communities) it gets social organizing efforts going. The rest of the job has to be the work of persons in areas that are extra-church – but not extra-kingdom – that is, in profane or societal (but not extra-faith) areas.[11]

There are several unresolved ambiguities here. First, it is not the church which is doing the 'priming', but those directly involved with the communities. The church for the most part is doing what it has always done. But secondly, the priming is not essentially theological. In practice what is happening is that individuals with higher education are raising the consciousness of the lay leadership about 'social reality'. Through the analytical tools of the social sciences, particularly of Marx, they are brought to an ideological awareness of hitherto concealed connections. They gain a unified picture of reality. Part of the discovery of the real behind the ideological is the disclosure of the part traditionally played by religion. All of this corresponds to Marx's demystification of social reality. However, and more ambiguously, Boff describes the end result differently: 'it creates a whole mystique of unity'. The mere fact that it is a priest who gives you directions to the race-track does not make it a religious action. The fact that Marx's social analysis is made available by a theologian does not make it a religious perspective. The danger is that 'mystique' is simply re-mystification. Thirdly, lay people who now have ideological awareness about social reality go on to perform secular tasks. Now that they have been shown the connections between their situation and the interests of the ruling class they can, for example, formulate and initiate political campaigns. But a drain, is a drain, is a drain. What is the theological interpretation of this non-theological reality? Early doctrinal contro-versies are characterized by the juxtaposition of two incompatible positions which are simply asserted to be identical. How is the 'extra-church' activity not 'extra kingdom'? How is a 'societal area' not an 'extra-faith area'? For liberation theology *that* the pairs can be rec-onciled is not demonstrated, simply asserted. We are not offered an argument, simply a hope.

For all the sophistication and erudition of the liberation theologians, I believe that liberation theology has failed intellectually. For all its insight and integrity in matters ethical and spiritual, it is based on theological premises which cannot be affirmed in the modern world. This kind of debate among academics has a certain importance, and it may well be that not a little ink will be spilt over it. It is an issue which will wear out many word-processor ribbons. However, it has only a relative importance. I am more concerned in the long term, as I have been throughout my adult life, with the pastoral and evangelical issues. Liberation theology has failed the academic community, but more importantly it has failed the very people to whom it is committed.

I recall a meeting of clergy when I worked in Rhodesia (now Zim-babwe) in a country district. One of them asked a rhetorical question: Why do people stop being religious when they move to the towns? At least I hoped it was a rhetorical question, and that he was not expecting an answer. There are of course sociological reasons for their loss of contact with the church, but I believe that the fundamental problem is theological. The theology with which they grew up fails them when they move into another social world. There are signs that this is already happening in Latin America. Liberation theology has indeed offered 'initial priming'. Some lay people – some of the most able – have been projected into a social reality which lies beyond liberation theology. The more committed they are, the more they are carried outside the church and outside its religious interpretation of the world, as much beyond liberation theology as beyond traditional theology.

Throughout this study I have acknowledged the scholarship of all the liberation theologians whose work we have so briefly examined. And I have also expressed my admiration for their moral – sometimes physical – courage in their commitment to the poor. In questioning

266

the outcome of liberation theology I retract nothing of this. But there is a dilemma, and it is expressed in the following words of José Bonino.

> To the extent that the theology of liberation is – and is made into – a new 'school', a set of self-contained theological tenets or positions, it will have its day and be gone. As a matter of fact, the pioneers in this movement are more and more unhappy with the very expression *theology of liberation*. But to the extent that we are here dealing with a task, the struggle for liberation, which lies as much ahead of us as ten or five years ago, which indeed in a certain sense always lies ahead of us, that task continues to be pertinent; a critical and committed Christian reflection of the people who have made this struggle their own and who understand it as the concrete witness to the freedom that has been promised to man in Jesus Christ.[12]

The task is real, and the commitment. But is the rest more than 'theological adornment' which will finally prove an obstacle to liberation? As the economies of Latin America are developed and as their societies are modernized, Christian activists will increasingly find themselves alienated from the religious interpretation from which they started out. And this is the tragedy, that liberation theology has failed not its least committed but its most committed lay people, both men and women. The problem is real and it is growing. The failure arises not from too much attention to Marx's social analysis, but from too little attention to his criticism of religion.

12

Religion in the Next Epoch

(a) Confirmation of historical materialism

The 1950s saw the rediscovery of the writings of Marx in Europe, especially the writings of the young Marx, which led to the Marxist-Christian dialogue. This decade, according to Gutierrez, was a time of optimism in the Third World, with the anticipation of genuine development. In the following decade political theology and the theology of hope appeared, theologies much influenced by neo-Marxism. But during this time the rhetoric of development was exposed and disillusionment ensued. At the end of the decade the theological initiative passed to the Third World, especially in Latin American theology of liberation. These three decades were characterized by criticism, suspicion, and hope for a new future. In all three aspects the influence of Marx was clear. The 1980s, however, saw a fundamental change.[1] It has been marked by a resurgence in capitalism, and a decline in socialism. Adam Smith's *The Theory of Moral Sentiments* has been dusted off, and *Capital* put back on the shelf. There has been a rapprochement between the USA and the USSR, while the European Economic Community moves towards a fully integrated market, already penetrated by Japan. If the previous three decades saw the division of the world into three, the new configuration may well be a world divided into two: rich/poor; north/south; 'white'/'coloured'. We should all like to think that we are living at an important juncture in world history, but there are objective grounds for thinking that during the 1980s we have entered a new epoch.

One of the weaknesses of historical materialism is that its 'broad outline' is too broad. The proposition that in any epoch the superstructure is determined by the base is as reasonable as any idealist or theological view of history, but with only a few examples of modes of

268

production, the theory does not explain the very substantial differences which take place within an epoch. A few months before he died Engels wrote a new Introduction to Marx's work *The Class Struggle in France*. Although he maintained that Marx had brilliantly applied historical materialism to the analysis of that period of upheaval, he admitted that this was possible only in broad terms. It would never be possible to account for day to day events by relating them to 'the *final* economic causes'.[2] For example, substantial developments in British constitutional government took place within the feudal period: the same base does not explain these very different arrangements. Historical materialism would seem to require a sub-division of modes of production. Thus capitalism might be divided into an early phase of industrialization, followed by subsequent phases of imperialism and technology. Each phase in the mode of production would give rise to fundamental changes in the superstructure – within broadly the same parameters. Marx, at least at the outset, expected capitalism to be replaced by socialism within a few years. In the same article to which I have just referred Engels was able to acknowledge this error, with hindsight. 'But history has also proved us mistaken and has exposed the position we held at that time to be illusion.'[3] Today Marx's followers speak of late capitalism, and look for signs of its imminent demise. But what if we have not yet seen mature capitalism? What if capitalism still has several phases yet to achieve?

The phrenetic voices of the sectarian Left are less strident today: the activists of 1968 are now dispensing mortgages; the prodigal sons of the Great Refusal have been welcomed home if not to a banquet of fatted calf, at least to a really interesting low cholestoral meal out with a few friends. Marx is not a popular subject of discussion over a glass of Glenmor Natural Spring water. On a national scale, the red rose has replaced the red flag as the symbol of the Labour Party. The entrepreneurial language of accountability and value for money has replaced the call for the nationalization of the means of production, distribution and exchange. On the world stage Mikhail Gorbachev has begun the process of democratization in the USSR and, unintentionally, decolonization. The leaders of the Chinese Communist Party ruthlessly suppressed the democratic movement in June 1989 so that they could resume the expansion of plans to co-operate with Western capitalism. Mrs Thatcher, despairing of finding real socialism anywhere in the UK or the USSR, has turned her Medusan glare on M. Jacques Delors and his social charter for the EEC. Far from being in the last stages of collapse, it would seem that capitalism is thriving in Europe, the USA and is being enthusiastically taken up throughout the world.

As it increases, and socialism decreases, so the conclusion is drawn that historical materialism is utterly discredited.

But not for the first time in history, data are capable of pointing towards precisely opposite conclusions. While these most recent developments may well discredit many contemporary forms of socialism and some who call themselves Marxists, the events themselves might well be taken as the confirmation of historical materialism. In Chapter 5 we saw that for Hegel we cannot jump over our time and place in history. It is not possible to bestow on a primitive people a democratic system of government which depends on the consciousness of individual liberty. We have found confirmation of this in post-colonial times. The settlers' jibe was: 'one man, one vote, once'. Instead of liberal democracy some African countries have reverted to tribalism (it could only be called racism if practised by white people). Let us also add in passing that along with tribalism there are other disturbing features. In particular there is the leader who is state president for life, who need not stand for election (or in some cases be subject to parliament). He not only knows the will of the common people, but in a real sense embodies it. Let us not be misled by the taking into public ownership of certain key industries or services. All of these features describe not Marxism, but National Socialism, or to give it its generic name, fascism. But none of these reversions discredits liberal democracy; rather they confirm Hegel.

The same argument can be used with regard to Marx. For Marx it is not possible for us to jump over our time and place in (economic) history. Since the superstructure is determined by the base, liberal democracy cannot develop before bourgeois capitalism. Of course Marx did not believe that liberal democracy is the highest form of political or societal life. But liberal democracy cannot be superseded by socialism until bourgeois capitalism has been superseded by communism. This many Marxists have failed to grasp. They have thought that communism succeeds capitalism, but this omits the Hegelian dialectic of history. It is capitalism which creates the necessary conditions for communism: without the transformation of society by capitalism, communism is impossible. It is capitalism which prepares society for the leap to communism. And it is not possible to leap over history. I have already discussed *The Communist Manifesto*, noting this aspect of the argument.

The bourgeoisie, historically, has played a most revolutionary part. The bourgeoisie, wherever it has got the upper hand, has put an end to all feudal, patriarchal, idyllic relations.

The importance of this claim can easily be overlooked by those

270

who are accustomed to Marx's condemnation of the bourgeoisie and capitalism. Yes, he does condemn that class and its exploitation of the proletariat, but each epoch supersedes its predecessor with a genuine revolution. It is not possible to move from feudalism to communism. Just as Marx makes a very positive claim for capitalism, so he clearly approves of its effects: it 'has rescued a considerable part of the population from the idiocy of the rural life'. Normally Marx is speaking of the subjugation of the proletariat by capitalism, but here he speaks of capitalism rescuing the peasants. Marx may be right or wrong, but for those who wish to make use of his social analysis peasants cannot be conscientized by religion, not even by the Book of Acts, into communism. They must go through capitalism.

According to historical materialism it is not possible to leap from a feudal society to a communist society. This is what many régimes have attempted to do in the period since World War II. Indeed this analysis might also be applied to the USSR and to China. Their failure has not discredited historical materialism, but at least in this respect has confirmed it. Only capitalism can prepare a society, culture or civilization for the qualitative leap to communism. Liberation theologians have encouraged their communities to believe that it is possible to move from feudalism to socialism, by-passing capitalism. The prospects for such a programme are not auspicious, but it is certainly not Marxism.

(b) The European way

Earlier I noted that Marx could deny that he was a Marxist. It would be too confusing to forbid the use of this adjective to describe his work, but we must have sympathy for a man whose name is taken by those who disregard his views. It is claimed that liberation theologians are Marxist, and yet, as we have seen, working within an essentially peasant and marginalized constituency their unmitigated rejection of capitalism is not simply at odds with Marx's position, but is entirely inconsistent with it. There is more, and it is worse. Liberation theology continually criticizes and rejects Europe as the model for Third World countries in general, and Latin America in particular. Yes, dear reader, as you may have guessed, this too is entirely inconsistent with Marx's position.

Although I have referred to liberation theologians, as if they formed a group or school, their positions are all different and their works have particular characteristics. As with other fine products, the connoisseur could probably distinguish one from another on the basis of a brief sample even if it were not identified by the author's name. In Chapter 9 we examined Jose Miranda's work on hermeneutics. Although he does not directly address Marx's second criticism of religion, his position has the most potential in this regard. In Chapter 10 we discussed his very well-informed study of *Marx against the Marxists*. His earlier exegetical work has had considerable impact on other liberation theologians, and his influence is clear even when they do not refer to his writings. However, this later work on Marx has had little influence, which is unfortunate, especially when he tackles the contentious issue of 'the intransigent occidentalism of Marx and Engels'.[4]

Miranda begins with the quotation given above from the *Manifesto* in which Marx has in mind the effect of capitalism in Europe. It has 'rescued a considerable part of the population from the idiocy of the rural life'. But this judgment would apply to any country. Even if industrialization is mainly in agriculture, this is very significant for workers who 'are plucked away from the idiocy of country life to belong to the industrial population'.[5] Engels expresses the same view, in language more extreme, when he writes of industrialization alone being able to 'deliver the rural population from the isolation and stupor in which it has vegetated almost unchanged for thousands of years'. (23.384) In a discussion of the shortcomings of Arnold Ruge, Marx describes the kind of person who is 'richly endowed with all the vices, the mean and petty qualities, with the slyness and the stupidity . . . of the peasant' (11.268). Miranda knows very well that on Marx's view it is necessary to pass through capitalism to reach socialism. Marx had no romantic tendencies whatsoever with regard to the rural life and the conditions of the peasants. The necessity of capitalism must be understood against the background of what Miranda calls Marx's 'mercilessly negative judgment of any and all so-called naturalism'.[6] Capitalism is therefore an instrument of civilization. Californian gold has drawn the Pacific islands into trade, thereby rescuing them from barbarism. Even colonialism can be defended on the same grounds. Whatever negative effects the British had on India, they ended the traditional isolation of the villages, a necessary advance, since 'the breaking up of these stereotyped primitive forms was the *sine qua non* for Europeanization'.[7] Capitalism, colonialism, civilization – in short Europeanization – are the necessary means by which socialism can eventually be achieved. It is ironic to think that all of these have been rejected in the name of Marx!

A further irony concerns anti-Americanism. The ritual abuse of America is also thought to be justified by Marx. Yet Marx had considerable admiration for American history, for example for Lincoln and his opposition to the 'pro-slavery rebellion', for American democracy and the separation of church and state. But on the necessary contribution of North America, 'the most progressive nation', to the development of world history he is emphatic. 'Only wipe North America off the map and you will get anarchy, the complete decay of trade and modern civilization' (38.102). If I concentrate on Europeanization it is first because that was a more central theme in Marx's work and because as a European I am particularly concerned about the constant criticism and rejection of the European way by liberation theologians. It is for Americans to respond to criticisms of their traditions. Whether many American theologians will want to criticize liberation theology for not being Marxist enough is another matter.

The communism which Marx advocates can only be achieved after the transformation effected by European capitalism. He rejects all forms of pre-industrial primitive communism. In Chapter 3 I discussed Marx's criticism of 'crude and thoughtless communism' as described in the Paris Manuscripts. Far from representing a higher form of civilization, it reduced people's lives to the lower level of a previous stage. In a letter to Kautsky in the year following Marx's death, Engels repeats this judgment. Primitive communism (*Urkommunismus*), as founded by the Dutch in Java, has the result of 'keeping the people at the level of primitive stupidity, and lays the broadest and most secure foundation of exploitation and despotism'.[8] In Chapter 5 I observed that the great movements of history are not achieved through human intentions. Marx did not claim that Europe had set out to serve others. But without the British Empire India would not have achieved the necessary social transformation. It threatened the 'idyllic village communities' which had always been the scene of 'oriental despotism', and brought an end to 'stagnatory and vegetative life'. Thus 'whatever may have been the crimes of England she was the unconscious tool of history in bringing about that revolution' (12.132).

Marx was never in any doubt about the evils of capitalism and colonialism, nor was he naive about the self-interests of Europeans as they explored the continents of the world. It has become fashionable to denounce European influence and decry its effects on Third World countries. This has spilled over to theology, so that as Nietzsche said of Wagner, Europe is taken to be the name of a disease. Those returning to Latin America have to undergo 'de-toxification'. Naturally this is not a view which I share, but that is of no consequence. What is more important is that it is not the view of Marx. In 1853 he wrote as follows: 'England has to fulfil a double mission in India; one destructive, the other regenerating – the annihilation of old Asiatic society, and the laying of the material foundations of Western society in Asia' (12.217–8). No one would suggest that Europe is beyond criticism; many of the widespread criticisms were first formulated by Europeans themselves. This is true of theology as of other spheres.

Liberation theologians, who to a man bear European names, learned to criticize European theology while in Europe. Before Gutierrez published his monumental book Moltmann had already turned Marx – that ultra-European philosopher – on his head. There can be no objection to others attempting to go their own way. In reality it is probably too late for that, but it would be ironic indeed if those who reject and denounce the European way thought that they could do so *as Marxists*. It is unfortunate that Miranda's study of what Marx actually said has not been read as carefully within Latin America as it has been in Europe.

If we wish to explore this 'intransigent occidentalism' further, there are two further issues which we must consider. They cannot be dealt with exhaustively, but they can at least take the form of an agenda. The first concerns the supersession of capitalism. The second concerns the place of religion in the next epoch, and at this point we must therefore once again address Marx's ontological criticism of religion.

(c)   Supersession of capitalism

The dominant feature in world history of the most recent times has been the resurgence of capitalism and its transformation of those societies which have adopted it. It has divided Christians in their response to it. The options normally on offer are equally unsatisfactory to anyone who holds a dialectical view of history.

Capitalism has many advocates throughout the world, not a few of them prominent Christians, both clerical and lay. Their enthusiastic defence often goes beyond its economic achievements to make moral and even religious claims on its behalf. The American Baptist evangelist Jerry Falwell, founder of Moral Majority, might be taken to illustrate this view.

> The free-enterprise system is clearly outlined in the Book of Proverbs in the Bible. Jesus Christ made it clear that the work ethic was a part of His plan for man. Ownership of property is biblical. Competition in business is biblical. Ambitious and successful business management is clearly outlined as a part of God's plan for His people.[9]

A more thoughtful and troubled position is represented by the English economist, Professor Brian Griffiths, a lay Christian and adviser to the Thatcher government.

> I have always believed and continue to believe that the advocacy of monetarist economic policies is perfectly compatible with a Christian view of the world, and indeed that if such policies are seen as part

of a general strategy to reduce the power of the state, give more power back to people, and to increase the participation of the individual family in economic life, then their basis is distinctly Christian.[10]

Falwell's position is simply a crude religious legitimation of American capitalism. Griffiths watchers, by contrast, can detect a development in his position as he struggles to maintain the priority of his Christian faith over his monetarist policies. The problem facing anyone travelling by this route is that capitalism has certain features which are not readily compatible with traditional Christian ethical values. Is it possible to use capitalism, given these characteristics, to achieve Christian goals?

On the other hand capitalism has many opponents, including the liberation theologians of Latin America. They take the straightforward view that capitalism is a bad thing, morally and religiously, and that in those countries where it functions it should be dismantled as quickly as possible, and that other countries should steadfastly oppose its introduction. On this view it would have been better if capitalism had never existed. As we have seen, this is not Marx's view, but its contradiction. Capitalism has a necessary effect in the transformation of economies, social institutions, consciousness and indeed civilization and culture: it is an indispensable step towards a goal. But capitalism is not that goal. According to Marx there must be something better than a capitalist society, but the route to it lies through capitalism beyond capitalism.

This considerably narrows down the choices for those who are Christians, and who consider that historical materialism is as good a model of historical motion as anything else on offer in philosophy, theology, sociology, history or biology. It means that on moral and religious grounds capitalism must be superseded, but that on historical materialist grounds it must be genuinely superseded and not simply rejected. This in turn raises two further problems. The first is the contradiction of planning for supersession, since that seems to contradict unintentional succession of one mode of production over another, and the determinate relationship of the base to the superstructure in historical materialism. The second, even if this problem could be overcome, concerns what would count as the genuine supersession rather than the complete rejection of capitalism.

The first matter is not as serious as it might at first appear. I am not raising the possibility that society could be fundamentally changed by an act of will, or by a moral or religious crusade. The premise of historical materialism is still affirmed, namely that fundamental change will take place only with change in the mode of production. The question is whether and to what extent human beings can actively participate in this process. But this is an issue which we have previously addressed in Chapter 10. According to Hegel history is marked by the progressive self-consciousness of Spirit. At a certain point, approximating on Marx's scale to the bourgeois revolution, the process becomes self-conscious. Man (i.e. Hegel) for the first time is aware of internal dynamic of the real. *Mutatis mutandis*, at a certain stage in historical materialism, namely the development of capitalism, man (i.e. Marx) becomes aware of the nature of the historical dialectic. In the previous discussion I said that at that stage human initiative enters creatively into the process itself. This does not mean that man can transform society according to some idealist or liberal notion of what ought to be the case. Rather it means that another mode of production can be chosen, on which a very different superstructure can arise, one in this case which reflects such considerations as morality, religion and aesthetics.

And this in turn leads us to the second matter, what would count as a genuine supersession of capitalism. The starting point would be a society which had already been transformed by capitalism, which had achieved the level of wealth creation, modernization, consciousness, civilization and culture made possible by it. That would be the starting point, but not the goal. The goal, embodying the moral, religious and aesthetic criteria to which we have already alluded, can be named variously utopia or the kingdom of God. The term 'communism' has now been so tarnished that it can no longer be held up as the new hoped-for age. In any case, Marx refused to raise communism as a 'dogmatic banner' and went on, in a letter to Arnold Ruge, to claim that 'communism, in particular, is a dogmatic abstraction' (3.143). The name is not the problem. Nor is this simply re-mystification. The outstanding problem is to discover what mode of production would enable us to achieve such a goal, overcoming the alienation and exploitation which are not accidental to but inherent in capitalism.

'Blessed are the poor' has become something of a slogan for liberation theology. It is good that the words of Jesus should be given central place in the life of Christian communities. It is also good that they have been restored to their original meaning. The Uruguayan Methodist Julio de Santa Ana undertook a study on behalf of the World Council of Churches, the results of which were published as *Good News to the Poor*.[11] As he points out, 'Blessed are the poor' soon became 'Blessed are those who give to the poor'. It is not easy to discuss this matter with complete honesty: it is easy to speak with bad faith. However, one of the features of the transition from feudalism to capitalism, from the ancient to the modern world was the creation of wealth. In the ancient world there was a fixed heap, and one person was rich at the expense of another. There was only so much wealth, and the moral issue was how it could be equitably divided. The most revolutionary feature of capitalism has been its capacity to create wealth. There is no fixed heap, and the moral issue is not how to share a finite amount, but how to create wealth in such a way that all could benefit from the process. This is the greatness of capitalism, and the reason why it has transformed social life more extensively and more rapidly than any single development in human history hitherto. Marx saw clearly that the wealth of nations was not to be measured simply in economic terms, but in the level of civilization and culture, of *human* life which could be attained thereby. The negative side of capitalism he identified as exploitation through commodity production and alienated labour. But he never advocated that society should return to the old privation and determinism of the fixed heap. The rhetoric of many Marxists, and of liberation theologians, suggests that it is possible to create a just and equitable society by moving from feudalism to pre-capitalist communism. That is to condemn the people of the Third World to live for ever in the ancient world. It is to adopt an idyllic view of the natural life which, as we saw in the previous section, Marx both rejected and despised as not fully human. Just as Marx rejected a communism which was a levelling down to the life which had not yet attained to private ownership, so the supersession of capitalism cannot be at the expense of a return to a fixed heap economy which is incapable of creating resources for human enrichment. 'Blessed are the poor.' Yes, and apparently 'Blessed are the merciful.'[12]

There is, however, one further consideration. Marx's 'intransigent occidentalism' designates his expectation that the future for every society must lie in following the European way. Yet as we saw in Chapter 6, Third World countries cannot develop as Europe once developed, for the simple reason that they exist in a world which is being dominated by European (American, Japanese) capitalism. The supersession of capitalism will therefore entail the creation of a system from which world alienation and exploitation will be eliminated.

But there is one final warning. There is a real danger that the world is being divided into rich nations and poor nations. It often seems as if the advocates of capitalism are working towards the entrenchment of this division. Given human nature, that is not perhaps surprising. What would be more distressing would be if those who have dedicated their lives to overcoming oppression and poverty, also and by a different route achieve the same entrenchment. The two groups we have already identified as likely to perform this unintentional function are

Marxists who do not understand Marx's view of the place of capitalism in historical materialism, and liberation theologians who recall people to that primitive religious socialism which Marx entirely rejected. How tragic it would be if from the highest moral and religious motives they fell into the trap described by Christians for Socialism: 'It often happens that groups which seem to be progressive or even leftist end up as strategic enemies of an authentic revolutionary process in the long run.'

(d) Religion and historical materialism

In *The German Ideology* Marx was making the transition from idealism to materialism and exposing the false consciousness by which familiar objects and relationships can be misrepresented and misunderstood. There is a section in his long rambling attack on Stirner where he discusses spirits. He makes a distinction between the practice of religion and the scientific study of religion. People who live within the religious sphere are inclined to view it as independent and autonomous,

> instead of explaining it from the empirical conditions and showing how definite relations of industry and intercourse are necessarily connected with a definite form of society, hence, with a definite form of state and hence with a definite form of religious consciousness (5.154).

It is all too easy to write a history of Christianity in a particular period as if it were determined either by supernatural guidance or by entirely internal factors. Marx criticizes Stirner for such an approach to the Middle Ages. If he had adopted Marx's method the outcome would have been very different:

> he could have found that *'Christianity' has no history whatever* and that all the different forms in which it was visualized at various times were not 'self-determinations' and 'further developments' 'of the religious spirit', but were brought about by wholly empirical causes in no way dependent on any influence of the religious spirit (5.154).

Most people with a genuine interest in religion will probably find this passage threatening and depressing. It seems to offer nothing but a reductionist explanation of religion. On a closer inspection, however, it is challenging and promising.

In the first place it is challenging, because it draws attention to something which is often ignored, namely that religion in many respects functions in exactly the same way as other social institutions. The churches have plant, capital, financial targets, personnel. They can allocate these resources well or badly. The fact that they are religious institutions does not protect employees from being treated in inhuman ways. They share the ethos of the day, and if they stand out against it in some respects it is very often out of loyalty to the ethos of a previous day. Paul made something of his capacity to be 'all things to all men',[13] but that achievement is as nothing compared to his successors who have been slave owners to the slave owners, feudal lords to the feudal lords, capitalists to the capitalists, colonial powers to the colonial powers and war-mongers to the war-mongers. In this sense Marx's claim is salutary: 'Christianity has no history whatever.' Its history is the common history of the nations.

But in the second place, is this not promising? Marx rejects religion as illusion when it deals with the non-empirical. He exposes its ideological character when it purports to explain history from outside history. He declares it to be the old idealist inversion of reality when it divorces itself from the real forces which determine secular history. But having said all that, he does not deny that religion is real, that it is part of the social life of mankind. If he rejects the ahistorical idealist account of religion, he proposes in its place a historical materialist account. Nor is he in any doubt that such an approach would be successful. Just do not ask him to spend time on it. But at least he indicates how it could proceed. If the historical materialist method is adopted, religion can be considered on the same basis as other social phenomena. Marx returns to this theme twenty years later in the first volume of *Capital*. By this time religion is no longer an important element in his work, but it is mentioned from time to time illustratively, often in the most seemingly unlikely contexts. In Book 1, Chapter 12, Marx discusses 'The Development of Machinery', insisting on relating the invention of machines to their historical contexts. Indeed a critical history of technology could be written, related to the mode of production.

> Technology reveals the active relation of man to nature, the direct process of the production of his life, and thereby it also lays bare the process of the production of the social relations of his life, and of the mental conceptions that flow from those relations.[14]

However, this is not true only of technology, and Marx continues this quotation by applying the approach to religion.

> Even a history of religion that is written in abstraction from this material basis is uncritical. It is, in reality, much easier to discover by analysis the earthly kernel of the misty creations of religion than to do the opposite, i.e. to develop from the actual, given relations

of life the forms in which these have been apotheosized. The latter method is the only materialist, and therefore the only scientific one.

As McLellan points out, this is not only a criticism of idealism, but of Feuerbach's ahistorical materialist approach.[15] By this time Marx has set aside the projection theory as an account of actual religion. The unpacking of anthropology from theology is still an exercise in the old idealist philosophy.

The main hesitation about a historical materialist approach to religion is the danger of reductionism. But reductionism is not always negative. With the development of secular consciousness the natural sciences were reductionist with regard to magical forces. Emancipated from religious dogma, they were able to investigate the origins of the universe as well as biological species. It is now widely accepted that many aspects of the religious world-view are obsolete. Reductionism can perform a positive function in clearing the decks for the real task. Of course reductionism can be carried too far. As I pointed out earlier, in Chapter 3, it is characterized at some point in the argument by a phrase such as 'nothing but . . .' Religion is nothing but a longing for the father (Freud). Religion is nothing but a declaration of allegiance to a set of moral principles (Braithwaite). These explanations have to be taken seriously, for there is an element of truth in them, but they arise not from empirical study but from positivist preconceptions of what must be the case. However, the misuse of reductionism does not argue against its merits.

There is, though, a continuing fear about possible reductionism in this historical materialist approach. Does it not deny the existence of the supernatural? Yes it does, and that is one of its strengths. The idea of the supernatural belongs to that world-view which has now been discredited. But that is more than compensated for by the fact that the natural turns out to be much more mysterious than the most fantastic dream. The real danger of reductionism is that we should adopt a static view of man, the universe and history. Religion has performed this function by offering us knowledge of these things 'from elsewhere'. It has thus inverted reality and created an ideology which has been all-pervasive. And this is Marx's second, ontological, criticism of religion. It does not apply only to bad religion, but to religion as such.

In Chapter 3 we claimed that it would be possible to continue with religion if this inversion could be itself reversed. The historical materialist approach offers this possibility. Religion arises from human experience, but this is far from saying that it is merely an expression of human feelings or moods. Like every other real experience it has two sides to it. It is not just experience, but experience of something. It is real, as it is a response to the real. In a historical materialist perspective this further entails that that experience will fundamentally change and develop from epoch to epoch. The experience and its conceptualization and institutionalization will change substantially with the new mode of production and the new consciousness arising therefrom. I wish to end, therefore, by illustrating this point in a non-religious example, before applying it to the religious.

In Chapter 3 I discussed the themes of the Paris Manuscripts, including Marx's critique of 'crude and thoughtless communism'. Historical materialism begins to emerge as he conceives of epochs through which civilization develops. But this first form of communism would not represent an advance; rather a reversion to a previous, lower and even sub-human level. Of all the indicators which Marx might propose in making this judgment no one could have predicted that he would have selected the relationship between man and woman. We might note in passing that in June 1843 Marx had finally been able to marry his fiancée, Jenny von Westphalen. Their first child was born on May Day, 1844. Since Marx claimed that social being should determine consciousness, it is not after all surprising that in that same year of 1844 he should make the relationship between man and woman normative in gauging the process of a civilization. At any rate this is how he describes it.

> From the character of this relationship follows how much *man* as a *species-being*, as *man*, has come to be himself and to comprehend himself; the relation of man to woman is the *most natural* relation of human being to human being. It therefore reveals the extent to which man's *natural* behaviour has become *human*, or the extent to which the *human* essence in him has become a *natural essence* – the extent to which his *human nature* has come to be *natural* to him (3.296).

In this fine Hegelian style Marx describes the supersession of the natural life of man. It is capitalism which frees him from his previous relationship to the natural world. Man has a natural, biological life, and this is expressed in the relationship of man and woman. But in the course of material history man supersedes this purely natural life. Nature becomes human nature. Human nature becomes man's nature. This takes place in the material world, not in its rejection, but in its supersession. I take this to mean that the new human relationship between man and woman makes use of the same biological process, but sexual intercourse is now undertaken for human and not purely natural reasons. Through the biological there is a transcendence of the biological. Through his material history man transcends the merely material. It is for this reason that the relationship of man and woman is the indicator of the real progress of a civilization. Let me say in passing that this is the importance of dependable forms of contraception for the development of human civilization. Those who insist that intercourse must still retain the possibility of procreation have entirely failed to comprehend this qualitative advance, and threaten to draw society back into the purely natural life.

The transcendence of the biological takes place within material history, and not in its rejection. It is a qualitative development, truly profound and awesome. The mystery of transcendence is not that it comes from beyond but that it leads us beyond. In this case beyond the natural, but certainly not into that obsolete quasi-dimension of the 'supernatural'. But what shall we call this form of experience, for it surely does not belong to any of the natural or medical sciences? Nor does it belong within the social sciences, though its significance has been noted by the German sociologist of religion Thomas Luckmann. Twenty-five years ago he criticized what he regarded as the trivialization of his discipline, and made this extraordinary claim:

> It is in keeping with an elementary sense of the concept of religion to call the transcendence of biological nature by the human organism a religious phenomenon.[16]

If previously we sought the human essence of religion, now we are confronted by the religious essence of the human. The mystery does not lie in another, supernatural dimension, yet as already noted, it is not merely a mood. Karl Jaspers, the Swiss philosopher understood that the experience is both subjective and a response to the objective. 'Transcendence is more than it is for me.'[17]

Liberation theologians have courageously led the way in ensuring that religion will no longer act as an opiate to the poor or an ideology in favour of the rich. In this they have accepted Marx's first and third criticisms of religion. But in steadfastly ignoring his second, ontological criticism, they have led the way into a cul de sac. Indeed they have not only ignored the ontological issue, they have deliberately rejected it. In this they have failed to comprehend the full implications of Marx's work. They have assumed that the ontological question is simply the European debate about the existence of God. Thus one group from Costa Rica confidently stand Shakespeare on his head. 'To be or not to be: that is *not* the question.'[18] But the ontological implications of Marx's work are more profound and extensive. Religion in its traditional form is inherently an inversion of reality. In this form it was appropriate and important in earlier epochs, but it is becoming obsolete in the modern world, and in this form deserves to be so. The future of religion, in the next epoch, depends on accepting Marx's ontological critique. It will require the most imaginative steps to reconceive of religion and to give it new institutional forms appropriate to contemporary experience. Nor would Marx object. In *The German Ideology*, at a point where the argument ends and in his intuition of things to come he is reduced to gnomic utterances Marx concludes:

Religion is from the outset consciousness of the transcendental arising from actually existing forces (5.93).

Notes

References to Marx's writings are from two standard editions.

(*a*) Karl Marx/Friedrich Engels, *Werke*, Dietz Verlag, Berlin 1964 referred to as MEW.

(*b*) Karl Marx/Friedrich Engels, *Collected Works*, Lawrence & Wishart, London. This ET is based on the MEW, and to avoid continual interruption references will be given in the text rather than in the following notes. Thus a quotation from the *Collected Works*, Volume 6 page 519, will appear in the text as (6.519).

Part One Marx's Criticisms of Religion

1. *Marx and Faith*

1. For further details see Saul K. Padover, *Karl Marx: An Intimate Biography*, New York: McGraw-Hill 1978, Chapter 1.

2. Karl Marx and Frederick Engels, *Selected Works: In One Volume*, London: Lawrence & Wishart, 1970, p. 430.

3. David McLellan, *Marx Before Marxism*, Harmondsworth: Penguin Books 1972, p. 66.

4. For further examination of this process see William Sargant, *Battle for the Mind: A Physiology of Conversion and Brainwashing*, Harmondsworth: Penguin Books, 1961.

2. *Religion as Reconciliation*

1. David McLellan, *Marx Before Marxism*, Harmondsworth: Penguin Books 1972, Chapters 1, 2.

2. Quoted in S. Korner, *Kant*, Harmondsworth: Penguin Books 1955, p. 129.

3. J. N. Findlay, *Hegel: A Re-examination*, London: Allen & Unwin 1958, p. 41.

4. G. W. F. Hegel, *Hegel's Logic*, Oxford: Clarendon Press 1975, p. 278.

5. G. W. F. Hegel, *The Phenomenology of Mind*, New York: Harper 1967, p. 776.

6. Charles Taylor, *Hegel*, Cambridge University Press 1975, p. 486.

7. G. W. F. Hegel, *The Philosophy of History*, New York: Willey 1900, p. 38.

8. Ibid., p. 39.

9. G. W. F. Hegel, *Hegel's Philosophy of Right*, London: Oxford University Press 1967, p. 168.

10. Hegel, *The Phenomenology of Mind* (n. 5), p. 164.

11. Hegel, *Logic* (n. 4), p. 142.

12. Hegel, *Philosophy of Right* (n. 9), p. 11.

13. Ibid, p. 10.

14. Hegel, *Logic* (n. 4), p. 9.

15. Hegel, *Philosophy of Right* (n. 9), p. 13.

Notes

16. Hegel, *The Philosophy of History* (n. 7), p. 19.
17. Ibid, p. 35.
18. Ibid, p. 33.
19. Albert Schweitzer, *The Quest of the Historical Jesus*, London: A. & C. Black and New York: Macmillan, p. 78.
20. Horton Harris, *David Friedrich Strauss and His Theology*, Cambridge University Press 1973, p. 51.
21. Quoted ibid, p. 77.
22. Schweitzer, *Quest* (n. 19), p. 85.
23. D. F. Strausss, *The Life of Jesus Critically Examined* (1846), reissued Philadelphia: Fortress Press and London: SCM Press 1973, p. 757.
24. General Superintendent Hoffmann, quoted by Harris, *Strauss* (n. 20), p. 40.
25. Bruno Bauer, 'The Trumpet of the Last Judgment', included in Lawrence Stepelevich, *The Young Hegelians: An Anthology*, Cambridge University Press 1983, p. 183.
26. Edgar Bauer, 'The Struggle of Critique with Church and State', ibid., p. 273.
27. Quoted in Frederick Gregory, *Scientific Materialism in Nineteenth-Century Germany* Dordrecht: D. Reidel 1977, p. 16.
28. Quoted in Eugene Kamenka, *The Philosophy of Ludwig Feuerbach*, London: Routledge & Kegan Paul 1970, p. 15.
29. Ibid.
30. Quoted in David McLellan, *The Young Hegelians*, London: Macmillan 1969, p. 29.
31. See Padover, *Karl Marx: An Intimate Biography* pp. 46–56.
32. I have preferred the translation given in T. B. Bottomore, *Karl Marx: Early Writings*, London: C. A. Watts 1963, pp. 43–4.
33. Virginia Berridge and Griffiths Edwards, *Opium and the People: Opiate Use in Nineteenth Century England*, New Haven: Yale University Press 1987.
34. Marx wrote this passage in the year following the end of the Opium War between Britain and China (1839–42) at a time when the metaphor was current. It was not original to Marx, even among the Young Hegelians, and had been used specifically by Bauer, Feuerbach and also Heine. For further references see 'Excursus on the expression "Opium of the People" ', in Helmut Gollwitzer, *The Christian Faith and the Marxist Criticism of Religion*, Edinburgh: The Saint Andrew Press 1970, pp. 15–22. See also Virginia Berridge, and Griffith Edwards, *Opium and the Poor: Opiate Use in Nineteenth-Century England*.
35. II Corinthians 5.19. All biblical quotations are taken from *The Revised Standard Version*.
36. Ludwig Feuerbach, *The Essence of Christianity* (1843), reissued New York: Harper & Row 1957, p. 1.
37. Ibid, p. 2.
38. Ibid.
39. Ibid, p. 152.
40. Strauss, *The Life of Jesus* (n. 23), p. 780.
41. Bottomore, *Karl Marx: Early Writings* (n. 32) p. 58.
42. Inevitably most theological terms were originally borrowed from secular language. When first used they would have considerable power of communication for this reason. The corollary is that when they are retained beyond their use in common speech they become specifically theological and lose this power. However, a movement in the opposite direction can also happen, when profound dimensions of secular events or movements can only be designated through a re-appropriation of theological terms. This is what has happened in the passage we have been discussing. In the ancient world the term ἀπολύτρωσις (redemption) was a secular word from the market place. It referred, for example, to the buying back of a slave. The unfortunate, who could not save himself, would be liberated by someone acting on his behalf. It was therefore a

powerful image when applied in the New Testament to the work of Christ. Thus Paul says that 'since all have sinned and fall short of the glory of God, they are justifierd by his grace as a gift, through the redemption which is in Christ Jesus . . .' (Romans 3.23–24). 'In him we have redemption through his blood . . .' (Ephesians 1.7). In both of these passages Luther translated ἀπολύτρωσις with the word *Erlösung*. I do not wish to pretend to the reader that this is the word used by Marx here: it is not. The question rather concerns his meaning. The actual text ends: 'also nur durch die völlige Wiedergewinnung des Menschen sich selbst gewinnen kann. Diese Auflösung des Gesellschaft als ein besonderer Stand is das Proletariat.' (MEW 1.390). Marx does not use the – by this time – theological term *Erlösung*, though it is echoed in *Auflösung*. Instead, he used the secular word *Wiedergewinnung*. It is a secular word, as were *Erlösung* and ἀπολύτρωσις originally. It means 'recovery' or 'reclamation'. But as I have just observed, there are occasions when the profound dimensions of a secular movement require the use of theological terms. Tom Bottomore bites the bullet and translates *Wiedergewinnung* as 'redemption'. That is exactly what Marx *means*, and it is the first duty of a translator to convey the meaning. By comparison the Moscow translation presents us with 'the rewinning of man'. It thus renders this important passage meaningless. It is difficult to avoid the conclusion that this has been deemed preferable to resorting to the use of a religious term.

3. *Religion as Reversal*

1. Ludwig Feuerbach, *The Essence of Christianity* (1843), reissued New York: Harper & Row 1957, pp. 29–30.
2. F. D. E. Schleiermacher, *On Religion: Speeches to Its Cultured Despisers* (1893), New York: Harper 1958, p. 1.
3. Ibid., p. 15.
4. Ibid., p. 39.
5. Ibid., p. 22.
6. Feuerbach, *The Essence of Christianity* (n. 1), pp. 10–11.
7. Ibid., p. 9.
8. Ibid., p. xxxvi.
9. Ibid., p. 13.
10. Ibid., p. 21.
11. André Liebich, *Between Ideology and Utopia: the Politics and Philosophy of August Cieszkowski*, Dordrecht: D. Reidel 1979, pp. 47–8.
12. David McLellan, *The Young Hegelians*, London: Macmillan 1969, p. 10.
13. T. B. Bottomore, *Karl Marx: Early Writings*, London: C. A. Watts 1963, p. 44.
14. Mark 2.27.
15. Alexander Gray, *The Development of Economic Doctrine*, London: Longman, Green & Co. 1931, p. 123.
16. G. W. F. Hegel, *Hegel's Philosophy of Right*, London: Oxford University Press 1967, p. 133.
17. Richard Norman, *Hegel's Phenomenology: A Philosophical Introduction*, London: Harvester Press 1976, p. 53.
18. Ibid., p. 24.
19. G. W. F. Hegel, *The Phenomenology of Mind*, New York: Harper 1967, p. 567.
20. Feuerbach, *The Essence of Christianity* (n. 1), p. 21.
21. Ibid., p. 39.

4. *Religion as Ideology*

1. Max Stirner, *The Ego and His Own*, London: Jonathan Cape 1971, p. 41.
2. Leszek Kolakowski, *Main Currents of Marxism*, London: Oxford University Press 1978, Vol. 1, p. 166.
3. Stirner, *Ego* (n. 1), pp. 99ff.

Notes

4. Ibid., p. 257.

5. Ludwig Feuerbach, 'Grundsatze der Philosophie', *Sämmtliche Werke*, Leipzig: Wigand, 1846, Bd II, p. 413.

6. Ludwig Feuerbach, *The Essence of Christianity* (1843), reissued New York: Harper & Row 1957, p. 140.

7. A. H. Armstrong, *An Introduction to Ancient Philosophy*, London: Methuen, 1977, p. 23.

8. Feuerbach, *Sämmtliche Werke* (n. 5), Bd. I, pp. xiv-v.

9. Feuerbach, *The Essence of Christianity* (n. 6) p. 60.

10. Ibid., p. 64.

11. Karl Marx and Friedrich Engels, *Selected Works: In One Volume* London: Lawrence & Wishart 1970, p. 182.

12. Ibid., p. 183.

13. Ibid., p. 585.

14. G. W. F. Hegel, *The Philosophy of History*, New York: Willey 1900, p. 45. See also H. M. Drucker, *The Political Uses of Ideology*, London: Macmillan 1974, Part I.

15. Karl Marx *Capital*, Harmondsworth: Penguin Books 1976, vol. 1, pp. 850ff.

16. Ibid., p. 825.

17. Alistair Kee, *Constantine Versus Christ: The Triumph of Ideology*, London: SCM Press 1982.

5. Historical Materialism as Religion

1. Quoted in Frank Sullaway, *Freud, Biologist of the Mind*, London: Fontana Books 1980, p. 14.

2. Frederick Gregory, *Scientific Materialism in Nineteenth-Century Germany*, p. xi.

3. George Lichtheim, Introduction to G. W. F. Hegel, *The Phenomenology of Mind*, New York: Harper 1967, p. xxx.

4. Leszek Kolakowski, *Main Currents of Marxism*, London: Oxford University Press 1978, Vol. 1, p. 158.

5. Karl Marx, *Capital*, Harmondsworth: Penguin Books 1976, Vol. 1, p. 91.

6. Ibid., p. 92.

7. Ibid.

8. Karl Marx and Friedrich Engels *Selected Works: In One Volume*, London: Lawrence & Wishart 1970, p. 95.

9. Marx, *Capital* (n. 5), Vol. 1, p. 63.

10. Ibid., p. 57.

11. Ibid., p. 63.

12. A. J. P. Taylor, Introduction to Marx/Engels, *The Communist Manifesto*, Harmondsworth: Penguin Books 1967, p. 36.

13. Hegel, *The Phenomenology of Mind* (n. 3), pp. 752–3.

14. F. Nietzsche, *The Joyful Wisdom*, The Complete Works of Friedrich Nietzsche, ed. Oscar Levy, London: Allen & Unwin 1910, Vol. 10, p. 275.

15. Walter Kaufmann, *Nietzsche: Philosopher, Psychologist, Antichrist*, New York: Meridian 1956, p. 142.

16. Quoted ibid., p. 127.

17. Marx, *Capital* (n. 5), Vol. 1, 103.

18. John A. Hall, *The Asiatic Mode of Production: Oriental Despotism, Historical Materialism and Indian History*, Oxford: Blackwell 1989.

19. G. W. F. Hegel, *The Philosophy of History*, New York: Willey 1900, p. 8.

20. G. W. F. Hegel, *Hegel's Logic*, Oxford: Clarendon Press ³ 1975, p. 13.

21. Ibid., p. 268.

22. Charles Taylor, *Hegel*, Cambridge University Press 1975, p. 112.

23. Hegel, *Logic* (n. 20), p. 268.

24. Taylor, *Hegel* (n. 22), p. 286.

Notes

25. Quoted by Grace Jantzen, in 'Human Autonomy in the Body of God', in Alistair Kee and Eugene Thomas Long, (eds.), *Being and Truth: Essays in Honour of John Macquarrie, London:* SCM Press 1986, p. 183.

26. Hegel, *Logic* (n. 20) p. 220.

27. Hegel, *The Philosophy of History (n. 19)*, p. 19.

28. Hegel, *Logic* (n. 20) p. 119.

29. J. N. Findlay, in Foreword to Hegel, *Logic* (n. 20) p. xiii.

30. Hegel, *The Philosophy of History* (n. 19), p. 63.

31. Richard Norman, *Hegel's Phenomenology: A Philosophical Introduction*, p. 86.

32. Hegel, *The Phenomenology of Mind* (n. 3), p. 760. London: Harvester Press 1976.

33. Taylor, *Hegel* (n. 22), p. 276.

34. Hegel, *The Phenomenology of Mind* (n. 3), p 789.

35. Tertullian, *Apology*, The Loeb Classical Library, London: Heinemann 1931, L.14.

36. Romans 8.28.

37. Marx, *Capital* (n. 5), Vol. 1, p. 113.

38. Quoted in Jose P. Miranda, *Marx Against the Marxists: the Christian Humanism of Karl Marx*, Maryknoll: Orbis Books and London: S C M Press 1980, p. 269. Miranda will be discussed in Chapters 9, 10 and 12 below.

39. Marx, *Capital* (n. 5), Vol. 1, p. 474.

40. MEW 38.363.

41. MEW 37.231.

42. Hegel, *Logic* (n. 20), p. 273.

43. Adam Smith, *The Theory of Moral Sentiments*, Oxford: Clarendon Press 1976, p. 36.

44. Ibid., p. 183.

45. Adam Smith, *An Inquiry into the Wealth of Nations*, Oxford: Clarendon Press 1976, p. 456.

46. Hegel, *The Phenomenology of Mind* (n. 3), p. 579.

47. L. Althusser, *For Marx* Harmondsworth: Penguin Books 1969, p. 162.

48. Hegel, *The Philosophy of History* (n. 19), p. 94.

49. Marx, *Capital* (n. 5), Vol. 1, p. 165.

Part Two   Marx and Liberation Theology

6.   *Redemption and Revolution*

1. Che Guevara, *Reminiscences of the Cuban Revolutionary War*, Harmondsworth: Penguin Books 1969, p. 243.

2. Hilda Gadea, *Ernesto: A Memoir of Che Guevara*, London: W. H. Allen 1973, p. xiv.

3. Rolando E. Bonachea and Nelson P. Valdes (eds), *Che: Selected Writings of Ernesto Guevara*, Cambridge, Ma.: The MIT Press, 1969, p. 48.

4. Jeremy Rifkin, *The Emerging Order: God in the Age of Scarcity*, New York: Ballantine Books 1979, p. 123.

5. Guevara, *Reminiscences* (n. 1), p. 235. The phrase 'unredeemed America' is repeated in the opening sentence of 'Latin America as Seen from the Afro-Asian Continent', *Che* (n. 3), p. 43.

6. Ibid., 183.

7. Che Guevara, *Guerrilla Warfare*, Harmondsworth: Penguin Books 1969, pp. 14–15.

8. Guevara, *Reminiscences* (n. 1), p. 262.

9. Ibid., p. 26.

Notes

10. Fidel Castro, 'Words to the Intellectuals', *Writers in the New Cuba*, ed. J. M. Cohen, Harmondsworth: Penguin Books 1967, p. 183.

11. Guevara, *Reminiscences* (n. 1), p. 264.

12. Guevara, *Guerrilla Warfare* (n. 7), p. 16.

13. Che Guevara, 'Man and Socialism in Cuba', *Venceremos!: The Speeches and Writings of Ernesto Che Guevara*, ed. John Gerassi, London: Weidenfeld and Nicolson 1968, p. 398.

14. Ibid., p. 398.

15. Guevara, *Reminiscences* (n. 1), pp. 45, 46.

16. Guevara, *Guerrilla Warfare* (n. 7), p. 18.

17. Ibid., p. 79.

18. Ibid., p. 13.

19. Ibid., p. 132.

20. Ibid., p. 45.

21. Ibid., p. 59.

22. Bonachea and Vales, *Che* (n. 3), p368.

23. Guevara, *Reminiscences* (n. 1), p. 255.

24. Guevara, *Guerrilla Warfare* (n. 7), p. 47.

25. 'Notes for the Study of the Ideology of the Cuban Revolution', in Bonachea and Vales *Che* (n. 3), p. 48.

26. Ibid., p. 50.

27. 'Development of a Marxist Revolution', Ibid., p. 247.

28. See 'Cuba' in Marcel Niedergang, *The Twenty Latin Americas*, Penguin Books 1971, Vol. 2, pp. 335–7.

29. Che Guevara, *Bolivian Diary*, London: Jonathan Cape 1968, p. 127.

30. Ibid.

31. 'Socialism and Man in Cuba', in Bonachea and Vales, *Che*, (n. 3) p. 169.

32. John Gerassi (ed.), *Camilo Torres: Revolutionary Priest*, Harmondsworth: Penguin Books 1973, p. 37.

33. Ibid.

34. For details of his early life see the account by his friend German Guzman, *Camilo Torres*, New York: Sheed and Ward, 1969.

35. Ibid., p. 5.

36. Gerassi, *Camilo Torres* (n. 32), p. 28.

37. Ibid., p. 162.

38. Ibid., p. 244.

39. Ibid., p. 297.

40. Ibid., p. 277.

41. Ibid., p. 297.

42. Ibid., p. 333.

43. Statement reproduced in full in Guzman, *Camilo Torres* (n. 34), p. 270.

44. Gerassi, *Camilo Torres* (n. 32), p. 25.

45. Ibid., p. 334–5.

46. John Alvarez Garcia and Christian Restrepo Calle, (eds.), *Camilo Torres: Priest and Revolutionary*, New York: Sheed and Ward 1968, p. 126.

47. Gerassi, *Camilo Torres* (n. 32), p. 66.

48. Camilo Torres, *Revolutionary Writings*, New York: Herder & Herder 1969, p. 15.

49. Gerassi, *Camilo Torres* (n. 32), p. 339.

50. Ibid., p. 374.

51. Ibid., p. 255.

52. Ibid., p. 258.

53. Ibid., p. 272.

54. Ibid., p. 169.

55. Ibid., p. 336.

56. The correspondence with the cardinal is reproduced in Guzman chapter 8.

57. Gerassi, *Camilo Torres* (n. 32), p. 334.

58. Ibid., pp. 337, 339.

59. Ibid., p. 352.

60. Albert Camus, *The Plague*, Harmondsworth: Penguin Books 1970, p. 209.

61. Gerassi, *Camilo Torres* (n. 32), p. 375.

62. Guevara, *Bolivian Diary* (n. 29), p. 106.

63. Helder Camara, *Church and Colonialism*, London: Sheed and Ward 1969, p. 109.

64. Some of the following biographical material is taken from the Epilogue of José de Broucker, *Dom Helder Camara: the Violence of a Peacemaker*, Maryknoll: Orbis Books 1969, but the account of his life begins with a mistake, giving Camara's date of birth as 1900. See p. 137.

65. Ibid., p. 154.

66. Miguel Arraes, *Brazil: The People and the Power*, Harmondsworth: Penguin Books 1972, p. 169.

67. Camara, *Church and Colonialism* (n. 63), p. 33.

68. Ibid., p. 7.

69. Ibid., p. 45.

70. Ibid., p. 108.

71. Helder Camara, *Spiral of Violence*, London: Sheed and Ward 1971, p. 40.

72. Camara, *Church and Colonialism* (n. 63), 107.

73. Camara, *Spiral of Violence* (n. 71), p. 45ff.

74. Not the one-hundredth anniversary of his birth.

75. John 10.10.

76. Camara, *Church and Colonialism* (n. 63), p. 20.

77. Ibid., p. 44.

78. Ibid., p. 20.

79. Quoted in de Broucker, *Dom Helder Camara* (n. 64), p. 29.

80. Camara, *Church and Colonialism* (n. 63), p. 27

81. See his 'Letter to the Executive Committee of the Brazilian Communist Party', in December 1966, in Carlos Marighela, *For the Liberation of Brazil*, Harmondsworth: Penguin Books 1971, pp. 183ff.

82. Camara, *Church and Colonialism* (n. 63), p. 120.

83. Camara, *Spiral of Violence* (n. 71), p. 32.

84. Camara, *Church and Colonialism* (n. 63), p. 16.

85. Ibid., p. 24.

86. Ibid., p. 112.

87. Ibid., p. 35.

88. Ibid., p. 104.

89. de Broucker, *Dom Helder Camara* (n. 64), p. 89.

90. Helder Camara, 'Thomas Aquinas and Karl Marx: The Challenge to Christians'. The text was issued by various co-operating bodies, including the Catholic Institute for International Relations, London 1982.

91. David Knowles, *The Evolution of Medieval Thought*, London: Longman 1988, p. 233.

92. de Broucker, *Dom Helder Camara* (n. 64), p. 106.

93. Ibid., p. 103.

94. Matthew 23.8–9.

95. Camara, *Church and Colonialism* (n. 63), p. 122.

96. Foreword by Leo Huberman and Paul M. Sweezy to Regis Debray, *Revolution in the Revolution*, Harmondsworth: Penguin Books 1968, p. 9.

97. Ibid., p. 90.

98. Ibid., p. 102.
99. Ibid., p. 112.
100. Marighela, *Liberation of Brazil* (n. 81), p. 164.
101. Ibid., 96.
102. Arraes, *Brazil* (n. 66), p. 209.
103. Marighela, *Liberation of Brazil* (n. 81), p. 23.
104. Text taken from Anne Fremantle (ed.), *The Papal Encyclicals*, New York: Mentor-Omega Books 1963, p. 393.
105. Ibid., p. 401.
106. Ibid., p. 404.
107. Quoted in Niedergang, *The Twenty Latin Americas* (n. 28), Vol. 1, p. 116.
108. Donald R. Campion, Introduction to the text of *Gaudium et Spes, The Documents of Vatican II*, London: Geoffrey Chapman 1967, p. 184.
109. Text published by the Catholic Institute for International Relations, London 1967, Section 13.
110. Ibid.
111. Ibid., Section 22.
112. Ibid., Section 24.
113. Ibid., Section 26.
114. Ibid., Section 28.
115. Ibid., Section 51.

7. *The Influence of Marx on Liberation Theology*

1. R. H. Preston, (ed.), *Technology and Social Justice*, London: SCM Press, 1971.
2. Gustavo Gutierrez Merino, 'The Meaning of Development: Notes on a Theology of Liberation', in *In Search of a Theology of Development*, Geneva: SODEPAX nd, p. 138.
3. Ibid., p. 116.
4. Ibid., p. 125.
5. Ibid., p. 133.
6. Ibid., p. 136.
7. Quoted ibid., p. 167 n.7.
8. Ibid., p. 147.
9. Ibid., p. 119.
10. Credited to Victor Hugo.
11. For the course of theology from the Marxist Christian Dialogue to the Theology of Liberation, see my collection *A Reader in Political Theology*, SCM Press 1974 (1978).
12. Gustavo Gutierrez, *A Theology of Liberation*, Maryknoll: Orbis Books 1973 and London: SCM Press 1974, p. 9.
13. Ibid., p. 32.
14. Galatians 5.1.
15. Gutierrez, *A Theology of Liberation* (n. 12), p. 48.
16. Ibid., p. 90.
17. Ibid., p. 89.
18. Ibid., p. 90.
19. Ibid., p. 11.
20. Ibid., p. 159.
21. Exodus 12.29. For a critical comment on the lack of socio-historical rooting of the Exodus among Latin American liberation theologians see Norman K. Gottwald, 'The Exodus as Event and Process: A Test Case in the Biblical Grounding of Liberation Theology'. This is one of the few critical contributions to an otherwise congratulatory collection, Marc H. Ellis and Otto Maduro (eds), *The Future of Liberation Theology: Essays in Honor of Gustavo Gutierrez*, Maryknoll: Orbis Books 1988. For an overdue recognition of the relative importance of the Exile over Exodus see Luis N. Rivera

Pagan, 'Toward a Theology of Peace: Critical Notes on the Biblical Hermeneutic of Latin American Theology of Liberation' in Dow Kirkpatrick (ed.), *Faith Born in the Struggle for Life: A Re-reading of Protestant Faith in Latin America Today*, Grand Rapids: Eerdmans 1988.

22. Gutierrez, *A Theology of Liberation* (n. 12), p. 174.

23. Ibid.

24. Ibid., p. 176.

25. Quoted by Paul Gallet in *Freedom to Starve*, Harmondsworth: Penguin Books 1972, p. 210.

26. Gustavo Gutierrez, 'The Historical Power of the Poor' (1978), included in his collection *The Power of the Poor in History*, Maryknoll: Orbis Books and London: SCM Press 1983, p. 90.

27. For further details see Marcel Niedergang, *The Twenty Latin Americas*, Harmondsworth: Penguin Books 1971, Vol. 1, pp. 59ff.

28. Quoted in Gutierrez, 'Theology from the Underside of History', in *The Power of the Poor in History* (n. 26), p. 203.

29. Gutierrez, 'God's Revelation and Proclamation in History' (1975), ibid., p. 9.

30. Ibid., p. 13.

31. Ibid., p. 16.

32. Gutierrez, 'Liberation and the Poor: The Puebla Perspective' (1979). ibid., p. 144.

33. Ibid., p. 18.

34. Ibid., p. 205.

35. Ibid., p. 18.

36. Ibid., p. 61.

37. Ibid., p. 184.

38. Ibid., p. 192.

39. Ibid., 193.

40. Gutierrez, *A Theology of Liberation* (n. 12), p. 267.

41. Ibid., p. 12.

42. Ibid., p. 271.

8.   The Use of Marx in Liberation Theology

1. Juan Luis Segundo, *Liberation of Theology*, Maryknoll: Orbis Books and Dublin: Gill and Macmillan 1977, pp. 8–9.

2. Harvey Cox, *The Secular City: Secularization and Urbanization in Theological Perspective*, New York: Macmillan and London: SCM Press 1965, chapters 1, 2.

3. Segundo, *Liberation of Theology* (n. 1), p. 17.

4. Ibid.

5. E.g. ibid p. 13.

6. Allan Boesak, *Black Theology/Black Power*, London: Mowbrays, 1978, p. 143.

7. James Cone, *Black Theology and Black Power*, New York: Seabury Press 1969.

8. Included in the collection, Jon Sobrino, *The True Church and the Poor*, Maryknoll: Orbis Books and London: SCM Press, 1985.

9. Jürgen Moltmann, *Theology of Hope*, London: SCM Press and New York: Harper and Row 1967, p. 21.

10. Sobrino, *True Church and The Poor* (n. 8), p. 34 n.23.

11. Ibid., p. 8.

12. Forward to Clodovis Boff, *Theology and Praxis*, Maryknoll: Orbis Books 1987, p. xiii.

13. Ibid., p. 198.

14. Ibid., p. 13.

15. Ibid., p. 32.

16. Ibid., p. 31.

Notes

17. Ibid., p. 56.

18. Ibid., p. 224.

19. Ibid., p. 266 n.8.

20. José Miguez Bonino, *Revolutionary Theology Comes of Age*, London: SPCK 1975, p. 87. Also published as *Doing Theology in a Revolutionary Situation*, Philadelphia: Fortress Press 1975.

21. Ibid., p. 52.

22. Ibid., p. 94.

23. Ibid., pp. 95–6.

24. Ibid., p. 97.

25. Ibid., p. 98.

26. Galatians 5.1.

27. Bonino, *Revolutionary Theology* (n. 20), pp. 99–100.

9. *Marxist Liberation Theology*

1. José Porfirio Miranda, *Marx and the Bible: A Critique of the Philosophy of Oppression*, Maryknoll: Orbis Books and London: SCM Press 1974, p. xvii.

2. Ibid., p. 250.

3. Ibid., p. 35.

4. Ibid., p. 40.

5. Ibid., p. 43.

6. Jeremiah 22.15–16.

7. Miranda, *Marx and the Bible* (n. 1), p. 44.

8. Amos 5.21–24.

9. Miranda, *Marx and the Bible* (n. 1), p. 57.

10. Matthew 22.34–40.

11. I John 4.12.

12. I Corinthians 11.17–33.

13. Miranda, *Marx and the Bible* (n. 1), p. 60.

14. Luke 20.4

15. José Miranda, *Communism in the Bible*, Maryknoll: Orbis Books and London SCM Press, 1982, p. 13.

16. E. Troeltsch, *The Social Teaching of the Christian Churches*, reissued New York: Harper & Brothers 1960, Vol. 1, p. 63. V. I. Lenin, *The State and Revolution*, Moscow: Progress Publishers 1969, p. 41.

17. I have discussed this issue in a related context in *Constantine Versus Christ*, London: SCM Press 1982, Chapter XII.

18. Acts 2.44–45.

19. Acts 4.32.

20. Miranda, *Communism in the Bible* (n. 15), p. 2.

21. Ibid., p. 4.

22. Matthew 25.35.

23. Miranda, *Marx and the Bible* (n. 1), p. 201.

24. Ibid., p. 278.

25. Harvey Cox, *The Silencing of Leonardo Boff*, Oak Park, Ill.: Meyer-Stone Books 1988; Norbert Greinacher (ed.), *Konflikt um die Theologie der Befreiung: Diskussion und Dokumentation*, Zurich: Benziger, 1985, IV.

26. 'Instruction on Christian Freedom and Liberation' was issued on 22 March 1986.

27. Quoted from the text as published in *The Tablet*, 4 September 1984, p. 868.

28. Juan Luis Segundo, *Theology and Church: A Response to Cardinal Ratzinger and a Warning to the Whole Church*, London: Geoffrey Chapman, 1985.

29. Cox, *The Silencing of Leonardo Boff* (n. 25), p. 28.

30. Leonardo Boff, *Church, Charism and Power: Liberation Theology and the Insti-*

tutional Church, New York: Crossroad Publishing Company and London: SCM Press 1985, p. 111.

31. Ibid., p. 63.
32. Ibid., p. 21.
33. Ibid., p. 10.
34. Quoted ibid., p. 142.
35. Ibid., p. 60.
36. Ibid., p. 133.
37. Ibid., p. 43.
38. Ibid., p. 33.
39. Ibid., p. 39.
40. Ibid., p. 110.
41. Ibid.
42. Ibid., p. 111.
43. Ibid.
44. Ibid., p. 122.
45. Alistair, Kee, 'Authority and Liberation: Conflict between Rome and Latin America', *The Modern Churchman*, Vol. 28, 1985.
46. Not that Boff was alone in this. See José Míguez Bonino, *Faces of Jesus: Latin American Christologies*, Maryknoll: Orbis Books 1984.
47. Leonardo Boff, *Jesus Christ Liberator*, Maryknoll: Orbis Books and London: SPCK 1978, p. 265.
48. Ibid., p. 266.
49. Ibid., p. 267.
50. Ibid., p. 274.
51. Ibid.
52. Ibid., p. 279.
53. Ernesto Cardenal, *The Gospel in Solentiname*, Maryknoll: Orbis Books 4 vols., 1976–82. The examples given here have been collected by Philip Berryman in *The Roots of Religious Rebellion: Christians in the Central American Revolutions*, Maryknoll: Orbis Books and London: SCM Press 1984, p. 101.
54. Hugo, Assmann, 'The Power of Christ in History: Conflicting Christologies and Discernment', in Rosino Gibellini (ed.), *Frontiers of Theology in Latin America*, Maryknoll: Orbis Books and London: SCM Press, 1980, p. 138.
55. Ibid., p. 141.
56. I Corinthians 4. 19–20.
57. Assmann, 'The Power of Christ in History' (n. 54), p. 147.
58. An English translation was published in 1975 by Search Press as *Practical Theology of Liberation*. In the same year Orbis issued this translation, but with the rather imaginative title *Theology for a Nomad Church*.
59. Ibid., p. 31.
60. Ibid., p. 34.
61. Ibid., p. 36.
62. Ibid., p. 46.
63. Ibid., pp. 54–5.
64. Ibid., p. 124.
65. Ibid., p. 143.
66. Ibid., p. 69.
67. Ibid., p. 62.
68. The text is given on pp. 3–6 of John Eagleson (ed.), *Christians and Socialism*, Maryknoll: Orbis Books 1975.
69. Ibid., p. 8.
70. Ibid., p. 9.
71. Ibid., p. 11.

Notes

72. Ibid., p. 24.
73. Ibid.
74. Ibid., p. 25.
75. Ibid., p. 26.
76. Ibid.
77. Ibid.
78. Ibid., p. 27.

10. *The Evaluation of Marx in Liberation Theology*

1. José Míguez Bonino, *Christians and Marxists: the Mutual Challenge of Revolution*, London: Hodder & Stoughton 1976, p. 19.
2. Ibid., p. 23–4.
3. Ibid., p. 42.
4. Ibid., pp. 48–9.
5. Ibid., p. 98.
6. Lawrence Bright, 'Christian and Marxist', in *What Kind of Revolution?* ed. J. Klugmann, and P. Ostreicher, London: Panther Books 1968, p. 125. Quoted in Bonino *Christians and Marxists* (n. 1), pp. 17, 143.
7. Juan Luis Segundo, *Faith and Ideologies*, Maryknoll: Orbis Books 1984, p. 15.
8. Ibid., p. 16.
9. Ibid., p. 31.
10. Ibid., p. 39.
11. W. Cantwell Smith, *The Meaning and End of Religion*, New York: Macmillan and London: SPCK 1962;*Belief and History*, Charlottesville: University of Virginia Press, 1977; *Faith and Belief*, Princeton University Press, 1979; *Towards a World Theology: Faith and the Comparative History of Religion*, Philadelphia: Westminster Press and London: Macmillan 1981. For a collection of Smith's descriptions of faith see the Appendix to Edward J. Hughes, *Wilfred Cantwell Smith: Theology for the World*, London: SCM Press 1986.
12. Mark 2.27.
13. Mark 7.19.
14. Segundo, *Faith and Ideologies* (n. 7), p. 50.
15. Mark 1.44.
16. Segundo, *Faith and Ideologies* (n. 7), p. 64.
17. Ibid., p. 62.
18. Ibid., p. 81.
19. Ibid., p. 182.
20. Quoted ibid., p. 197 n.20.
21. Ibid., p. 338.
22. Antonio Pérez-Esclarín, *Atheism and Liberation*, Maryknoll: Orbis Books and London: SCM Press 1980, p. 1.
23. Ibid.
24. Ibid., p. 2.
25. Ibid., p. 53.
26. Ibid., p. 119.
27. Friedrich Nietzsche, *Der Antichrist*, Munich: Carl Hanser Verlag, second revised edition 1960, Bd 2, p. 1233.
28. Pérez-Esclarín, *Atheism and Liberation* (n. 22), p. 127.
29. Ludwig Feuerbach, *Sämmtliche Werke*, Leipzig: Wigand 1846, Bd 1, p. 14.
30. I have discussed Feuerbach's projection theory and its relation to *mimesis* in idealist philosophy in *Constantine versus Christ*, London: SCM Press 1982, chapter 10.
31. Sigmund Freud, *The Origins of Religion*, The Pelican Freud Library, Vol. 13 in Penguin Books 1985, p. 40.
32. Pérez-Esclarín, *Atheism and Liberation* (n. 22), p. 196.

33. Ibid., p. 160.

34. José Porfirio Miranda, *Marx Against the Marxists: the Christian Humanism of Karl Marx*, Maryknoll, Orbis Books and London: SCM Press 1980.

35. Quoted ibid., p. 71.

36. Quoted ibid., p. 6.

37. Ibid., p. 47.

38. Ibid., p. 180.

39. Mark 2.27.

40. Matthew 6.24.

41. Mark 10.25.

42. Miranda, *Marx Against the Marxists* (n. 34), p. 201.

43. Quoted ibid., pp. 204–7.

44. Marx, *Capital*, Harmondsworth: Penguin Book 1976,Vol. 1, p. 163.

45. Ibid., p. 172.

46. For further reference see the following: Willem den Boer, (ed.), *Le Culte des Souverains dans l'Empire Romain*, Geneva: Foundation Hardt 1973; Lily Ross Taylor, *The Divinity of the Roman Emperor*, Middletown, Conn.: American Philological Association 1931; Ulrich Wilckens, 'Zur Entstehung des hellenistischen Konigskultes' (1938), reprinted in Antonie Wlosok, *Römischer Kaiserkult*, Darmstadt: Wissenschaftliche Buchgesellschaft 1978.

47. Miranda, *Marx Against the Marxists* (n. 34), p. 224.

48. Henry Fielding, *Tom Jones*, London: J. M. Dent & Sons 1955, Vol. 1, Book III, Chapter 3.

49. Quoted in Miranda, *Marx Against the Marxists* (n. 34), pp. 227–37.

Part Three   Beyond Liberation Theology

11.   *Marx and the Failure of Liberation Theology*

1. Feminists, some of whom cannot tell a friend from a foe, will have observed that I have not discussed the work of any feminist theologians from Latin America. There are very few, and that has its own significance. The basis of my selection, however, was whether and how Marx was incorporated into the subject's theology. Some eminent theologians were therefore omitted, regardless of gender. In her beautiful study of the legend of Quetzalcoatl Elsa Tamaz, from Costa Rica, is able to refer to the writings of more than twenty feminist theologians dealing with a wide variety of Latin American experiences. 'The Power of Nudity' in Dow Kirkpatrick (ed.), *Faith Born in the Struggle for Life: A Re-reading of Protestant Faith in Latin America Today*, Grand Rapids: Eerdmans 1988.

2. Quoted in José Purfiria Miranda, *Marx Against the Marxists*, Maryknoll: Orbis Books and London: SCM Press 1980, p. 280.

3. Alfredo Fierro, *The Militant Gospel*, Maryknoll: Orbis Books and London: SCM Press 1977, p. 198.

4. Clodovis Boff, *Feet-on-the-Ground-Theology*, Maryknoll: Orbis Books 1987, p. 4. It may be that Boff seeks to disguise this attitude towards the people of the north, and in any case they may not be conscious of it. Those of us who live in the north of the UK are not only aware of being viewed in this way, but those who treat us as marginals and lesser beings do not trouble to disguise the fact. This is one reason for a very particular interest in liberation theology in Scotland.

5. Ibid., p. 21.

6. Ibid., p. 148.

7. Ibid., p. 106.

8. Ibid., p. 142.

9. Ibid., p. 114.

10. For a penetrating, even alarming account of corresponding conservatism in

Notes

Protestant leadership, see Rubem A. Alves, *Protestantism and Repression: a Brazilian Case Study*, Maryknoll: Orbis Books and London: SCM Press 1985. For a discussion of its significance see Alistair Kee, *Domination or Liberation*, London: SCM Press 1986, Chapter 4.

11. Boff, *Feet-on-the-Ground Theology* (n. 4), p. 70.

12. José Miguez Bonino, *Revolutionary Theology Comes of Age*, London: SPCK 1975 (see ch. 8, n.20), p. xvii. Or to put it in historical materialist terms, 'it will disappear along with the socio-economic conditions that presently called it into being and made it topical', Fierro, *Militant Gospel* (n. 3), p. 208.

12. *Religion in the Next Epoch*

1. I have covered this contrast in *Domination or Liberation: The Place of Religion in Social Conflict*, London: SCM Press 1986.

2. MEW 22.509.

3. Ibid., p. 513.

4. Jose Porfirio Miranda, *Marx Against the Marxists*, Maryknoll: Orbis books and London: SCM Press 1980, p. 252.

5. MEW 26/2.476.

6. Miranda, *Marx Against the Marxists* (n. 4), p. 242.

7. MEW 28.268.

8. MEW 36.109.

9. Jerry Falwell, *Listen, America!*, New York: Bantam Books 1980, p. 12.

10. Brian Griffiths, *Monetarism and Morality: an Answer to the Bishops*, London: Centre for Policy Studies 1985, p. 8. For an original critique of the religious dimensions of capitalism see Franz Hinkelammert, 'The Economic Roots of Idolatry: Entrepreneurial Metaphysics', in Pablo Richard et al., *The Idols of Death and the God of Life: A Theology*, Maryknoll: Orbis Books 1983, pp. 165–93. Hinkelammert, a German economist who has spent a number of years in Costa Rica and Honduras, has also written a full-length study on a related theme. See especially Part One, 'On Marx's Analysis of Fetishism', in *The Ideological Weapons of Death: a Theological Critique of Capitalism*, Maryknoll: Orbis Books 1986.

11. Julio de Santa Ana, *Good News to the Poor*, Geneva: World Council of Churches 1977.

12. Matthew 5.7.

13. I Corinthians 9.22.

14. Karl Marx, *Capital*, Harmondsworth: Penguin Books 1976, p. 493, n. 4. Marx had brought this point out more than twenty years previously in a letter to Annenkov, in which he discussed his criticisms of Proudhon (38.98–99).

15. David McLellan, *Marxism and Religion*, p. 26. This is also a favourite passage of Juan Luis Segundo, e.g. *Faith and Ideologies*, Maryknoll: Orbis Books 1984, pp. 100, 132, 237. But just as Marx's criticisms of religion are only partially applied, to other people's religion, so Segundo does not care to adopt this method for religion as such.

16. Thomas Luckmann, *The Invisible Religion*, New York: Macmillan 1967, p. 49.

17. Karl Jaspers, *Philosophy*, University of Chicago Press 1971, Vol. 3, p. 21.

18. Introduction to Pablo Richard et al. *The Idols of Death and the God of Life: A Theology* (n. 10), p. 1.

Index

Index